The Phone Hacking Scandal

Journalism on Trial

EDITED BY
RICHARD LANCE KEEBLE
and JOHN MAIR

Published 2012 by Abramis academic publishing

www.abramis.co.uk

ISBN 978 1 84549 533 6

Printed and bound in the United Kingdom

Typeset in Garamond 11pt

Abramis is an imprint of arima publishing.

arima publishing
ASK House, Northgate Avenue
Bury St Edmunds, Suffolk IP32 6BB
t: (+44) 01284 700321

www.arimapublishing.com

Contents

Acknowledgements

These 'hackademic' books – this is the sixth in the series for Arima – require the hard work and goodwill of many people to hit the library and bookshop shelves so quickly and achieve much short, medium and long-term impact. The proof of that pudding is in the reading. Richard Lance Keeble and John Mair would like to thank:

ICE, the Institute of Communication Ethics, which put on the annual conference in London on 28 October 2011 that begat so much of the book.

Fiona Thompson, member of ICE's executive group, for diligently and carefully organising a splendid conference down to the last tiny detail and sandwich.

The individual authors who have contributed chapters to this book. None gets a fee. All produce splendid copy in record unacademic time with little complaint.

Richard Franklin, our publisher at Abramis, who is always calm and collected in getting the books to market in a record turnaround time. Richard Franklin's 'new publishing model' deserves more recognition and more copying if the academe is to have any influence in the real world...

Madeleine Atkins, Vice-Chancellor of Coventry University, who has been unwavering in her support for the Coventry Conversations enterprise over six, at times turbulent, years. She makes Coventry a worthwhile place to work.

All those who have contributed to the crucial debate on media ethics over the last decade – and more recently within Lord Leveson's Inquiry and beyond...

Finally, our families who have had to put up with us creeping in and out of home offices at unsocial hours to achieve this project in such a timely fashion. They have been very very tolerant. This book is dedicated to them.

John Mair, Oxford, 22 December 2011

Richard Lance Keeble, Withcall, Lincolnshire, 22 December 2011

The editors

Richard Lance Keeble has been Professor of Journalism at the University of Lincoln since 2003. Before that he was the executive editor of the *Teacher*, the weekly newspaper of the National Union of Teachers and he lectured at City University, London, for 19 years. He has written and edited 21 publications including *Secret State, Silent Press: New Militarism, the Gulf and the Modern Image of Warfare* (John Libbey, Luton, 1997); *The Newspapers Handbook* (Routledge, 2005, fourth edition); *Ethics for Journalists* (Routledge, 2008, second edition); *The Journalistic Imagination: Literary Journalists from Defoe to Capote and Carter* (Routledge, 2007, with Sharon Wheeler) and *Communicating War: Memory, Media and Military* (Arima, Bury St Edmunds, 2007, with Sarah Maltby). He is also the joint editor of *Ethical Space: The International Journal of Communication Ethics* and the winner of a National Teacher Fellowship in 2011 – the highest prize for teachers in higher education.

John Mair is Senior Lecturer in Broadcasting at Coventry University. He has won the Cecil Angel Cup for enhancing the prestige of Coventry University in 2009 and 2010. He invented and produces the weekly Coventry Conversations. He is a former BBC, ITV and Channel Four producer/director on a wide range of programmes from daily news to investigative documentaries on *World in Action* to more considered pieces on *Bookmark*. A Royal Television Society Journalism Award winner, he publishes widely in the media and journalism press including the *Guardian*, bbc.co.uk/journalism and journalism.co.uk. This is his seventh co-written or edited book. For the BBC, he co-wrote *Marx in London*, with Asa Briggs, in 1981. With Richard Lance Keeble, he edited *Beyond Trust* (2008) *Playing Footsie with the FTSE? The Great Crash of 2008 and the Crisis in Journalism (2009)*, *Afghanistan, War and the Media: Deadlines and Frontlines* (2010), *Face the Future: Tools for the Modern Media Age* (2011), *Investigative Journalism: Dead Or Alive? (2011)* and *Mirage in the Desert? Reporting the Arab Spring* (2011), all published by Arima, of Bury St. Edmunds. He is on the editorial board of *Ethical Space* and chairs the Institute of Communication Ethics. He is also a judge for the RTS Journalism Awards, the Muslim Young Writers and the Society of Editors Press Awards.

Preface

Exposed: The 'Swaggering Arrogance' of the Popular Press

John Lloyd

Journalism has more means of self-advertisement that most professions, and doesn't hesitate to use them in the service of its proclaimed role – that is, at root, that it is a necessary attendant to democratic life and to a civil society. And this is a true claim. No society can claim the status of free with unfree news media; free media cannot, in practice, exist in an unfree state.

But that cannot be extended to a claim that everything free media publish, in whatever form, contributes to greater freedom. News media can deprive citizens and other institutions of rights and freedoms through their actions. If we didn't know it before, we know it now.

In pursuit of the proclaimed democratic role, the news media say that they can construct a reliable hierarchy of the significant events in the world, and in the societies they serve which, though it may (and should) vary among different news media according to their leaning, nevertheless makes sense as an attempt to distinguish what matters most, what least; and give accounts of significant events which have as their aim the telling of the truth. Even where it is recognised (as it must be) that the position of responsible news media is Sisyphean – forever rolling the boulder of investigation up a hill towards truth, and never accomplishing the entire journey – still the temptation to argue that 'all truth is relative' has to be resisted, if the project of journalism itself is to be saved. Modern newspapers have these fundamental goals:

- to hold power to account – that is, to examine how far power, especially but far from only political power, actually does what it says it is doing, and in doing so, produces the effects it says it expects and desires;

1

- to provide a space for competing views from as wide a spectrum as possible, including those which large majorities may find distasteful.

In attempting these difficult and often expensive goals, modern newspapers are an expression – a high expression – of an enlightenment philosophy, based on the belief that the truth is available to be discovered, that public business and public figures should be accountable to the rest of society and their actions made as transparent as possible and that debate is necessary for a democratic and civil society. That is not because, as both John Milton and John Stuart Mill believed, that truth will always win out: it often won't. Rather it is because if such debate is suppressed, so freedom will also be curtailed.

What we have learned about phone hacking at the *News of the World*, and about the general behaviour of the tabloid press which is being illuminated, bit by bit, by the Leveson Inquiry, is destructive of these principles which newspapers, and their owners, insist they live by.

Outrages Practised on Citizens
The scale of the outrages practised on significant numbers of citizens include, above all else, wanton invasions of privacy through phone hacking, deceit, disguise and sometimes robbery; the giving over of most space in the most popular newspapers to the trivial, ignoring that which is significant in the world; the construction of wholly or partly fictional narratives; the at least implicit blackmailing of politicians with threats of exposure if they prove 'unhelpful'. All of this has been contained within an attitude which assumed immunity from legal or other challenge, because of the immense power which mass readerships was assumed to bring.

These attitudes flourished in the past three to four decades, when the belief that journalists could not be brought to account was conflated with the belief that whatever they did was an expression of freedom, and whatever they were prevented from doing was an expression of censorship or worse. This was best expressed by a sentence in the Press Complaints Commission code, which stated flatly that 'freedom of expression is itself a public good' – an absurd claim, but brilliantly expressive of the working philosophy of many newspapers.

The swaggering arrogance which these beliefs engendered is now undergoing a slow exposure in the Leveson Inquiry. That inquiry has a considerable time to run: but from its beginning, the large question of it has been: will it change anything? Or, after appropriate rituals of humiliation (already undertaken by the Murdochs, father and son) will business return to normal, constrained only by the loss of power and reach of newspapers because of cuts in circulation and in advertising revenues? Much will have to change if that is not to happen.

- Privacy must be respected. It will always be in balance with, not so much free speech, as the public interest investigations by journalists, which at times require intrusion. Thus, the weighing of the respective claims of privacy as against public interest which is made necessary by the Human

Rights Act is a reflection of reality: but such judgments as that made by Judge Eadie over the Max Mosley case – that his sexual preferences were his own affair, and exposure of them not in the public interest – is to be welcomed.

- The law covers journalists as much as anyone else. It should be applied to their activities as robustly as to any other citizens.

- The police are valuable sources for journalists, and journalists valuable to the police in their investigations. That necessary relationship must not be corrupt.

- Politicians rely increasingly on the media, since parties – which had in their time of mass memberships, carried their messages – are now weak. That reality cannot be allowed to cow them – especially the leaders – into acquiescence and, worse, the granting of favours.

- The media, if they wish to claim the status of the carriers of news and opinion and this be part of that which democracies offer to their citizens, should realise what that means in terms of fidelity to the truth.

The essays in this volume flesh out these and other reflections. They are more than usually valuable. When the activities of the news media are in the public eye and that public has been made aware of the civic cost of much of the content of what they read and watch, we should hope for public pressure for a better journalism for all. Since journalism, however funded, is inescapably constrained by market pressures in a free society, that will be the largest determinant of what it is.

Note on the contributor
John Lloyd is a Contributing Editor for the *Financial Times* and Director of Journalism at the Reuters Institute for the Study of Journalism at the University of Oxford.

Section A. Journalism at the Crossroads

Richard Lance Keeble

Over the weekend of 8 and 9 October 2011 I attended a wonderful conference in London celebrating the 75th anniversary of *Peace News*. More than 1,100 people packed a hall at the Institute of Education to hear the maverick intellectual Noam Chomsky give his spin on the Occupy Wall Street movement in the United States; scores of workshops covered a vast range of issues – the role of the trade union press, peace journalism, citizen journalism, feminist media, radical publishing and so on. One session looked at 'Surveillance, Privacy and the State in the Digital Age', another at 'Films, Photos and Dissent' and another 'Unheard Voices: Youth, the "riots" and the media'. Present were academics, Fleet Street progressives and media activists from Britain, South Korea, America, Lebanon, Israel and elsewhere.

Hackgate (the scandal engulfing the mainstream press) did feature in some of the discussions. I, for instance, chaired a session at which Professor James Curran, of Goldsmiths College, suggested that any inquiry into the press which failed to take into account the political economy of the industry would be a waste of time. Another session looked at the role of radicals in the mainstream. The blurb ran: 'How can an aspiring radical journalist avoid becoming, in George Monbiot's words, 'a specialist in the moronic recycling of what the rich and powerful deem to be news'.

But I would guess that for many of those present at the conference, the preoccupations of the Leveson Inquiry – the illegal excesses of tabloid hackery, the closeness of the ties between the Fleet Street, the police and politicians – were all too predictable and too narrowly focused on the mainstream. Leveson was likely to take little account of the valuable role of the alternative, internet based media – with their progressive, anti-racist, pro feminist, internationalist campaigning stances. Moreover, while Leveson was billed to examine the links between politicians and the press, should it not also probe the far more important ties between Fleet Street hacks and the spooks? The Hutton Inquiry into the strange death of weapons inspector Dr David Kelly, after all, had significantly failed to grasp the nettle and delve into the influence of the intelligence services on the news agenda.

Corruption at the Heart of the Mainstream Press

Yet Hackgate – with its seemingly daily stream of 'revelations' – is, indeed, highlighting the corruption, illegality and distorted news values at the heart of British mainstream journalism in an unprecedented way. How can press standards be improved? What kind of regulation, if any, is required? These are just two of the many questions now being asked with a new sense of urgency.

In the first chapter, writer and journalist Huw L. Hopkins provides his own, lively timeline of the Hackgate controversy to help guide the reader through its seemingly never-ending twists and turns. He begins his story this way:

> The phone hacking saga turned from journalists doing something dodgy to get a story to complete public outrage on 4 July 2011. Then it was revealed by the *Guardian* that 13-year-old Milly Dowler, who went missing in 2002, had her phone hacked. At the time this caused the parents to believe their child was still alive and it led the police up a non-existent path. There had been rumblings of a hacking nature when the *News of the World* published some trivial but private details about a royal in 2005. In the end, a *NoW* journalist and a private detective went to jail in 2007. But it was the Dowler revelation in July 2011 that caused national outcry. No longer did it seem the press focused only on the self-obsessed celebrities, or the discredited politicians or royals. Phone hacking now affected 'ordinary' members of the public.

Where will it all end? The coalition government has set up the Leveson Inquiry to look into the culture, practices and ethics of the British press (see www.levesoninquiry.org.uk) with its hearings watchable live on the website. Various royal commissions have pronounced on the press in the past but achieved little. Will Leveson be any different?

Richard Peppiatt, who resigned from his journalist job on the Richard Desmond-owned *Daily Star* in protest at its Islamophobia, reflected on his experiences in a remarkable, theoretically adventurous talk at the annual conference of the Institute of Communication Ethics on 28 October 2011 in London (where many of the contributions to this text first saw the light of day). Here he argues persuasively that too much mainstream journalism occupies the realm of story-telling. Journalism is, in effect, closer to fiction than fact. And Peppiatt suggests that the truth-seeking impulse of journalism proper will always be tainted by the excesses of its entertainment-driven cousin.

Wonderfully Irreverent

Chris Atkins' wonderfully irreverent *Starsuckers* film exposed the way in which the tabloid press and the BBC (with their celebrity obsessions) could so easily be hoaxed into carrying nonsensical, totally fabricated 'news' stories. In an edited extract from his evidence to the Leveson Inquiry, Atkins relates some of the conversations he had with tabloid journalists while he was researching his film undercover. He concludes: 'I believe that *Starsuckers* shows that there are serious problems at the heart of the British media, in particular the tabloid press. These are problems that the media itself is incapable of investigating or solving, which is why I support stronger regulation of the press that is completely independent of both the press and government.'

Brain Cathcart, founder of the Hacked Off campaign and Professor of Journalism at Kingston University, gave one of the keynote speeches at the ICE annual conference. Here he argues that news organisations should be asked to make increased and systematic use of paper trails in news as a way of highlighting the ethical responsibilities of the individual journalist:

> As for the use of such audit trails, they would have obvious practical applications in internal post mortem examinations, after problems have arisen. They might conceivably be made accessible to a new regulator. Adoption of the practice might serve as a protection in law.

Revelations to the Leveson Inquiry about unethical behaviour by the press will come as no surprise to anyone who has taken an interest in media standards since World War Two, according to Mike Jempson and Wayne Powell, of the media ethics campaigning organisation MediaWise. But they conclude with a certain degree of optimism:

> The journalism of the future will not be in the hands of a select band of hacks who consider themselves the gatekeepers of public taste and morals, free to operate as they please. It will be subject to constant scrutiny and open to a far wider range of participants – and best of all it should become fertile ground for high quality investigative reporting which recognises people rights, considers consequences, and expects public servants and power elites to operate as ethically as the media professionals will now be expected to behave.

White heat of Anger and Prejudice Directed at British journalists

Tim Crook, Senior Lecturer in Media Law and Ethics and Head of Radio at Goldsmiths, University of London, next argues that the white heat of anger and prejudice directed at British journalists as a result of the Hackgate scandal is in danger of 'consuming the oxygen of libertarian tolerance'.

Finally in this section, Teodora Beleaga, a student on the MA Interactive Journalism, City University, London, wonders why anyone would want to commit themselves to a career in journalism when the public standing of reporters has fallen to rock bottom in the wake of Hackgate.

During a recent debate at City University led by Professor Roy Greenslade on the Hackgate controversy, she and her fellow students were challenged as to whether they would ever agree to using information acquired through hacking phones. She writes: 'Amongst the many wannabes, less than a handful said they would categorically not resort to hacking or any other dark arts. Now, what does that tell us about the future of journalism in this country?' Indeed.

'Nobody likes a rotten apple, but someone picks them'

Huw L. Hopkins traces the long and winding history of Hackgate from its beginnings way back in 2000. After jailings there came silence. But then a constant stream of revelations, arrests, and resignations have all hit the headlines since those heady days in July 2011. Where will it all end?

The question is not: 'How far back does it go?' it is, in fact: 'Who knows how far back this thing has gone?' The phone hacking saga turned from journalists doing something dodgy to get a story to complete public outrage on 4 July 2011. Then it was revealed by the *Guardian* that 13-year-old Milly Dowler, who went missing in 2002, had her phone hacked. At the time this caused the parents to believe their child was still alive and it led the police up a non-existent path.

There had been rumblings of a hacking nature when the *News of the World* published some trivial but private details about a royal in 2005. In the end, a *NoW* journalist and a private detective went to jail in 2007. But it was the Dowler revelation in July 2011 that caused national outcry. No longer did it seem the press focused only on the self-obsessed celebrities, or the discredited politicians or royals. Phone hacking now affected 'ordinary' members of the public.

Over the next six-months the hacked victims came out thick and fast. Each story piled more pressure on the media and politicians – particularly as links between the press and David Cameron's government were revealed. Calls for action from the public and lobbying groups intensified. The result – Prime Minister David Cameron announced a judge-led investigation into the ethics of the press. But let us now return to the start of the scandal – in the year 2000.

2000 – Rebekah Wade (later Brooks) became Editor of *News of the World*.

The *News of the World* was one of the biggest papers in the world well before the turn of the millennium. In 1950, it had a weekly sale of 8,441,000. By May 2011, its circulation figure had dropped to just 2, 660, 000. In 2000, Rebekah Brooks took over from Phil Hall as Editor and immediately her presence had an impact. Her three years in charge brought about the hugely controversial but highly marketable 'Sarah's Law' campaign, with the tabloid carrying the names of paedophiles in an attempt to gain public access to the Sex Offenders Register. There were misnamings, mistaken identities and protesters holding 'PEADO' signs outside the homes of paediatricians. During this time Brooks befriended the mother of the Sarah Payne, (of Sarah's Law) and gained her trust.

2002 – Milly Dowler disappears.

The 13-year-old girl who would ultimately be the NoW's undoing was reported missing in March. Her body was discovered six months later, on 18 September.

Andy Coulson, Editor of *News of the World*

2003 – Andy Coulson took over as Editor of the *NoW*; Brooks flies closer to the *Sun*.

Despite the controversy, Brooks left her mark on the *NoW* by the time she had left in July 2003. While she moved next door as Editor of the *Sun*, her Deputy Editor, Andy Coulson, took her place. They sat together at a select committee shortly after the swap and Brooks stated boldly: 'We have paid the police for information in the past.' Coulson interjected quickly assuring the world that it was 'within the confines of the law'. There was little follow-up by both the press and police.

2005 – Clive Goodman writes about Prince William in the *NoW*.

Somehow Clive Goodman, the *NoW* royal correspondent, became the best investigative reporter the world had ever seen. He managed to convince the otherwise private and respected royal family to tell him about personal conversations they had had as a family. Not only that, they allowed him to print these private stories in one of the biggest selling newspapers in the world. A fantastic achievement. But the truth is Goodman used underhand and illegal methods to discover a knee injury to the future king.

2006 – Goodman arrested, along with private investigator Glenn Mulcaire.

2007 – Jail terms handed out but editors move on to bigger and better things.

Whether the two events are linked does not matter. Andy Coulson left the newspaper at the end of January and a few weeks later the two men arrested in the royal phone hacking scandal were jailed. Rupert Murdoch seemingly ordered a 'rigorous internal investigation' of the *News of the World*. Les Hinton, News International Chief Executive, confirmed that there was no widespread hacking taking place at the newspaper and the Press Complaints Commission later confirmed this in May. Coulson, the ex-Editor who fell from grace several months earlier, was appointed Director of Communications and Planning for the Conservative Party. To top off the year, the head honchos have a shuffle. Rupert Murdoch steps down as Sky's non-executive chairman and his son, James, takes over the running of News Corp's UK newspapers, Asian TV and Star TV.

2008 – News International pays Gordon Taylor £700,000

Testing period for James Murdoch

Under a bus. In the deep end. Pick your metaphor. The first few months at the helm of News Corp's European and Asian operations proved a testing period for James Murdoch. In April, News International paid the chief executive of the Professional Footballers Association £700,000 in legal costs and damages on the condition that Gordon Taylor signed a gagging clause to prevent him speaking about the case.

2009 – As Brooks became CEO of News International, the *Guardian* revealed new levels of illegality.

Brooks took over 'Fortress Wapping' in September as she was appointed CEO of News International. The company manages the three subsidiaries; Times Newspapers Ltd, News Group Newspapers (NGN) and NI Free Newspapers on a large site in Wapping, East London. In July, the hefty payment made in the previous year to the PFA executive became public knowledge. The *Guardian* also revealed several other illegal activities by NGN, including the hacking of more than 3,000 phones, misleading the PCC, the police and the public. Coulson told the Commons culture, media and sport committee that he had 'never condoned the use of phone hacking, nor do I have any recollection of the incidences where phone hacking took place'. The PCC released a statement confirming that there was no evidence that phone hacking was continuing.

2010 – Coulson feels the heat and the hacking spreads.

The Commons culture, media and sport committee released the report of their findings in February stating it was 'inconceivable that Goodman acted alone'. A month later Nick Davies, of the *Guardian*, continued his long list of Hackgate scoops. One involved Max Clifford's acceptance of more than £1million to keep quiet about the interception of his voicemail whilst Coulson was the Editor of the *NoW*. In May, the Conservative Party formed a coalition government with the Liberal-Democrats after failing to secure an overall majority. The leader of the Lib-Dems, Nick Clegg, was reported giving advice to Cameron over his choice of press secretary, Andy Coulson. When autumn fell, an ex-*NoW* reporter revealed in an interview with *The New York Times* that phone hacking was 'encouraged' at the Sunday tabloid. The interviewee, Sean Hoare, also later said that Coulson helped spread the practice which had become 'endemic'. This led to Coulson being interviewed by the police in November, but only as a witness.

2011 – Inquiries begin and the spotlight turns on the Murdoch family.

Media Rolling Stone Gathering Moss and Other Disgusting Forms of Life

This is the year when the media rolling stone really began gathering moss, stones, dirt and all other disgusting forms of life, as the Hackgate scandal simply refused to go away. The year began with three high profile claims of hacking which led to Operation Weeting being set up by the police: Ian Edmondson; news editor the *NoW*, was suspended on 5 January over allegations of phone hacking in 2005-6. And Andy Coulson resigned from his position as Director of Communications at No. 10 on 21 January, blaming the coverage of the hacking scandal.

February saw Glenn Mulcaire being called to reveal the names of who commissioned him to hack phones. From one rogue reporter to one rogue newsroom. The *News of the World* had three journalists arrested in April: Ian Edmondson, James Weatherup and Neville Thurlbeck. The paper then set up a compensation scheme for those affected. The following month actor Sienna Miller and sports commentator Andy Gray received damages after their voice mails were intercepted.

July was the knockout month for the *News of the World*. On 4 July, Rebekah Brooks said it was 'inconceivable' that she knew about the hacking of Milly Dowler's phone as she was on holiday when it was carried out. The following day, evidence showed the victims of the London 7/7 bombings, the families of the murdered Soham schoolgirls and the parents of Madeleine McCann (snatched while on holiday in Portugal in May 2007) were all targeted over phone hacking. The *Guardian* reported 'messages were deleted by *NoW* journalists in the first few days after Milly's disappearance…As a result friends and relatives concluded wrongly that she might be alive'. This quickly put pressure on the Murdoch's to make a bold decision about their newspaper. On 6 July, the Hacked Off campaign, calling for a full public inquiry into the hacking scandal, was launched (headed by Professor Brian Cathcart, of Kingston University) and finally James Murdoch announced the closure of the 168-year-old *News of the World* on the following day.

On 10 July, the newspaper apologised in its final edition (with its front page declaring: 'Thank you & goodbye'). But the closure of the tabloid did not mean the end of the problem at hand. Two days earlier, the Prime Minister announced that a judge-led inquiry into press standards would take place. On 13 July, Rupert Murdoch's News Corporation withdrew its bid to take over the rest of BSkyB, just as MPs were to vote on a motion, with cross-party support, calling on Murdoch to scrap the bid.

Then Rebekah Brooks resigned. Les Hinton resigned. And so the bricks of Murdoch's empire started toppling. Then Sir Paul Stephenson, the most senior police officer in the country, resigned (after criticism of his links to former *News of the World* Deputy Editor Neil Wallis). Even Met Police Assistant Commissioner John Yates resigned.

Sean Hoare, the first *NoW* journalist to come forward bravely and speak on the record about hacking, was found dead at his home (though the police indicated there were no suspicious circumstances).

Gotcha! Rupert Murdoch eats 'Humble Pie'

What happened on 19 July has gone down in the annals of history. How Jonathan May-Bowles managed to walk into the select committee hearing with a paper plate and shaving foam, completely unnoticed, is bizarre. How he managed to make the foam pie, walk out of the public seating area, in front of the cameras and the desk where the Murdochs sat, and launch the pie at Rupert's face before being tackled, is totally baffling. During the ruckus, his wife, Wendi Deng, managed to strike a blow to May-Bowles. But pictures of Murdoch with 'humble pie' on his face and the caption 'Gotcha!' went worldwide.

During this turbulent select committee hearing (watched live on television by millions) both Murdochs claimed they knew nothing of phone hacking. Several days later, *NoW* staff, including the senior legal adviser, Tom Crone, and the last editor, Colin Myler, claimed they had told James about the hacking in an email marked 'For Neville'. On the 28th, the close friend of Rebekah Brooks, Sara Payne, was told by investigators that a phone that Brooks had given to her had been hacked into. This announcement came less than a month after Payne had written a column in the final ever edition of *News of the World* thanking the tabloid for its support through the traumatic time of the loss of her daughter.

The next day found Baroness Buscombe, chair of the PCC, resigning. The PCC's failures to investigate the phone hacking allegations adequately ultimately made her position untenable. Glenn Mulcaire also defended himself by saying he was merely working 'on the instructions of others'.

From 2 August, arrests began taking place left, right and centre, each one being *NoW* staff or former employee. Interestingly, a *Guardian* reporter, David Leigh admitted to phone hacking on 5 August. But he claimed that when it took place in 2006 he was investigating bribery and corruption, not 'tittle tattle'.

On 17 August, the *Guardian* revealed an explosive letter written by Clive Goodman to Les Hinton. Dating from March 2007, it stated Coulson knew of the hacking and that the practice was 'widely discussed'.

As the saga entered September, Tom Crone, the former *NoW* legal manager, and the former editor, Colin Myler, were called to the select committee. They stated that an email titled 'for Neville' was seen by James Murdoch. The email was meant for Neville Thurlbeck and should have led him to knowing about the illegal practices.

On 17 September, it was reported that policeman John Yates secured a job at Scotland Yard for the daughter of *NoW* executive Neil Wallis. He was later cleared of improper behaviour on this action. On the same day, James Murdoch finally admitted the £700k payout to Gordon Taylor of the PFA.

Two days later, Rupert Murdoch paid £2million to the Dowler family and a personal donation of £1m to their chosen charity. Later, a Scotland Yard detective was arrested for leaking phone hacking evidence to the *Guardian*. And on the 26 September Glenn Mulcaire revealed the full list of people that paid him for illegally sourced information.

Over the next month a number of further and re-arrests were made. Tom Crone told the select committee that one of the reasons Murdoch had for settling one case was because he knew of the 'for Neville' email. Operation

Weeting also increased the amount of police officers assigned to 200 to assist with the investigation.

On 25 October, a third of News Corporation's investors voted against the Murdoch sons being re-elected to the board. The following day the Metropolitan Police find a phone that was used for more than 1,000 instances of illegal hacking.

Rogue Newsroom becomes Rogue News Company

Entering November, one rogue newsroom became a rogue news company as the *Sun* had its first journalist arrested for paying police officers. Jamie Pyatt was released on bail until March 2012 – as have all the others arrested. The Metropolitan Police calculated that 5,795 people had been victims of phone hacking but this figure could actually increase. One of these cases is the father of Josie Russell who survived an attack in which her mother and sister were killed. Shaun Russell, the father, sued News International.

On 5 November, reports surfaced that a former police officer was hired to spy on the lawyers representing phone hacking victims. Shortly after a second private detective claimed that he had followed more than 90 people under orders from *NoW*. Derek Webb continued to work for them right up until the close of the newspaper.

The following morning, James Murdoch was questioned again by the select committee since his previous appearance was considered misleading by some. Tom Watson, a Labour MP, accused him of being 'the worst Mafia boss in the world'.

On 14 November, the Leveson Inquiry officially started. This inquiry over the next few weeks would see celebrities, witnesses, victims and journalists all give evidence. Some of the high profile cases involved Hugh Grant and Charlotte Church, along with comedian Steve Coogan. It became clear that the scandal was no longer just about phone hacking. Lord Justice Leveson is now looking at the ethics of journalism as a whole. Certain newspapers, such as the *Daily Mail*, are being asked to write apologies and are coming under severe pressure. Whether or not any more newspapers will close, no one knows but one thing for sure is that no newspaper is safe. The *News of the World* is shut, the *Sun* is trying to distance itself from the scandal, the *Mail* and *Daily Mirror* are facing all sorts of pressures – and the *Guardian* has also admitted being involved in hacking – but 'in the public interest'. The latter newspaper has been instrumental in the revelations and is largely responsible for the campaign building up such momentum.

On the 12 December, the Metropolitan police made a statement to the Leveson Inquiry saying it was 'unlikely' Glenn Mulcaire, whilst working on behalf of the *News of the World*, deleted any of Dowler's voicemail messages. The *Guardian* had reported this as fact, having been briefed to that effect by the Surrey police. It apologised and amended the relevant reports online.

Leveson: Allowing the Public see the Damage after a Car Crash

Lord Leveson is effectively allowing the public see the damage caused after a car crash. The victims can air their grievances. Not only has Leveson interviewed celebrities, but also affected members of the public. 'We're just ordinary people,' said Milly Dowler's mother. The lack of journalism ethics isn't just affecting the rich and famous, it's hurting the people who want no part of it.

The fishing for stories, rummaging of bins and the hacking of phones will undoubtedly be very hard to do in the near future. Next year, Leveson will recommend a path to take. One of many. Together they could bring about a monumental change in how journalism is conducted and regulated in the UK. As Jon Snow, the Channel 4 news presenter, said in a Coventry Conversation: 'There are many people with great integrity in the media, there are also some rotten apples.' It's time to throw the rotten apples out and focus on the fruit that is still healthy and does some good for the public.

Note on the contributor

Huw L. Hopkins is a writer and journalist. In 2009 he graduated with a combination of Honours from University College Plymouth Marjon and is currently on the MA in Global Journalism at Coventry University. He works with AltSounds magazine online and has written for CUToday. He also manages his own website, www.huwlhopkins.com, and you can follow him on Twitter @HuwLHopkins.

The Story Factory: Infotainment and the Tabloid Newsroom

Richard Peppiatt, who resigned from the _Daily Star_ over its Islamophobia, argues that too much journalism occupies the realm of story-telling. And he fears that the truth-seeking impulse of journalism proper will always be tainted by the excesses of its entertainment-driven cousin

2011: Year of the great tabloid existential crisis. Of course, some industry voices will seek to write the history rather differently; that of the great red-top witch hunt, that of the politicians' revenge (helped in no small part by some meddling mummies in leafy Hampstead). Yet even those who have insisted on burying their heads in the sand are finding their rose-tinted spectacles now somewhat scratched. Most will admit the constant jab, jab, of the Leveson Inquiry, media select committees and phone hacking revelations are forcing them to fight for their very right to exist.

Tabloid journalists, too, are feeling punch drunk. Public trust is in single digits and falling, and the new spotlight on their practices is leaving them hamstrung in the pursuit of the sort of slap n' tickle scoops some have spent years cultivating into an art form. Others (particularly if lubricated with a few post-deadline drinks) will admit they welcome a reappraisal of the industry's _modus operandi_. Public figures may rightly have complained to Leveson about weeks of looking from inside their homes to see reporters camped along the driveway, but as any coalface hack would care to add, it's even less fun huddled on the outside, looking in. Even in the relative comfort of the newsroom many are disillusioned with being forced to fit the squareness of fact into the round hole assigned by their editors.

Sitting before Lord Justice Leveson in November, I was struck by how, as much as giving evidence about my former employers at the _Daily Star_, I was also testifying against myself. The picture I was painting of my red top exploits, be it the ideologically driven distortions or tittle-tattle inventions, betrayed my behaviour as something other than journalistic. What is less clear is what that other is.

Look up 'journalist' in the dictionary and you will be told it's 'a person who writes for newspapers or magazines'. The definition of 'journalism' is no more illuminating, defining itself as 'the activity or profession of writing for newspapers or magazines'. Seeking to escape this frustrating semantic loop, I turned to a definition offered by Professor Brian Cathcart. He describes journalism as an activity that is 'demonstrably valuable to society. It tells us what is new, important and interesting in public life, it holds authority to account, it promotes informed debate, it entertains and enlightens'.[1]

It struck me as an excellent definition, if a sobering one. Very little of my work in tabloids fell within these parameters. Sometimes what I wrote was *new*, but more often than not it was cannibalised from other news sources. Even that appearing new was caged within pre-defined narratives and well-worn stereotypes.

Self-interested Ideological or Commercial Reasons

On occasion my writing *held authority to account*, but it was often simply as a by-product of one powerful institution flexing its muscles against another for self-interested ideological or commercial reasons. Negative tabloid coverage of the BBC as bloated, left-leaning and increasingly debased fits this profile. Some of the stories may have justifiably shone a light on a public service body, but the light was primarily pointing in their direction because the likes of News International, Associated Newspapers and Northern & Shell have a commercial interest in undermining a powerful rival.

Far from *promoting informed debate* and *enlightening* the reader my writing tended to deliberately obfuscate the issues and skew the terms of reference, creating binary arguments and offering reductive solutions, leaving any semblance of balance until the very last, safe in the knowledge few ever make it that far.

Whether it dealt with what is *important* and *interesting* in public life is more difficult because of the subjectivity of the terms, but let it be said that on the awe-inspiring day last spring millions took to the streets of Egypt to demand freedom, the *Daily Star* front page read: 'Jordan…the movie.' This was not a reference to the Middle East.

So if it wasn't journalism I was doing, what was it?

Jonathan Caplan QC, lead counsel for Associated Newspapers, inadvertently lifted the lid during his opening statement to the Leveson Inquiry. 'Our aim,' he said, 'is to entertain – to engage the reader.' To entertain. Despite the fullness of Brian Cathcart's definition of journalism, my experience in tabloids is that entertainment usurps all other facets. Everything I wrote was designed to appeal to the emotional over the rational, the knee-jerk over the considered, assumptions reinforced rather than challenged and all presented in an easily digestible style that celebrated its own triviality.

Journalism Essentially a Form of Story-Telling – to Entertain

Back to my dictionary I came across another word, described as 'an account of imaginary or real people and events told for entertainment'. The word? Storytelling. Journalism is a form of storytelling, both being simulacra-building enterprises. But the obligation of journalism proper must be an attempt at The Truth, while a storyteller's only obligation is to entertain – to keep your audience diverted and engaged.

Storytelling is not constrained by the parameters Professor Cathcart chalks out for journalism. Yet the common assumption, as seen from the dictionary definition, is that because something is printed in a newspaper, it is therefore journalistic and that anyone providing content to a newspaper is, therefore, a journalist. It's a fallacious leap of logic that has contributed as much as anything to the industry's current crisis.

Entertainment has to some degree always formed part of a newspaper's output. Crudely, news informed, comment entertained. But today the prerogative to entertain has superseded that to inform, with comment indistinguishable from news, fact indistinguishable from conjecture. This type of discourse is having a devastating impact not only on the quality of our social dialogue, but on individuals too.

Ask the likes of Chris Jefferies (wrongly accused by a number of newspapers over the murder of Jo Yeates) or Rebecca Leighton (hounded by the press after the contamination of saline solution at Stepping Hill Hospital in Greater Manchester) what it's like to be caught in the crosshairs of a media whose imperative is not to truth, but entertainment. They have witnessed from the inside the staggering speed in which the simulacra overtakes the real, the crude reductionism of their lives into grotesque caricatures. The point of reference used by journalists writing about them was not the real; it was the hyperreal. It was the calculating killers and creeping oddballs of the movie screens that were simply imprinted upon the names and images of an innocent retired schoolmaster and young nurse to create blockbuster storylines. Both Chris Jefferies and Rebecca Leighton have described how they simply cannot tally the person represented on tabloid news pages with the image they have of themselves.

Consider further that if a friend tells you they've met a famous person, most will add: 'They were different in real life than I'd expected.' The image we hold of all those in the public eye is filtered through the prism of mass media, increasing sections of which have abandoned any attempt to anchor their simulations within the sphere of the real. Instead, real-world images are re-appropriated as the building blocks upon which a storytelling narrative can be constructed.

Fear and Anxiety Key Emotional Drivers

I resigned from the *Daily Star* chiefly over its coverage of Islam, which in the absence of any individual vulnerable enough to have their image kidnapped by the newsroom storytellers, was the newspaper's caricature *du jour.* It is important here to stress that entertainment in this context is not solely about provoking positive emotional reactions. Fear and anxiety are also key emotional drivers, and powerful tools of rhetoric.

Much has been said and written post 9/11 about the politics of fear as a form of social manipulation, one facet of which is its influence on consumption. Crudely, when people are scared, they spend. These are parallel cycles that lie at the very heart of agenda-rich tabloid storytelling. The potent narrative formula of provoking fear, often through demonisation of the disenfranchised – be they Muslims, or the working class, or immigrants – juxtaposed with the aspirational materialism of celebrity culture offers both the illness and the cure within a single, bite-size package, and as such has less in common with journalism than another pervasive medium – advertising. George Monbiot's following words are about the advertising industry, but much could unnervingly be applied to tabloid news too:

> Pervasiveness and repetition act like a battering ram against our minds. The first time we see an advertisement, we are likely to be aware of what it's telling us and what it is encouraging us to buy. From then on, we process it passively, absorbing its imagery and messages without contesting them, as we are no longer fully switched on. Brands and memes then become linked in ways our conscious minds fail to detect. As a report by the progressive think-tank Compass explains, the messages used by advertisers are designed to trigger emotional rather than rational responses. The low attention processing model developed by Robert Heath at the University of Bath shows how, in a crowded advertising market, passive and implicit learning become the key drivers of emotional attachment.[2]

The increasing reliance of newspapers on advertising has a commercial foundation, but also an ideological one. Both advertising and much current journalism passively sell a particular worldview through their storytelling that is founded not on a public-interest to inform (and secondarily to entertain) but on the self-interest to entertain (and secondarily to inform) and in doing so maximise profit. The difference is that with advertising the self-interest is explicit. Currently much of that which is passing for journalism is self-interested storytelling attempting to seek cover behind public-interest defenses.

But just as with advertising we have little choice as to whether we consume the hyperreal narratives of the newsroom because they have come to dominate popular culture, with storytellers as much involved in shaping its content and values as they are disinterested reporters upon it. Docu-soaps or scripted reality shows such as *The Only Way Is Essex* and *Made in Chelsea* have exploded in popularity, hugely fuelled by a tabloid agenda that has recognised a fertile new storytelling pasture.

The nature of the format means the shows stars simultaneously occupy the spheres of both the real and the hyperreal, a concept perhaps best contained beneath Jacques Derrida's neologism 'artifactuality'.[3] The persons submitting themselves to such representation abandon any meaningful separation of the public and private spheres, instead enthusiastically embracing their passive role as the malleable characters of whatever storyline TV producers – and to no lesser extent tabloid editors – decide upon. More than ever before journalists are not passively reporting on the behaviour of these persons, but shaping the very path of their real-world lives for our hyperreal consumption. It is journalist as scriptwriter, as storyteller. This is a cultural shift – we have passed a point where the public has to be cajoled or deceived into becoming participants of the simulacra building process; they are queuing up and literally desperate to do so.

The Simulacra Rapidly Overtakes the Real

The cross-media nature of this storytelling has been instrumental in legitimising the simulacra-building process of the newsroom. Within minutes of rolling off the print presses (or more likely today published first online) the stories are reproduced across the TV, radio and the internet. 'Never wrong for long' may be a newsroom gag on the pressures to be the first on breaking news, but there is another meaning. 'Never wrong for long' can also refer to the instantaneous process of reinforcement across media platforms which adds veracity to storytelling narratives. The simulacra rapidly overtakes the real. In many regards the fictional *becomes* the factual, the storytelling *becomes* akin to journalism solely because the force of repetition legitimises it as a form of truth. This process is an insidious force upon public discourse because it robs the participants of a democracy of the ability to participate fully. They are denied the access to the legitimate realm of truth regarding the society in which they live. They are treated not as citizens to be respected, but consumers to be manipulated.

A less discussed effect, but one that has contributed greatly to the current phone hacking scandal and wider ethical crisis within the press, is the impact mass media storytelling has on the storyteller. As much as journalists consider themselves as the special beings that can see through the matrix, their arguments – the very same arguments that I have preached from many a barstool – betray them. Take this one: 'Celebrities are fair game. They make millions off their image, so they can't just turn it off and claim privacy when it suits them.'

This argument is constructed around the premise that the simulacra and the real are one and the same. The underlying assumption is that the celebrity of the red carpets and chat shows *exists* beyond a media construct. I'd allow myself to buy into my own storytelling because it's easier to write intrusive, speculatory and sometimes hurtful things when the subject is a character in a story rather than it is a person existing in the real world; it's easier to listen to the phone messages of Alan Partridge than it is Steve Coogan.

The moral and ethical standards one applies to their real world behaviour can be suspended when adopting the role of the storyteller whose main imperative beyond all others is to entertain. This attitude is betrayed in its full ugly glare by Owen Beanie, owner of the World Entertainment News Network (WENN), a global celebrity photo and news agency. Speaking about the 2008 paparazzi harassment of Britney Spears, he boasts:

> What she actually does makes no difference. Whether she's in hospital, and we don't get pictures of her, we sell pictures of her before she went into hospital, or she's out of hospital, goes out for dinner and gets her haircut, doesn't make a difference, as long as we're there to cover it, we make our money. They are not people to us. When we have cameras that take nine pictures a second, so when someone gets out of a car and walks into a door which takes three seconds, I've already got 40 pictures. Now that's just one photographer – I have three photographers on it – 20, 30, 40 whatever – there's a shit load of pictures. For the amount of pictures you get, especially when flashes are going off, for expressions – pictures where you look good, pictures where you look bad. We can decide which ones we send out…From our point of view, we just want to sell the photos. From the publications' point of view, they just want things that people are going to pick up and buy. And that is always going to be bad news. We are forced into giving them bad news (see *Starsuckers* 2009).

While few in the tabloid industry would publicly express Mr Beanie's sentiment in such brash terms, I can attest that it is in some sections a predominant perspective. In my years spent in tabloid newsrooms I strain to remember a single instance in which discussion over content included empathetic consideration on the subject of the coverage, be it celebrity or simply someone in the public eye. While some may be unmoved that *News of the World* reporters and editors gave scant regard to the emotional impact on former F1 boss Max Mosley when they invaded his privacy to expose his sexual proclivities[4], consider the Sun's front-page fascination with 'Britain's youngest Dad' in the spring of 2009.[5]

For weeks a boy of 13 and girl of 15 were subjected to the full glare of a tabloid feeding frenzy, frothing comment passed on their upbringing, education and morality. Was the welfare of these vulnerable teens and the impact such acute coverage would have on their lives given consideration? I would suggest not. The oft-heard defence that the subjects of many, but not all, of these types of stories are paid and therefore complicit is disingenuous. The photographers are on the doorstep long before the chequebook is produced – the subjects are often forced into the so-called 'Faustian pact' as the better of two evils; if their images are going to be exploited by the newsroom storytellers regardless, they may as well get paid. The argument is also diversionary. It sidesteps the ethical concern by reframing it as a monetary issue. One does not necessarily inform the other.

Groupthink for those Cocooned in a Newsroom Bubble

This dubious self-justification based on a hyperreal interpretation of the world becomes a type of groupthink for those cocooned in a newsroom bubble of fellow storytellers, each incentivised, sometimes through bullying and manipulation, to suspend real-world moral judgments in pursuit of their newspapers' agenda. The increasingly deskbound nature of the job exasperates the situation, the main interaction not being with real-world contacts, but a computer screen, itself perhaps the epitome of hyperreal consumption. This immersion only extenuates a dangerous disassociation from empathic judgment.

Let us take the case of Milly Dowler. Did private investigator Glenn Mulcaire and the *News of the World* journalist who allegedly commissioned him see her as a 13-year-old schoolgirl in the same way they saw a niece or neighbour's daughter, or did they simply see a narrative they were under pressure to develop? The pretty, young kidnap victim from the suburbs, the search, the whodunit. Were these people callously amoral, or were the reference points for their behaviour no longer grounded in the real?

Although I could not quantify it at the time, it was the dull thud of reality that convinced me to abandon my career in tabloids. During the beginning of the *Daily* Star's flirtation with the far-right in the spring of 2011[6] I had confronted the fact that my agenda driven storytelling about Muslims and immigrants could well be the trigger to real world violence. Further, a suppressed recognition surfaced that the simulacra world image of terror, fear and social division I perpetuated in newsprint began to be recognisable in my own real-world community. It may be the age-old chicken and egg scenario, but logically as such it is impossible to absolve myself; I was kicking at the cracks in society in the pursuit of profit for my employer. In the words of Charlie Brooker I felt I was 'wasting my life actively making the world worse'.[7]

The writer George Saunders sets out the current tone of our mass media discourse brilliantly in his essay *The Braindead Megaphone*. In it he imagines the voice of the mass media as a man at a dinner party, shouting into a loudspeaker and thus coming to dominate the individual conversations of his fellow guests. He writes:

> Megaphone guy is a storyteller, but his stories are not so good. Or rather, his stories are limited. His stories have not had time to gestate – they go out too fast and to too broad an audience…The best stories proceed from a mysterious truth seeking impulse that narrative has when revised extensively; they are complex and baffling and ambiguous; they tend to make us slower to act, rather than quicker…If the story is poor, or has an agenda, if it has come out of a paucity of imagination or is rushed, we imagine these other people as essentially unlike us: unknowable, inscrutable, inconvertible. In surrendering our mass storytelling function to entities whose first priority is profit, we make a dangerous concession: 'Tell us,' we say in effect, 'as much truth as you can, while still making money.' This is not the same as asking: 'Tell us the truth.'[8]

Pre-Defined Narratives

Journalism proper, driven by a truth-seeking impulse grounded in the real, is vastly more exhausting both financially and temporally than the type of agenda-rich storytelling that dominates the news market. The conditions of the modern newsroom, particularly, but not exclusively, tabloid ones, mean that journalists walk in the door and are forced by circumstance to behave as storytellers, abiding by the pre-defined narratives as part of an entertainment-seeking impulse.

If any doubt exists why this matters so much let's consider the invasion of Iraq. The British public were convinced of its necessity significantly because of the allegation that Saddam Hussein could launch chemical weapons within 45 minutes. It was a great story; it fitted the right narratives; it was presented on a plate with little need for investigation – it was duly splashed across front page after front page. Later it was discovered it had absolutely no grounding in reality. By then we were at war.

As we enter a period of profound change in the print media, we are already seeing the newsroom storytellers working around the clock to claim the narrative upper hand. Tabloid versus broadsheet, politician versus press, self-regulation versus state-regulation. For me the real battle here is between journalism and storytelling, or more specifically storytelling masquerading as journalism. With storytelling the consumer is encouraged to suspend belief, while with journalism they are encouraged to do the opposite – to trust. With this in mind we must give more scrutiny to what journalism actually is, and what we want it to be. The breadth of what we consider journalism at present is so vast as to beg the question of whether a catch-all form of regulation is possible, or even desirable. A system which allows public interest journalism to flourish whilst reigning in self-interested storytelling feels to me an almost insurmountable challenge.

Just as under the current PCC system, scope given to the 'quality' end of the market will likely be exploited by the tabloids towards entertainment-centric ends. This is no less complicated by the fact that tabloids on occasion do some brilliant, thrusting journalism. The shift between storyteller and journalist can be a fluid one. This is not about deriding celebrity gossip or tabloid fun because it certainly has its place within the media ecosystem. To me this is about recognising the true nature of the activity being pursued. I take no pleasure removing my career from the sphere of the journalistic, and assigning it to the realm of storytelling.

But until a distinction between the two is recognised I fear the truth-seeking impulse of journalism proper will always be tainted by the excesses of its entertainment-driven cousin, and in doing so public trust will remain in the gutter. If the public don't believe the journalism they read then a vital trust facet of that transaction is lost. All journalists become storytellers by default, the implications of which are devastating.

Notes

[1] See http://inforrm.wordpress.com/2011/09/11/opinion-the-code-breakers-part-1-brian-cathcart/, accessed on 1 December 2011

[2] See http://www.monbiot.com/2011/10/24/sucking-out-our-brains-through-our-eyes/, accessed on 1 December 2011

[3] See Jacques Derrida and Bernard Stiegler (2002) *Echographies of Television: Filmed Interviews*, Cambridge: Polity Press

[4] See http://www.guardian.co.uk/media/2011/nov/24/max-mosley-news-world-publisher, accessed on 1 December 2011

[5] See http://www.thesun.co.uk/sol/homepage/news/article2435283.ece, accessed on 1 December 2011

[6] http://www.guardian.co.uk/media/greenslade/2011/feb/10/dailystar-english-defence-league, accessed on 1 December 2011

[7] http://www.guardian.co.uk/commentisfree/2011/apr/18/phone-tapping-victims-tabloid-hacks, accessed on 1 December 2011

[8] George Saunders (2008) *The Braindead Megaphone*, London: Bloomsbury

Note on the contributor

Richard Peppiatt is a former tabloid reporter, who quit the *Daily Star* in 2011 in protest at what he regarded as their Islamophobic news agenda. He is now a freelance journalist, writer, broadcaster and campaigner for press reform.

How to Fool the Tabloids Over and Over again…

Chris Atkins specialises in making films that cause trouble. His 2009 film, *Starsuckers*, put the cat firmly among the tabloid pigeons. Here, in an extract from his evidence to the Leveson Inquiry, he reveals just how he fooled the red tops over and over again

Starsuckers was made over two years and released in 2009 and looks at the different ways that media corporations use the allure of fame and the impact this has on society. We wanted to explore how the news media and, in particular, the tabloids, obtain their celebrity stories.

The public have to pay for news through advertising, cover price and online subscriptions, but are largely kept in the dark about how the information is gathered and its veracity. We were struck by how rarely tabloid journalists, editors or executives went on record to discuss their work. When they did they rigidly held the corporate line that all their activities were within the law and the PCC code.

Researching the subject, we were told off-the-record by working tabloid journalists that their papers routinely fabricated news and broke the law to deliver scoops. We made many requests for on-the-record record interviews with people working for the tabloids and they all refused, apart from one ex-journalist Emma Bussey, who used to write for the *People*. We asked to film behind-the-scenes in newsrooms and were also turned down.

The only means left open to investigate the workings of the tabloids, where there was abundant *prima facie* evidence of wrongdoing, was to use subterfuge. Our investigations were planned using high ethical standards, and we made sure that any subterfuge was fully justified in the wider public interest. We were always intending that the film would one day be screened on television, so we knew we would have to meet Ofcom standards.

Fake Stories

We set out to feed untrue stories to tabloid newspapers to see if they would be printed without checks, and observe how the stories were relayed to the public. We created fictional celebrity stories that had no factual basis whatsoever, apart from the physical location of a celebrity at a certain time. We avoided fabricating anything malicious or defamatory to the celebrity themselves, and did not take any of the money that was offered in return for the stories. We called the numbers advertised within newspapers encouraging members of the public to call in and sell stories.

Researching our first story, we learned that the Canadian singer, Avril Lavigne, had been to the nightclub Bungalow 8. The next morning, on 18 March 2009, our researcher Jen Richardson called the *Daily Mirror* news desk pretending to be French party girl 'Gigi', with the story that Lavigne had fallen asleep in Bungalow 8, and started snoring. Jen had spent a large amount of time (and expense) visiting celebrity nightclubs, and working on Gigi's character, in order to make her stories convincing. From this first call it was clear that this research was redundant – the journalist at the *Daily Mirror* simply wrote down what Jen said, and didn't probe further. Our fabricated story appeared in the newspaper the following day without checks. Jen was told to send in her bank details to receive the £50 payment for the story, which we did not do.

As the investigation continued we created more and more outlandish stories to see at what point suspicions would be raised. We went on to feed fabricated stories successfully to the *Daily Star*, the *Daily Mirror* again, the *Sun* and the *Daily Express*. As the tales became more absurd, the effect was not that they received more scrutiny, but that the payments offered increased along with the coverage.

Amy Winehouse's 'flaming hair' story

The next story was about the singer Amy Winehouse. A friend had visited a party at the singer's house the previous evening. During an impromptu jamming session several guitars and amps were plugged in, and the resulting surge in power overloaded the mains and the lights went out. In the dark, Winehouse and a guest attempted to change the fuses, but they were both given an electric shock. Winehouse's companion was knocked out, but Winehouse herself merely twitched, and her famous hair started smouldering. Jen called this story into several tabloid news desks, and despite it appearing to come from a friend of the source rather than the actual witness, it appeared without checks in the *Daily Mirror*, and the *Daily Star*. The *Daily Star* added its own fictional element to the story: 'A friend was called in and ended up punching Flamey Amy's head to put out the blaze.'

The Amy Winehouse hair fire story then got picked up by other news outlets in the UK and overseas, who simply copied the *Mirror*'s story from its website, and presented it to their readers as fact....In all, six fake celebrity stories were created and fed to the tabloid press in a two-week period in March 2009:

- Guy Ritchie injuring himself juggling cutlery in restaurant (Bizarre column in the *Sun*);
- Russell Brand admitting wanting to be a banker as a child during the G20 protests (*Daily Express*);
- Pixie Geldof confessed to padding her bra out with sweets (*Daily Mirror*).

The 'Sarah Harding Secret Fan of Quantum Physics' Hoax

Our biggest story was in the *Sun*, revealing that Sarah Harding from Girls Aloud was secretly a fan of Quantum Physics. It ran as a lead story in Gordon Smart's Bizarre column. Smart's article also included a fabricated quote: 'There is a lot more going on under that blonde barnet than Sarah is given credit for. She's a smart cookie and does read an awful lot.' This quote didn't come from Jen, showing that the *Sun* will add fictitious quotes into their articles, as well as not running basic checks. At the time, Girls Aloud appeared regularly in the *Sun*, so it would have taken minutes to check with the agent or PR if there was any truth to our story. The Harding physics story was then was picked up by dozens of news sites around the world. Had we claimed it, the story fee would have earned us £600 from News International.

All of our hoaxes were picked up by at least one national tabloid, apart from a ridiculous story about Alan Sugar. We since discovered that Sugar is extremely litigious and newspapers are extremely wary of running stories other than PR for the *Apprentice*.

Tabloid 'Criminality'

Later in the media section of *Starsuckers* we look at the culture of criminality in tabloid newspapers. We talked to several journalists and ex-journalists off-the-record, who told us that the Goodman and Mulcaire convictions were just the tip of the iceberg. These sources explained that tabloid journalists, from the Sunday papers in particular, were still routinely breaking the law to get stories without any public interest. Our research also indicated that this behaviour was institutionally ingrained in tabloid culture, rather than the 'rogue reporters' whom newspaper editors claimed were responsible.

We wanted to test the Sunday tabloids to see if their journalists were willing to break the law, and the PCC code, to obtain private information about celebrities that was not in the public interest. The scenario was constructed to present the newspapers with a story that would involve them breaking the rules, and see which newspapers would engage with us.

I would pose as an intermediary who was selling the details of celebrities plastic surgery operations, but was ignorant of the rules of modern tabloid reporting. I would claim that I was the ex-boyfriend of a nurse who worked in a plastic surgery clinic and who had evidence of high profile celebrities having operations. Given the intrusive nature of such stories, the newspapers would be likely to need to obtain proof that these stories were true in order to print them. Any such proof would inherently involve a breach of the Data Protection Act, which prohibits the sale of medical records. Even harvesting information to research the stories would involve a breach of the DPA, as this would constitute a fishing expedition.

The DPA does have a general opt-out for journalists where the information is in the public interest. A recent case where the authorities said they would not prosecute due to public interest grounds was over the MPs' expenses revelations. So we deliberately created stories that, while of interest to a tabloid readership, could never be classed as being in the public interest. The PCC code also makes it clear that health issues are extremely sensitive. In parliament, Paul Dacre, in his role as chair of the editors' code of ethics, said there was an absolute prohibition on journalists accessing medical records.

Stories that would breach the DPA

To initiate the investigation, on 20 March 2009, 1 called the news desks of the *Sunday Express*, the *News of the World*, the *Sunday Mirror* and the *People*. All these newspapers had been accused of printing stories that would breach the DPA without public interest. The first call was to the *Sunday Express*, and I explained the story I had to offer (which I kept the same for all the news desks):

> Chris Atkins (CA): This is quite sensitive, but a friend of mine has some information, I think quite interesting information, about a variety of well-known people. She basically she works in a cosmetic surgery clinic.
> *Sunday Express*: Right
> CA: And I've been on at her for years saying 'Look, you could make a fortune out of some of the things you know' and she's been like: 'No, no, no, no.'. She's an ex-girlfriend basically, she's um – I don't know what's happened – I think she's fallen out with her boss, and she's interested. So she's asked me to sort of make some discrete enquires.

The person on the *Sunday Express* news desk made it clear why the PCC prevented them touching stories from such a source:

> *Sunday Express*: I think we'd find it very difficult because under the Press Complaints Commission Charter you cannot go into people's health issues: it would be a gross breach of ethics basically…it would be regarded as some sort of breaching their medical trust... I think you'd find that you could be taken to the court for cleaners especially since the Max Mosley case where it's – you know – someone having masochistic sex is protected…from our point of view there would be three really difficult areas: a privacy side of it. There's the privacy side with the fact that it's a health issue which makes it even more private and then from her point of view I think it would be regarded as sort of a breach of confidentiality as well. I think you'll find it a very difficult thing to get a newspaper interested. I mean there might be others who have got a different view on it but I just think from our point of view it would be a legal minefield.

'We're definitely interested in these sorts of stories'
I then called the news desks of the other three Sunday tabloids on our list with the same cover story. They all seemed interested in the information, and requested meetings.

> Nick Owens, *Sunday Mirror*: To be honest with you it's extremely sensitive in the case of that patient confidentiality thing but, you know, if you want to set up a relationship with a journalist to start feeding information through then that's absolutely fine.

> Sarah Jellema, the *People*: We're definitely interested in these sorts of stories. Obviously we've got be very careful with you know there's a new wave of privacy laws but you know lots of people in the public eye are quite open about the work that they've had done, and you know stuff we can elaborate on and it does depend entirely on who the individuals are and how high profile.

> Sara Nuwar, *News of the World*: It sounds like definitely something that's worth meeting up to speak to you about... and we can look at ways of doing it because obviously if you're ex-girlfriend is worried about losing her job and everything there's other issues that come into play there about how we'd be able to present it.

I arranged to meet all three of the interested journalists on 26 March 2009. Given their statements over the phone, we were advised that we were justified in secretly filming the meetings. We were investigating the journalists in their place of work and not focusing on their private lives. All the journalists worked for newspapers which demanded high moral and ethical standards in all professions, and regularly used undercover recording to expose perceived wrongdoing.

How the *Sunday Mirror* fares
The first meeting was with Nick Owens (NO) from the *Sunday Mirror*.

> NO: I think the best thing is for you to give me some information about what you have got and we can see on the basis of that. I'll let you have a confidentiality agreement. I'll go back to them and see what we can do with the information and how much it's worth. I'm normally able to give you quite a good idea because I work on the news desk as well. And I have the eye and the ear of the news editor and editor as well. Which is quite handy...

> CA: Because for me you know what I do – I am a salesman – it's now, you know, a problem for me if someone said: 'Oh, it was him that sold that story.' I would not want that to happen, I don't want that to happen, it's not going to happen. That wouldn't ruck me up with my job – but for her it's her whole life – you know what I mean?

NO: I understand that. I cover a lot of health stories, and I work with a lot of health professionals. You know I work with people in that area as well.
CA: Really?
NO: Yeah I do. So, I understand that issue…

NO: Let's give you an example right. You take Fern Britton. She's on the front of the papers, she had a gastric band – that was a big story – not only because it was Fern Britton had a gastric band and everyone was amazed by her weight loss but it was a big story because she had said in public many times that she had got a huge keep-fit regime, and all that shit, turned out to be wrong…there's a public interest in reporting that story – what there probably isn't a public interest in doing is just reporting that someone had a gastric band operation, unless they are a massively big name then you might make a decision…

NO: That is why it is quite important to get an idea of who we are looking at – we have celebrities obviously at the top of the list.
CA: People you like to write about – people who sell.
NO: Yeah – same thing. They are going to be at the top of the list and we are interested and if they are the kind of guys who you have access to…can get information on, then there's a chance – it is always up to the editor – put it in front of the editor, and say: 'Look, we've been given this bit of information about this person' – it's 'going to cost this amount of money if we want to run the story, what do you reckon?' She will make the call – she will make the decision…

NO: If someone has had that operation – and it is true – correct, and you go to them.., the problem you can have – you always have – you can come to me and say: Fern Britton has had a gastric band and we go to Fern Britton and she says: 'No, I haven't' and her agent says: 'No, she hasn't' we are in a difficult spot then because it is a flat denial and it can happen – often they lie – but then you are faced with the situation whereby we might say to you guys: 'Look, we are not going to use this information – but can you give us anything else other than just your word? Is there a document somewhere – a piece of paper – is there an email – something that would prove she had it?…'

CA: I was just thinking this: 'Through, you know, in terms of our work – we're going to come to you and say '35 Y and Z' – what would you need to substantiate it? I mean I could just be anyone…sorry.
NO: Yeah, you could be exactly. Substantiate it… I guess. Difficult isn't it, I have never had any cosmetic surgery – but I suspect there is a record in the clinic of that surgery taking place, it is not like the NHS obviously where you phone up and they tell you about an operation that's happened on such a date as it's private…

NO: But, the way round it is to say to your friend: 'Look, this is how it works.' Look, she won't know how it works.

CA: No, she hasn't a clue – that's why she has come to me.

NO: Exactly so, hey look. It is not just a case of you saying that this person has had X surgery – there could be a situation whereby we'll need…perhaps you have to produce something – have you got anything available now. Do it in one? That is the way round it…

Fabricated operations of celebrities

I then gave him several fabricated operations of real celebrities:

CA: Well – one of Girls Aloud.

NO: One of?

CA: One of boob job, consultation.

NO: Oh really – OK – that's good.

CA: Mr Hugh Grant had a bit of a face tuck – that's happened a while ago.

NO: Face tuck?

CA: Yeah.

NO: That's OK.

CA: Rhys Ifans – tummy.

NO: Oh really – Rhys? Tummy tuck.

CA: Yeah, again don't know how long that was.

NO: He's not going back for more?

CA: I don't know – I don't know.

NO: OK.

CA: I don't even know what this is – but Guy Ritchie apparently – chemical peel…

CA: This is the one which is literally quite recent is Gemma Arterton… a gastric.

NO: That's surprising, isn't it?…

NO: I think Rhys is funny – cos, you know, Rhys Ifans wanting a tummy tuck is a very funny story. But, then again, is it justified in the public interest? That's the problem. We could get away with Gemma – that's massive, good story that…because as you see she does not need one. You have got to ask yourself why? Why is she bothering? That age as well. So that's all great.

CA: What sort of figure, this would never be…but so I've got a ball park.

NO: Think you are looking to get over three grand minimum – that is a start. How it works is right, page lead in the paper is a grand – but the further it gets to the front of the paper, the more it is. Get a spread – well you won't get a spread out of this as it's one fact. That is the problem – unless you get some kind of…Fern made a spread cos of the issues surrounding her. This one is 'Nicola's got a boob job.' It is a one fact story…there's no getting around it. As a journalist you write that story up, there's almost a point where you put a full stop and you've finished the story. Then you have to write round it.

CA: Just rehash old stuff?

NO: Yeah, you have to…

NO: [About Rhys Ifans] having a tummy tuck to get rid of his beer belly isn 't it? It's a fucking good story that – but out of all of them you could do Rhys – if you wanted to do one you could probably do Rhys Sunday…

NO: Having a tummy tuck to get rid of his [Rhys Ifans] beer belly isn't it? It's a fucking good story that – but out of all of them you could do Rhys – if you wanted to do one you could probably do Rhys Sunday, but we're not gonna do that. But looking at it, Rhys you could probably get away with because it's so funny. The other two you have got to wait – Gemma and Nicola you have got to wait.

CA: Yes, but which ones would she need to.

NO I don't think we would need anything more on Nicola because it would be there – in plain view for all to see.

CA: But what if... we don't want to be in a situation where they deny it – and they come back to us and say I need something tomorrow, or it's dead, do you know what I mean?

NO: Yes the thing is – with that she'll need – in my opinion is that with an operation like that it is quite a big operation – they will normally need a couple of weeks off – so it will come when there's a gap in their thing – we'll be able to work it out – no one has seen them for a few weeks – where has she been? I think we will be fine on that – I mean, I think we will be all right – and obviously it looks like she has got bigger tits we can easily say she has had a boob job and we will be all right. Gemma Arterton we'll need if possible some documentation. The thing to say to your friend is 'What can you get?' Because the more the better really. If she can 't get anything then fine.

CA: She is an administrative nurse, that's the thing, so she probably can

NO: If she can, yeah get a document on everything.

When the public interest requirement is set aside

In summary, Owens, acting under guidance from the *Sunday Mirror* news desk, was looking to pay us £3,000 a story in return for wholesale mining of as many medical records as possible from our clinic. He explained how the public interest requirement is set aside by editors if the celebrity is big enough or the story is funny. Simply by collating the information and taking it back to his news desk mean that the *Sunday Mirror* were appointing themselves judge, jury and executioner of what was publishable.

This was, in effect, setting the *Sunday Mirror* up as the data controller, in clear breach of the DPA. Had our medical information been real, this conversation would have been illegal even if the material was never published. Owens also hinted that he had been involved in similar health stories in the past. Owens called several times following the meeting, leaving messages pushing to run the stories.

How the News of the World fares

The next meeting, on the same day, was with Sara Nuwar, from the *News of the World*. The following are excerpts from her meeting:

> Sara: Anything medical these days you just have to steer clear of but it all depends because there could be public interest or at least there could be other reasons for doing it…

> Sara: Which is kind of bizarre because in a way someone having elective surgery it should be different from if someone has a serious medical condition which obviously we just wouldn't stray into but it's kind of a grey area but er definitely just the best way is to see story by story piece by piece how we could do it and if the lawyers are happy clearing it...

> Sara: We deal with so many different topics where we protect our sources for that very reason and we have to obviously have proof of what the story is and proof that the facts are facts and then as long as we're happy with that we don't.
> CA: When you say proof what would you?
> Sara: It kind of depends what the stories are and how…what legal…all the guidance comes from our legal department so it's 'kind of on a story-by-story basis' and there might be obvious proof or there might be a certain celebrity that is really anti the media and anti the press and they might have quite a strong backlash.

I went on to list the same celebrities having fictitious plastic surgery operations as with the conversation with Nick Owens.

> Sara: But that's something we can talk to you about when it's being done, and then the kind of proof that we'd need I'd obviously have to speak to the lawyers to see what we'd need to get.
> CA: But you'd need something?
> Sara: Yeah we'd need something…

> Sara: You could get a decent payment out of that and also it's the kind of story that just runs and runs and that one did it was picked up everywhere then we revisited it again. Especially when someone denies it and then someone comes out and says it's true it takes on a life of its own then.
> CA: A feeding frenzy yeah.

Sara: So, yeah that can always make the fee greater but I think we can say in the region of 10 [thousand]
CA: In the region of 10 [thousand]. It's just so we can…
Sarah: Maybe we could be looking at 20 to 30 for a front page or you could be looking at a staggered…if the story's strong enough you could carry a couple of weeks you could be looking at 60 to 80. It just depends…

Sara: Well it's good to get the background. I'll take those titbits back and just run them past the legal guys and just see. I mean, the one that I just don't think we'd touch is Hugh Grant. I just think he's so hyper sensitive about his own public image.
CA: Yeah.
Sara: With the others, maybe there's more leeway.

While Nuwar as much more cautious than Nick Owens, she was asking us to verbally impart large amounts of private medical information to her so that she can then distribute it to numerous colleagues at News International. They would then discuss and retain this information and judge what should be published. Were this information true, it would involve a breach of the DPA, even if it were not published, and that a breach of the DPA would have no public interest defence. Nuwar does claim that they would only print stories in the public interest. But in our view, the public interest could never justify buying private medical records of celebrities having plastic surgery. The public interest would only excuse buying health records of, say, a politician who had a serious illness that prevented them doing their job, that they were hiding from the public. Nuwar also said that there was 'leeway' with some of the stories, especially if they involved very big names, and that it was a 'grey area', both indicate she is at best confused with the PCC and DPA rules.

How the *People* fares
The third and final meeting that day was with Sarah Jellema (SJ), from the *People*.

SJ: Well obviously it's very legally dodgy, a lot of it….Heather Mills recently sued the *Sunday Mirror* as they accused her of having a boob job. We've been told that story as well and I think it's true actually…but she's a very litigious celebrity anyway…erm ..so a lot of the stuff we might not be able to use but there's sort of… I was batting round with my news editor who spoke to you before Tom.
CA: Yep, yep.
SJ: Sort of ideas about how you might do it – ideas of maybe a spread of silhouettes of people hinting who might have done it….Or with some celebrities you might be able to get an agent to say: 'Yes it might boost her appeal or something.'
CA: Something to get their name in the papers?
SJ: Yeah, if it's going to be really obvious. But if it's someone like Heather Mills who would rather die than have people know they've had work done,

rather than eating healthily. So it would all depend, I mean, if you saw the Fern Britton story, you can just expose people like that. It really does depend on the people, what they've had done, and what the lawyers say. Obviously as well the first thing we want to know is 'What back up we have.'...

SJ:... it will be something written or whatever. Just something for the file. I'll find out on that sort of basis.
CA: Yeah.
SJ: I'm sure they'll want something...I'm not sure what exactly.
CA: Some kind of documentary proof, yeah?
SJ: Yes.

I gave her the same list of operations as I had presented to the other journalists. I refused to say which member of Girls Aloud was having consultations for breast enlargements.

SJ: Even if it wasn't Cheryl you could do a teaser on the front and people wouldn't know until they got inside.
CA: So you wouldn't even put the name on the front you'd go 'Girls Aloud'?
SJ: It would depend. If it was her...
CA: She'd be front.
SJ: But f it wasn't they'd do a teaser, and everyone would be like 'Ooh is it Cheryl?' And even fit's not, they're all attractive girls.

SJ: Guy Ritchie and stuff...maybe not if it's not that drastic then...maybe not him (points to celeb), he's not that litigious. He seems to just let the media run its course. I don't know how Rhys Ifans reacts to stuff. Again, it will be how much we can get out of the story in terms of...obviously and we'd need all of the nitty gritty we could get.
CA: Yeah.
SJ: And back-up documents if they were available...

SJ: Again, with her [Heather Mills], they were very very careful and I think because of her now it ended up with her suing them or whether she just put in a PCC for a complaint for a breach of privacy.
CA: Right.
SJ: Which...getting a PCC isn't great, but a lot of papers just kind of brush it aside. All it is a little apology, somewhere in the paper you get a slap on the wrists if you get reported by the PCC, But there's no money.
CA: Oh really?
SJ: Yep, it's a really odd situation.
CA: So, it's a slap on the wrist.
SJ: And the PCC is run by the newspaper editors.
CA: Really?

SJ: Yes, it's a self-regulating...
CA: Right, of course, yeah, I remember reading about this.
SJ: It's really odd. And that's why a lot of people are saying it's not enough now to have that but while that's still there...
CA: So, it even if something is shown to be kind of wrong in the way you got the information and all that it goes to the PCC little apology slap on the wrist.
SJ: Yeah.
CA: We've still got our money, you've got your circulation.
SJ: Yes...so they will tend to take more risks if they think a PCC will be revolved.

Jellema had been told by her news editor, Tom Carling, to harvest as much private medical information as possible. She indicated that they would need some form of documentation to corroborate any story. She outlined how they would overcome public interest issues if it was a big enough name or if the celebrities were not litigious. She also explained how they could mask the source to avoid revealing that the source was inside the clinic. Her comments on the PCC speak for themselves.

The following week Jellema called me and left a voicemail. The message said that they were very keen to do the stories. She had consulted with her news desk and legal team and they had asked her to ask us to provide a copy of the appointments book of the surgery, or similar, to prove that the celebrities had been in and what they were in for. This would, of course, had been a clear breach of the DPA – without public interest, and sanctioned by her superiors.

Failure of PCC to follow up Starsuckers revelations
To our knowledge, the PCC did not, in any way, investigate any of the allegations made by *Starsuckers*, even though three of the four newspapers we tested seemed willing to breach the PCC code and the DPA. Nick Owens, the journalist whose behaviour was the most blatantly over the line, is still writing for the *Sunday Mirror* at the time of going to press (December 2011).

I believe that *Starsuckers* shows that there are serious problems at the heart of the British media, in particular the tabloid press. These are problems that the media itself is incapable of investigating or solving, which is why I support stronger regulation of the press that is completely independent of both the press and government.

Note on the contributor
Chris Atkins started out producing low budget theatrical fiction films, including Richard Jobson's *Sixteen Years Of Alcohol* and *A Woman in Winter* which was nominated for a Scottish BAFTA for best film. In 2006, he directed a documentary on the loss of civil liberties in the UK called *Taking Liberties*, despite having no experience in either directing or documentaries. Helped by Michael Moore's producer, the film was released theatrically to coincide with Tony Blair's departure in June 2007 and was given excellent reviews in the national broadsheet and tabloid press. It played in more than 100 cinemas

around the UK and was one of the highest grossing documentaries of 2007. In 2008, Chris Atkins was nominated for a BAFTA for Best Writer and Director in his first feature film. As a follow up, he set out to make a film about the toxic effect that the media and celebrity are having on our world. Two years later, *Starsuckers* was premiered at the London Film Festival in October 2009, and received unprecedented press attention, taking up the front page of the *Guardian* for two days running and then making the news in countries all over the world. The film fought off legal challenges from the *News of the World*, Max Clifford and Bob Geldof and was released to rave reviews. More recently, he faked an urban fox hunting film that was taken seriously by most of the British press and the BBC.

The Press, the Leveson Inquiry and the Hacked Off Campaign

Brian Cathcart, founder of Hacked Off campaign, argues that news organisations should be asked to make increased and systematic use of paper trails in news as a way of highlighting the ethical responsibilities of the individual journalist

The Hacked Off campaign was born, as an idea, in the spring of 2011, when the outlook for the British national press seemed very different from the outlook towards the end of the same year. In January, News International had finally yielded to the weight of evidence and admitted that the hacking of voicemails by journalists at the *News of the World* was more than a problem of one rogue reporter. In other words, after four years the company had abandoned its insistence that Clive Goodman, the royal editor jailed in 2007, had been the only journalist involved. Meanwhile, the Metropolitan Police, which for almost as long had maintained the position that there was nothing to investigate, had launched Operation Weeting, and this was evidently working towards new prosecutions for voicemail hacking by News International employees in 2004-6.

By April, however, there were once again grounds for concern that the full facts about hacking, and about the covering up of hacking by News International executives in 2006-2011, might never be known. The company had begun to settle the civil cases brought against it by victims, and appeared to be doing so in assertive fashion. Notably, it obliged Sienna Miller, the actress whose vigorous litigation had done a great deal to expose the extent of the problem, to end her activities by the simple measure of offering her every penny she asked for. Even if she had wanted to, she could not have proceeded.

There was evidence that others in the forefront of legal action were under similar pressure, reducing the chance that there would eventually be a full public trial of the claims involving five or six test cases, as had been envisaged in the courts. Meanwhile the company was also establishing a mediation and compensation scheme for claimants which would operate behind closed doors. While no one could regret the prospect that claimants might at last receive compensation to which they were entitled, long-term observers of the scandal had grounds to worry that what had been the principal lever available to turn over stones at News International and reveal wrongdoing was being taken away.

As for Operation Weeting, there was reason for optimism that it would be an energetic and vigorous investigation in sharp contrast to what had gone before, but here again, in the spring, new doubts were beginning to creep in. I had been specialist adviser to the House of Commons select committee on culture, media and sport (the 'CMS committee') when it investigated libel, privacy and press standards in 2008-10, and since the publication of the committee's report had written about the unfolding hacking scandal on the *Index on Censorship* free speech blog and in the *Guardian* and the *Independent* newspapers. I had found common ground on both the scandal and its implications with Martin Moore, director of the Media Standards Trust. In April and May, we began to feel that the outlook was darkening, and our concerns were sharpened in conversations with lawyers representing hacking claimants, who were among the people best informed on the issues. They asked the question: what if every journalist charged with hacking pleads guilty?

The answer, we knew, was that there would be no hacking trials, merely sentencing hearings at which the only real evidence to be presented would be minimal agreed narratives relevant exclusively to each defendant's case. Under such circumstances, the public would learn very little about what had happened. Foot-soldiers might be held to account, but only them, and no light would be shed on the management of these foot-soldiers or on the four-year cover-up by News International. How likely were guilty pleas? As the lawyers pointed out, it was exactly what had happened in the case of Goodman and the private investigator Glenn Mulcaire in 2007, an outcome that effectively placed a lid on the affair for four years. The CMS committee had later wrung from News International an admission that both of these men, after their release from jail, received substantial payments from the company, an arrangement which prompted the MPs to observe: '... we are left with a strong impression that silence has been bought'. (It was not known at that stage that the payments to Goodman had amounted to £243,000.)

A Campaign is Launched
This combined prospect of the buying up of the civil cases and the possible muting and limiting of the criminal dimension through guilty pleas appeared to us to amount to a new cover-up, a fall-back defence that would have the twin effects of preventing the public from learning anything like the full story of phone hacking and at the same time of protecting those News International executives who had been in charge at the time hacking took place and during the period of the 'one rogue reporter' defence. We decided to launch a campaign for

a public inquiry, because an inquiry seemed to be the only way to ensure that the facts would come out and that those responsible would be held accountable.

We were motivated by a conviction that the affair was more than one of simple wrongdoing by journalists and more also than a case of corporate misconduct. Its ramifications spread to the Metropolitan Police, which had not only failed to investigate the matter adequately in 2006-7 but had also, in unison with the company, long maintained the line that there was just one rogue reporter. And it extended to the political sphere, where the Prime Minister, David Cameron, was particularly close to the News International chief executive, Rebekah Brooks, and had until January 2011 employed former *News of the World* editor Andy Coulson as his chief media adviser inside 10 Downing Street. Rupert Murdoch, the chairman of News Corporation, also enjoyed access to the prime minister apparently at will, and their meetings usually went un-minuted. In all this, we and many others felt, there were plenty of questions a public inquiry might ask, if only to put the public mind at rest. By the same token, an inquiry might ask a question by then on many lips: did voicemail hacking stop at the *News of the World* or was the technique used at other newspapers?

It is worth saying that at this time the odds against the establishment of a public inquiry were very high: such decisions are in the hands of politicians and not only were the Conservatives close to News International but the Labour Party, though no longer in that position, had a long record of associating with the company while in power. An inquiry, in other words, threatened to embarrass both of the biggest parties in parliament. It thus seemed likely that any campaign for an inquiry would have to be a long one, and in that light I admit we did not hurry our preparations.

By the first days of July 2011 we had a website, a mission document and more than 100 endorsements from leading journalists and journalism academics, a cross-party range of politicians, lawyers and victims or possible victims of hacking. We were two days from our launch when the *Guardian* broke the story that the *News of the World* had hacked the voicemail of the Surrey teenager Milly Dowler after her abduction in 2002, and had even deleted messages in an apparent attempt to see what new messages might land. The public revulsion which greeted this revelation transformed the terms of the debate, and the principle of a public inquiry was conceded by all parties almost immediately. We at Hacked Off now found ourselves in a position to influence the shape of the inquiry.

Through our legal connections we were the nearest thing to a body representing the actual and potential hacking victims and on the strength of our sustained engagement with the issue we were among the few who had given thought to what might be the scope and remit of an inquiry. We lobbied the three main party leaders and the chairs of three relevant select committees and made a case to which they all proved largely sympathetic. We argued, among other things, that the inquiry should have the power to look beyond hacking at other forms of illegal information gathering, that it should look beyond News International at other parts of the press, and that it should be able to examine relations between the press and politicians and the press and the police. A number of our suggestions found their way into the final remit document for the Leveson Inquiry.

The Leveson Remit

That remit and the general form of the inquiry are unusual for reasons that could not be avoided. Notably, because of the continuing police investigation some aspects of the remit could not be addressed until legal proceedings were at an end, which might be a matter of years. We at Hacked Off argued vigorously that this should not be used as a 'long grass' excuse, that even if some delay to some work was inevitable it was essential to seize the moment and establish the inquiry with a strong remit rather than give the company and any allies it might have the time and opportunity to wriggle away from scrutiny. The politicians agreed with us; indeed, they were all alert to this issue before we met them. The result was a two-phase inquiry which, contrary to the normal process, addresses general issues of press ethics and regulation before it examines the specifics of illegal information-gathering. It is not perfect, but it is better than the alternatives that were available in those turbulent summer weeks.

Does the inquiry really need to examine broad issues of regulation affecting the whole press, when the scandal emerged from one practice at one newspaper (which has been closed)? There are two answers to that. The first is that in July 2011, and still at the time of writing (December 2011), we did not know and do not know whether phone hacking or comparable illegal information-gathering activities were restricted to one newspaper. Indeed, there were always good grounds to suspect that that was unlikely. This was, after all, a competitive market in which journalists, staff or casual, moved between titles. It seemed unlikely that the *News of the World* could have kept its activities, carried out over at least four years, secret. Equally, it seemed open to doubt that its rivals, if they knew what it was doing, would have resisted using the same techniques. It was clearly in the public interest to know the scope, or the limits, of the problem.

Hacking also had a context which was not limited to the *News of the World*. It was not the first grave scandal to affect the press in recent years and to raise public doubts about the ethics and standards of journalists and newspapers and about the effectiveness of the Press Complaints Commission as a regulator or self-regulator of the industry. The CMS committee report of February 2010, Press Standards, Privacy and Libel, looked not only at hacking but also at other cases, notably the coverage of the Madeleine McCann abduction in Portugal in 2007-8 (CMS 2010). With unanimous, cross-party committee endorsement, it condemned much of the McCann coverage on several counts and, in particular, criticised the PCC for failing to intervene to uphold its code of practice. It also highlighted the scale of abuse, noting that a dozen papers had subsequently admitted publishing between them hundreds of false articles on the case over a period of more than half a year.

Nor was this the only case. In the same month that the Milly Dowler revelation was published, eight national newspapers acknowledged in court that they had printed dozens of false stories about the retired Bristol teacher Christopher Jefferies which the Lord Chief Justice, Lord Judge, would describe as vilification. In this context it seemed that it would have been perverse to limit the scope of the inquiry to hacking at the *News of the World*. Indeed, there were grounds to believe News International itself would almost certainly have challenged such a decision, which would have implied that only its journalists had hacked voicemails. And once the remit went wider the PCC automatically came into play because it has for 20 years been held up to parliament and the public as the body responsible for upholding press standards. It was, therefore, an inevitable consequence of the hacking scandal that reform of regulation should form part of Lord Justice Leveson's considerations.

Events marched on. The CMS committee, formally investigating the question whether it had previously been misled about hacking, continued its hearings with a view to producing a report which at the time of writing seems likely to criticise several former News International executives and possibly one or more former Metropolitan Police officers. A joint parliamentary committee on privacy and injunctions, established shortly before the Milly Dowler story broke, also began taking evidence. Operation Weeting continues its work and stated that the number of people whose voicemails may have been hacked was 5,785 at the latest count and was still rising.

Allegations were made (and not disputed) that, besides hacking voicemails, *News of the World* journalists commissioned surveillance by a single private detective of more than 150 people, including politicians, celebrities, royal princes and dozens of people described as ordinary members of the public. Further, it emerged that as recently as 2010 News International commissioned surveillance of two lawyers representing people claiming to be victims of hacking, something the company swiftly admitted was unacceptable.

The Future of Regulation

Not surprisingly in this context, a public debate about the press has begun that is almost certainly unprecedented in its range and depth, and which anyone with an interest in communications ethics can only welcome. Matters once regarded as obscure and academic are now the stuff of headlines and public speeches, and it is beyond doubt that the centre of gravity in the debate is in a new place.

The Press Complaints Commission, having seen one chair, Baroness Peta Buscombe, resign, and welcomed a new one in, Lord Hunt, has been working hard on reform proposals. Lord Hunt has written in *The Times*: 'What is needed is a new structure that will include a body with teeth, a body with credibility' (Hunt 2011). He wrote also of the need to monitor and police agreed standards of behaviour, and of the need for the new body to be robust and truly independent of politicians on one hand and proprietors and editors on the other. This was a dramatic change of position for the PCC. As recently as 2010 it had completed what it called a governance review which concluded, despite the strongly contrary views of, for example, the CMS committee, that no fundamental reform was necessary.

Paul Dacre, the editor-in-chief of Associated Newspapers and probably the most powerful journalist in Britain today, told a Leveson Inquiry seminar in October that regulation must change, and that a first step must be to solve the 'Desmond problem' – the ability of any paper or group of papers simply to opt out of PCC jurisdiction as Richard Desmond's *Star* and *Express* titles have done. Dacre declared: 'While I abhor statutory controls, there's one area where parliament can help the press. Some way must be found to compel all newspaper owners to fund and participate in self-regulation' (Dacre 2011). He also responded to the common criticism that the PCC lacked teeth, suggesting the appointment of a newspaper ombudsman, whom he described as follows:

> An ombudsman, possibly a retired judge or civil servant, and possibly advised by two retired editors from both ends of the newspaper spectrum, could have the power to investigate, possibly with specialists co-opted on to his panel, potential press industry scandals. The ombudsman could also have the power to summon journalists and editors to give evidence, to name offenders and, if necessary, in the cases of the most extreme malfeasance, to impose fines.

His words found some echo in a speech by the Lord Chief Justice. Lord Judge defended the PCC against the charge that it had failed, principally on the ground that it had never had the powers or remit to do more than it had done. And then he went on to take it as read that the PCC must be strengthened and improved, and that it should have new powers. Without saying how this might be achieved, he stated that it must be all-inclusive – the 'Desmond problem' again – and he suggested ways in which appointments to the commission could be made more independently (Judge 2011).

There have been many other important contributions to the debate, of which perhaps the most notable is a speech in November 2011 by Alan Rusbridger, the editor of the *Guardian*, who advocated self-regulation on new terms. He suggested the establishment of a Press Standards and Mediation Commission, which might both take over the mediation work of the PCC and also deal with many cases which presently end up in the courts. He also supported Paul Dacre's call for an ombudsman with fining powers (Rusbridger 2011).

Rejected outright as unnecessary by most of the industry as recently as 2010, and regarded then by many outside the industry as a political impossibility, serious reform of press regulation was thus widely seen by late 2011as a certainty and a necessity. Increased powers and some form of compulsion to membership were taken as read; the argument was over form and method. Moreover, it appeared that, for most participants, the old, binary view of self-regulation versus statutory regulation was no longer accepted. The many shades of grey in between – expressed in terms of diverse models of regulation borrowed from a great variety of spheres, or under general headings such as independent regulation or co-regulation – were recognised.

Also recognised was the need to ensure that any new regulatory regime protected and did not threaten freedom of expression. The Lord Chief Justice issued a warning on this; the leaders of all three main political parties had spoken of it, as had the Justice Secretary, Kenneth Clarke, and many Members of Parliament; newspaper editors and leading journalists have raised the issue and Lord Justice Leveson has made clear it is in his mind (Clarke 2011). It may be worth stating that this concern also animates Hacked Off. Our manifesto binds us to campaign for an independent regulatory regime that affords the maximum freedom for ethical journalism in the public interest while bearing down on journalism which breaches accepted professional codes of practice. On a personal note, as a journalist who has written extensively about the Stephen Lawrence case, the Barry George case, the Deepcut affair and the hacking scandal, and as a teacher of young journalists, I am under no illusions about the preciousness of our freedom to speak out through the press.

The Role of Hacked Off

Hacked Off has continued in existence, with funding largely from the Joseph Rowntree Charitable Trust and support in kind from the Media Standards Trust. We have participated in the debate, made submissions and given evidence. We have continued to have a role making links between, advising and occasionally speaking for the victims and possible victims of voicemail hacking. Our website carries reports, updates and links relating to the Leveson Inquiry and other public events. And we try to push debate forward in areas we see as important.

One such is the character and role of the public interest in journalism, sometimes a subject of confusion. At the time of writing we are working on an initiative to develop a workable definition of the public interest for legal purposes and to review areas of legislation where public interest defences are absent or inadequate. Ultimately we hope this will yield a submission to the Leveson Inquiry and the joint parliamentary committee on privacy and injunctions whose purpose will be to reduce the pressures on, and impediments to, journalism that is conducted in the public interest.

The Personal Responsibility of Journalists

Another aspect of the crisis in the press that the debate has only touched on at the time of writing, and which is of interest to Hacked Off, is the responsibility of individual journalists. Our discussions are not advanced, and what follows is a personal view. The law and regulation may be able to solve some of the problems of unethical conduct but nothing can make so much difference as a change in the culture of journalists and newsrooms which raises the status of ethics, of the public interest and of relevant codes of practice. The working environment on some newspapers in recent years appears in some respects to have had the opposite effect. When Peter Hill, who edited the *Daily Express* at the time of the McCann coverage, was asked by the CMS committee whether any journalist or editor had been reprimanded or disciplined for the mistakes which cost the newspaper more than £500,000 in damages, he replied: 'I have reprimanded myself because I was responsible' (CMS report 2010 par. 372).

When the *News of the World* lost the Max Mosley case there was no internal inquest into the catalogue of journalistic abuses laid bare in the trial and judgment, and the chief reporter on the story remained in his job, unchallenged about his methods. This kind of general indemnity can be presented as editors 'standing by their reporters', a form of professional loyalty in the face of external pressures that we tend to admire. But it mocks those high principles if, beneath the umbrella of editorial protection, there is no questioning, no reflection, no learning from mistakes. The McCann and Mosley cases point to an apparent lack of consequences for mistakes and failures besides the writing of cheques for damages, and that is a state of affairs almost guaranteed to deliver more mistakes and failures.

A further example of the problem at work is the decline in credibility of bylines. When the *Daily Mail* published online, briefly and accidentally, a false account it had prepared of the climax of the Amanda Knox appeal, it turned out that the reporter whose name appeared on the story was not involved in any way. The very fact that we know such abuse of bylines to be commonplace erodes the meaning of bylines themselves: the copy may have been written by anyone, and so no one is publicly responsible for it, with the possible exception of the editor.

One possible means of driving change in this area of responsibility, as part of wider reform, might be an expectation that news organisations make increased and systematic use of paper trails or audit trails in news. Reporters writing and submitting stories would attach all their source materials permanently to the electronic file, including audio files from interviews and internet links. (Incidentally, we have surely reached a point where we should be able to assume that all interviews are recorded unless there is a good reason not to.) A record of the story as written at that time would also be preserved. Associated with this might be a brief series of questions and answers establishing that the reporter had considered the possible ethical complications of the story. Alan Rusbridger has suggested a five-point questionnaire derived from one in use in the security services (Rusbridger 2011). They ask, in brief, whether a story will cause harm, how the harm is justified and whether there is proper authority for causing such harm. As the story advances through the editorial process all changes and additions are recorded, with the identities of those involved, and the questions may be asked and answered again at more senior levels.

Importantly, this would be an active process and not merely an automatic electronic record to be unearthed and considered if things go wrong. It would take some investment of time, though less than might be imagined with the use of appropriate modern software (and it is less in bureaucratic terms than we expect of others with important, responsible jobs, such as doctors and police officers). To what use could it be put? There are several possibilities, but first it is worth noting that it would institutionalise early consideration of the public interest in a way that is apparently not current in some news organisations, and this alone would be likely to bring benefits. It would also raise awareness of the individual responsibility we bear or should bear as journalists for the consequence of our work.

As for the use of such audit trails, they would have obvious practical applications in internal post mortem examinations, after problems have arisen. They might conceivably be made accessible to a new regulator. Adoption of the practice might serve as a protection in law, a little like the operation of the Reynolds defences. There is certainly a risk of abuse, for example in the bullying or scapegoating of reporters, but equally there is considerable potential for such a system to protect conscientious reporters.

The appropriate levels for decision-making in public interest matters would be defined and clarified, and key choices and responsibilities could not be shuffled downward. These are, once again, methods which journalists have for years been insisting should be in place in other walks of life. Chains of command, checks and balances, and good record-keeping are what reporters and editorial writers demand to know about when there is a railway crash or a breakdown in the child welfare system. They are part of society's new culture of accountability, described by Baroness Onora O'Neill in her Reith Lectures in 2002 (O'Neill 2002). Journalists have the power to wreck reputations and cause great misery; the public has some right to expect that when they do so it is after careful consideration, in line with some formal procedures and with some record to show for it afterwards.

- This chapter is based on the keynote presentation Brian Cathcart gave on 'Hacking, Leveson and the Individual Responsibility of Journalists' at the annual conference of the Institute of Communication Ethics, in London, on 28 October 2011.

References

Clarke, Kenneth (2011) Address to the annual conference of the Society of Editors, Egham, Surrey, 14 November 2011. Available online at http://www.guardian.co.uk/media/2011/nov/14/no-threat-to-press-freedom-ken-clarke, accessed on 15 November 2011

Dacre, Paul (2011) The Future for Self-Regulation? Presentation to a seminar of the Leveson Inquiry, 12 October 2011. Available online at http://www.levesoninquiry.org.uk/wp-content/uploads/2011/11/Paul-Dacre.pdf, accessed on 14 November 2011

House of Commons select committee on culture, media and sport (2010) *Second Report: Press Standards, Privacy and Libel HC-362-1*. Available online at http://www.publications.parliament.uk/pa/cm200910/cmselect/cmcumeds/362/36202.htm, accessed on 15 November 2011

Hunt, David (Baron Hunt of Wirral) (2011) This 'toothless poodle' will grow some teeth, *Times*, 14 November p. 24

Judge, Igor (Baron Judge of Draycote) (2011) Speech to the Human Rights Law Conference, London, 19 October 2011. Available online at http://www.journalism.co.uk/news/full-text-lord-chief-justice-s-speech-on-press-regulation/s2/a546417/, accessed on 20 October 2011

O'Neill, Onora (Baroness O'Neill of Bengarve) (2002) A Question of Trust: The Reith Lectures 2002. Available online at http://www.bbc.co.uk/radio4/reith2002/, accessed on 14 November 2011

Rusbridger, Alan (2011) Hacking away at the truth: The 2011 Orwell Lecture. Available online at http://www.guardian.co.uk/media/2011/nov/10/phone-hacking-truth-alan-rusbridger-orwell, accessed on 13 November 2011

Note on the contributor

Brian Cathcart is Professor of Journalism at Kingston University London and a founder of Hacked Off. He began his career in journalism at Reuters and was later on the founding staffs of both the *Independent* and the *Independent on Sunday*, becoming deputy editor of the latter paper. He is the author of several books, including *The Case of Stephen Lawrence* (1999) and *Were You Still Up for Portillo?* (1997) and has also been assistant editor and media columnist at the *New Statesman*.

Blame not the mobile phone, 'twas ever thus

Mike Jempson and Wayne Powell look back on decades of questionable behaviour in the national press

Revelations to the Leveson Inquiry into press culture, practice and ethics will have come as no surprise to anyone who has taken an interest in press standards since World War Two. There have been periodic outbreaks of concern about press intrusion and sensationalism and demands for statutory controls, none of which have had much impact in terms of curtailing press excesses. Public revulsion over the hacking of a murder victim's phone may have brought things to a head, and while there remain many untold stories about the harm done by intrusive, inaccurate or sensational press coverage, much of what is being said to the inquiry has been said before, and to little avail.

In his memoirs, Fleet Street investigative reporter Gerry Brown (1995), who worked for News International and Mirror Group titles, claimed to have invented what he called 'tabloid-techno' using the latest technology to obtain sound and images. He explained that a scanner costing a few hundred pounds could home in on selected mobile phones, and with a 'Celltracker' – a mobile phone linked to a laptop – it was possible to lock on to signals and even make calls from the numbers under surveillance.

He cited the audio tapes of Princess Diana complaining to her lover James Gilbert about a previous lover James Hewitt, allegedly scanned by a retired bank manager, and by another Oxfordshire resident, and supplied to the *Sun* in 1990. At the time, David Calcutt QC was conducting an investigation into press invasions of privacy (Calcutt 1990), and the 'Squidgygate' tapes were not published for another two years (*Sun*, 23 August 1992). Shortly afterwards, an erotic conversation between Prince Charles and his then-lover, Camilla Parker-Bowles, was similarly intercepted. First published by *New Idea*, one of Rupert Murdoch's Australian magazines, his UK titles quickly followed suit, days after the now Sir David Calcutt had proposed statutory controls in a government sponsored review (Calcutt 1993) of the effectiveness of the Press Complaints Commission (PCC).

Although some doubts arose about whether the tapes were direct recordings or if the scanners had picked up deliberately rebroadcast recordings, the Press Complaints Commission (PCC 27 January 1993) was adamant: 'Bugging of private telephone calls is manifestly an invasion of privacy, no matter who does it. As such, it is contrary to the industry's code and the commission deplore the publication of the so-called Camillagate tapes. We recognise, however, that unethically and illegally obtained material may still be published abroad and republished in Britain.' Rejecting the Calcutt proposals, the PCC nonetheless admitted: '…exceptional circumstances may arise which would justify the publication. For these reasons we think it is essential that there should be legislation defining the boundaries of the law.'

Hint at more Sinister Practices

The incident highlighted the apparent contempt with which Murdoch's newspapers in particular held any attempt by the British establishment to curtail the activities of the press. Brown also hinted at more sinister practices. He claimed that Robert Maxwell bugged his own staff and kept under lock and key the names and pictures of two senior Conservative MPs who made use of the services of a Wigmore Street massage parlour but was happy to publish stories about the visits of showbiz celebrities and Major Tom Ferguson, father of the Duchess of York.

The careers of several prominent members of the Conservative administration had been targeted by the press during the 'Calcutt years' – notably the Secretary of State for National Heritage, David Mellor, who had warned that the press were 'drinking in last chance saloon'. He resigned after several scandalous revelations about him were published. The sexual antics of Environment Minister Tim Yeo and former Transport Minister Steven Norris were exposed soon after Calcutt's call for statutory regulation. In 1994, two parliamentary private secretaries, Hartley Booth and David Ashby, Transport Minister, the Earl of Caithness, and the Tory Whip, Michael Brown, were forced out of office.

However, the power of the press had given cause for concern long before these latter-day press barons held sway. A National Union of Journalists (NUJ) campaign for an investigation into how commercial pressures were driving news values once newspapers had been freed from wartime censorship and shortages of paper and ink, brought into being the first Royal Commission on the Press of 1947.

The industry was slow to agree to its main proposal, the creation of a self-regulatory General Council of the Press (GCP), until statutory controls were imposed in the form of the Defamation Act 1952. Criticism about inaccurate or intrusive stories, mostly featuring establishment figures and foreign dignitaries, had been largely ignored by the industry until tougher libel laws provided a wake-up call. The GCP was set up in 1953. Following a second Royal Commission (1962) it would become the Press Council (PC) but, in general, the industry displayed a marked reluctance to comply with the recommendations of three separate Royal Commissions (the third came in 1974-1977). This may have been a signal to indicate a desire to remain independent of outside influences, but it was also seen as evidence that proprietors and some editors saw their papers as a law unto themselves. It is an interpretation that has held good to this day.

The Press Council's first Declaration of Principle, in 1966, was that 'no payment should be made for feature articles to persons engaged in crime or other notorious behaviour where the public interests does not warrant it'. As veteran journalist Tom Bairstow recalled (Bairstow 1984), this followed the discovery that a key prosecution witness in the Moors Murder trial of Myra Hindley and Ian Brady had received payments from the press for information. Yet a decade later the *Daily Telegraph* was criticised for offering to double its fee for the memoirs of former Liberal MP Peter Bessell if Liberal Party leader Jeremy Thorpe was found guilty of conspiracy to murder. Bessel was a prosecution witness at the 1979 trial.

'Gross Misconduct' over Reporting of Ripper
Four years after that the PC found the *Daily Express*, the *Sun*, the *Daily Star*, the *People*, the *Mail on Sunday* and the *Daily Mail* guilty of 'gross misconduct' for making payments to members of the family of Peter Sutcliffe, the 'Yorkshire Ripper'. The PC had compiled a massive dossier of press misbehaviour, accusing newspapers of 'callous harassment' of relatives of his victims to whom offers of 'blood money' had been made.

The *Mail*'s then-Editor, the recently knighted Sir David English who had refused to attend a hearing before the Press Council, claimed an offer of £90,000 to Sutcliffe's wife Sonja had just been a ploy to get her to talk. His newspaper had also tried to buy the story of a prostitute whom Sutcliffe was with at the time of his arrest, and the *Mail on Sunday* had done a deal with the Chief Constable of Yorkshire to publish his 'Ripper File' when he retired. Sir David's response to the council's ruling was robust: 'This a most unfortunate decision by a body that should be devoting itself to protecting the freedom of the press. Newspapers, for all their faults, are guardians of the public interest,' he said dismissing the adjudication as 'short-term, short-sighted and smug [proving] yet again that the Press Council does not truly understand the concept of a free press'.

Almost thirty years later the journalism ethics charity PressWise (now MediaWise) had to alert the Press Complaints Commission (PCC) chair that potential witnesses and relatives of victims in the Fred and Rose West murder trial were being similarly harassed and offered money for their stories. Even though Lord Wakeham then warned all newspaper editors of the risks, at the subsequent trial of Rose West no fewer than 19 people admitted to being party to financial deals with national papers.

Around this time the *Daily Mail* and the *Daily Mirror* were criticised, respectively, for paying £300,000 for extracts from a book by gaoled Barings' rogue trader Nick Leeson and for offering cash to convicted fraudster Darius Guppy. By now Sir David English had become Chairman and Editor-in-Chief of Associated Newspapers, and Chair of the Press Board of Finance (PressBof) editors' code committee. On the morning he was called to account before the national heritage select committee (27 November 1996), Sir David announced a change to the editors' code outlawing such payments. However, he neglected to mention he had been one of the editors at fault when he dismissed the PC's earlier condemnation of the practice as 'some grandiose announcement…around the time of the Ripper trial'.

The 'particularly unwarranted intrusion' into the lives of Sonja Sutcliffe and the mother of his last victim also flew in the face of a Press Council Declaration of Principle on privacy. In 1976, it had insisted that 'the publication of information about the private life of individuals without their consent is only acceptable if there is a legitimate public interest over-riding the right of privacy, not merely a prurient or morbid curiosity'. Demonstrably, this had had as little impact then as the new PCC would have when it replaced the PC in 1991. It was the industry's response to a new threat of statutory regulation following David Calcutt QC's investigation of press breaches of privacy (Calcutt 1990).

During the 1980s the excesses of the press had given rise to three, unsuccessful, Right of Reply Bills, sponsored by Labour MPs Frank Allaun, Ann Clwyd, and Tony Worthington, and a Privacy Bill, tabled by Tory MP John Browne. All were unsuccessful but were indicative of growing public concern. Tabloid coverage had also claimed the life of talented young actor David Scarboro (*Grange Hill, EastEnders*). He leapt to his death from Beachy Head in 1988 after the *News of the World* published a photograph of the psychiatric hospital in which he was receiving treatment. He had been hounded by the tabloids over many months and begun libel actions against several for inaccurate and intrusive stories. After his suicide his parents left the UK in disgust. His brother, Simon, presented a moving account of his mistreatment by the press in a documentary (see http://www.youtube.com/watch?v=QBnCNlWS88Q).

Hurtful and Inaccurate Stories
The mother of the 'Worst brat in Britain' (the *Sun*, July 1989), also quit the UK after failing in her initial efforts to obtain redress for a series of hurtful and inaccurate stories about her son whose behavioural problems had been caused by childhood illness. In 1991, he became the first child in the UK to win a libel action.

The ineffectiveness of the Press Council had been most clearly demonstrated by its response to complaints that the *Sun* had fabricated an interview with the widow of a Falklands War hero in 1982. The *Daily Mirror* (22 October 1982) accused its rival of publishing deliberate lies, and Maria McKay told the *Observer* she had never spoken to the *Sun*. The PC did not contact her directly and dismissed this evidence as hearsay (Robertson 1983: 54-57).

There was further public outrage in 1990 when it became clear that a *Sunday Sport* journalist had sneaked into the hospital where popular sit-com actor Gorden Kaye was recovering from brain surgery after a serious car accident, taken photographs and claimed to have interviewed him. To add insult to injury Kaye failed to win his court action for invasion of privacy.

Evidence of the radical reform the PC went though under the chairmanship of Louis Blom Cooper QC, who would later chair the journalism ethics charity MediaWise (www.mediawise.org.uk), was its final act. It published an excoriating critique of coverage of the Strangeways prison riots of April 2000, when the press had fallen 'into the serious ethical error of presenting speculation and unconfirmed reports as fact' (Blom-Cooper 1991).

Newspapers had claimed that up to 20 prisoners had been murdered and others tortured or castrated during a stand-off that lasted for weeks. One *Daily Mirror* front page announced 'Prison Mob "Hang Cop"' (3 April 2000). The PC report made clear that 'many of the more gruesome events reported in the press had not occurred – nobody had been systematically mutilated, there had been no castrations, no bodies had been chopped up and flushed in the sewers. Though there was inter-prisoner violence in the first hours of the riot, torture on the scale suggested by many of the early reports did not take place'.

When TV Kept Watchful Eye on Press Excesses

This was an era when television, in particular, began to keep a watchful eye on such excesses, with Channel Four programmes such *Hard News* and *Right of Reply* holding journalists to account. *Hard News* went on air in April 1989 and won a Royal Television Society award for its rigorous investigations into the truth behind intrusive and sensational headlines in the press. Its presenter, journalist Raymond Snoddy, would later write a challenging book about press standards and regulation (Snoddy 1992). Its point was 'a very simple one', he wrote. 'It is that all journalists, broadsheet no less than tabloid, have got to make the time to get off the treadmill of deadlines to think a little more about what they do, the effect it can have on their fellow citizens and the impact their work is having on the reputation of the press.'

Snoddy's first two examples contrasted the resources of a media-savvy government minister, MP Peter Bottomley, with those of a man devastated by the loss of his wife and two children in an accident in Greece. Both had received rough treatment by the press – Bottomley by the *Mail on Sunday* ('Minister in Sex Case Row', 21 May 1989), Tom Evans by the *Daily Mirror* (9 August 1989) which had distressingly misrepresented an interview he gave to an agency reporter while visiting his one surviving daughter in hospital. Evans eventually won an apology and was sent a cheque for £100 by way of compensation. Bottomley received substantial undisclosed damages in an out-of-court settlement, but no apology. It was a telling example of the inequities in the relationship between the press and its readers, whether well-connected or not.

His book came out as a second Calcutt Inquiry got underway questioning whether the two-year-old PCC was sufficiently effective to preclude the necessity of statutory intervention. Meanwhile, Labour MP Clive Soley was making parliamentary history by setting up an all-party committee to hear evidence for and against his proposal for an Independent Press Authority to investigate complaints and defend press freedom. Soley's Freedom and Responsibility of the Press Bill did not make it on to the statute book but the essential idea is among those that have resurfaced for consideration by Lord Leveson.

During the Soley hearings MPs heard traumatic stories of lives being ripped apart by unthinking, inaccurate or intrusive stories (Jempson 1993), again highlighting the unequal struggle ordinary people face when trying to set the record straight. Former royal maid Linda Townley and her brother spoke of the stress they had endured when she had been falsely accused (by the now defunct *Today*) of stealing love letters from Princess Anne, and how they had been pursued by the press pack even after she had cleared her name. A young couple told of the upset caused when the *Daily Mirror* misrepresented research findings giving them false hopes that their child might be cured of a debilitating illness. One witness, a journalist from Northern Ireland, had to give his evidence *in camera* because inaccurate reports in a 'quality newspaper' that he was part of an alleged ANC/IRA plot to assassinate Margaret Thatcher had put his life in danger.

Having documented the Hillsborough football stadium tragedy in 1989 when 96 people lost their lives (Scraton, Jemphrey and Coleman 1995), criminologist Professor Phil Scraton told the Soley hearings about a journalist whose request for a photograph of a child killed at the stadium had been refused by the parents. He then went to the grandmother and told her he had a photograph of the child dead but would prefer to use one of the boy alive. Both images were then published as 'before' and 'after' pictures. It was one example of a lengthy catalogue of insensitive, inaccurate and sensational stories: some newspapers carried photographs of the dead and dying crushed against fencing. After the *Sun* claimed that Liverpool fans had urinated on the dying crowds, it saw its readership in Liverpool drop by up to 40 per cent as the public responded to its crass and hurtful coverage.

During the hearings, Quentin Davies MP asked Keith Parker, of the Guild of British Newspaper Editors, about 'the great sensational stories of 1992…the bugging of [government minister] Mellor's telephone conversations, the theft of the lawyer's letter relating to [the then-Liberal Democrat leader Paddy] Ashdown's private life, and the purloining of photographs and the bugging of telephone conversations allegedly held by members do the royal family' (Jempson 1993).

Were the methods used to obtain information for these stories 'illegitimate?' he asked. 'Yes,' replied Parker, although he could not be certain 'that newspapers themselves were necessarily engaged in the activities'. Pressed on the point that newspapers 'had rewarded financially those who were engaged in these illegitimate activities', Parker admitted that this 'could indeed be said to be an excess' (ibid).

It was such 'excesses' that had given rise to the first Calcutt Report which, in turn noted that similar concerns were examined by the Younger committee on privacy which reported in July 1972. Sir David Calcutt's review of self-regulation appeared just after the Soley hearings and was withering in its disdain for the Press Complaints Commission. 'Nothing that I have learnt about the press has led me to conclude that the press would now be willing to make, or would in fact make, the changes which would be needed,' he wrote. 'I do not doubt that the commission commands the confidence of the industry, but it cannot, in my view, command the confidence of the public. The pressing social need which has to be addressed is protection against unjustifiable infringements by the press.' He wanted it replaced by a statutory tribunal, operating to a tough code and with power to impose fines, and initiate investigations, not unlike one of the proposals placed before Lord Leveson by the Co-ordinating Committee for Media Reform, a group of academics and media activists (see Chapter 30).

Founding of PressWise (later MediaWise)

As if to demonstrate distain for their critics, no journalists turned up at the public meeting Clive Soley organised in the Grand Committee Room at Westminster to which he had invited the national press along with some 70 people who wanted to explain how they had been hurt and how things might be improved. Annoyed by what they saw as the arrogance or lack of comprehension among editors and journalists, the 'victims of media abuse' who did turn up spoke of the sense of isolation and powerlessness that overcame them when the inaccurate or intrusive stories were published. They recorded their displeasure at the non-appearance of the press by resolving to set up an organisation that would provide advice and support for complainants and challenge the media.

Since then PressWise (which changed its name to MediaWise in 2005) has handled thousands of inquiries from individuals and groups about mistreatment by the press. They have included black and minority ethnic groups, gypsies and travellers, mental health service users, gays, lesbians and transgender groups, single parents, surrogate mothers, young people, people with disabilities, asylum-seekers and refugees, victims of crime and families of prisoners. In short, some of the most vulnerable groups in society have found that the popular press are more often their adversary rather than their friend.

The tabloids turned Essene Rabbi Desiree Ntolo into a figure of fun, then derision. A former teacher from Cameroon, she had built an oratory from mud in her back garden, only to be told by Redbridge Council that it required planning consent. Persuaded that publicity would help her cause she spoke to the *Sun* ('Nice Hut With All Mud Cons'), the *Daily Star* ('Des Res is a Mud Hut in Dagenham') and the *Daily Mail* ('Out in Dagenham'). All these stories appeared on the same day (25 June 1992) but it was to be the start of a media assault on her dignity that lasted for months. One reporter she found climbing over her wall offered her money if he could pretend to have stayed in the building over night, but when she told a *Daily Star* reporter he should pay for wasting her time his newspaper ran with 'Mud Hut Mum Begs For Cash'.

All of the stories misrepresented her, and none of the nationals recorded that she later won her court battle with the council – but only after the oratory had been demolished. One of the most damaging examples of bad journalism came in an appalling piece by columnist Barbara Amiel (*Sunday Times*, 26 March 1993). Relying entirely on inaccurate information culled from cuttings, she vilified Ms Ntolo, whom she did not realise was a fellow Jew. Using highly pejorative language, she attacked 'the madness of immigration without integration' under the headline 'Here's Mud in Your Multicultural Eye' and suggested that the mother of six should leave England. The family received racist hate mail and death threats and her 12-year-old son was attacked at school. She did not know about the PCC and never received redress for her ill-treament, but survived to write her own story (Ntolo and Cohen 1994) and to help found PressWise.

The Excesses of Cheque-Book Journalism
Her story was one of many that highlighted the practice of cheque-book journalism. Trading in stories has long been lucrative and journalist Christopher Browne claimed (Browne 1996: 55) that in 1994 the *Sun* alone was paying its agency and freelance journalists £8million for stories and tips. Then an ex-directory phone number was worth £100, and informants included police officers, chauffeurs, taxi drivers, airport staff, bar staff and hairdressers. And if sufficient leads had not come in as deadlines approached at the *Sunday Sport* and *Daily Sport*, he claimed 'the news editor sometime instructs six or seven reporters to go into a private room for the afternoon and concoct stories zany and outrageous enough to titillate their readers'.

The tabloids and so-called human interest magazines have been openly offering inducements for years. The lure of easy cash has persuaded many to sell tittle-tattle as well as hard factual information.

Editors have often claimed that it is greed which fuels the trade. There was distressing evidence of this at the trial of two juveniles accused of the murder of 10-year-old Damilola Taylor in 2002. The key prosecution witness, a 14-year-old girl, demanded the £50,000 offered by a national newspaper to give evidence of what she had seen.

But it is the newspapers that offer the lure, produce questionable contracts to obtain exclusive access and leave notes offering blank cheques for people's stories. Those despised for 'kissing and selling' often turn out to have been victims themselves. MediaWise has heard time after time from young women who have effectively been blackmailed into giving 'their side of the story' or risk sensational exposure with no means of redress after a third party has tipped off the press about their encounters with married or famous people.

MediaWise dealt with the case of a young woman who hoped to pay off her student debts by selling information about her encounter with a convicted rapist. Isolated with a friend in a London hotel by a tabloid her photograph was taken before a lengthy 'debrief'. When she objected to posing on a bed in her underwear, the newspaper reneged on the agreed payment on the grounds that the story did not meet the terms of the entirely self-serving contract it had drafted.

In another case a hard-up young couple who were offered money to strip for a visiting sheikh in his London hotel room found themselves at the centre of an elaborate trap set by the *News of the World's* Mahzer Mahmood. The tabloid was trying to expose a solicitor who, it believed, was running a sexual services scheme from his workplace. The couple were plied with drinks and handed drugs for the sheikh before being taken to his room in the Savoy. But the newspaper named the wrong law firm and had to publish a fulsome apology the following week and pay damages. Meanwhile the young couple were ostracised by their family at a time when the woman's mother was dying in hospital. Although they had committed no crime, they received no apology and did even receive the promised fee.

PCC's Reluctance to Investigate

The PCC has always seemed strangely reluctant to investigate the methods used to obtain stories, perhaps relying too heavily upon assurances from editors that their staff would never misbehave in such a way. Often MediaWise has had calls from people besieged in their homes by 'media scrums'. They are always advised to try to keep their cool, since displays of fear – driving away at speed – or anger – threatening or actually striking out at photographers or reporters – provide the new angle the pack are waiting to seize upon. One teacher, who had in earlier days worked for an escort agency, described how a reporter had marched around her house calling out: 'Come on out, we know you're in there. We know you were a whore.' This was, of course, denied by the newspaper.

A single parent who had left the police force after winning compensation three years earlier for what the *Daily Mail* had described as 'a sustained campaign of harassment [by police colleagues] which undermined not only her professional confidence but also her health', was horrified to discover that two people had been peering into her house and asking questions of her neighbours. She had moved home for her own protection. The following week the *Daily Mail* identified its location and described her home as 'tastefully decorated with old-style farm furniture and expensive ornaments'.

Although the *Mail* had earlier opined: 'She had every justification for taking her case to an industrial tribunal…which she had deservedly won', like other newspapers it had always quoted a sum concocted by journalists after the hearing. Constrained by the terms of her settlement from revealing details of the award, the woman felt helpless to challenge the frequent repetition of this exaggerated figure, which was now being used by the *Mail* along with some of the sexist jibes she had endured, as part of its campaign against 'the compensation culture'. The PCC wanted evidence that the incident had affected her health, and the *Mail* claimed 'public interest' in justification of its repeated references to her.

Other complainants had also been asked to reveal medical or even police records to the PCC with no guarantee that they would not be seen by the newspapers which had made inaccurate or intrusive claims. Some even suggested that the PCC was being used as a backdoor means of confirming what was only suspected, or of legitimising information which had been illicitly obtained.

Another woman called MediaWise from her bedroom where she had taken refuge after being told by a neighbour that two men were skulking around her isolated house, and peering through her downstairs windows. She had earlier refused to talk to a reporter and photographer from the *Daily Mail*. MediaWise called the news desk to insist that the men be called off. Despite denials of their presence, they withdrew shortly afterwards. This woman, who had been trying to expose sharp practices by a mortgage company, had become terrified when she realised that someone was accessing her telephone records illicitly. This was before mobile phones had become ubiquitous. She had been hounded by a man claiming to be a journalist but who she suspected of being a private investigator. Years later the revelations of the Information Commissioner (Thomas 2006) confirmed what so many MediaWise clients had always suspected, that newspapers routinely hired investigators to collect data which staff could not readily access.

Role of Freelances

Their other sources are the news agencies and freelances who provide an ever more essential information gathering service as the number of staff journalists has reduced over the years. Their earning capacity depends upon adding value to stories which may arise from court cases or local news outlets, and to provide local background for national stories. This is one of the significant structural issues, along with 'citizen journalism', blogging and Twitter which will continue to have an impact upon newsgathering techniques and media standards.

Two European Commission funded projects are currently investigating what all this might mean in terms of both policy and practice (see www.mediaact.eu and http://www.mediadem.eliamep.gr/). The new PCC Chair, Lord Hunt, already believes he has got the measure of the task in his reform proposals to persuade bloggers to register and adopt a standards 'kitemark'. However, it remains one of the greatest challenges both to regulators and to the Leveson Inquiry.

Hackgate and the forensic investigation of stories and information gathering techniques that the inquiry has brought on, may have opened up UK journalism to unfamiliar scrutiny but that will do little to resolve the problem of unethical behaviour when the pressure for stories that will sell is more likely to increase than decrease if newspapers and magazines are to survive. All of the cases quoted here occurred long before the *News of the World* royal editor Clive Goodman was jailed in 2007 for using phone intercepts. Opportunities to gain private information about people have since increased exponentially as access to the internet has spread and social networks have encouraged the sharing of intimacies.

Three months after the Scottish *Sunday Express* published its disgraceful 'Anniversary Shame of Dunblane Survivors' (8 March 2009), the PCC announced that the newspaper had made a 'serious error of judgment', since the young people whose Facebook pages had been trawled for evidence of their life styles 'were not public figures in any meaningful sense, and...had done nothing to warrant media scrutiny'. Yet by the end of March the newspaper had already removed the offending article from its website and published an apology, in response to an online petition which attracted 11,186 signatures.

It may well be that in future those subjected to unwarranted harassment by the media will begin to use more effectively the internet to set the record straight, or get their own back, as an alternative to approaching the regulator. Bob and Sue Firth famously exacted revenge on *News of the World* reporter Neville Thurlbeck by posting on the internet a video of him in the nude and evidently not 'making his excuses and leaving' while visiting their naturist bed and breakfast in 1998. His employers were quick to get the site shut down and visited the couple to find out how best to resolve matters. The Scientologists tried a similar technique by filming John Sweeney while he put together a *Panorama* programme about them. Ahead of the BBC broadcast in May 2007, they posted on YouTube a sequence of him losing his cool (see http://www.youtube.com/watch?v=hxqR5NPhtLI). It is unlikely that many others will emulate this approach to keeping journalism in order, but such examples and the evidence assembled by Leveson serve as a warning that the 'good old bad old days' are over.

Journalism of the Future under Constant Scrutiny

The journalism of the future will not be in the hands of a select band of hacks who consider themselves the gatekeepers of public taste and morals, free to operate as they please. It will be subject to constant scrutiny and open to a far wider range of participants – and best of all it should become fertile ground for high quality investigative reporting which recognises people rights, considers consequences, and expects public servants and power elites to operate as ethically as the media professionals will now be expected to behave.

References
Bairstow, Tom (1984) *Fourth Rate Estate*, London: Comedia

Blom-Cooper, Louis (1991) *Press at the prison gates: report of the inquiry by the Press Council into press coverage of the Strangeways Prison riot and related matters*, London: Press Council

Brown, Gerry (1995) *Exposed! Sensational true story of Fleet Street reporter*, London: Virgin Books

Browne, Christopher (1996) *The Prying Game: The sex, sleaze and scandals of Fleet Street and the media mafia*, London: Robson Books

Calcutt QC, David (1990) *Report of the Committee on Privacy and Related Matters*, Home Office, London: HMSO Cm 1102, ISBN 0 10 111022 7

Calcutt QC, Sir David (1993) *Review of Press Self-Regulation*, London: HMSO Cm 2135

Chippindale, Peter and Horrie, Chris (1992), *Stick it up your Punter, the rise and fall of the Sun*, London: Mandarin

Cookson, Richard and Jempson, Mike (2004) *Satisfaction Guaranteed? Press complaints systems under scrutiny*, Bristol: MediaWise

Cookson, Richard and Jempson, Mike (2005) *The RAM Report: Campaigning for fair and accurate coverage of refugees and asylum seekers*, Bristol: MediaWise

Hooper, David (1986) *Public Scandal, Odium and Contempt*, London: Coronet

Jempson, Mike (1993) *Freedom and Responsibility of the Press: Report of special parliamentary hearings*, Bristol: Crantock

Jempson, Mike (2002) *And the consequence was…* Berry, David (ed.) *Ethics and Media Culture: Practices and Representations*, Oxford: Focal Press pp.278-296

Ntolo, Desiree and Cohen, Phil (1994) *The Sacred and the Profane*, London: UEL/NEU

Robertson, Geoffrey (1983) *People Against the Press: An Enquiry into the Press Council*, London: Quartet

Scraton, Phil, Jemphrey, Ann and Coleman, Sheila (1995) *No Last Rights: The denial of justice and the promotion of myth in the aftermath of the Hillsborough disaster*, Liverpool: Liverpool City Council

Snoddy, Raymond (1993) *The Good, the Bad and the Unacceptable: The hard news about the British Press*, London: Faber and Faber

Thomas, Richard (2006) *What Price Privacy?* London: HMSO

Thomas, Richard (2006) *What Price Privacy Now?* London: HMSO

Younger, Sir Kenneth (1992) *Report of the Committee on Privacy*, London: HMSO, Cmd 5012

- Among the many website offering to buy or sell stories (accessed on 15 December 2011): www.featureworld.co.uk/sellyourstory.html; www.cashforstories.com; www.cash4yourstory.co.uk/; www.famousfeatures.co.uk/sell_story; www.featureworld.co.uk/sellyourstory.html; www.firstfeatures.co.uk/; www.frontpageagency.co.uk/SellStories; www.mirror.co.uk/sell-your-story/; www.moneyforyourstory.com; www.nationalstoryseller.co.uk/; www.photo-features.co.uk; www.sell-my-story.co.uk; www.sellyourstorynow.co.uk/; www.sellusyourstory.com/; www.takeabreak.co.uk/send-us-your-story; www.talktothepress.co.uk; www.thesun.co.uk/sol/homepage/article240522.ece; www.takeabreak.co.uk/send-us-your-story.

Note on the contributors

Mike Jempson was a co-founder of PressWise (now MediaWise, see www.mediawise.org.uk) and is now its Honorary Director. He has some 40 years experience as a journalist in newspapers, radio, television, public relations and in parliament. He has devised and delivered training programmes in more than 45 countries, working with UN agencies, the International Federation of Journalists, Media Diversity Institute, IREX, the OSCE and the British Council. He has been Visiting Professor in Media Ethics at the University of Lincoln (UK) since 2006, and a Senior Lecturer in Journalism at the University of the West of England since 2007. He is Vice Chair of the NUJ Ethics Committee, the longest serving member of the Campaign for Press and Broadcasting Freedom, and is leading the UK end of an international research project on media accountability systems (see www.mediaact.eu).

Wayne Powell, a history graduate from the University of the West of England, has been handling administrative and research duties MediaWise for almost a decade. He is a Research Assistant on the 14-nation EU-funded Media Accountability and Transparency in Europe Project (www.mediaact.eu) on which UWE is leading for the UK.

Infantilising the Feral Beasts: Criminalising the bad boys and girls of popular journalism and Hackgate's boomerang

Tim Crook argues that the white heat of anger and prejudice directed at British journalists as a result of the Hackgate scandal is in danger of 'consuming the oxygen of libertarian tolerance'

The Hackgate scandal and Leveson Inquiry are profoundly humiliating experiences for any British journalist. The charge, with compelling evidence, that reporters and media institutions with the help of private detectives and corrupt police officers obtained scandalous stories about celebrities and head-start 'scoops' in murder inquiries by snooping on mobile phone messaging, planting viruses to hack computer email accounts, and passing wads of cash to bribe public servants, is shameful.

British journalism is considered socially so bad it needs scores of detectives in multiple police inquiries, parliamentary committees, and a team of lawyers headed by an Appeal Court Judge to investigate and fashion regulatory solutions. Crimes may well be prosecuted at the Crown Court. There is the approaching vista, should arrests lead to charges, of journalists and their former editors appearing for trial in the dock of the Old Bailey. How many police officers will be joining them for taking bungs in exchange for tip-offs and betraying the very people they should have been protecting? Wanton Stasi-style surveillance, intimidation, blackmail and harassment have been added to the political indictment and, no doubt, are being followed by forensic legal consideration.

Problematising Journalism

The 'Hackgate discourse' problematises all forms of journalism, and reduces long established media texts and institutions into an underclass of social outcast and outlaw spinning them into the nexus of democracy, the protestant ethic and punishment syndrome (Newburn and Sparks 2004: 84-91). There is an acute risk that the democratic and libertarian function of a free press to challenge the abuse of power of the rich and powerful has been and is continuing to be disempowered. Those on the lower rungs of social and economic injustice risk being abandoned by the Fleet Street diaspora. In the midst of Leveson witnesses describing how their loved ones have been driven to suicide by media hounding, such homilies seem so very pompous. But before we begin to intellectually abuse a tolerance for freedom without responsibility we do need some robust George Orwell-style resistance to praise Joseph Stalin because he has thrown his lot in with the allies against Nazi Germany (Orwell 1998: 98-108).

It would seem that leading elements of the popular media have been preoccupied with competitively and illegally pursuing a voyeuristic intrusion into the private lives of celebrocrats rather than challenging the unequal vortex of their wealth and privilege. But at the same time the moral panic directed at the bad boys and girls of popular journalism continues to gestate censorial laws that are emotionalised as protecting dignity, honour, reputation, and identity. The language of rape, murder and suicide constitutes a vocabulary of outrage against journalistic and photographic communication.

The immaterial has been reified into materialised horror: J. K. Rowling's five-year-old daughter's schoolbag violated by a reporter's letter (Leveson 24 November 2011); Max Mosley's son driven to an overdose (ibid); Sienna Miller chased down dark alleys, and spat at by mobs of male paparazzi (ibid); Milly Dowler's parents photographed trying to grieve privately over their murdered daughter, given false hope that she might have been alive as a result of a reporter(s) allegedly deleting her phone messages (Leveson 21 November 2011). Lord Justice Leveson exercises a foreboding inquisitorial authority as the litany of disgust and disgrace unfolds in the number 73 court of the Royal Courts of Justice. Yet his inquiry in a curious way represents the very best of that mutually protective meeting place of the wig and the pen.

Leveson and his lawyers along with the super-media public access of camera, microphone and online streaming are giving sanctuary and honour to many of the witnesses who seem to feel safe for the first time. I thought there was something tremendously reassuring to observe a clearly stressed J. K. Rowling clutching a large file to her chest after giving evidence and looking like a PhD student who had just survived a particularly terrifying *viva voce*. Leveson brings humanity to people who had been dehumanised and that includes journalists as well as their victims. And it is the inquiry that has questioned the *Guardian* claim that Milly Dowler's messages were deleted by the *News of the World* (Leveson, 12 December 2011). It may have simply been a matter of automatic deletion by the technology of the mobile phone.

The risk of boomerang lies in the potential constitutional confiscation of democratic and irreverent scrutiny and mockery. Could it be the case that the 'tabloid' media had wrongly presumed that its largely working class and lower-middle-class 'residuum' readership had demanded an unrelenting diet of nasty and sensationalist, though entertaining, gossip and tittle-tattle, oblivious and uncaring of whether the storytelling was fiction or fact? If the presumption had been correct and we are in the process of seeing this 'constitutional service' outlawed and eradicated what does this mean for democratic polity? What is to be gained by the victory of bourgeois, elitist and middle-class values and their full control and censorship of mainstream popular media? The given in academic circles is that privacy laws are good, and first amendment culture is bad and, indeed, Max Mosley feels journalism academics are best qualified to enforce with statutory powers the rules of the Press Complaints Commission (Mosley 2011).

The 1947 US Hutchins Commission that supposedly did for the sewer rats of American journalism what the Leveson Inquiry is doing for the gutter press of British journalism, was constituted entirely by academics and was fiercely criticised for being so (Crook 2009a: 296). The First Amendment was invoked in the civil rights period of US history to stop Ku Klux Klan white supremacists killing black generals on the road to Georgia. Watergate and the Pentagon Papers happened because of the First Amendment. The British Watergates and Pentagon Papers never got to press because we have never had a First Amendment. The First Amendment is not the driving force and ignition spark of journalistic lying and hounding with words.

Lord Justice Leveson appears to be treading in the footsteps of a well-remembered and influential line of investigations into press ethics. In 1990 and 1993 Sir David Calcutt's committees made recommendations on privacy that through legislation and judicial activism, referencing European jurisprudence via the Human Rights Act, has begun to impose a legal *cordon-sanitaire* around the sexual peccadilloes and private embarrassments of celebrities and public figures (115-35). Statutes such as the Protection from Harassment Act 1997, the Data Protection Act 1998, and the Regulation of Investigatory Powers Act 2000 have created crimes and civil wrongs in connection with the methodology of all forms of information gathering.

The Legal Boomerang Accelerates

Year by year statutes and case law have cumulatively bitten on and restricted the tactics and content of the tabloid market. Leveson might be invited to consider whether the harsh English libel laws, so expensive and claimant friendly, drove scandal mongers to break the law in the pursuit of information that could be guaranteed to be the truth rather than merely provable on the balance of probabilities.

The judiciary and government law officers appear to be comfortable with a curious double-think in articulating assertions about the importance of press freedom, but at the same time pursuing media freedom restrictive and punitive legalism. The Attorney General, Dominic Grieve (Grieve 2011), and the Lord Chief Justice of England and Wales, Igor Judge (Boycott and Watt 2011), appear to agree on the idea that media reporting of parliamentarians breaching judicial gagging orders is unlawful. This would render the freedom of expression provision enshrined in the 1689 Bill of Rights for MPs and Peers somewhat meaningless in a 21st century society where democratic politics cannot function without media representation of their political debates and proceedings.

Media contempt laws used to be about deterring a substantial risk of serious prejudice to juries. But recent case law has decided that the media should be convicted of criminal liability with heavy fines for a temporary and mistaken publication of a photograph online unseen by the jury (AG v Associated 2011), and prejudicial coverage of a suspect after his arrest nearly a year away from the trial who had already collected substantial damages for the attack on his reputation through libel litigation (AG v MGN and Others 2011). It would seem the court in its ruling was creating a new dimension of media contempt rooted around the idea that the vilification of a suspect under arrest should be considered a potential impediment to the course of justice. Is it possible that this is the new criminal libel, an offence abolished by parliament several years previously? Media responsibility is to be legally measured against speculative unknowns and hypothetical possibilities:

> ...such material may deter or discourage witnesses from coming forward and providing information helpful to the suspect...This may arise, for example, because witnesses may be reluctant to be associated with or perceived to be a supporter of the suspect, or, again, because they may begin to doubt whether information apparently favourable to the suspect could possibly be correct...it is not an answer that on the evidence actually available, the combination of the direction of the judge and the integrity of the jury would ensure a fair trial. The problem is that the evidence at trial may be incomplete just because its existence may never be known, or indeed may only come to light after conviction (Lord Judge CJ [at 31] ibid).

Compared to our common law cousins in the US, British media institutions have had to come to terms with the crossing of the constitutional Rubicon in ways that would be intolerable in San Francisco, Dallas or Washington DC. The generation of new media contempt powers and challenging the Bill of Rights parliamentary immunity follows the legal interdicting of global communications to deter civil disobedience of privacy court orders on Twitter, the extension of Official Secrets Act liability to accidentally reporting information that might be part of an *in camera* hearing (Crook 2009a: 357), retrospective prohibition of media publication already in open court or the public domain (*Times* and Others and R 2007), the consolidation of gagging truth through prior restraint privacy law rather than a remedy through post-publication damages, the expansion of secret policing and judicial processes, and the cult of anonymity and concealing accountability (ibid: 117-121).

The latest constitutional shift has emerged in section 13 of the Education Act of 2011 which prohibits by criminal prosecution anything that could lead to the identification of teachers accused and arrested for criminal offences against children. It is only a matter of time before anyone arrested for any criminal offence will have the same protection. These are disturbing trends. Britain's media laws are becoming more authoritarian. There may well be a connection with the construction of British popular journalism as a Mafiosi protection racket bullying, suborning and porno-gazing across the debris and detritus of private grief and misfortune.

The authoritarian tendency haunts existing legal needs and rights for all forms of journalism. What happens when an investigative reporter challenging high level political corruption can only obtain the evidence required by phone hacking? No public interest defence is available for a section 1 RIPA offence. The public interest for unlawfully obtaining private information under the 1998 Data Protection Act is under threat with a renewed call for custodial penalties on conviction. There are calls to repeal the statutory protection for journalistic materials and confidential information under the Police and Criminal Evidence Act 1984. As the *Guardian* realised when New Scotland Yard came knocking over leaks from the new phone hacking inquiry, there are no public interest defences for the ambit of conspiracy law surrounding misconduct in public office, official secrecy and the day-to-day, non press bureau sourcing from detectives and civil servants of crime stories. The everyday contact of journalists with their sources is subject to the new legal jeopardy of the 2010 Bribery Act.

The campaign for more media friendly defamation laws, combating the exponential rise of media litigation and compliance costs exhaustion through conditional fee agreements and lawyer success fees looks wrecked on the storm of Hackgate, which through the Leveson Inquiry raises the spectre of statutory regulation of the print media. This could be a return to state licensing and control that had been abandoned in the middle of the 19th century.

Freedom of Expression the First Casualty

Despite this alarming helter skelter spiraling towards the authoritarian tendency, political and public opinion is offering little sympathy to journalism as a defendant in an inquisitorial trial of ethics. There may well be an excessive and distorted moral panic exploited by the political expediency to reap revenge on newspapers for the parliamentary expenses scandal and distract from the Faustian pact politicians had with Rupert Murdoch's media empire. There is little sign that the public cares. There is no rush to buy more newspapers, pay for online content, or give the BBC more money through the licence fee so that it can produce more journalism. There are no demonstrations demanding more news and current affairs programmes on the radio or television. At least one million Sunday *News of the World* readers have disappeared without switching their allegiance to any other title (Plunkett 2011).

If anything there is a climate of embarrassment and unease that British society has fostered and cultivated cheap and sordid journalism. There is a palpable sense that public opinion may quietly be of the same view as the legendary CBS broadcaster Ed Murrow who, in 1955, poignantly signed off his exposure of the notorious persecutory bullying of Senator Joseph R. McCarthy with the words from Shakespeare's *Julius Caesar*. 'Cassius was right, the fault dear Brutus is not in our stars, but in ourselves' (Sperber 1998: 414).

The sociological moral panic analysed and defined by cultural theorists such as Stanley Cohen and Stuart Hall (see Cohen 1973, Hall 1978 and Critcher 2003) can be seen in the intensifying of moral hue and cry and expanding margin of liminality unleashed by the rhetorical charge of hacking Milly Dowler's phone and that of the terrorism victims of 9/11, and 7/7 and the parents of child murder victims Holly Wells and Jessica Chapman. It is certainly reminiscent of the social and political action arising out of the legend of chase, photographic intrusion and media exploitation of Diana, Princess of Wales in 1997 where socially the paparazzi were held culpable in her road death.

Yet it took ten years and a multi-million pound London inquest, avoided by the 'paparazzi' themselves, before any legal responsibility was issued by court ruling. The moral panic associated with Diana's death led to European Council assembly resolution 1165 that has become a benchmark on the drive and aspiration for applying a shield of immunity and protection within the zones of private and public interaction of people defined as individuals *par excellence* (Crook 2009a: 230-232). But culturally and historically this shield of social prohibition and inhibition is a temporary construction and is dealing with the functions of capitalism not upholding *a priori* issues of sacred human identity. As Terry Eagleton so bracingly puts it: 'Nothing in human life is inherently private. Certainly not urinating, defecating and copulating, which only a few centuries ago could be performed in public with no sense of shame' (Eagleton 2011).

Devils and Angels

Hackgate can be seen as a scaling up in the moral panic over tabloid predatory harm. The political language resembles the longstanding discourse in youth justice where young offenders are divided between angels and devils, an intellectual narrowing frequently criticised by academics such as Julia Fionda in her seminal text *Devils and Angels: Youth Policy and Crime* as a dichotomy of false consciousness (Fionda 2005: 3-7).

There is no doubt that this is a political and media power struggle with horns of absolutist rhetoric locking into battle. The 'popular and tabloid' media have become synonymous with deviance, delinquency, and the anti-social Other, requiring crime control, behavioural treatment, or retributivist and punitive conditioning. Cast in the role of angels are *Guardian* investigative writer Nick Davies and Editor Alan Rusbridger, hacking victim lawyer Mark Lewis, along with the campaigning Labour MP, Alan Watson. We can also add a highly talented line-up of celebrities: the actor Hugh Grant whose adventures on Los Angeles's Sunset Boulevard reportedly launched Divine Brown on a modeling career worth more than one $1million (*Daily Mail* 2007), Steve Coogan, otherwise known as Alan Partridge; and the former president of Formula One motor racing, Max Mosley, at the time of writing (December 2011) a very happy resident of the principality of Monaco. There are many other angels, though when stripped of the metaphorical labeling, they have disclosed a more visceral and human presence in the Leveson Inquiry witness box.

Cast in the role of devils are Rupert Murdoch and his former *News of the World* editors and executives, along with counter-celebrocrats such as former *Sun* editor, Kelvin MacKenzie who was responsible for the notorious edition that wrongly accused Liverpool football supporters of hooliganism at the Hillsborough stadium disaster of 1989. A judicial public inquiry by the late Lord Justice Peter Taylor, as he then was, decided that the suffocation and fatal crushing of 96 men, women and children arose out of decisions made by South Yorkshire police officers who failed to control crowd entry.

Paul Dacre, the Editor in Chief of the *Daily Mail* – believed to have a salary package well in excess of £2 million (Sweeney 2011) – is struggling to avoid the sobriquet of devil though he is very much in the firing line. Former *News of the World* reporter and now pub landlord, Paul McMullan, continues to advocate intrusive and illegal phone-hacking of celebrities (Leveson 29 November 2011) and was bugged himself by Hugh Grant in a reversal of fortune celebrated by *New Statesman* magazine. Mr. McMullan has had the misfortune of being described as 'rat-like' and so easily fits into former Prime Minister Tony Blair's description of the tabloid media pack resembling feral beasts: 'The former *NoW* hack Paul McMullan was as twitchy as a laboratory rat when he was interviewed on Newsnight' (Pearson 2011). The writer Will Self characterised him as 'a kind of rat-like feral persona' (Self 2011). Taken together, MacKenzie, Dacre and McMullan are hardly the most effervescent parade of journalistic defenders of the faith.

The adjective 'feral' has comfortably sat alongside the plural noun 'youths' for many years. There is certainly a sense of near poetic justice in the media being demeaned as 'feral churnalists' when it continues to be the conduit for demonising 'feral youths' who alongside the developing Hackgate scandal were seen as the main 'sick' instigators of the summer rioting. The media is saturated with recurrent images of childhood deviance from 12-year-old sex offence defendants giving the media 'the finger' outside court, to the moral panic about 'fat kiddies' with even the seemingly innocent over-consumption of ice-cream being condemned as waddling on the path to obesity. There is no shortage of 'feral youths' being condemned for excessive crime, eating, sex, anti-social behaviour, and excessive stupidity in thinking they are performing better each year in grade inflation flawed examination GCSE and A level papers (Fionda 2005: 262-270). Recent media coverage characterised the country's youth as a generation of drunks hurtling toward alcoholism and premature death through liver disease.

The so-called respectable media has no trouble giving itself a taste of its own malignant medicine. There is no recognition of insight and irony that the bigoted and dehumanising language prevalent in political media discourse about 'problematised youth' and young people is deployed against popular journalism. Public interest BBC and *Guardian*-style middle class, bourgeois journalism is good. Popular 'tabloid' working class journalism for CDE marketing categories is bad.

Privately educated children of celebrocrats are good and children who are unfortunate enough to be educated in state schools are bad. The class labels of private educational institutions such as Eton, Westminster, Marlborough and a few surviving grammar schools along with the stress of unseen examinations, learning classical Latin and Greek, and now computer coding rather than 'pressing buttons', and aspiration for the dreaming spires of Oxford and Cambridge are elevated and super-charged. State educational institutions are 'demonised' and diminished.

The state teaching profession is belittled as feckless as their unruly 'out of control' pupils and their examination successes are dismissed as 'grade inflation', new modern and pragmatic subjects such as psychology, business, law and media studies are dismissed as 'soft' even though the latter is the very academic subject that questions and analyses the abuse of media power. State education is problematised as needing the military forces culture to discipline and 'teach properly' (an added irony is that teachers in private education do not need state accredited teaching qualifications). Hence the rapid deregulation and privatisation of state education through free schools and academies. A new language and labeling is needed to replace old and discredited comprehensive education. The humanities in Higher Education are stripped of direct state funding and diminished *vis-à-vis* pure sciences and modern languages. Once universities were discoursed as a solution; now they are discussed as a problem to be avoided, reformed and improved by privatisation rather than continuing any kind of 'public service'.

The Internal Divide Extends to Attitudes Towards the Leveson Inquiry
The media has certainly mastered the art of dividing itself in the internecine warfare about whether and how it should change. It is confused about the purpose of the Leveson Inquiry. Freedom of expression and US First Amendment enthusiasts generally in the tabloid and 'red top' corner raise the issue of whether it is a symptom of political witch hunt, is duplicating multiple police inquiries, has an unrepresentative panel bereft of tabloid and regional newspaper expertise, is lacking a research budget and strategy, is quasi-judicial and adjudicatory rather than ameliorating and conflict resolving, is a disproportionate frame exaggerating minority criminality to represent the general situation and as far as putting the tabloid press in another last chance saloon is nothing new.

The arguments that 'dog eat dog' is a tired and time-honoured journalistic narrative, that present day journalism is being judged by the sins of the past, and that because the previous Metropolitan Police inquiry in 2006-7 resulted in criminal convictions and jail sentences for a *News of the World* journalist and a private detective, there is a suggestion that the current exertions are akin to *res judicata* and *autrefois convict*, tend to receive a slow handclap.

There are a few penitent moral entrepreneurs in journalism conscious of a wider academic consensus that Leveson brings social and cultural advantages in being a judicial, accountable and public inquiry distanced from executive, exploring the rights as well as the responsibilities of the press, appreciating the wider context of competitive pressures on the press and their impact on journalism, avowedly expressing support for a free press and an aspiration for higher standards in the approach to regulation and apparently inclusive in the way the inquiry is inviting contributions and submissions with an ongoing deadline, that could constitute a source of effective external research (Kampfner 2011 and Petley 2011).

The Political and Policing Bystanders
Prime Minister Tony Blair spoke on media ethics in 2007 and most of his words seem to be central to the subject of the current inquiry, but it was also the start of the media feral beast insult:

> But misconduct is what has impact. Third, the fear of missing out means today's media, more than ever before, hunts in a pack. In these modes it is like a feral beast, just tearing people and reputations to bits. But no-one dares miss out. Fourth, rather than just report news, even if sensational or controversial, the new technique is commentary on the news being as, if not more important than the news itself. (Blair 2007).

The language alienates and dehumanises individual journalists caught up in a toxic equation of fear, ego, ambition, competition and self-loathing. It pollutes the political atmosphere with the cordite of revenge.

Political, dramatic and literary texts have always been replete with exaggerated and negative representations of journalists. Joseph Conrad's *Heart of Darkness* (1899 in magazine, 1901 in novella) had a central character called Kurtz (similar to *kurz*, meaning short in German) who was a journalist. The famous catch-phrase of this charismatic and corrupted legend, lost up river in European colonial madness, was 'the horror, the horror' (Conrad 1996: 86). But he also shrieked in his dying despair 'Exterminate all the Brutes!' (ibid: 66). It might be argued that one could substitute the word 'beasts' for 'brutes'.

Prime Minister Stanley Baldwin, in 1931, spoke of 'power without responsibility' in an attack on the press barons Beaverbrook and Rothermere over their papers' sponsorship of a political party that libeled him and peddled in:

> ...direct falsehood, misrepresentation, half-truths, the alteration of the speaker's meaning...What the proprietorship of these papers is aiming at is power, but power without responsibility – the prerogative of the harlot through the ages' (Margach 1978: 30-31).

But he went on to declare he would not sue for damages as he did not wish to sully his pockets with their money. This exercise of restraint and good judgment in politics is not as common now as it should be. To what extent is the hunt for justice and the feral beast being pursued with more vehemence than MPs' expenses? It might be argued that the deployment of so many detectives in the investigation of thousands of crimes committed so many years ago appears to be a discrediting of discretionary policing – often seen as the mark of democratic policing. What has been achieved by the parliamentary jeering of experienced, distinguished and independent police officers who in the popular imagination have been reduced to being the feral beast's geezer?

The Agenda for Press Reform

Broadcasting journalism culture does not want to be involved. The BBC's director general advised against merging press self-regulation into a general infrastructure of state regulation and licensing. This could be seen as somewhat ironic since it is being argued that 'press' and not 'media' freedom needs to be preserved. Is it not the case that 'press' 'online' and 'broadcasting' media are interpenetrating and this compartmentalising of 'press' media is anachronistic and a false chimera? This may be symptomatic of a lack of industrial solidarity with an old broadsheet and tabloid divide and the *Guardian* seemingly at war with the Murdoch-owned News Group Newspapers/News International. Where is the moral confidence and entrepreneurial leadership to revitalise the ethical and commercial heart of popular journalism?

The Leveson Inquiry was politically commissioned with the declared assumption by the Prime Minister that the Press Complaints Commission self-regulation had failed, and there is no shortage of opinion condemning the PCC as discredited and irrelevant. The PCC might counter that institutional criminality is not within the PCCs remit. Yet restorative justice measures advanced and operated by the PCC with little praise and recognition, are now fashionable because they are non legal adjudicatory and based on negotiation, mediation, conciliation, arbitration, and non dispute resolution. These are low cost, high volume, non-litigious outcomes.

It might be argued that the PCC could add inquiry to its remit so that the process of regulation is more inquisitive and responsive to complaints pointing to ethically and legally problematical patterns of journalistic methodology and publication. The rhetoric over the need for 'press regulation with teeth' could be an unhelpful and distracting sideshow. Any regulatory regime with teeth chomping out fines would simply add to the financial hemorrhaging of already burdensome media costs through criminal and civil law litigation and regulatory compliance.

If it is argued that we need more educated, ethically trained journalists and public interest journalism, is it not time to consider constructively restorative and developmental remedies? Ofcom's penalties go into the consolidated fund – when they could be invested in community radio or television. Hackgate is sapping News International of tens of millions of pounds instead of investing in new openings for journalism students at university, and the high quality investigative journalism seen as the holy grail of the fourth estate's democratic function.

There appears to be a double standard of state and self regulation between broadcasting and the press and without any recognition of the multimedia context. Large scale criminal fraud in UK broadcasting (radio and television) when millions of pounds were stolen from the public in fake and rigged competitions and phone votes was not investigated by the police and criminally prosecuted. It was left to Ofcom to investigate and regulate by fines. Yet the press is indicted by a call for non-discretionary police inquiry. The cry is for no stone to be left unturned, every victim to be contacted and alleged crime investigated and a following of the evidence wherever it should go.

It does not look very likely that parliament, public opinion and the full spectrum of British multi-media are prepared to agree a sophisticated constitutional settlement in capping the damages and costs for privacy and libel at a reasonable and sustainable level, living with an end to prior restraint, and channeling complaints and infractions through compulsory restorative justice, arbitration, inquiry, conciliation and mediation processes.

However, there is a low-cost and constructive reform measure that might be seen as a threat to the body politic, political establishment and media institutions. The individual journalist's conscience clause if made mandatory in all employee contracts (whether staff, contract or casual) would challenge editorial autocracy and oppressive, unlawful, unethical, immoral media professional cultures that serve extremist and cynical business and political agendas (Phillips 2008). The conscience clause has always been advanced and campaigned for by the NUJ – in the past an effective frame for ethical and professional mentoring and the first self-regulator. The clause would move the battleground on irresponsibility and criminality to the employment tribunal. Journalists and media employees would have the right to say no to breaking the law and breaching codes of ethics, a right to compensation for reprisal by sacking, and black-listing, and proper employment law protection.

Conclusion

I have argued for many years (Crook 2009a: 308-314 and 2009b) that human communication generates harm that is largely emotional and immaterial and that civil legal remedies and criminal sanctions should be proportionately restorative and avoid the temptation for popular penalism. Our penal institutions are overfull with young offenders and no useful social purpose would be served by feral youths being joined by the feral beasts of journalism. Intriguing though I found Max Mosley's adoption of John Stuart Mill in support of his plea that he should have the right to practise his unorthodox and minority strand of sexuality, I am not sure he fully appreciated the argument advanced by Mill and his wife Harriet Taylor in *On Liberty* that truth should always be allowed to collide with error and should not be suppressed and censored unless there is a real and present danger of damage to the individual, at the threshold of shouting fire in a crowded theatre and maiming and causing death by stampede.

My late father always used to say there was nothing wrong with the offensive, embarrassing and uncomfortable breeze of truth apart from the halitosis of social attitude. I gladly quoted him in *Comparative Media Law and Ethics* as stating that 'There are only two steps from tyranny: the first is when you deny a journalist the right to ask unpopular questions: the second is when you deny a lawyer the right to defend unpopular causes' (Crook 2009a: 6). Campaigning *Guardian* journalist Nick Davies and tenacious solicitor Mark Lewis had every right to think they might have been in these positions when they stood strong against a tide of political and legal skepticism and condemnatory pressure.

However, I fear that the aggression and retributive atmosphere of the Hackgate scandal and Leveson Inquiry, the white heat of anger and prejudice directed at British journalists and journalism is consuming the oxygen of libertarian tolerance and confidence in giving the media a necessary though potentially uncomfortable freedom without responsibility. Could it be that inquiry, negotiation, mediation, arbitration, conciliation, apology, forgiveness and emotional restitution are solutions that prey too greatly on the egos of the high and mighty? Surely restorative justice and media freedom are preferred options to the multi-million pound adjudicatory sequestration and incarceration of the scoundrels and miscreants of British journalism?

References

Blair, Tony (2007) Prime Minister Tony Blair's Reuters speech on public life on 12 June, BBC News. Available online at http://news.bbc.co.uk/1/hi/uk_politics/6744581.stm, accessed on 3 October 2011, accessed on 17 November 2011

Bott, George (1958) *George Orwell: Selected Writings*, London: Heinemann Educational Books

Bowcott, Owen and Watt, Nicholas (2011) Judges challenge use of parliamentary privilege, 21 May. Available online at http://www.guardian.co.uk/politics/2011/may/21/judges-challenge-use-parliamentary-privilege, accessed on 17 November 2011

Cohen, Stanley (1973) *Folk Devils and Moral Panics: The Creation of the Mods and Rockers*, St Albans: Paladin

Conrad, Joseph, (1996) *Heart of Darkness*, New York: Bedford Books

Critcher, Chas. (2003) *Moral Panics and the Media*, Maidenhead: Open University Press.

Crook, Tim (2009a) *Comparative Media Law and Ethics*, London and New York: Routledge

Crook, Tim (2009b) Reforming UK libel, privacy and media standards through the creation of a Media Law and Restorative Justice Commission' in a constitutionally reforming 'Media Freedom and Restorative Justice Act. Available online at http://www.publications.parliament.uk/pa/cm200910/cmselect/cmcumeds/memo/press/m13002.htm, accessed on 4 November 2011

Daily Mail (2007) Vice girl turned millionairess Divine Brown can't thank Hugh Grant enough, 6 July. Available online at http://www.dailymail.co.uk/femail/article-466250/Vice-girl-turned-millionairess-Divine-Brown-thank-Hugh-Grant-enough.html#ixzz1f241A6Lt, accessed on 15 October 2011

Davison, Peter (ed.) (1998) *The Complete Works of George Orwell, Volume Eight, Animal Farm: A Fairy Story*, London: Secker and Warburg

Eagleton, Terry (2011) Leveson Inquiry: the frontiers of privacy, 28 November. Available online at http://www.guardian.co.uk/commentisfree/2011/nov/28/leveson-inquiry-frontiers-of-privacy?, accessed on 1 December 2011

Fionda, Julia (2005) *Devils and Angels: Youth Policy and Crime*, Oxford and Portland, Oregon: Hart Publishing

Grieve, Dominic QC MP, Attorney General (2011) Contempt – a balancing act, 1 December. Available online at http://www.attorneygeneral.gov.uk/NewsCentre/Speeches/Pages/ContemptAbalancingact.aspx, accessed on 2 December 2011

Hall, Stuart et al. (1978) *Policing the Crisis: Mugging the State, and Law and Order*, London: Macmillan

Kampfner, John (2011) Leveson Inquiry: The tabloids don't get it, *Guardian*, 22 November. Available online at http://www.guardian.co.uk/commentisfree/2011/nov/22/leveson-inquiry-tabloid-newspapers, accessed on 1 December 2011

Leveson Inquiry (2001) Official web-site. See http://www.levesoninquiry.org.uk/evidence/, accessed on 1 December 2011

Margach, James (1978) *The Abuse of Power: The War between Downing Street and the Media from Lloyd George to Callaghan*, London: W. H. Allen

Merrills, J. G. (2005) *International Dispute Settlement*, Cambridge: Cambridge University Press, fourth edition

Mosley, Max (2011) Rules for the press are there. They just need enforcement, *Guardian*, 27 November. Available online at http://www.guardian.co.uk/commentisfree/2011/nov/27/press-rules-need-enforcement, accessed on 2 December 2011

Newburn, Tim and Sparks, Richard (2004) *Criminal Justice and Political Cultures: National and International dimensions of crime control*, Devon: Willan Publishing

Pearson, Alison (2011) Phone hackers have dragged us deep into the gutter, *Daily Telegraph*, 6 July. Available online at http://www.telegraph.co.uk/news/uknews/phone-hacking/8621705/Phone-hackers-have-dragged-us-deep-into-the-gutter.html, accessed on 26 November 2011

Petley, Julian (2011) Louis Blom-Cooper: Leveson Inquiry 'A Golden Opportunity', *Index on Censorship*, 29 November. Available online at http://www.indexoncensorship.org/2011/11/louis-blom-cooper-leveson-inquiry-a-golden-opportunity/, accessed on 2 December 2011

Phillips, Angela (2008) Are there any desirable reforms that would improve the effectiveness of the regulatory regime? Available online at http://www.publications.parliament.uk/pa/ld200708/ldselect/ldcomuni/122/122we13. htm, accessed on 1 December 2011

Plunkett, John (2011) *Sunday Mirror* holds on to gains after *News of the World*'s demise, *Guardian*, 14 October. Available online at http://www.guardian.co.uk/media/2011/oct/14/sunday-mirror-news-of-the-world, accessed on 10 November 2011

Self, Will (2011) *Newsnight*, BBC Two, 8 July. Available online at http://www.youtube.com/watch?v=mT1BVPuPTIc&feature=related, accessed on 1 December 2011

Sperber, A.M. (1998) *Murrow, His Life and Times*, New York: Fordham University Press

Sweeney, Mark (2011) Paul Dacre's pay soars 70% to £2.8m, *Guardian*, 12 January. Available online at http://www.guardian.co.uk/media/2011/jan/12/paul-dacre-pay-daily-mail, accessed on 17 November 2011

Legal cases

Times Newspapers Ltd. and Ors v R. [2007] EWCA Crim 1925, 30 July 2007

Attorney General v Associated Newspapers Ltd & Anor [2011] EWHC 418 (Admin), 3 March 2011

HM Attorney-General v MGN Ltd and Anor [2011] EWHC 2074 (Admin), 29 July 2011

Note on the contributor

Tim Crook has been a journalist/writer for 36 years and is currently Senior Lecturer in Media Law and Ethics and Head of Radio at Goldsmiths, University of London. His recent publications include *Comparative Media Law and Ethics* (Routledge 2009), *The Secret Lives of a Secret Agent: The Mysterious Life and Times of Alexander Wilson* (Kultura 2010) and *The Sound Handbook* (Routledge 2011). Throughout his career he has campaigned for freedom of expression and helped secure the right to appeal court reporting bans in 1989. He blogs at http://libertarianspirit.wordpress.com and http://comparativemedialawandethics.wordpress.com.

Hacking our Future: What are trainee journalists to learn from the Hackgate saga?

Journalism student Teodora Beleaga wonders why anyone would want to commit themselves to a career in journalism when the public standing of reporters has fallen to rock bottom in the wake of Hackgate

Sleepless nights, bullying, low pay, scarce jobs, dark arts, social disregard: why would anyone in their sane minds train to be a journalist? In the academic year of 2010–11 alone, more than 15,000 wannabes have taken the National Council for the Training of Journalists (NCTJ) exams[1], a number that does not include those studying for a degree in journalism requiring different examinations for completion purposes or those on otherwise accredited courses.

At the same time, thousands of jobs are being cut in the industry, with the BBC alone laying off as many as 2,000.[2] Predictions of a dying industry's due date are also made online (@themediaisdying has almost 25,000 followers[3]) and you can actually track the timeline of job losses. For example, journalism.co.uk has embedded an interactive index of articles on the topic in an attempt to 'track cutbacks and layoffs across the industry'[4]. Simultaneously, print circulations have been dropping constantly for years, as McAthy writes: 'Figures published by the Audit Bureau of Circulation show a decline in circulation across the popular press month-on-month' (2011).

However, as a couple of trainees[5] testify below, the reasons why they chose to study journalism include a moral duty to report on wrongdoings and a genuine enjoyment of being at the forefront of handling raw information, which is also in a nutshell why most are still drawn to journalism. Incidentally, it is also what lecturers are after, as the director of the investigative journalism course at City University London, stressed at a conference that turned into the second book of this series, *Investigative journalism: Dead or Alive?*: people 'who want to change the world and have a little fun while doing it'[6] are being sought after.

Still, as a trainee also points out, the scandalous events of last summer have 'outraged the public', thus bringing the social standing of journalists at potentially its lowest point in history. If we are to go by Jeremy Paxman's statement that 'in popular regard journalists are somewhere between estate agents and second-hand car salesmen,'[7] we have to wonder if we have reached rock bottom and, subsequently, what's the impact on trainees and the future of the journalism they will play a part in?

What we are taught: Law, Ethics and Codes of Practice: But who's listening?

'Media law is something journalists can't avoid,' argue Bloy and Hadwin, adding that 'ignorance of the law can certainly be expensive in terms of damages, costs and even a spell in prison' (2011: 1) Yet, as they go on to explain, unlawful practices are usually weighted against the story, leading to incidents where journalists disobey the law. 'Many journalists, and editors, will come across a story that they want to tell badly enough – for principled and/or commercial reasons – to take that risk. Some will pay a heavy price' (ibid: 2). Still, those paying the price are rarely, if ever, the reporters alone; but also other players involved in the story and, of course, future generations of reporters.

Moreover, the law itself allows for 'grey areas'. 'Since 2000 and from now on, cases will be judged in terms of pitting the journalist's Article 10 rights [of the Human Rights Act] against other human rights, particularly the Article 8 rights of individuals to protect their privacy and the Article 6 rights to a fair trial' (ibid: 2). As a result of this vagueness, journalists are left with a considerable 'room for manoeuvre' which evidently doesn't always play to their advantage.

Furthermore, 'ethical inquiry is crucial for all media workers', according to Richard Keeble, one of the editors of this book. 'It encourages journalists to examine their basic moral and political principles; their responsibilities and rights; their relationship to their employer and audience; their ultimate goals' (2009: 1). But it also 'implies freedom to choose' (ibid: 3) and, consequently, a complete ethical inquiry needs to answer both these requirements. As Nick Davies told Lord Leveson: 'You've got this huge intellectual puzzle in front of you; how do you regulate a free press?'.[8]

In addition, Brock points out: 'If you train the next generation of reporters, the first simple and obvious truth is that newsroom culture counts' (2010: 21). And according to Marr: 'Different papers have different cultures... but today newspaper cultures are blurred, and there is a far less clear distinction between broadsheet and tabloid journalists' (2004: 4). Therefore, the ethical inquiry might easily be said to be left to the individual journalist who, in turn, cannot possibly be blamed for opting for the 'sleazy shortcuts'[9] at least once in a while. But what does this practice teach wannabe journalists?

Moreover, we are required to learn and abide by several codes of practice from the Press Complaints Commission, the Office for Communications and the National Union of Journalists. As Campbell argues, 'with all these concerns and problems it is no wonder that most countries have tried to provide some kind of ground-rules for newsgathering practices, most often in the form of professional codes of practice, which lay down the rights and responsibilities of journalists' (2004: 148). A study he made of common principles in such European codes shows truthfulness, honesty and accuracy of information to be present in 90 per cent of the codes alongside correction of errors (ibid: 149). Nevertheless, these codes are fundamentally flawed in that 'they don't have legal force in the majority of the countries' (ibid: 149), including Britain, thus making them to a certain extent ineffective.

With such discrepancies between what we are taught, what we learn though work experience and what we read, listen to and watch as being relayed from the Leveson Inquiry, what are we, as prospective journalists, to make of ethics? What does it all mean, if anything? For both the academia and the industry have clearly agreed to disagree here, particularly on the definition of '*the public interest*'; as Nick Davies said in his testimony to the Leveson Inquiry: 'We don't know quite where the lines are supposed to lie. Different journalists have different definitions of the public interest.'

What is more, 'regulation in any sphere reflects a mix of economic, political and cultural concerns and approaches', and 'the political aspects of regulation are a strong part of the mix' (Bloy and Hadwin 2011: 361). This is why media ethics need to be discussed in the much larger context of current developments within the industry. On the one hand, they need to take account of the issues concerning both the existing and emerging business models, as well as their short and long-term sustainability, and the economical, social, cultural and political factors impacting on media standards.

On the other hand, the craft of journalism is technically evolving at a high speed; networked journalism, participatory journalism, alternative journalism, citizen journalism all come with new skills to master, new tools and devices and software to learn and play with. But how are we to perform any of the new journalisms without a clear and clean ethical basis that is not only acknowledged, but also abided by across the board?

In a recent debate at City University led by Professor Roy Greenslade on the Hackgate controversy, we were challenged as to whether we would ever agree to using information acquired through hacking phones. Amongst the many wannabes, less than a handful said they would categorically not resort to hacking or any other dark arts. Now, what does that tell us about the future of journalism in this country?

The Dark Arts of the Press and the Trainees' Testimonies

'The dark arts are free to flourish,' wrote Nick Davies (2008: 286) two years before his phone-hacking investigation was to shake the press industry to its very core. But are they still flourishing today and, better still, will they be flourishing in the future?

The question of the 'dark arts' being an option for the fourth estate aside, another more emergent question arises. As nowadays reporters are increasingly asked to turn around a considerable amount of copy in a short time span and are thus 'reduced to churnalism, to the passive processing of material which overwhelmingly tends to be supplied for them by outsiders' (Davies 2008: 73), why would any reporter add the required sweat, creative thinking and whatever else is needed in order to obtain some fact or piece of information that is anyway easily obtainable through some 'dark art' skill(s)?

Moreover, questionable means of obtaining or verifying information have been around for longer than we might care to research and/or admit. Professor George Brock, of City University London, intriguingly points to the philosopher Sissela Bok's inquiry into some practices behind Watergate. Sissela Bok 'was astonished that they [Bernstein and Woodward] were allowed to lie so casually, not only on that occasion [to their principal source, Deep Throat, in order to confirm facts] but on others' (Brock 2010: 24). She wrote: 'No one seems to have stopped to think that there was a problem in using deceptive means.' (ibid: 24) According to Brock, the philosopher warned 'that this was dangerous for the future because it would shape the view of both the public and those about to become journalists' (ibid: 24). Well, if Bernstein and Woodward's actions had questionable implications for trainees, then surely the practices of phone-hacking have allowed for a complete shift to such a danger zone.

In addition, all journalists' work is questionable in this danger zone. Take, for example, the *Panorama* episode 'Tabloid Hacks Exposed', of March 2011.[10] Towards the end of the reportage, the presenter, Vivian White, asks one of the private investigators named in the Hackgate scandal, Jonathan Rees: 'What about the work you did accessing people's bank accounts?' In reply, the private investigator asks: 'What about the information that you've got?' with his lawyer adding: 'How did *Panorama* get this information?' The intriguing exchange of lines continues with the BBC presenter asking: 'So you don't deny that you've paid serving police officers for information?' to which Mr. Rees replies: 'Are you denying that you've paid serving police officers for information, because you've got information that could only come from police officers?' The presenter then goes on to clear *Panorama*'s research team and their means of sourcing, but concludes: 'The dark arts are still not fully exposed.'

I spoke with a trainee journalist who completed work experience at the *News of the World* back in 2009. He said: 'I don't think there is any suggestion that phone-hacking continued in 2009' and, while he insisted he would not resort to phone-hacking in his career. He added: 'I don't feel uncomfortable about the experience. I was there, I did some work, some of which I am quite pleased with and I don't feel that I supported phone-hacking in any way. The only thing now is I have *News of the World* in my CV and I am a little bit worried about it, but I've not seen any evidence that it's been detrimental to my career so far.'

Another trainee journalist who admits to having resorted to subterfuge while on work experience in Vietnam confessed: 'If in a newsroom someone asks me to do something morally questionable, I would have to think carefully about it, because now I have much more awareness of the dark side of journalism. But if it's something that I believe the public has a right to know or should know, I would not have much compunction about using a less than honest approach to get the information I needed to make a case. But it would have to be something pretty important and I would always seek advice from my supervisor and take legal advice as well.'

Journalism: How Will we Define it in the Future?

Let's look at the reasons given by the two trainee journalists I interviewed as to why they decided to study journalism. One said: 'I think it's quite fun and it's quite enjoyable to be at the forefront of getting information and disseminating that information,' while the other said: 'I fell into journalism by accident while covering a new angle of a story. It made me realise that I wanted to write about issues that hadn't been covered before and that needed to be covered. Part of it is moral duty, but I just find it really interesting and if I can tell one person about some injustice or something they should know about, I feel like part of my job is done.'

Are these not reasons that could have easily been given 10 or even 50 years ago? If so, what does it mean? As an article titled 'The Future of Journalism: Artificial Intelligence and Digital Identities'[11] introduces the concept of a built in 'DNA of journalism content', one might wonder whether the abovementioned reasons should change as our approach to journalism changes? Starting from the argument that all stories have a 'DNA of elements', the authors suggest data analysis tools will be used in the future to match stories to consumers based on their digital identities. 'These attempts to discover good story elements and persuasive drama were not written from an information-retrieval perspective but provide the literary "blobs" that will let researchers dissect, in our case, a journalism story along its content elements.'[12] To a large extent, then, does entering journalism now require a different mindset?

Notes

[1] The figure is taken from the NCTJ annual report. Available online at http://www.nctj.com/about-us/annual-reports, accessed on 13 December 2011

[2] The announcement was made on their news website. Available online at http://www.bbc.co.uk/news/uk-england-15204257, accessed on 13 December 2011

[3] Available online https://twitter.com/themediaisdying, accessed on 13 December 2011

[4] The interactive timeline made in Dipity includes layoffs from 2008-2010. Available online at http://www.journalism.co.uk/news-features/journalism-job-losses-tracking-cuts-across-the-industry/s5/a533044/, accessed on 13 December 2011

[5] For the purpose of this chapter, a couple of trainee journalists have been interviewed, one who had completed work experience at the *News of the World* and one who posed as someone else in order to obtain information while working for a publication in Vietnam

[6] A statement by Rosie Waterhouse at the 'Investigative Journalism: Dead or Alive?' conference at Coventry University, March 2011

[7] Jeremy Paxman speaking at the 'Is world journalism in crisis?' conference in October 2009 at Coventry University

[8] Nick Davies speaking this to Lord Leveson when he testified for the Levoson Inquiry into the culture, practices and ethics of the press on 29 November 2011. Available online at http://www.levesoninquiry.org.uk/hearing/2011-11-29am/, accessed on 13 December 2011

[9] The phrase is used by George Brock in 'Road to regaining the high ground' in the *British Journalism Review* and referenced below

[10] The episode was first aired on 13 March 2011 and is available on the BBC Panorama website and on YouTube for residents outside the UK. The example mentioned takes place at the very end of the reportage in the last couple of minutes. Available online at http://www.bbc.co.uk/programmes/b00zn7hk or http://www.youtube.com/watch?v=nB-Q33zLFP4&feature=list_related&playnext=1&list=SP081F62A7DBCE086A, accessed on 21 December 2011

[11] Article by Noam Lemelshtrich Latar, of Sammy Ofer School of Communications, Israel, with David Nordfors, of the Stanford Centre for Innovation and Communication, US, in February 2011. Available online at http://isaleh.uct.ac.za/AI%20andThe%20Future%20of%20%20Free%20Journalism%20%20vf2.pdf, accessed on 13 December 2011

[12] Ibid: 12

References

Bloy, Duncan and Hadwin, Sara (2011) *Law and the Media for Print, Broadcast and Online Journalism*, London: Sweet & Maxwell

Brock, George (2010) Road to regaining the high ground, *British Journalism Review*. December, Vol. 21, No. 4 pp 19-24

Campbell, Vincent (2004) *Information Age Journalism: Journalism in an International Context*, London: Arnold

Davies, Nick (2008) *Flat Earth News*, London: Vintage

Keeble, Richard (2009) *Ethics for Journalists*, London: Routledge, second edition

Marr, Andrew (2004) *My Trade: a short story of British Journalism*, London: Macmillan

McAthy, Rachel (2011) Popular press circulations fall in November across the board, Journalism.co.uk. Available online at http://www.journalism.co.uk/news/popular-press-circulations-fall-in-november-across-the-board/s2/a547136/, accessed on 13 December 2011

Note on the contributor

Teodora Beleaga is a student on the Interactive Journalism MA at City University London, fully funded by the Arts and Humanities Research Council. She graduated from the BA in Journalism and Media at Coventry University in July 2011. She is also blogging for helpmeinvestigate.com, socialmediadna.co.uk and cityinterhacktives.wordpress.com. A collection of her online presence is available at about.me/TeodoraBeleaga. She is originally from Romania and loves to travel.

'...But what comes after?'

For Kevin Marsh, the tabloid press's business model has become so dependent on trashing the reputations of 'ordinary people' – as well as celebrities, politicians, people in public life – that it is now nothing other than a machine to convert harassment, intrusion, misery, sneering and mockery into cash. Leveson, he concludes, will have got it right if his solution makes the press truly accountable to us, the public

'We were just ordinary people.'

At the end of November 2011, a steady stream of 'ordinary people' whose lives and reputations the tabloid press had trashed gave their accounts to the Leveson inquiry.[1] Bob and Sally Dowler – who were just 'ordinary people' until someone murdered their daughter. Gerry and Kate McCann – who were just 'ordinary people' until their daughter Madeleine disappeared in Portugal. Or Jim and Margaret Watson – who were just 'ordinary people' until their daughter was murdered and their son, Alan, committed suicide.

Or even the father of footballer Garry Flitcroft – 'collateral damage' in the tabloids' revenge on his son who dared to try to protect his privacy. Flitcroft's father could not be at the inquiry. He killed himself, unable through depression to watch his son on the football field.

It was impossible to listen to these accounts without a sense of profound sadness mingled with downright rage. Impossible, too, not to wonder what it takes for someone calling himself a journalist or an investigator assisting a journalist to find himself so distant from common human decency. Leveson has become subtitled 'the phone hacking inquiry'. It's very much more than that. Phone-hacking is just one small part of something that's become very, very sick in our culture and our society.

A tabloid press whose business model had become so dependent on trashing the reputations of 'ordinary people' – as well as celebrities, politicians, people in public life – that it is now nothing other than a machine to convert harassment, intrusion, misery, sneering and mockery into cash.

Anger and vindictiveness are its default settings. Papers sell on the depths of their inhumanity. Columnists are judged by the frequency and inventiveness of the offence they cause.

No Defence

By the end of just one week of these accounts to the Leveson Inquiry, it was clear the game was up. Almost no-one was prepared to defend the way the tabloids use their immense power. And while it may still be far from clear how the world will change for them, change it will.

Few tabloid editors, even, are prepared to take the stand to defend what they do. And listening to one who did, the *Daily Mail's* Paul Dacre, you can understand why.[2] True, Dacre was prepared to break cover and deserves some credit for that. But there the credit ends. And though he was speaking to the Leveson Inquiry before that long queue of 'just ordinary people' gave their accounts, he misjudged the public mood catastrophically.

Claiming what he and fellow editors did – and, presumably, how they did it – was in the public interest. Asserting his and his fellow editors' absolute and unqualified freedom of expression. Standing on their right to expose corruption and hold power to account. This is hypocrisy of the most snivelling sort. Worse, it pollutes the arguments we need to protect the best in journalism by trying to justify the worst.

Yes, it's vital that we protect our freedom of expression. Yes, it's vital that no-one can be silenced when they call power to account or root out corruption or ruthlessly examine and embarrass powerful institutions. Yes, it's vital that we insist power is exercised transparently and that we can hold it to account. And it's vital that we protect the right of the press to do all of these. But the truth is, that's not what the tabloids do.

For every MPs' expenses exclusive – not a tabloid exclusive incidentally – there are thousands of 'ordinary people' harassed, vilified, libelled. For every court battle that lifts injunctions to expose evil corporations – not something the tabloids have ever indulged in – there are dozens to assert the tabloids' right to report that yet another dog has bitten yet another man. Or rather, another premiership footballer has been caught with his shorts off. Defending the tabloids' right to do what they want to who they want how they want is nothing to do with protecting free speech. Or protecting the press.

Powerful Institutions

The fact is that tabloid newspapers are mightily powerful institutions themselves. And amongst the least accountable and transparent, defending that lack of accountability and transparency in the name of 'protecting sources'. Actually, it's about hiding the yobbish behaviour and lazy omissions that go into their vindictive journalism. Or to cover up the fact that a story was planted by a PR agency. Or bought from someone who, at the sight of hard cash, would say whatever a journalist asked them to.

These powerful opaque institutions care nothing about your or my freedom of expression. In fact, they suppress it if your freedom of expression in telling the truth lessens their potential to make money with a lie. As a society, we have the right and the duty to expect of this powerful institution exactly what we demand of others. To determine how they should exercise that power. To impose on it responsibilities. To insist they're accountable to us for the way they use their power.

We demand it of our police, our hospitals, our politicians. We cry foul when institutions far less powerful than the press seem out of reach of our insistence that they behave in our interests rather than theirs – the bonus grabbers in the City or bond dealers, for example. So it is with the press. The phone-hacking scandal has done no more than bring to a head the boil we know had been festering for years.

People Not Like Us

After hearing account after account of harassment and distortion at the Leveson Inquiry, it began to seem that the tabloid press is peopled by beings who are not like us. Or perhaps and more likely, people who started off like us but have been transformed by the mean minded, mean spirited, macho culture in every tabloid newsroom

The lack of the most basic, human, decent regard for the family of a murdered girl is simply the worst excess in an ethic that has no regard for anyone. Celebrity or 'ordinary person'. Victim or villain. Powerful or powerless. A total refusal even to consider the effects and consequences of what they are doing. The rest of us know it's not just about phone hacking. The rest of us know that the game is up. The rest of us know we can't go on with this powerful interest group – the press – behaving like the Stasi, restrained by nothing. We can't even assume any more that common human decency will restrain them.

The American journalist Janet Malcolm began a book she wrote in 1990 called *The Journalist and the Murderer* like this: 'Every journalist who is not too stupid or too full of himself to notice what is going on knows that what he does is morally indefensible.'³ People were prepared to argue with her then. Only tabloid editors would argue with her today. As the *Daily Mail's* Paul Dacre did in a performance before Leveson that was defiant, disingenuous and in denial.

'No-one Died'

He could only just bring himself to condemn phone hacking and bribing police officers – even though both are illegal. Neither are such a big deal, he insisted – showing contempt for Mrs Dowler's tears and her husband's gnawing fear. Britain's cities weren't looted because of phone hacking, nor did the banks collapse because of it. 'No-one died,' he sneers. Actually, that's only just true. Charlotte Church's mother attempted suicide after the *News of the World* hacked into the singer's phone. And I wonder how much any tabloid editor would have cared if someone had died. It was a chilling insight into a warped mindset.

In his speech to Leveson, Dacre claims that the public's revulsion over phone-hacking derives only from 'hypocrisy and revenge' in the political class – i.e. MPs – because the papers 'dared to expose their greed and corruption'. Nothing to do with the years of harassment, thieving, blagging, distortion, lies, deception, monstering. Nothing to do with the tabloids' default assumption that reputations – big and small – are there only for his power and business to trash.

Nothing to do with every tabloid editor's usurpation of the right to decide who is evil. To decide who must be pursued and vilified – based only on which victim will yield the best financial return on the outlay. The issue isn't that newspapers must be free to tell it how it is. It's that we're fed up with them using that freedom to tell it how it isn't. To harass, distort and lie in the name of profit.

Tabloid editors defend what their papers and their journalists do in their name because, as Dacre has argued at both the Society of Editors[4] and before Leveson, they have to 'leaven their papers with sensation, exclusive pictures, scandal, celebrity gossip and dramatic human stories' in order to cover serious news, politics and campaigns. On the face of it, that's not just reasonable. It's self-evidently true. For the tabloids to stay in business, they have to appeal to their readers' less lofty instincts. And so long as they're in business, they can bolt onto that titillation and sensation and gossip some serious news, scrutiny, reporting, opinion, campaigning. In other words, serve some useful purpose.

Beyond Useful Purpose

That used to be true – but as everyone now knows, we've gone way, way beyond that. What used to be the 'leavening' is now the purpose of most tabloids. The sole content of some. And instead of serving any useful purpose, it poisons our view of ourselves and corrodes our culture and our society.

Dacre is fond of quoting two former senior judges – judges, incidentally, he would in most other circumstances revile as the people who really run the country. Lord Woolf, who a decade ago when he was Lord Chief Justice, put it like this: 'If newspapers do not publish information which the public are interested in, then there will be fewer newspapers published, which will not be in the public interest.'[5] While Baroness Hale, now a Supreme Court Judge, said:

> Newspapers should be allowed considerable latitude in the intrusions into private grief so that they can maintain circulation and the rest of us can continue to enjoy the variety of newspapers and other mass media which are available in this country.[6]

Both judges were talking, there, about a balance that no longer exists – a balance that everyone in the country, apart from tabloid editors, knows no longer exists. We have, instead, what one hacking victim called 'sociopathic' fixation with intrusion and scandal. The sociopathic fixation of a powerful institution that has the unbridled power to ruin the lives of those it and it alone decides deserve it. But let's assume just for a moment that tabloid editors such as Paul Dacre are right. And that we need the papers to stay in business, however that can be achieved, because if they were to disappear that would 'diminish our democracy'.

True, of course. And we have seen some of this in the carnage in the local press. As local papers fold, Dacre tells us: 'Courts go uncovered. Councils aren't held to account. And the corrupt go unchallenged. That is a democratic deficit that in itself is worthy of an inquiry.' It would be impossible to disagree with that. So let's take a closer look at the *Daily Mail's* attitude to the courts and the processes of justice.

Remember the case of what the *Mail* called 'The Strange Mr Jefferies'? The retired schoolteacher who had the misfortune to be Joanna Yeates' landlord. Who, though entirely innocent, was briefly arrested and questioned. How did the *Mail* and the other tabloids report the inquiry? With respect for the courts and for the innocence of any suspect until proven guilty?

We all know the answer. The *Daily Mail* and other tabloids spared no effort in portraying Mr Jefferies as a weirdo. After all, he was a bachelor and had funny hair that he once dyed purple. Subtext? We all know the message the tabloids were screaming at us. He had campaigned for a 'gun range and prayer books'. Subtext? How weird is that? Shades of gun-toting Christian fundamentalism. And had a fixation for Christina Rossetti, a poet obsessed with death.

It's true, the *Mail* wasn't the worst – but it was in the pack, securing its place in that pack, making money from trashing Christopher Jefferies. Turning contempt for him and for the proper process of justice into profit. Respect for the courts? Or for Mr Jefferies' right to have the truth told about him? Free speech? Protecting the press's right to report the facts fearlessly? It was none of these. It was a naked, calculated commercial risk – that any financial cost would be outweighed by the income it brought in. And when it came to acknowledging its part in trashing Mr Jefferies, the *Mail* was as surly and grudging as an adolescent caught shoplifting:

> Eight newspapers apologised to Mr Christopher Jefferies in the High Court yesterday. Reports of the investigation into the death of Joanna Yeates had wrongly suggested that Mr Jefferies, who was arrested but released without charge, was suspected of killing Ms Yeates, may have had links to a convicted paedophile and an unresolved murder. It was also wrongly alleged that the former school master had acted inappropriately to pupils. The newspapers, including the *Daily Mail*, agreed to pay Mr Jefferies substantial damages and legal costs.[7]

The *Mail* could not even bring itself to say – 'We're sorry.' When it was totally, completely, 100 per cent banged to rights in its race to the bottom as tabloid outdid tabloid in contempt and defamation all in pursuit of market position and profit.

Balancing the Financial Cost of Lies

We saw something similar in the way that Richard Desmond's papers – the *Daily Express* and *Daily Star* – libelled the McCanns and Robert Murat week in, week out – over 100 times. As Leveson heard in that week of tabloid shame at the end of November, these libels weren't slight things. Ambiguities dressed up as sensationally as possible. 'Maddy "sold" by hard-up McCanns' . was one. Allegations that they had stored her body in a freezer, another. Did they run these stories because their newshounds were fearlessly tracking down the facts? Holding the Portuguese police's feet to the fire, keeping them up to the mark with their insistent scrutiny?

No. These 'journalists' were sitting in a bar in Portugal, filing the latest odious rumour so that back in London, editors could make a simple calculation. What's the financial risk if we run this lie? If we're sued, will we have made more through lying than we stand to lose in court?

There's even a myth that the tabloids are better behaved and disciplined than they were in the seventies. Then, as Paul Dacre told the Leveson Inquiry, reporters would steal photographs from homes; blatant subterfuge was common; invasion of privacy was unrestrained; harassment was the rule. And he sketched a typical scene in a typical tabloid newsroom. A scene where editors and executives stroked their chins in careful contemplation of the editors' code. A scene that is as touching as it is fantasy:

> When a photograph is presented, the question is immediately asked: Did the subject of the picture have a reasonable expectation of privacy? In stories, executives question whether the privacy of the person's family or health is being invaded and whether their children are being protected. Were we harassing people?

Now I find this very difficult to reconcile with Hugh Grant's account of *Mail* and other tabloid journalists' behaviour towards Tinglan, the mother of his child. A woman and baby, the tabloids decided, who needed a bit of harassment and a sound trashing.

How Tabloid Photographers Really Behave

Take this. Grant's description of arriving home one evening to find reporters and photographers besieging Tinglan and her baby:

> I asked them if there was anything I could do or say to make them leave a new and frightened young mother in peace. They said show us the baby. I refused. I asked them if they thought it was acceptable for grown men to be harassing and frightening a mother and baby for commercial profit. They just shrugged and took more pictures.[8]

Does a mother in her own home with her baby have a 'reasonable expectation of privacy'? Clearly not, as far as journalists acting in Paul Dacre's name are concerned. It makes you wonder what that 'reasonable expectation' might ever amount to in the tabloid mind.

Perhaps, though, we should cut the tabloid greybeards some slack as, back in the newsroom, they carefully weigh whether or not to run these pictures and these stories. Perhaps they won't make the cut once the editor knows how the photographers and journalists behaved? Think again. In his evidence to Leveson, Grant named the *Mail* journalist leading the charge:

> He is also the person behind most of the texting and phoning of Tinglan since the birth...Some of the pictures that are printed of Tinglan when pregnant, taken either covertly...or openly and expressly against her will, are the ones used in the *News of the World* article back in April. The *Mail* appears therefore to be picking up where the disgraced *News of the World* left off (ibid).

And it's not just young mothers and their babies in their own homes that the tabloids now consider appropriate victims of their thuggish harassment. Here's more of Hugh Grant's statement:

> Tinglan's mother, a lady of 61, started to take photos of one photographer parked outside. He immediately turned his camera on her, took some pictures and then accelerated hard towards her so fast that Tinglan's mother had to jump out of the way. Then he did a U-turn at the end of the street and drove fast towards her again in a deliberately menacing way. She was, and remains, extremely frightened (ibid).

I'm wondering what the *Daily Mail* headline would have been if, instead of a tabloid photographer trying to run down a 61-year-old granny in the street, it had been a failed asylum seeker. Or a traveller from Dale Farm. Or some other *Mail* hate figure.

But it wasn't. It was a tabloid photographer from the world that tabloid editors like Paul Dacre have created. A world where there is no regard for anyone and where there is a mocking, sneering culture. A world and culture that John Lanchester described so precisely when he reviewed Nick Davies' book *Flat Earth News* in the *London Review of Books*. Too many journalists, he wrote, are:

> ...indifferent to their own best traditions of independence, recklessly indifferent to the central functions of reporting and checking facts...and in far too many respects, simply indifferent to the truth. There is a growing, industry-wide failure to be sufficiently interested in reality.[9]

By the end of 2011, Leveson – and the rest of us – had heard account after account of the most unacceptable behaviour and attitudes. Behaviour and attitudes that, if they existed in any other sector of society, the tabloids would condemn day in, day out in page after page of spume flecked outrage. They would ask what kind of person wouldn't just hack a dead girl's phone but stalk her parents when they walked their daughter's last journey. Or print the private diary of a mother whose child has been stolen away. Or wear disguise to gatecrash a private funeral to photograph a father's grief.

'What kind of ethics can you teach this kind of journalist,' one of the lawyers asked at the Leveson Inquiry. Rhetorically, one has to assume. Expecting the answer – none. It's just not possible.

What To Do?

The question is, though, what to do? A question Lord Leveson plans to answer, perhaps in full perhaps in part, towards the end of 2012. And he may well try to answer the question that before, during and after the phone hacking scandal has been repeatedly asked. Can the press regulate itself? Or do we need statutory regulation?

The trouble is, that's the wrong question. This is no longer about replacing the failed Press Complaints Commission nor re-casting the utterly discredited editors' code. There is, instead, a much more important, prior question that now demands an answer. What do we require a free press to do on our behalf? And what do we want it not to do in order to be a civilised player in a civilised society?

How do we make sure we have a free press that really can expose MPs' greed; corporate corruption and crime; police, doctors social workers and the rest who really are incompetent. A press that can bear witness on our behalf; campaign for justice; argue the hell out of everything that matters to us. But do it without divesting itself of every shred of decency. Without the harassment, the lying, the blagging, distortion, vindictiveness that's become the norm in this powerful institution.

There's no easy answer and it would be foolish to pretend there is. But one thing I do know. The last people you want to make or monitor any set of rules are the crooks themselves. Imagine if you will the *Mail's* spitting outrage if paedophiles were invited to draft new child protection laws and enforce them. Or if illegal immigrants and people traffickers were to be given control of Britain's border. Quite.

The tabloid press has proved beyond any doubt that it can't be trusted to regulate itself. But if the answer doesn't lie in regulation, where might it lie? The fact is that the British media, including the press, is already surrounded by a forest of legislation. Legislation that, if it were enforced it as the legislators intended and as most decent, reasonable people thought proper, would constrain most if not all of the tabloid's bestial behaviours.

The libel laws. The Human Rights Act that, effectively, balances rights to privacy and to freedom of expression. The Data Protection Act; the Freedom of Information Act; the Official Secrets Act; the Bribery Act; the Contempt of Court Act and so on. But this forest of laws is a mess. Some is statute, some common law. Most is effectively unenforceable or a real brake on responsible journalism because of the costs and time involved. Some have a public interest defence; some don't. Some is closely defined, some a question of balance between conflicting statutes or precedents.

It is a massive thing to suggest and I do so aware of the monumental, probably insurmountable difficulties in the way. But we can still consider ideals and in that an ideal word, we would have a new legal settlement for the media. A clear body of law that applied to people and businesses committing deliberate acts of journalism, whether paid for or not.

And one of the key characteristics of that body of law would be that all parts of it had a clear, public interest defence. And while it's easy to get hung up on defining 'public interest', there is a model for this kind of defence in the so-called Reynolds defence – or common law privilege – in a libel action. It's otherwise known as the defence of diligent and careful journalism done in the public interest. Tied to this new body of media law, however, we need rapid, low-cost resolution. Both victims and newspapers argue – rightly – that the cost of pursuing or defending a libel action is prohibitive. That, and the time involved, turns the righting of that particular wrong into a thermonuclear option. Yet most victims don't want massive damages. An apology, explanation and putting the record straight is all most require. Quickly and prominently.

The one thing the PCC did, in fact, do well was to organise speedy mediation and resolution, particularly in the local press. And we also have the models of the small claims court and professional arbitration panels to draw on – models that limit costs and damages and aim to resolve disputes quickly and simply.

Streamlining and simplification like this would strengthen both free expression and the public's ability to keep the press honest and accountable. But there should be more. Even with more rational media law, we'd still need an editors' code – though one not written by the tabloid editors themselves – underpinning an independent, statutorily established regulator whose main job would be to investigate, rather than simply resolve, breaches of the code.

A burden? Perhaps. But here's the thing. Newspapers could choose whether to be inside a system like this or not. Inside, you'd sign up to the whole package – complete with public interest defence and limited costs and damages. Outside, you could do what you liked – much as the tabloids do now.

Except for this. Outside would be very, very cold and hostile indeed. You'd have no public interest defence. Unlimited costs and damages. Juries and judges would, inevitably, take into account your decision to stay outside the system when they were apportioning those costs and damages. And, as is already the case with libel, the balance of proof would be against you – you'd have to prove you hadn't harassed, distorted, misrepresented. It wouldn't be up to the complainant to prove that you had.

When Leveson finally writes his report, it's very unlikely he'll take a many steps in this direction. It would be a step – may be more than one step – too far. But it's not a bad 'high water mark' against which we can judge whatever recommendations he does finally produce. But he's already made it clear he's not going to walk away and do nothing about this massively powerful, profit led institution that's gone so far off the rails, it no longer knows where the rails once were.

Getting the Thugs off the Street

How else might we judge whether Leveson has got it right? In the long queue of 'just ordinary people' and celebrities who gave Leveson their accounts of tabloid harassment there was one that struck me especially forcefully. It was Sienna Miller's. She told how up to fifteen men would stalk her every day. How they would spit on her to get a reaction. How they would chase her, alone, down dark streets at midnight.

The men weren't just your ordinary, common-or-garden stalkers, perverts and muggers. They had been given licence by their editors – men like Paul Dacre – to leave decency behind and 'legitimised' by Miller's celebrity and the cameras they carried. Miller was just 21 years old. The same age my daughter is now. That gave her account, for me, a painful resonance and piquancy.

Leveson will have got it right if his solution makes the press truly accountable to us, the public. If he brings some responsibility to the last unaccountable power in the land. If the tabloid press has to take more care than it does now that that it's honest and fair and has more than a passing relationship with the truth. If it can tell the difference between challenging power and trashing the lives of the victims of crime. If we, the public, can put wrongs right quickly and fairly.

And if young women, whether a celebrity like Miller or 'just ordinary people' like the rest of us are no longer be terrorised by thuggish yobs, turning that terror into cash for the power that is the tabloid press.

Notes

[1] Details of evidence to the Leveson Inquiry can be found at http://www.levesoninquiry.org.uk/evidence/, accessed on 12 December 2011

[2] Paul Dacre's submission to the Leveson Inquiry. Available online at http://www.guardian.co.uk/media/2011/oct/12/paul-dacre-leveson-speech?INTCMP=ILCNETTXT3487, accessed on 12 December 2011

[3] Malcolm J (1990) *The Journalist and the Murderer*, New York: Vintage

[4] Dacre P (2008) Speech to the Society of Editors. Available online at http://www.societyofeditors.co.uk/page-view.php?pagename=thesoelecture2008, accessed on 12 December 2011

[5] The case was heard as A v B & C [2002]. Available online at http://www.bailii.org/ew/cases/EWCA/Civ/2002/337.html, accessed on 12 December 2011

[6] Campbell v MGN 2004. Available online at http://www.publications.parliament.uk/pa/ld200304/ldjudgmt/jd040506/campbe-1.htm, accessed on 12 December 2011

[7] *Daily Mail* 29 July 2011. Available online at http://www.dailymail.co.uk/home/article-2020289/Chris-Jefferies.html, accessed on 12 December 2011

[8] Hugh Grant's witness statement at the Leveson Inquiry. Available online at http://www.guardian.co.uk/media/2011/nov/23/hugh-grant-leveson-inquiry-statement, accessed on 12 December 2011

[9] Lanchester J. Riots, Terrorism etc *London Review of Books* 2008. Available online at http://www.lrb.co.uk/v30/n05/john-lanchester/riots-terrorism-etc, accessed on 12 December 2011

Note on the contributor

Kevin Marsh is Director of OffspinMedia (www.offspinmedia.co.uk) and a host/facilitator at Coventry Conversations/BBC College of Journalism events. He was formerly Executive Editor of the BBC College of Journalism and Editor of *Today*. He produced investigations into the Brighton Bomb, the Cyprus Spy Trial, the Ponting Trial and is currently an executive producing a new investigation into the Nazi's Treblinka camp. His latest book, *Stumbling Upon the Truth*, about Lord Hutton, New Labour and the BBC, will be published by Biteback in September 2012.

Section B. The Murdochs: An Everyday Tale of Media Folk?

John Mair

Rupert Murdoch made Orson Welles' Citizen Kane look like a midget. By the beginning of the twenty first century, Rupert and his News Corporation empire be-straddled the globe owing huge chunks of media real estate in Europe, the USA, Australia – and beyond. The scion of an Australian media magnate, 'Roop' had truly internationalised the Murdoch brand and even changed his nationality to American (it is said for business reasons) in the process. One wife had been divorced to be replaced by a younger model but three of the products of that first union – Elizabeth, Lachan and James – were at one time or another pro-consuls in the Murdoch media empire spanning newspapers and television. The Murdoch story is anything but that of an ordinary media family. Their tentacles were, and are, just about everywhere.

Veteran (ex BBC) political journalist Nicholas Jones (the brother of George Jones, one of Lord Leveson's panel of expert advisers) has observed the Murdoch effect on British politics over three decades. Parties and Prime Ministers were at his beck and call. Tony Blair flew halfway round the world to worship at his feet and gain his approval for 'New Labour', the back and front doors of No. 10 Downing Street were always open to him (though he seemed to prefer the anonymity of the back).

Prime Minister David Cameron even took a former Editor of Murdoch's *News of the World*, Andy Coulson, into Downing Street with him as Director of Communications when he became Prime Minister in May 2010. Coulson had resigned from the *NoW* in disgrace after his Royal Editor was jailed for phone hacking, Cameron took him into the Tory fold on the advice of George Osborne saying 'everyone deserves a second chance'. Coulson helped 'tabloidise' Cameron the Tory toff and played no small part in the May 2010 election victory

Coulson later had to leave Downing Street under a cloud after eight months, has since been arrested and bailed and his future in freedom does not look bright. Jones looks at the Cameron/Coulson relationship and asks why and what went wrong and was there a cover up?

Ivor Gaber, of City University, is an equally seasoned interpreter of the British political scene. He looks at the front and back door political influence of the Murdochs, their links with the political elites and the increasing trend for British Prime Ministers simply to ignore parliament for the powerful such as media moguls. For example, was the so-near-to-completion News Corp bid for the rest of BSkyB (which would have yielded huge profits to News Corporation) ever subject to proper and rigid parliamentary scrutiny before the Hackgate scandal blew up in July 2011.

There seemed to be an awful lot of log fire rolling deals taking place in Oxfordshire country cottages rather than deep interrogation of the deal. Gaber thinks that the phone hacking scandal may prove a turning point – a moment of truth – in the re-assertion of backbench MP power over the executive and, more importantly, over the media which they held in awe for too long.

Finally, Patrick Barrow, a seasoned PR professional in the media, offers some advice to Murdoch the damaged brand as he and they try to restore a relationship that *so* nearly went toxic. Indeed, so bad that Murdoch cut loose his first British newspaper, the *News of the World*, in four days rather than try to rescue it from infamy. Barrow's advice – broad shoulders and spread the blame to all tabloid newspapers. In summary: 'We were at it but then so was everyone else!' The Murdochs – indeed, far far from an everyday story of ordinary media folk.

How did a British Prime Minister come to depend on an Ex-Editor of the *News of the World?*

Nicholas Jones traces the tabloid career of Andy Coulson and his performance as chief spin doctor for David Cameron. He concludes: 'In three years as the Conservatives' top spin doctor and eight months in Downing Street, Coulson had barely put a foot wrong'. But then to come was his sensational fall from grace…

An understanding of the reasons why David Cameron chose to rely on the advice of Andy Coulson might to help answer one of the most troubling questions underlying the *News of the World* scandal: Why did successive British Prime Ministers become so fearful of the Murdoch press? Political collusion of one form or another is in the DNA of the national press and over the decades, as they built up mass circulations, the owners of daily and Sunday newspapers did all they could to exploit a close working relationship between their journalists and politicians. The most successful publishers established themselves as formidable players on the political stage, be it the Lords Northcliffe, Rothermere and Beaverbrook of earlier years or more latterly Rupert Murdoch. They have all been feared and also courted by the Prime Ministers of their day but none so more than Murdoch. For well over thirty years his national newspapers were deployed to gain maximum political and commercial advantage.

In recent years phone hacking was just one of a number of covert techniques used by what for so long was the UK's biggest-selling newspaper as it struggled to continue commanding the tabloid agenda. Its Fleet Street reputation relied on a constant supply of exclusive stories about, perhaps, the sex life of a politician, a misbehaving celebrity or another comparable scandal. Because its proprietor had the deepest pocket, the *News of the World* commanded the market place in the highly-competitive trade for sensational information – information which all too often was gained by questionable if not illegal means.

On the one occasion I walked along the corridor at Wapping which led to the *News of the World's* inner sanctum, I could not take my eyes off the framed copies which lined the walls. There on display were the front pages of the editions which had rocked the government of the day, stunned show business or perhaps scandalised the world of sport. The framed front covers were like the trophies on display at a football club; one could only imagine the pride of the reporter whose scoop had earned a place in the *News of the World's* hall of fame.

My visit was in October 2006, the month before the newspaper's royal editor, Clive Goodman, pleaded guilty to conspiracy to intercept voicemail messages. I was in the company of a group of Norwegian journalists who were visiting London and who had asked my help to explain why successive British governments were prepared to collude with media proprietors such as Murdoch. I had called in a favour to gain access to Wapping and we were invited to a presentation on the *News of the World's* success in being named Newspaper of the Year at the 2005 British Press Awards, a much-prized accolade for the then-editor Andy Coulson.

We were each handed an information pack which opened with a glowing tribute from the Prime Minister and Chancellor of the Exchequer. They had given their 'first-ever joint interview' exclusively to the *News of the World*. Tony Bair: 'My wholehearted congratulations. Well done.' Gordon Brown: 'What a great achievement.' Listed on the next three pages were the scoops which demonstrated why the *News of the World* had fulfilled 'in an unprecedented fashion...the primary role of a popular newspaper...to set the news agenda'.

Coulson and his staff had collected a hat trick of awards: Newspaper of the Year, Scoop of the Year, and Young Journalist of the Year. Three of the scoops which had taken pride of place were the secret affair of a cabinet minister and two infamous kiss-and-tells: Rebecca Loos's story of her secret relationship with the footballer David Beckham; the affair between Football Association secretary Faria Alam and the former England football coach Sven-Goran Eriksson; and the scoop which 'stunned the nation' when the *News of the World* revealed that the Home Secretary, David Blunkett, was having a 'secret affair with a married woman'.

My Norwegian guests admitted they were 'gobsmacked' – certainly that was the translation they gave me – by the breath-taking scope of these exclusive stories. Nonetheless, most of their questions were greeted with enigmatic smiles by our hosts. One of the visiting journalists recalled how reporters across Scandinavia had got wind of 'Sven's affair' but such were the privacy laws there had been no mention of it in the local news media. 'Of course that all changed when the story appeared on the *News of the World's* website; once that happened we could all write about it because we could quote the *News of the World* and we could use that as our source.'

Another member of the group asked why the British Prime Minister and Chancellor of the Exchequer were so complimentary about the *News of the World* when it had just exposed the private life of their cabinet colleague, the Home Secretary, and had obviously caused him great personal anguish. Another Delphic smile and a further aside about the phenomenal success of *News of the World's* journalistic formula; the group were told that media organisations around the world were always keen to know much more about the newspaper's ability to publish so many scoops. But we were not about to learn any tricks of the trade; the shutters came firmly down when the visitors tried to probe the tabloid's news-gathering techniques.

On leaving Wapping, I told my guests they could hardly have found a more telling illustration of the love-hate relationship between British politicians and the Murdoch press. However appalled Blair and Brown might have been by the *News of the World's* invasion of David Blunkett's private life, they clearly felt they had no option but to be gushing in their praise of the newspaper's scoops.

The awards ceremony, in March 2005, was the pinnacle of Coulson's career after almost twenty years of hard graft with the Murdoch press, first on the *Sun's* Bizarre column and then as Deputy and finally Editor of the *News of the World*. On the back of his success, Coulson gave a rare interview to the London *Evening Standard* in which he declared that Princes William and Harry were fair game for tabloid reporting. 'The royals shouldn't be treated any differently to anyone else...the kids are of an age now where they have no special rights.'[1] Eighteen months later Clive Goodman and a private investigator Glenn Mulcaire were arrested for tapping the mobile phones of the princes' royal aides.

Another give-away remark after the 2005 awards ceremony was from chief reporter Neville Thurlbeck, who broke the Beckham scoop after Rebbeca Loos was paid a reported £300,000 for her story. He said the secret was simple: 'To be brutally honest, we pay big money for big stories.'[2] Half-page advertisements published by the paper each Sunday promised to pay 'big money for tips and pics...for sizzling shots of showbiz love-cheats doing what they shouldn't ought to, A-listers looking the worse for wear and Premiership idols on the lash the night before a crucial game'.[3]

Cameron as Desperate as Blair to Woo the Murdoch press

In the summer of 2005, not long after Coulson received his award, the *News of the World* had another scoop: 'Top Tory, coke and hooker' was the headline over an allegation by a former 'vice girl' that George Osborne, then David Cameron's leadership campaign manager, had a 'youthful fascination with cocaine', a claim that he vehemently denied. Despite the difficulties surrounding his dealings with the paper, Osborne formed a favourable impression of Coulson's abilities as a tabloid editor, a recollection which came into play in early 2007 when the Conservative Party was searching for a new director of communications in preparation for the long haul to the 2010 general election. Coulson had resigned from the *News of the World* in January 2007 after the jailing of Clive Goodman and Glenn Mulcaire. Several weeks later he was sounded out among others by Osborne, then shadow chancellor, who told him the party needed some 'really serious firepower' in dealing with the news media.

Coulson's comeback caught the Westminster village on the hop. His appointment in May 2007 as Cameron's chief spin doctor was a genuine surprise and one which caused consternation among the Labour Party's media strategists. In interviews the previous summer Rupert Murdoch had left the door firmly ajar to the prospect of his newspapers switching their support to the Conservatives. What Cameron lacked was a media technician with the clout and experience who could help shape and manage an agenda which would appeal to the popular press and hopefully win the support of the proprietor of Britain's two most widely read tabloids.

Cameron was convinced Coulson would make 'a formidable contribution' to building 'a most effective' election-winning strategy. When asked to justify the appointment, he said he was satisfied Coulson 'was not aware' that a journalist under his control had engaged in telephone tapping but as editor he 'did the right thing, took responsibility and resigned'. Nonetheless, in view of the criticism of New Labour for having been all spin and no substance, Cameron had adopted a high-risk strategy in following Tony Blair's example in appointing a high profile journalist as his leading propagandist. Coulson, like Blair's infamous press secretary Alastair Campbell, was well versed in the media mindset and he knew precisely how low tabloid reporters were prepared to stoop in search of a story.

During his 2005 campaign for the Tory leadership, Cameron had castigated Blair and Campbell for their cynical manipulation of the media. But my own conclusion was that by early 2007 Cameron had become as desperate as Blair had been in the mid 1990s to woo the Murdoch press. An insight into the gear shift which was taking place within the Tory high command emerged in the autumn of 2011 in a speech by the Conservative MP George Eustice, who was Cameron's press secretary at the time of Coulson's appointment. He revealed that initially, on being elected party leader, Cameron tried to adopt a distant relationship with the print media: the party's analysis was that under Blair there was too much emphasis on getting the headlines right. 'Our position was not to respond to page one headlines...but it was very hard to sustain that and abandoned in 2007.'

Eustice was also in no doubt that before Coulson's appointment Cameron would not have followed the example of Blair and Campbell who in 1995 travelled to Hayman Island, Australia, to meet Rupert Murdoch and his executives. 'It was our position that if we were invited to News International's worldwide conference we'd have politely declined.'[4]

Connecting Cameron to Murdoch's Political and Commercial Agenda
When Coulson started work at Tory headquarters in July 2007, Cameron and Osborne were bracing themselves for a possible snap general election. Gordon

Brown, installed as Prime Minister the previous month, was continuing to savour a short-lived political honeymoon and the Labour Party was recording a lead in the opinion polls ranging between 7 and 9 per cent. Coulson's priority was to reconnect the Conservatives to the agenda of newspapers such as the *Sun*. To begin with it was an uphill struggle as Brown remained in close contact with Murdoch and the Downing Street press team was doing all it could to feed exclusive stories to the News International titles.

My first sighting of the engaging nature of the Cameron-Coulson partnership in action was in March 2008 at the annual lunch of the Journalists' Charity. Cameron was guest speaker and his new publicity chief sat at a table with his former colleagues, evidently enjoying their company, there being no sign of any hard feelings. By then Gordon Brown had lifted the threat of an immediate general election and Labour were digging in for the long haul to 2010. For his part, Coulson was hard at work looking for ways to transform the Conservatives' ability to respond to the dictates of the popular press. His bridge-building skills were well to the fore at the lunch and he was clearly succeeding in helping Cameron to steer party policy towards News International's commercial interests, as well as its political agenda.

Without prompting, but no doubt as a result of Coulson's advice, the Tory leader knew precisely which buttons to press at an event where the guests included several influential Murdoch executives. He praised Britain's great tradition of campaigning journalism and singled out the *Sun* for its reports into the plight of forces families; he also praised the *Observer*, *Mail on Sunday* and *Sunday Times* for their investigations into the scandal of fraudulent television phone-in programmes and the financial irregularities of MPs at Westminster. There could hardly have been a friendlier meeting of minds: Cameron had flagged up perhaps Coulson's greatest strength, his undoubted talent in understanding how to create a tabloid campaign, get Cameron on board and spin the Conservatives' line.

Despite the darker side to his work and his affinity with the murky world of cheque book journalism, Coulson had previously spoken with pride about the *News of the World's* success in exposing grievances and in using the paper's influence to change government policy. He believed the British tabloids could justify their claim that they did more for the people of the country than 'any other newspapers of the world'.

He was prepared to be judged on his achievements. His flair and ingenuity as a campaigning editor had helped to secure the introduction of 'Sarah's law', the right of parents to discover whether their children were at risk from paedophiles living in their neighbourhoods. When the *News of the World* began publishing pictures of sex offenders in the summer of 2000 to highlight the background to the murder of six-year-old Sarah Payne there was a storm of protest about the danger of 'mob rule' but the then-editor, Rebekah Wade, and her deputy, Coulson, held their nerve, published more photographs the following Sunday and then launched a mass petition.

Coulson continued the campaign when he succeeded Wade as editor in 2003 and the Labour Home Secretary, John Reid, finally responded in June 2006 by promising to study 'Megan's law' in the United States, the first of a series of initiatives which culminated in March 2010 with the Labour government's decision to give all parents the right to check whether people with access to their children were sex offenders.

Generating a million signatures in support of 'Sarah's law' was said by Coulson to have been an experience which more than anything else strengthened his belief in the campaigning role of newspapers and their ability to represent the views of their readers. Another of his campaigns was for an 'end to the terror of devil dogs'. Each Sunday, illustrated with ever more graphic photographs of injured children, the newspaper promoted a petition calling on the government to change the law to make owners of dangerous dogs criminally responsible for all attacks on public and private land.

Cameron Hitches a Ride on Tabloid Story Lines

Under Coulson's guidance Cameron was about to learn how to hitch a ride by exploiting the populist story lines which the tabloids were able to manufacture; the Conservatives could not have found a greater expert on the issues which excited the Murdoch press. The *Sun's* long-standing demand for better wages and conditions for 'Our Boys' was an obvious first step. In October 2007, as the returning casualties from the wars in Iraq and Afghanistan continued to mount, the *Sun* launched its 'Help Our Heroes' campaign. Cameron responded through a series of exclusive interviews and signed articles, promising that a future Conservative government would improve pay rates and also do more to support the rehabilitation of the injured. Each pledge was trumpeted by the *Sun* and generated further criticism for what the newspaper claimed was Gordon Brown's failure to uphold a duty of care towards service personnel.

Deciding when and how best to take advantage of fast-moving stories is a constant challenge for a political spin doctor and Coulson's deft touch ensured that Cameron was able to shape rather than simply react to the headlines. After a mother and stepfather were convicted at the Old Bailey in November 2008 for killing Baby P, Coulson seized the opportunity to take advantage of the outrage expressed by the *Sun*. Next day when the paper launched a petition which demanded that the social workers in the case should be sacked, it was endorsed with a signed article by Cameron, the first and only party leader who tried to exploit the Baby P case. After attracting more than 1.4 million signatures, the *Sun* proclaimed victory on the 26th day of the campaign when Sharon Shoesmith, head of children services for the London Borough of Haringey, was dismissed.

Coulson's effectiveness in sharpening the Conservatives' media offensive against the Brown government had not gone unnoticed in newsrooms of national newspapers and, as his influence increased, so did the way he was viewed by political journalists. They realised he had become a close confidant of

Cameron and was firmly in the driving seat of the Conservatives' publicity machine; the Westminster lobby correspondents needed no reminding of the importance of maintaining a good working relationship with a future Downing Street press secretary. Unlike Alastair Campbell, Coulson was not addicted to personal promotion, clearly having no wish to become the centre of attention. Nor was he tempted to antagonise lobby correspondents by adopting Campbell's tactic of divide and rule when dealing with journalists or in attempting to intimidate those considered 'unhelpful' to the government.

Despite the initial controversy surrounding the appointment of a former red-top editor as the Tories' spin supremo, Coulson was able to prove beyond doubt that his expertise in crisis PR was more than a match for the No.10 press office. His sure touch had been demonstrated in June 2008 when Cameron appeared to be threatened by the unexpected resignation of the then shadow Home Secretary, David Davis, in protest at the government's latest proposals for the detention of terrorist suspects. To the consternation of colleagues, Davis, whom Cameron had defeated in the run-off for the party leadership, stood down from both the front bench and parliament in order to fight a by-election which he hoped would provoke a debate about the erosion of civil liberties.

Coulson's handling of what had been a potentially destabilising event was cited by Danny Rogers, editor of *PR Week*, when Coulson was named public relations professional of the year in October 2008. He was said to have gained control of the Davis story by responding 'quickly and decisively'. In the event, a messy shadow cabinet resignation was a mere dress rehearsal for the stress test which unfolded in May 2009 when the *Daily Telegraph* began publishing its highly-acclaimed run of exclusive stories exposing the scandal over MPs' expenses.

Cameron was about to face the most challenging set of circumstances since his election as party leader. Extravagant claims submitted by Tory grandees to subsidise the running costs of their country homes were among the most outrageous. But again, on the strength of his inside knowledge of the newspaper industry, Coulson was able to devise media strategies which helped the Tory leadership keep one step ahead of the Prime Minister and ride out a wave of public anger. Cameron was able to pre-empt each fresh round of disclosures with headline-grabbing initiatives designed to show that the Conservatives were taking the toughest action against the MPs whose abuse of the expenses system had scandalised the public, a strategy which kept the Labour government firmly on the defensive.

Coulson's network of contacts was far superior to his counterparts in Downing Street and, armed with tip-offs from sympathetic journalists, he was in a far better position to exploit the *Daily Telegraph's* ploy of using the late-evening television news bulletins to trail the revelations to be published in next morning. As a flood tide of scandal engulfed the House of Commons and put the party leaders on the spot, Coulson tailored his strategy of damage limitation to meet the deadlines of the unfolding news agenda. On the eve of disclosures about the expenses claimed by some of Cameron's closest colleagues, the party issued a statement at eight o'clock expressing regret; there were follow-up interviews for the late-evening television news bulletins.

'Cameron says sorry' was the headline on the BBC's *Ten O'Clock News* which then named the six shadow cabinet ministers whose questionable claims were to be revealed next morning. Both the government and the House of Commons had been unwilling or unable to offer a collective apology and Cameron's contrition on behalf of Conservative MPs was widely reported, only adding to the criticism of Brown and the Speaker Michael Martin for failing to respond to public anger. Cameron repeated the exercise at other key moments becoming not only the first party leader to apologise but also the first to promise that his MPs would be required to repay excessive claims and that the worst offenders would not be reselected as candidates in the forthcoming general election.

An indication of the success of Coulson's hands-on operation in organising the presentation of the Conservatives' response was revealed in the *Daily Telegraph's* book on the scandal, *No Expenses Spared*. When the paper's journalists alerted Tory headquarters to the timing and likely extent of their disclosures about Cameron and his colleagues, Coulson and the party's head of media Henry Macrory co-ordinated the collation of statements from the MPs involved and, as a result, were judged to be in a 'far stronger position to answer questions than their Labour counterparts'.[5] At a subsequent lunch of the Journalists' Charity, the newspaper's editor, Will Lewis, praised Cameron for the way he had 'tapped into the public's anger' and responded far more effectively.

As he approached the completion of his second year as the Conservatives' Director of Communications, Coulson could hardly have been in a stronger position. Not only had he gained the respect of the party's press officers and the Westminster lobby correspondents, but he was also well on the way towards achieving Cameron's goal of un-coupling Murdoch's newspapers from Labour, re-connecting them to the Conservatives and assisting the shadow cabinet to formulate policies designed to appeal to the commercial interests of the press and broadcasting sector.

Cameron Ready to be as Accommodating to Murdoch as Thatcher

At his first joint outing with Coulson in March 2008, Cameron promised that the Conservatives would support the continued self-regulation of the newspaper industry through the Press Complaints Commission. His pledge was of particular interest to executives at News International, Associated Newspapers (*Daily Mail*) and the Telegraph Media Group, the three most vocal cheerleaders for self-regulation, because the PCC – rather than the government-funded broadcasting regulator Ofcom – had been allowed to take on the additional role of regulating the editorial content of video and audio material on newspaper and magazine websites.

Finding ways to expand their audio-visual services had become a priority for press proprietors and within three weeks of Cameron's speech the Conservatives published a discussion document which warned that the BBC's 'dominant online presence' created a 'real danger' of crowding out innovation in a multi-channel, multi-platform era. An early warning shot across the bows of the corporation was the first indication that a Cameron-led government had every intention of heeding the clamour of media companies for less regulation in the broadcasting sector and a curb on the continued expansion of BBC output, especially online.

Before the BBC Trust had time to reply, the management were engulfed in the damaging furore which ensued after Radio 2 presenters Jonathan Ross and Russell Brand left obscene messages on the telephone answering machine of the *Fawlty Towers* actor Andrew Sachs. Failure to honour guidelines on taste and decency left the BBC's hierarchy at the mercy of the legendary hostility of the Murdoch press. 'BBC £14 million fat cat scandal' was the *News of the World's* banner headline over a report revealing that more than fifty of its executives earned more than the Prime Minister. Coulson needed no further encouragement. Cameron leaped into the controversy next day with a signed article in the *Sun*: 'Bloated BBC out of touch with viewers.'

Here was a ready-made opportunity for Cameron to put in writing the Conservatives' pledge to rein in a BBC which had 'over-reached' itself and 'become bloated with many of its executives overpaid'. Another bold headline in the *Sun* in March 2009 underlined the depth of the Conservatives' commitment to scale back the BBC: 'Cameron: We'll freeze the licence fee.' His pitch for endorsement by the News International titles could not have been any more blatant: if the Conservatives were elected they were ready to be as accommodating as Margaret Thatcher had been when her government waved through Murdoch's take-over of the *The Times* and *Sunday Times* in 1981 and gave the go ahead for the launch of Sky Television in 1989 and the merger with British Satellite Broadcasting in 1990 to form BSkyB.

No opportunity was missed as Cameron pursued his bid for the kind of patronage which the Murdoch press had no shame in exercising. When Ofcom became embroiled in a dispute about pay television, Cameron singled out the broadcasting regulator as a prime example of a quango – quasi-autonomous non-governmental organisation – which had become heavy-handed and unaccountable; under the Conservatives its policy-making functions would be returned to government. His promise of a 'bonfire of the quangos' was hailed by the *Sun* as signalling the axing of a 'hugely expensive brigade of bossy boots'.

James Murdoch could hardly have orchestrated a timelier curtain raiser to his MacTaggart lecture at the 2009 Edinburgh Festival. He ratcheted up the anti-BBC rhetoric by arguing that in an expanding digital and online market place the corporation was spearheading 'a land-grab, pure and simple' which in the 'scale and scope of its current activities and future ambitions is chilling'.[6]

Phone Hacking Scandal Returns to Haunt Cameron and Coulson

In the two years that he had worked for Cameron, Coulson had gone a long way towards detoxifying public perceptions about his own share of the blame for the phone-hacking scandal. He had kept firmly below the radar, maintaining the lowest possible profile. Whenever political correspondents wrote about his influence and handiwork they had been forced to rely on second-hand insights; there were no direct quotes which could be attributed to him. But Cameron and his publicity chief were in for a rude awakening: on 9 July 2009, the second anniversary of the day Coulson started work at Tory headquarters, his photograph stared out from the *Guardian's* front page under the headline: 'Revealed: Murdoch's £1 million bill for hiding dirty tricks.'

Following months of work, the newspaper's investigative reporter Nick Davies suggested that 'suppressed evidence' showed that Clive Goodman was not the only *News of the World* journalist who had commissioned Glenn Mulcaire to hack into mobile phones. Davies's claim that there could be 'hundreds more legal actions by victims' immediately called into question Cameron's judgment. But when asked to comment on leaving home that morning, Cameron dismissed calls for Coulson's dismissal and said he believed in 'giving people a second chance', a justification which he would come to use repeatedly.

After the Metropolitan Police ruled out a further investigation on the grounds there was 'no additional evidence', and the Press Complaints Commission also took no further action, Coulson had little difficulty in keeping MPs at bay at a reconvened session of the culture, media and sport select committee. When editing the paper, his staff worked within the PCC's code of practice. If a 'rogue reporter' had behaved in any other way, he was not sure there was 'an awful lot more' he could have done.[7]

My own assessment at the time of reaction among correspondents, reporters and producers, across press and broadcasting, was a widespread feeling that Coulson had shown himself worthy of the 'second chance' which Cameron had afforded him. Having a former tabloid editor in a key role at the heart of the Conservatives' media machine found favour with most political journalists because they preferred dealing with a communications director who was well versed in the rules of the game when it came to offering preferential access or exclusive interviews.

And, after having had two years in which to monitor the transformation which had taken place in the Conservatives' handling of the media, I had also formed a clear impression that Coulson relished the opportunity to use his expertise to further political objectives which he clearly believed in. The hacking scandal was in the past, or at least appeared to be receding, he had reinvented himself and as Cameron would later acknowledge the two men had struck up a friendship which would only strengthen Coulson's commitment to the Tory Party.

A general election was only months away and traditional political loyalties were beginning to kick in. Conservative-supporting newspapers had no intention of giving currency to what they dismissed as nothing more than the Guardian's on-going obsession with a left-wing vendetta against the Murdoch press. Similarly, most political correspondents had no wish to jeopardise their relationship with the Tories' media team by resurrecting Coulson's link with the phone-hacking scandal just when the story seemed to be going nowhere. Journalists faced far more pressing challenges, such as the struggle to keep abreast of the behind-the-scenes manoeuvring over the possibility of the first-ever televised debates between the three party leaders, an innovation which was eventually agreed after lengthy negotiations in which Coulson played a pivotal role for the Conservatives.

Pre-election jockeying between the news media and the rival parties took off in earnest at the 2009 Labour Party conference when, on the morning after Gordon Brown's speech, the *Sun*'s front-page banner headline said 'Labour's lost it', the first public confirmation that Murdoch had switched sides. There had never been much doubt that the *Sun* would back the Conservatives but the pre-planned brutality of its attack on the Prime Minister in the middle of his final pre-election conference stunned even Labour's hard-bitten media handlers. Next day Cameron was pictured holding the 'Labour's lost it' front page and alongside was his promise not to take '*Sun* readers for granted' and to 'earn their votes'.

Once the election campaign began in earnest the Murdoch press was unanimous in calling for a change of government and on polling day all four titles endorsed the Conservatives. Coulson's influence over access to Cameron and his wife delivered an exclusive 'David and Samantha' interview for the *News of the World* on the last Sunday of the campaign in which the Tory leader revealed that he still found time to 'slip off for afternoon "cuddles" with his wife Sam'. The *Sun*'s election-day front page was a brazen piece of political propaganda: above the headline 'Our only hope' was Cameron's face superimposed on the image of an iconic American election poster depicting Barack Obama. As perhaps might have been predicted, Cameron's first signed article as Prime Minister on behalf of the newly-installed Conservative-Liberal Democrat coalition government provided a two-page spread for the *News of the World*.

The indecisive result of the 2010 general election, and the resulting hard bargaining which led eventually to a deal between Cameron and Nick Clegg, was an unprecedented chapter in post-war British politics and of far greater significance to journalists than a run-of-the-mill announcement that the two top jobs in the coalition's media operation had gone to Coulson and his opposite number Jonny Oates, the Liberal Democrats' Director of Election Communications.

If Cameron harboured any further doubts about having taken with him into Downing Street a former *News of the World* editor to head up the No.10 press office, they were quickly dispelled by the leadership which Coulson displayed in welding together two highly-partisan teams of propagandists who had just spent an election campaign making it their daily business to oppose each other. Of all the apparatchiks at Westminster spin doctors are by far the most tribal but Coulson managed to smooth out any lingering rivalries and despite the underlying policy differences, there was hardly any evidence in those early months of the anonymous and negative counter-briefing which became a way of life for Blairites and Brownites and which did so much damage to the reputation of New Labour.

Such is the novelty of a newly-elected government that an incoming Prime Minister is almost always assured a political honeymoon in the media and the *Sun* was only too happy to co-operate, conscious no doubt of the aspirations of Rupert and James Murdoch and the need to encourage Cameron to fulfil the Conservatives' undertakings over reining in the BBC and adopting a relaxed approach towards cross-media ownership. Engineering coverage to promote the government's narratives is the daily grind of the Downing Street press office and once again Coulson's ability to develop story lines and then sustain them must have endeared him to Cameron.

Cutting the bill for welfare payments was one of the key objectives of the coalition's post-election emergency budget. Later, in August 2010, with the Prime Minister's written endorsement, the *Sun* launched a hotline for readers to expose 'feckless benefit claimants' to 'help us stop £1.5 billion benefit scroungers'. Week after week, following tip-offs from neighbours, the paper published stories about 'disabled spongers cheating the benefit system'. Another ongoing challenge was thinking up ways to promote Cameron's vision of a country which encouraged people to shoulder greater responsibility for their own communities. The *Sun* obliged in October 2010 by providing space for a two-page article by the Prime Minister in support of another re-launch of the 'Big Society'.

Within five months of the election Cameron honoured his promise to curb the excesses of a 'bloated' BBC. A six-year freeze in the licence fee was one of the measures included in the October 2010 comprehensive spending review; the resulting 20 per cent cut in the BBC's spending power meant it would have to reduce spending by £1 billion a year by 2015, triggering extensive reductions in programme output and large-scale job losses.

No doubt having felt gratified on seeing such savage retrenchment within the BBC, Rupert and James Murdoch must have had every hope of an equally-swift delivery of their paramount post-election reward – government approval for News Corporation's bid for full control of BSkyB. But the consultation process dragged on for months and at the very point in July 2011 when the government finally said it was 'ready to give clearance' the *Guardian* revealed that the *News of the World* had hacked into messages left on the mobile phone of the murdered schoolgirl Milly Dowler. Such was the outrage that even the paper's dramatic closure was not enough to save the BSkyB deal and within the space of a week News Corporation had withdrawn the proposed takeover.

Well before the Murdochs' *denouement* the steady drip, drip of revelations about the true scale of phone hacking at the *News of the World* had forced Andy Coulson's resignation. In January 2011, he finally acknowledged that given the mounting intensity of the media focus on who-knew-what at News International, his role as the government's director of communications had become untenable. In a brief comment, he stuck firmly to his previous denials of responsibility: 'I stand by what I've said about those events but when the spokesman needs a spokesman it's time to move on.' Coulson was arrested three days after the *Guardian*'s revelation about Milly Dowler and, after being questioned in connection with 'allegations of corruption and phone hacking', he was released on bail.

In three years as the Conservatives' top spin doctor and eight months in Downing Street Coulson had barely put a foot wrong. Cameron could claim with every justification that there had been no complaints about the way Coulson had dealt with the news media or handled government information. His departure was a setback for the Prime Minister, not least because of the absence of Coulson's steady hand during all too frequent media firestorms. 'If only Andy was here, we'd know what to do' became a common refrain at Tory headquarters and No.10. But there was no escape for the Prime Minister. One of the most troubling unknowns about Cameron remained the extent to which he was aware of illegal phone hacking at the *News of the World*, an unanswered question at the heart of the collusion between politicians and media proprietors.

Notes

[1] Coulson, Andy: interview, London *Evening Standard*, 3 March, 2005

[2] Thurlbeck, Neville: interview, London *Evening Standard*, 3 March 2005

[3] *News of the World* (24 October 2004) advertisement

[4] Eustice, George, MP speech to *Guardian* seminar, 'After Hacking: How Can the Press Restore Trust?', 29 September 2011

[5] Winnett, Robert and Rayner, Gordon (2009) *No Expenses Spared*, London: *Daily Telegraph* Books

[6] Murdoch, James, MacTaggart Memorial Lecture, Edinburgh Television Festival, August 2009. Available online at http://www.broadcastnow.co.uk/comment/james-murdochs-mactaggart-speech/5004990.article, accessed on 9 December 2011

[7] Coulson, Andy, evidence, House of Commons Culture, Media and Sport Select Committee, July 2009. Available online at http://www.publications.parliament.uk/pa/cm200910/cmselect/cmcumeds/362/90721 18.htm, accessed on 9 December 2011

Note on the contributor

Nicholas Jones was a BBC industrial and political correspondent for thirty years. He has written extensively on the relationship between politicians and the news media. His books include *Strikes and the Media* (1986), *Soundbites and Spin Doctors* (1995) *The Control Freaks* (2001) and *Trading Information: Leaks, Lies and Tip-offs* (2006). His most recent book was *Campaign 2010: The Making of the Prime Minister*. News archive: www.nicholasjones.org.uk

Moment of Truth: What Hackgate tells us about the Changing Relations between the Media and Politics

In recent years there has been a clear trend of ministers and political journalists paying less and less attention to backbench MPs. However, Hackgate shows that this trend could be reversing with MPs beginning to re-assert themselves over both the government and the media, argues Ivor Gaber

The extent of the influence on British politics of the Murdoch Empire in general, and Rupert Murdoch in particular, has long been well-established. But the events of the latter half of 2011 suggest that we could be in the midst of significant changes in the overall relationship between politics and the media.

The revelation that David Cameron, or one of his senior ministers, met Rupert Murdoch, or one of his senior executives, at least 27 times between the election of the Coalition government in May 2010 indicates the extraordinary intensity of the contacts between the government (or at least its Conservative parts) and News International. But what is equally significant is that these meetings were not between Murdoch's political journalists and politicians, but between Murdoch's editors and executives and the politicians. (A similar trend was also revealed about News International's contacts with the Metropolitan Police.)

The precise list of meetings was made available by the Prime Minister following intense pressure on him to reveal the government's dealings with News International in the course of the negotiations around Murdoch's bid for BSkyB. Before examining the list it is worth bearing in mind that, whilst it gives details of face-to-face meetings between cabinet ministers and Murdoch executives, it does not show the range of phone and email conversations that took place between these two groups over the year under review. And it is perhaps significant that whilst relatively junior ministers such as Michael Gove and Jeremy Hunt held a number of meetings with Murdoch and his colleagues, the Deputy Prime Minister and the Business Secretary were noticeably absent from this list – is it coincidental that neither are Conservatives?

Whilst the headline figure for these meetings is 27, on closer inspection it can be seen that, in terms of contacts between the Cameron and Murdoch teams, there were at least 86 such encounters (this is because some of the events involved more than just one participant from either side). A detailed breakdown of the figures reveals the following:[1]

Table 1. Meetings between members of the government and News International, May 2010 to June 2011. Source: 10 Downing Street.

	Rupert Murdoch[i]	James Murdoch	Rebekah Brooks	Dominic Mohan	James Harding	Colin Myler	John Witherow	Elizabeth Murdoch	Jeremy Darroch	Not specified	Total
Cameron (27 events attended)[ii]	2	2	7	6	7	3	3	-	-	2	32
Osborne (17)	2	4	5	1	5	2	2	1	-	1	23
Gove (11)	6	2	8	1	2	2	1	-	-	-	22
Hunt (9)	3	2	1	-	-	-	1	1	1	-	9
Total 62	13	10	21	8	14	7	7	2	1	3	86

A number of observations arise from this list. First, it is worth remarking on that the Prime Minister, in the course of the 14 months, had 32 encounters in 27 meetings with Murdoch and his executives. His Chancellor, George Osborne, had 17 meetings and 23 encounters; just one behind was the Education Secretary, Michael Gove, whose 11 meetings involved 22 encounters and the Culture Secretary, Jeremy Hunt, who had 10 encounters in nine meetings.

Cameron's 'Relationships' with the Editors of the *Sun* and *Times*

It is perhaps significant that, on the Murdoch side, the person who was most frequently involved in these encounters, was the News International Chief Executive, Rebekah Brooks, who had 21 encounters, including seven with the Prime Minister (of which five were social engagements with two taking place at Chequers, the Prime Minister's country retreat). Cameron also engaged in an almost equally intensive 'relationship' with the editors of the *Sun* and *The Times*, meeting them, respectively, six and seven times during the year. Most intriguing, but least explained, is the high ranking of the Education Secretary, Michael Gove, who met with Rupert Murdoch six times, far more than any other minister and with Rebekah Brooks on eight occasions, again more than any of his colleagues. What were these meetings about? The only meeting of Gove's that has its content described is the one in January 2011 with Rupert Murdoch and one of his senior American lieutenants, when the subject was reportedly 'US education policy'.

But there is one other topic that gets a specific mention in the information published by Downing Street, which perhaps explains why there was such a frequency of meetings, and why the Culture Secretary only got to one social event whilst all the rest of his encounters were business-like one-to-ones; and that topic is BSkyB. The Culture Secretary is recorded as meeting with Jeremy Darroch, the Chief Executive of BSkyB, on one occasion, but it is a fair assumption that his boss, Rebekah Brooks, who participated in no fewer than 21 encounters with senior ministers during the year under review, might also just have referred to News International's interest in securing approval for its plans to take over BSkyB.

But there could be another, or at least a contributory, explanation for the intensity of these encounters; and this is simply: after 13 long years of opposition followed by an indecisive election result, the Conservatives were desperate to retain and, if possible, deepen their ties with the Murdoch Empire. Back in 1992, the day following the Conservatives' surprise General Election victory under John Major, the *Sun* ran its now notorious headline, 'It's the Sun Wot Won it' – a headline that some Tories subsequently sought to distance themselves from. Nonetheless, those Conservatives who believed it was true could only have had their views reinforced as in the years following Major's victory they watched the *Sun* switch its support away from the Tories to New Labour as Tony Blair went on to win successive election victories in 1997, 2001 and 2005; and then, no doubt, watched in awe as the paper switched its support back to the Tories, as a precursor to Labour's defeat in 2010. Without going into the debate as to the impact of newspaper readership on voting behaviour it is worth quoting the American sociologist Michael Schudson who wrote:

> The power of the media resides in the perception of experts and decision makers that the general public is influenced by the mass media not in the influence of the mass media on the general public. That is to say the media's political appeal lies less in its ability to bend minds than in its ability to convince elites that the popular mind can be bent (Schudson 1995: 121).

Whatever the truth of the situation there is little doubting the fact that both Labour and Conservative politicians, and their advisers, either strongly believed that winning Rupert Murdoch's support was crucial or, at the very least subscribed to a 'Murdochian' version of Pascal's Wager.[2]

How the BBC is Shunned

It by no means represents robust empirical evidence but the 1994-1997 diaries of Alastair Campbell, who was Blair's first press secretary, indicate the extent to which New Labour courted Murdoch in the run-up to Labour's 1997 election victory. Campbell's diaries for this period contain 43 references to

Rupert Murdoch, whilst the editor of the *Sun*, (then as now Britain's most popular newspaper) gets just 24. But perhaps the starkest revelation, in terms of how Blair and his entourage saw their media priorities, is the fact that the head of the country's largest news organisation the BBC gets just six mentions.

Murdoch has been so successful in persuading politicians of his power to swing elections for three reasons. The first, and most obvious, is that anyone who controls more than 40 per cent of the British press (as Murdoch did before the closure of the *News of the World*) is objectively very powerful, even if he can't actually decide the result of elections.

But second, Murdoch has shown a ruthless guile and promiscuity in switching his, and his newspapers', political support, sublimating his own ideological preoccupations in the interests of the greater good of News Corporation's. It began in Australia when he and his newspaper group, which had been long-standing and firm supporters of the right wing, conservative governments which had held power in Australia through the 1940s to the 1970s, switched support to Gough Whitlam, the Labour leader, when it looked likely that Whitlam would win the 1972 General Election. Murdoch reportedly claimed he had 'single-handedly put the present government into office' (Millken 1994) But when, three years later, public opinion turned against Whitlam, the Murdoch press plunged the knife into the tottering Labour administration.

Murdoch demonstrated the same political ruthlessness in the UK. Even though he had been a strong supporter of Margaret Thatcher, and briefly of John Major, when Blair was elected to the leadership of the Labour Party in 1974, he intimated that he could envisage switching support to New Labour. An Australian commentator at the time warned:

> Murdoch's overtures to Labour Party politicians in Australia have always come at a price and have sometimes turned out to be dangerously mercurial. The Murdoch-Labour relationship here has a turbulent history, the bottom line of which is less to do with political principle than with Murdoch's desire to keep expanding his commercial empire (ibid).

But whilst New Labour continued to serve Murdoch's corporate interests, and did not too greatly offend those political principles that were personally important to him (e.g. by not entering the Euro and supporting the United States wars in Iraq and Afghanistan) Murdoch kept his papers loyal to New Labour. But once it was clear that new leader, Gordon Brown, was unlikely to win the 2010 election, Murdoch switched his support back to the Conservatives.

It is this very promiscuity that made politicians so nervous about Murdoch; they knew his political beliefs but they never felt sure about his loyalty, hence they made great efforts to try to maintain his support or, at the very least, not to incur his wrath. But the narrative above makes it clear that Murdoch, far from being the mighty Svengali of Australian and British politics; is rather a canny observer of the political scene and, having put his finger to the wind, switches his papers' support to what he sees, usually rightly, as the winning side.

The political influence of journalists is clearly of relatively limited importance although thanks to Murdoch's support for Blair, the Political Editor of the *Sun* was dubbed 'Britain's most influential political journalist' by a slightly breathless interviewer in the *Evening Standard*, who described Kavanagh as 'the man with the hotline to Rupert Murdoch who is feared and revered at Westminster, especially when an election looms' (a reporter having a 'hotline' to his own proprietor would be a slightly odd sobriquet were that proprietor not Rupert Murdoch) (Rowan 2005).

Legendary Reporting

Kavanagh's scoops during Blair's time in office were legendary: they included naming the dates of forthcoming elections and, most spectacularly, revealing the detailed findings of the Hutton Inquiry – set up by the Blair government following a major clash between the BBC and the Government over the build-up to the war in Iraq. Speaking about the scoop Kavanagh has only said that an 'unnamed source' telephoned him with details of the inquiry's findings the night before it was officially published. Could that 'source' have been Rupert Murdoch who learnt the details directly from Tony Blair?

This speculation is made on the basis of this author's own experience. Back in 2000, the author was assisting Alexander Litvinenko, the Russian spy who was later to be poisoned, in the drafting of his application for political asylum in the UK. Litvinenko's presence in this country was supposed to be a closely guarded secret, but mysteriously the *Sun* broke the story of his clandestine arrival with a front page splash, under the byline of Trevor Kavanagh. In an attempt to find out where the leak had come from this author discovered that one of the few people who knew of Litvinenko's whereabouts was his patron Boris Berezovsky, the Russian oligarch.

Beresovsky was adamant that he had not spoken to Kavanagh, but then speculated as to whether his mentioning it to Rupert Murdoch over dinner the previous night, might have had some connection with the *Sun's* exclusive. It seems reasonable to assume that if this was the route as to how one *Sun* exclusive came to hit the front page, then, if Berosovsky was telling the truth, it is a reasonable assumption to make that other stories also travelled this same pathway.

An additional issue, explaining Murdoch's influence on British politicians is that there has long been a belief in and around Westminster that to attack Murdoch, or his newspapers, was to risk making oneself a target for bilious attacks and character assassination. Without specifically referring to Murdoch, David Cameron, speaking at the height of Hackgate said: '.. your bins are gone through by some media organisation, but you hold back from dealing with it because you want good relations with the media'. (quoted in Lloyd 2011: 5). And writing in the *Guardian* just the day before, Peter Mandelson, regarded by many as the architect of New Labour 'spin', said: 'We simply chose to be cowed because we were too fearful to do otherwise' (Mandelson 2011).

Decline in the Power of the Legislature

But there's another aspect to the way that Hackgate might be changing the relationship between the media and the political class and that relates to the decline in the power and influence of the legislature, both in terms of the government and the media. In recent years there has been a clear trend of ministers, and political journalists, paying less and less attention to backbench MPs. However, there are some indications that this trend could be reversing with MPs beginning to re-assert themselves over both the government and the media.

The re-assertion began with a passionate debate in the House of Commons in July 2011, with MPs from all sides strongly denouncing the role of News International, both in terms of phone hacking and the political influence wielded by Rupert Murdoch and his senior executives. Conservative MP Zac Goldsmith, speaking during the main Commons debate on hacking, said:

> We have seen, I would say, systemic abuse of almost unprecedented power. There is nothing noble in what these newspapers have been doing. Rupert Murdoch is clearly a very, very talented businessman, he's possibly even a genius, but his organisation has grown too powerful and has abused that power. It has systematically corrupted the police and in my view has gelded this parliament to our shame (quoted in Watt: 2011).

During the course of this debate Prime Minister David Cameron was forced to announce the establishment of the Leveson Inquiry which is (at the time of writing, December 2011, is currently investigating the relations between the media and politics) but he was also obliged to release the detailed information referred to earlier in this chapter about meetings between him, his colleagues and News International executives.

However, perhaps more significantly, MPs have been reasserting themselves through the Select Committee system. This system, established in its present form in 1979, has only recently received high profile media attention, but more than 20 years ago research indicated that its influence, if not power, even then was beginning to build (Barnett and Gaber 1992).

As a result of the hacking revelations two of the Commons committees set to work. The home affairs select committee began a series of hearings into relations between News International and the Metropolitan Police; the close ties between the two revealed during the course of the hearings led directly to the resignations of three of the Met's senior officers and a number of internal investigations that are still on-going at the time of writing.

But it is the hearings into the phone hacking itself, undertaken by the culture, media and sport committee, that really caught the public's attention and demonstrated this new found power of MPs. Since March 2011 the committee has held six public hearings into the scandal including one which will surely become one of the emblematic broadcasts of the modern age in which Rupert and James Murdoch appeared before the committee and Murdoch senior began his evidence by saying 'This is the most humble day of my life.'

Apart from being gripping television this moment signified two trends – one being that this was the first occasion when Murdoch and News International had been called to public account for the misdeeds of the *News of the World* , but second, the holding to account was not done either by ministers or the media but by backbench MPs. And millions watched the process, either live or on later television news bulletins, thus denying political journalists their central storytelling role and giving the public an unmediated insight into the central characters in the drama, with the MPs, rather than the journalists, the key inquisitors.

This attempt by the legislature to make up for the government's failure to regulate effectively the media sector was a re-run of what happened in 2009 when, following the banking crisis, the Treasury select committee's own investigations and hearings were seen to be a more effective means of holding the banking industry to account, than anything devised by government regulators.

So we stand at a crossroads. Will News International, or any other media proprietor for that matter, ever again be able to muster the sort of the political influence that Rupert Murdoch was, until recently, able to employ? And will backbench MPs be able to maintain their new-found authority, or will they sink back into acquiescence as the whips re-assert their power? And finally what of the lobby: is it undergoing merely a temporary blip in its central role in the political/media nexus, or are we watching the decline of a once powerful body, replaced either by MPs gaining in confidence in terms of communicating with the public, or by media executives and editors regaining the shadowy influence that, for those from News International at least, Hackgate has so endangered?

Notes

[1] In the case of the editors of the Murdoch newspapers, whilst the majority of their encounters are specified, it is assumed that when one of the ministers attended an event organised by the relevant newspaper, the editor would have been on hand to meet and greet his distinguished guest. Left to right: Rupert Murdoch, Chief Executive Officer, News Corp; James Murdoch, Chairman News International; Rebekah Brooks, CEO News International; Dominic Mohan, Editor the *Sun*; James Harding, Editor *The Times*; Colin Myler, Editor *News of the World*; John Witherow, Editor *Sunday Times*; Elizabeth Murdoch, daughter of Rupert; Jeremy Darroch, CEO BSkyB. The total number of meetings is greater than the total number of events attended because some of these meetings involved more than one representative from either side. The full list is available at http://www.guardian.co.uk/news/datablog/2011/jul/27/news-corp-meeting-david-cameron?INTCMP=SRCH, accessed on 12 December 2011

[2] Pascal's Wager is the suggestion by the French philosopher Blaise Pascal that even if one had no reason for believing in God it was best to live one's life on the assumption that God did exist because the potential benefits of believing, in the after-life are so great that it was a better bet than not believing. The Murdochian equivalent is the belief that even if Murdoch could not swing the result of elections, courting his support, at the very least, could do one's electoral prospects no harm

References

Barnett Steve. and Gaber, Ivor (1992) Committees on Camera: MPs and Lobby Views on the Effects of Televising Commons Committees, *Parliamentary Affairs*, Vol. 45, No 3 July pp 409-419

Lloyd, John (2011) *Scandal: News International and the Rights of Journalism*, Oxford: Reuters Institute for the Study of Journalism

Mandelson, Peter (2011) It was fear, not principle: Labour chose to be cowed rather than reforming the media. But self-regulation can still work, given teeth, *Guardian*, 12 July

Milliken Robert (1994) A man of selfish loyalties: Rupert Murdoch's apparent overture to Tony Blair strikes a chilling chord among Australian politicians he has supported, *Independent on Sunday*, 14 August

Rowan, David (2005) Interview: Trevor Kavanagh, of the *Sun*, *Evening Standard*, 12 January

Schudson, Michael (1995) *The Power of News*, Cambridge: Harvard University Press

Watt, Nicholas (2011) Phone hacking: 'Evasive, dishonest or lethargic'? The Met were one of those three': Police accused of knowing about this week's revelations in 2006 as MP says News International boss is behind 'cover-up', *Guardian*, 7 July

Note on the contributor

Ivor Gaber is Professor of Political Journalism at City University, London, and Professor of Media and Politics at the University of Bedfordshire. He is also a broadcaster, writer, and media consultant. His journalistic career has included senior editorial positions at the BBC, ITN, Channel Four and Sky News. Now, as an independent radio and television producer, he makes and presents programmes for BBC Radio and Television and Channel Four. His main field of academic expertise is political communications. He has authored or co-authored three books and numerous chapters and articles on this topic and is a frequent expert contributor to BBC 5Live, Radio 4, the World Service BBC TV, ITN, Sky News and a host of foreign broadcasters.

Repairing a Damaged Reputation: My Advice to Rupert Murdoch

Patrick Barrow argues that all is not lost for Rupert Murdoch in the wake of Hackgate. 'Murdoch and his newspapers have become, increasingly, one of a gang of tabloid players all doing what everyone has long suspected, behaving badly. The rest, to the world at large, is detail. Right now, any decent advisor would be telling him that'

My advice to Rupert Murdoch: seize the initiative, the worst is over. Because, unfashionable though it may be to suggest it, Rupert Murdoch, CEO of News Corp, owner of disgraced and defunct Sunday tabloid the *News of the World* (*NoW*), *eminence grise*, *bête noire* and all round bad lot, may, just may, be out of the reputational woods.

To examine why, and establish the basis of any advice he should be given, the evolution of allegations, events and happenstance need to be explained. Circumstances have changed from a point that once looked hopelessly bleak to a point where he may emerge with Mark Twain on his lips, 'reports of his demise greatly exaggerated'.

After the initial furore, and perhaps as much by luck as design, events have begun to run in his favour. Of course, unforeseeable revelations may arise and once again set him back, perhaps irredeemably. At the time of writing (December 2011) that is impossible to predict. But, like the skin beneath a scab, his reputation slowly re-knits, albeit with a very ugly scar. Because the debate is now moving on to wider issues of newspaper malpractice and has retreated from the public mind into one confined more and more within the self-interest of the media.

Murdoch and his newspapers have become, increasingly, one of a gang of tabloid players all doing what everyone has long suspected, behaving badly. The rest, to the world at large, is detail.

Right now, any decent advisor would be telling him that.

The Damage Done

This is not to say that his various reputations as newspaper magnate, successful businessman and associate of the powerful have not been damaged. They have. In fact, they have been damaged, stained and tainted to a point that, in much the same way as there is a corner of Tony Blair that is forever Iraq, the scandal of how the *News of the World* went rogue will be a chain shackled forever to the ankles of his personal history.

His capacity to influence the powerful is greatly diminished. The politicians that so assiduously courted him have publicly disowned him and his executives. They are the devils with whom no one can be seen to dance. This applies not just in the UK epicentre of the scandal but across the Atlantic too where suggestions that phone hacking extended to victims of the 9/11 attacks provoked the emotions one would expect. American politicians angrily demanded criminal investigations under the Foreign Corrupt Practices Act.

As a businessman, Murdoch's reputation and fortunes have also suffered badly. At the most basic, he has lost Britain's best-selling newspaper, closed down in the face of initial public outrage and the pressure exerted by advertisers desperate to distance themselves from the stink of disgrace. They deserted in droves. His then imminent attempt to purchase BSkyB simply died on the spot. Already the centre of a controversy in which Business Secretary Vince Cable was caught by a *Daily Telegraph* sting, the messy politics got messier. It became an untouchable and the bid was withdrawn (Goldfarb, Beales and Dixon 2011).[1]

A doddering performance at the initial House of Commons Parliamentary Select Committee hearing into what had happened at the *News of the World*, raised questions over whether the once mighty Murdoch hand was quite as steady as it could and should be on the tiller of empire. Newscorp's share price plummeted, major backers raised concerns over the fitness of son James Murdoch for continued business governance (Wilson 2011)[2] and, it was reported, daughter Elisabeth was raising similar points with considerable vehemence. The very fabric of the intertwined Murdoch business and family, of which former *NoW* and *Sun* editor Rebekah Brooks was widely deemed to be part, seemed to be under threat.

Turning the Tide – the *News of the World* Shut Down

The advice now would surely be to move decisively, be bold and reassume command of events. Murdoch did exactly that. He shut down his best-selling UK paper. Those desperate firebreak attempts at first seemed to fail. First, the closing down of the *News of the World* was accompanied in seconds by suggestions on the various live feeds set up by rival media organisations that a *Sun on Sunday* would be up and running as soon as the dust settled.

The failure to fire executives including Rebekah Wade, under whose editorial regime some of the worst excesses of hacking appeared to have occurred, was seen as an attempt only to use them as lightning conductors, drawing fire from the beleaguered Murdochs. Sacking them immediately would, of course, have instantly meant an accusation that they were scapegoats for greater Murdoch empire sins. A line already being used by the now redundant staff at the *News of the World*, embittered, angry and claiming themselves to be 'all unspotted' by previous practice.

But Murdoch kept his nerve, even when cynicism reigned, himself apologising to the family of murdered schoolgirl Mille Dowler for the hacking of her phone, the single act which had propelled the scandal from marginal to general public opprobrium.

Crisis Management – Human, Accessible, Credible

If crisis management is about being human, accessible and credible, he had dealt with point one. A family man had apologised to a family and, albeit under duress, he had made himself accessible to parliamentary scrutiny, underlining once again his human credentials by professing himself 'humbled'. Only 'credible' remained. But, first, further sessions of parliamentary select committees loomed as disgruntled journalists promised further revelations on precisely who knew what and the Leveson Inquiry into media practice was announced, promising a drip, drip of allegations not only from journalists but from victims.

Stakeholders Alienated

That corrosive damage looked the more threatening for the sheer emotional weight it would carry. The Dowler family, the McCanns, themselves parents of a child lost in appalling circumstances, could not be dismissed as celebrities caught in the ambivalence of seeking media attention but wanting it only on their own self-serving terms. Worse, preliminary sessions of the inquiry saw former *Sun* Editor and Murdoch favourite Kelvin MacKenzie caricaturing the aggressive, unapologetic tabloid journalist. He condemned the inquiry as 'ludicrous', the political classes as 'nauseating' and proclaimed the *Sun* as 'a bit of fun'.

'So, where is David Cameron today? Where is our great Prime Minister who ordered this ludicrous inquiry? After all, the only reason we are all here is due to one man's action; Cameron's obsessive arse-kissing over the years of Rupert Murdoch. Tony Blair was pretty good, as was Brown. But Cameron was the Daddy,' MacKenzie opined.[3] For those to whom Murdoch's reputation was forever wound about the *Sun* of the Eighties, this was a further piece of clinching evidence.

Among those in the Labour Party weaned on the notion that their political exile during the Eighties and a good chunk of the Nineties was due to a 'Tory press' and 'The *Sun* Wot Won It', MacKenzie's outburst was simple confirmation of undue political influence. Those included former Deputy Prime Minister John Prescott, himself a victim of hacking, and Tom Watson MP, long-time pursuer of all things Murdoch and prominent member of the select committee investigating him.

Conservatives, fighting off the scandal associated with former *NoW* editor Andy Coulson's role as David Cameron's director of communications, must have been similarly unimpressed. Ditto the public whose view of political reputations, befouled by expense abuses revealed, ironically, through the pages of a newspaper, the *Daily Telegraph*, had been given a ringing endorsement. If two sets of stakeholders were being systematically alienated, a further one, the media, was not failing to take advantage of the opportunity a rival's difficulties were presenting.

Not satisfied with the demise of the *News of the World*, the *Independent*, meanwhile predicted Leveson would be the end of the *Sun*. 'The past few days have been the worst that anyone can remember at the *Sun*, where there are genuine fears that the paper could follow its sister publication's path to oblivion, taking its place among thousands of other defunct titles in the archive of the British Library,' wrote journalist Ian Burrell.[4]

Opportunity Presents Itself – Closing Down *NoW* Pays Out and Leveson Terms Favour Murdoch

Rarely can Rupert Murdoch's reputation have been at a lower ebb. And yet it is from here on that things have changed for Rupert Murdoch, presenting him – and any advisor – with an opportunity once again to take charge of his reputation. Take charge is classic advice, before events and competitors do so to your detriment. Firstly, whatever was now thrown at the *News of World*, the newspaper was dead. He had had the rogue beast put down. Flogging it further hardly mattered. There was, by now, also no sign of an imminent replacement. Had it ever been planned, that route was now cut off.

Despite what must have been Murdoch's worst fears, the circulations of other titles in the News International stable, including *The Times* and *Sunday* Times but more importantly the bigger selling tabloid *Sun*, either held up or reflected only the trend decline in newspaper circulation. Advertisers felt they were sufficiently free of contamination to hold on. Confidence was returning. That key element of the PR stakeholder map that is 'business' was keeping its faith in the reputation of Murdoch publications.

Wade, arrested, questioned, kept in the limbo of a police investigation, resigned. In so doing, she took with her whatever sins she had committed. To those among the business stakeholders, the right executive changes were finally being made. And the terms of the Leveson Inquiry were announced. Importantly, their focus lay not on Rupert Murdoch, News International nor the *News of the World* but on press practice as a whole.

Where News International is mentioned at all, it is as one of a host of media organisations whose behaviour was to be examined. Add to that an examination of the behaviour of the Metropolitan Police and politicians plus the brief to look at and recommend a regulatory regime, and suddenly Murdoch was only one face among a crowd in the dock.[5] An advisor looking at the terms of reference would instantly have seen a chink of light. Counsel for the inquiry, Robert Jay

QC, characterised phone hacking as 'a thriving cottage industry' in his opening remarks and helped almost straight away. He specifically included the now-defunct *News of the World* as a part of that industry. But he had very soon implicated the *Daily Mirror* too. The names of *Mirror* reporters were found in the notebooks of Glenn Mulcaire, the man at the centre of phone hacking allegations, he revealed.

Hugh Grant, inquiry witness, actor and long-time campaigner against press intrusion, fingered the *Mail on Sunday*. Comedian Steve Coogan, another celebrity witness, named the *News of the World*, still dead, in his testimony but added the *Daily Mirror* and the *Daily Mail*, alive and now issuing denials. The powerful testimony of Kate McCann, mother to missing daughter Madeleine, was bitterly critical of the *News of the World* and its final editor Clive Myler. But the *News of the World* had gone, the *Daily Express*, which accused her and her husband of having been so hard up as to sell their daughter, had not. Nor had the *Daily Mail* which knowingly printed a photograph of a girl seen in India suggesting it was Madeleine when the McCanns knew emphatically that it wasn't her.[6] The process was no longer about Murdoch. Or at least Murdoch alone.

At about the same time, allegations brought by *NoW* journalists to a second hearing of the select committee suggesting that James Murdoch had known about and condoned hacking at the *News of the World*, were described as 'less than compelling' by Louise Mensch MP and committee member. For a second time, James Murdoch escaped a select committee without anyone finding a smoking gun.

Stakeholders Reachable and Unreachable

Tom Watson's frustration was evident as he accused Murdoch Junior, saying: 'You must be the first mafia boss in history who didn't know he was running a criminal enterprise.' It made a good sound bite and was widely reported but there was eye-rolling and tutting in the committee room and James Murdoch dismissed the remark with no further comment than it was 'inappropriate'. A good advisor would now be pointing out what some, including perhaps those observing Watson, had already guessed; that a section of largely Labour politicians were appearing in that part of a classic stakeholder map which says 'those we cannot reach'.

As *NoW* journalist Neville Thurlbeck, implicated in phone hacking by a transcript of an email (for Neville) passed to the *Guardian*, said of examination by Watson: 'My evidence did not fit the pre-ordained frame of his argument "I'm old Labour so Murdoch is a lying, capitalist bastard. Right, I've ticked that box".'[7]

And for now, one would advise, that didn't matter. Exiled at least for now from power and reliant on a popular media to either return to it or be an effective opposition, the separation could only be temporary.

Benefiting perhaps from his classical education, David Cameron had already alighted on the eternal rule of politics: *nulli permanentes amici nulli permanentes inimici* (no permanent friends, no permanent enemies) and used Murdoch's *Sun* to appeal over the heads of public sector workers in advance of an imminent national strike. Rupert, one would be tempted to advise, it appears your reputation no longer puts off Prime Ministers.

Elsewhere, the stakeholder position occupied simultaneously by media and competition had been forced into a corner by the terms of Leveson, forcing them to defend their perception of press freedom, and implicitly News International as part of the press. *Guardian* editor Alan Rusbridger, whose newspaper had revealed the misdeeds of Glenn Mulcaire and the *News of the World*, was in a particularly difficult position, telling Leveson:

> The coming period of examination of the press will doubtless be an uncomfortable one in some respects. We're sure you will have in your mind the good things that journalists do which, more than ever, need protection as well as the work of the 99 per cent of British journalists who wouldn't have a clue how to hack a phone and who don't go to work to snoop into the private lives of others.[8]

Simple maths tells you that this means 99 per cent of Murdoch journalists also. Simon Jenkins, columnist and former editor of *The Times*, rowed back further in an irascible performance on BBC Radio 4's *The Moral Maze*. Conceding that the *News of the World* newsroom had been 'systematically corrupted', he went on to suggest that what followed 'had been blown out of all proportion' and that 'no-one died'.[9]

In fact, Milly Dowler had. And someone had hacked her phone as desperate attempts were made to find her. But that unfortunate fact remains an obstacle to a press now united in fear, less of Murdoch, than of the common enemy of regulation. Your enemy's enemy, one would advise Rupert Murdoch, has just become your friend.

Advice on Exploiting Circumstances – Guiding Regulation

And, with those pieces in place, the final element of the crisis mantra 'human, accessible, credible' comes into play. Credibility hinges on believable behaviour and that requires action. In this, Murdoch can take the initiative.

Truth and Reconciliation?

It would be easy to suggest a truth and reconciliation exercise. A year zero approach, confessing all and everything in a way that lances the boil and expunges the opportunity for any further damaging accusations. 'We know,' would come the response, 'we admitted it, conceded it and apologised for it.' *Mea culpa, mea culpa, mea maxima culpa*. Before forgiveness, true repentance.

However, the 'collateral damage' from such an exercise would be colossal, dragging in informants, whistle-blowers, politicians and businessmen, soldiers, doctors, priests and prisoners. Murdoch journalists would never again be trusted, their discretion never relied upon, the relationships on which both

Murdoch's influence as a media magnate are based and on which journalistic operations can continue, would be blown.

As an option, however attractive to the public it might be, would be deeply undesirable and, far from fixing Murdoch's reputation, sink it without trace.

Public Atonement, Informing a New Regulatory Process

Others have suggested the endowment of chairs and academic positions in media and media ethics; an approach which has, in the past, worked to cleanse the reputations of US newspaper proprietors. But this is invisible, obscure, esoteric. A publicly sullied reputation needs public mending. What does remain open to him, however, is the regulatory process.

This he can both influence and inform, construct and comply with and do so with an unbridled enthusiasm which leaves his commitment to reform open to no doubt. What one cannot change, embrace, would be the advice. To do that will demand an element of sacrifice. What information he chooses to yield up to Leveson and elsewhere to satisfy that, only he can know. That would, however, compromise the Murdoch family line that phone hacking and related bad practice was a matter of which they were largely unaware.

Murdoch would suggest, and to a degree rightly, that the shutting down of an old established and profitable title such as the *News of the World* was sacrifice enough and certainly an explicit acknowledgement that what went on was wrong. Cynics will say that the market did the work. However, that can't detract from the essential fact of its closure and that gives Murdoch a moral platform from which to operate in a way that rival titles now facing fire such as the *Express* and *Mail* cannot claim.

Acknowledging the realities of both the newspaper market and the means which journalists use to extract information from those who would prefer to conceal it would be his first port of call. By getting this right, and Alan Rusbridger in the extract already used largely makes his case for him, he ensures the support of his rivals. The media stakeholder is bound back in.

However, outside that he must be seen to administer justice to those in his empire who are in breach of whatever regulatory regime he helps construct. Prominent apologies must be published, journalists must be disciplined, even fired *pour encourager les autres*. This need not blunt the teeth of a rigorous press. The *Telegraph* used a sting to trap Vince Cable and the chequebook to gain information on MPs' expenses. *The Times* received a leaked internal report to blow the lid on the England rugby team's disastrous 2011 World Cup. Those are legitimate means of journalism.

But, in instances where the law or whatever new code is broken, Murdoch newspapers must act swiftly, decisively and publicly.

Who fronts up?

Supplementary to this must be the regular appearance across the airwaves of Murdoch himself and senior journalists from his publications to state often and repeatedly their determination to be at the forefront a clean-up in journalism. The message must be clear. Reform is being driven from the top. Reputations are at stake.

Precisely who fronts up is important. Rupert Murdoch must be more than the old man who looked so baffled by the select committee process. His son, James, now resigned from his News International board posts, is a man to be used sparingly. Not only is he inextricably linked to the investigation – his father has been well advised in assuming a background role that distances him from events in what remains a small part of his empire – but his Ivy League business school monotone is not engaging and less than the 'human' for which crisis management practice calls. His role would seem now largely over, a fact implicit in his departure from NI.

New executives, trusted executives, if necessary poached from elsewhere would cleanse the face of Murdoch.

In Murdoch We Trust

Meanwhile, internally, there should be no illusion that the new regime is a nod-and-a-wink refuge from due scrutiny. Management needs to enforce the headline behaviours unequivocally. The philosophy behind this is a simple one and it hinges on trust, the ultimate reputational marker. All that Murdoch now does must be an exercise in the re-establishment of trust in him and his media outlets.

To politicians, this would illustrate that once again they may be seen in his company. To businessmen, it would reinforce confidence, de-risk investment and re-engage advertisers. To the public, a message of reform would reinforce behaviour that they had never really abandoned anyway – buying Murdoch newspapers. To competitive media, it would set a challenge to which they would be obliged to respond and to regulators and law makers, the idea of Murdoch as straight player would be hard to refute.

Win. Win.

For some, the building of a trusted Murdoch may be an uncrossable Rubicon but with the press collectively daubed with the brush of roguery, an honest villain may become the most attractive option. My final advice to Murdoch would be to embrace that inner villain.

Notes

[1] See http://www.nytimes.com/2011/07/14/business/murdoch-discount-in-news-corp-stock.html?_r=1, accessed on 21 November 2011

[2] See http://www.telegraph.co.uk/finance/newsbysector/mediatechnologyandtelecoms/media/8893060/Pirc-tells-BSkyB-investors-to-oust-James-Murdoch.html, accessed on 17 November 2011

[3] See http://www.telegraph.co.uk/news/uknews/phone-hacking/8823558/Phone-hacking-Kelvin-MacKenzies-speech-in-full-to-Leveson-inquiry.html accessed on 22 November 2011

[4] See http://blogs.independent.co.uk/2011/11/14/leveson-inquiry-could-this-be-the-end-for-the-sun/, accessed on 14 November 2011

[5] See http://www.levesoninquiry.org.uk/about/terms-of-reference/, accessed on 23 November 2011

[6] See http://www.telegraph.co.uk/news/uknews/leveson-inquiry/8911318/Leveson-Inquiry-I-wanted-to-climb-into-a-hole-I-felt-so-worthless-says-Kate-McCann.html, accessed on 27 November 2011

[7] See http://www.pressgazette.co.uk/story.asp?sectioncode=1&storycode=48263&c=1, accessed on 25 November 2011

[8] See http://www.guardian.co.uk/media/2011/nov/16/alan-rusbridger-statement-leveson-inquiry?INTCMP=SRCH, accessed on 24 November 2011

[9] See http://www.bbc.co.uk/iplayer/console/b0174hs8, The Moral Maze, accessed on 24 November 2011

Note on the contributor

Patrick Barrow has over twenty years' experience in reputation management for corporations and individuals. He worked for BBC News during the Birt years and was head of corporate affairs for the Telegraph Group. Formerly Director General of the Public Relations Consultants Association (PRCA), the professional body for PR, he has also advised corporations across a wide range of sectors, particularly during crisis and transition. Currently running Reputation Communications, he also blogs on reputational issues as Forsooth at www.forsooth.blog.co.uk.

Section C. Guardian angels? How Hackgate places the Mainstream under the Microscope

Richard Lance Keeble

Perhaps the most fascinating aspect of the whole Hackgate affair is that it took so long to erupt. Years ago there was clear evidence of journalists operating illegally – but nothing was done. In 2006, Information Commissioner Richard Thomas claimed to have a list of 305 journalists who had obtained information using methods in possible breach of the Data Protection Act (see Davies 2008: 259-86).

And Mark Watts, author of a seminal study of Benji ('the binman') Pell who trawled the dustbins of the rich and famous for juicy information to sell to newspapers (2005) reported that many journalists were routinely breaking the law in their investigations. As investigative journalist David Leigh, of the *Guardian*, commented (back in 2008): 'These newspapers know very well what they are doing is disreputable and illegal. That is why they sub-contract the work to private detectives who in turn often subcontract it further down the food chain. The real villains hide behind minor criminals, who have to be willing to take the fall if necessary.' In my *Ethics for Journalists* (2009: 154), I wrote:

> Messages can generally be accessed remotely using a password code. These systems typically have default code settings, such as four zeros. A hacker can intercept such messages if the user has failed to change the default settings or uses obvious passwords such as birth dates. Journalists on rival newspapers, and sometimes working for different departments on the same title, have even tapped into each other's voicemail messages.

But is not the rise of 'private detective-led journalism' in response to the growing powers of PR to control so much of what goes into newspapers? According to Mayes and Hollingsworth (see Watts op cit), 'an insatiable appetite for celebrity and royal gossip has increased the commissioning of private detectives. Many journalists now act as managers of information uncovered by private detectives'.

All this should not discount the fact that deception *can* play a place in public interest journalism. David Leigh, for instance, has admitted he listened to company executive's phone messages while looking into corrupt arms deals. *The Sunday Times* also used impersonation and secret tape recordings to kick off the cash for honours story (see Wilby 2007).

Goodman – First Journalist Jailed for 44 Years

News of the World reporter Clive Goodman was jailed for four months on 26 January 2007 for intercepting phone messages of Prince William and two other royals. He was the first journalist to be jailed in the UK in 44 years. Goodman's private investigator Glenn Mulcaire, a former Wimbledon footballer, also pleaded guilty to a further five counts of unlawful interception of communications under the Regulation of Investigatory Powers Act 2000, a law brought into recognise technological advances in telephony and research.

A PCC inquiry into the affair cleared the *News of the World* of any misbehaviour on the (somewhat surprising) grounds that no one at the paper knew of Goodman's activities. Andy Coulson resigned as editor but was not called to answer to the PCC's inquiry. Instead, Clive Myler who succeeded him as editor was. Strange.

And things went strangely quiet until the Guardian's Nick Davies and his team of investigative reporters started to dig. The rest is history…Here, Alan Rusbridger, editor-in-chief of the *Guardian* and *Observer*, reflects on the 'extraordinary 12 months' for his newspapers and websites. And he goes on to make five major proposals:

- Lord Justice Leveson could make it a condition of belonging to a voluntary regulation regime that any newspaper over a certain size – say, 100 editorial staff – should employ, on a properly independent basis, a readers' editor to correct and clarify material promptly and prominently – and to be able to demonstrate this to the regulator.

- The setting up of a regulator 'with teeth' and powers to fine transgressors.

- A new organisation, the Press Standards and Mediation Commission, to act as a one-stop shop disputes resolution service so that people never have to go to law to resolve their differences with newspapers. 'It would be quick, responsive and cheap. We could even make this a carrot to tempt people into the fold of independent regulation – i.e. newspapers that signed up to PSMC would have clear advantages to newspapers that didn't.'

- Journalists need to agree a definition of the 'public interest' – and stick to it.

- Finally, journalists need to learn from others: 'Issues to do with privacy and intrusion are not unique to journalists: indeed, they are issues to which every citizen is becoming more and more attuned. The police, security services, public authorities, health services and private corporations are all working out the new rules of the game posed by technologies which have the potential to lay bare, store and analyse every aspect of our lives.'

Next Daniel Bennett and Judith Townend, in examining some of the reasons why the media went mum following the original convictions over the phone hacking scandal, argue persuasively: 'The vigour of journalism and healthy democratic debate is not merely dependent on the effective regulation of what is reported, it is also dependent on ensuring that harmful illegal activity is regarded as sufficiently "newsworthy" to be investigated and reported.'

'Serious Media' More Spectacle than Substance
Hackgate is often represented as a triumph of investigative reporting – by the *Guardian*'s Nick Davies in particular. But Justin Schlosberg, focusing on the mainstream media's treatment of the WikiLeaks revelations, argues that the watchdog function of the serious media (including the *Guardian*) remains ultimately more spectacle than substance and more ideological than counter-hegemonic. He concludes:

> Though the Leveson Inquiry into the ethics and practices of the press has set itself a wide ranging remit by any standards, the reaction of the British press has been to close ranks around the narrative that any significant change to the way the media is owned, structured or regulated is, in simple terms, bad news. Such *en masse* resistance does not bode well for the prospects of reform and is compounded by a framing which situates the problem in one particular sub-sector of the press, and in one particular rotten apple which was the former *News of the World*. The tacit implication of this framing is that the mainstays of serious, quality journalism are governed by a professional and credible commitment to serving the public interest above all else.

Finally, in this section, Tim Luckhurst, Professor of Journalism at the University of Kent and a speaker at the ICE conference on Hackgate, pursues an entirely different angle arguing that the main question facing British policymakers is not how to prevent the hacking of telephones – nor even how to limit the political influence of an octogenarian media magnate who has already lost the confidence of several major shareholders. It is how to finance an ethical future. He says:

> I welcome Lord Justice Leveson's inquiry into press ethics and practices in relation to the public, politicians and police. It is an appropriate response

to a profoundly troubling episode in public life. It is essential that operations Weeting and Elveden (the Metropolitan Police investigations into telephone hacking and alleged payments to police) be pursued thoroughly. But when each of these appropriate reactions to egregious conduct is complete, journalism's core crisis will remain. The pressing question that deserves more thought than hacking is how to fund expensive investigative, foreign and public interest reporting in the multimedia age.

References

Davies, Nick (2008) *Flat Earth News*, London: Chatto and Windus

Keeble, Richard (2009) *Ethics for Journalists*, London: Routledge, second edition

Leigh, David (2008) Licence to steal, *Guardian*, 7 April

Watts, Mark (2005) *The Fleet Street Sewer Rat: Exclusive – The Muckraker Who Got Rich Scavenging Celebrities' Binbags*, London: Artnik

Wilby, Peter (2007) Would Goodman be in trouble if he'd found a decent story, *Guardian*, 29 January. Available online at http://www.guardian.co.uk/media/2007/jan/29/mondaymediasection, accessed on 1 January 2008

Hackgate 'Reveals failure of Normal Checks and Balances to Hold Power to Account'

Alan Rusbridger, editor-in-chief of the *Guardian* and *Observer*, suggests the setting up of a Press Standards and Mediation Commission as a new regulator 'with teeth'

The events leading to the Leveson judicial inquiry were shocking: for what they revealed about one powerful and dominant company; about the responses of the police and the flawed nature of regulation; about the limitations of parliament and the initial unwillingness of much of the press to write about what had been going on at the *News of the World*. There was, in short, a failure of the normal checks and balances in society to hold power to account. For why did the News International and the police fail to take revelations in the *Guardian* seriously? Why did it take four inquiries before the police took it seriously?

The issue of plurality and competition also needs to be explored by the Leveson Inquiry. In October 2011, the tiny family-owned Kent Messenger group was prevented from taking over seven Northcliffe titles because of the distortion of the newspaper market in East Kent. Yet, until the post-Milly Dowler intervention of MPs, there appeared to be nothing anyone could do to prevent News Corp from effectively doubling its already-remarkable dominance of the British media market by acquiring the 61 per cent of BSkyB it did not already own.

Extraordinary year for the *Guardian*

The Leveson inquiry comes at the end of an extraordinary 12 months for the *Guardian*. Most improbably, we have been chased by a number of major film studios wanting to make films about both the hacking stories and the WikiLeaks revelations. Stephen Spielberg was one of a number of producers who snapped up different rights to the WikiLeaks saga.

My most crushing moment came when the American magazine, *Adweek*, ran a profile of me, headlined 'the Ben Bradlee of phone hacking' – a reference to the legendary *Washington Post* Editor at the time of Watergate. In the film he was a proper cigar-chomping, braces, growling, feet-on-the-desk kind of editor. Well, that wasn't the crushing moment. That was rather nice. It was the sentence: 'But if you had to pick a man for this role from Central Casting, you almost certainly wouldn't pick Rusbridger...he looks more like Harry Potter's lonely uncle than the kind of man capable of bringing down Rupert Murdoch.' So Bradlee is Jason Robards while I am the Charles Hawtree of editors.

What would the film of phone hacking look like? It could actually be made as comedy, thriller or family psycho-drama. You can imagine both Paul Greengrass and Stephen Frears behind the camera.

The obvious thing, if you were making a film about the phone-hacking saga, would be to concentrate on the extremely dramatic events of July 2011 – a month that saw revelations that plumbed new depths in journalism. There were resignations, arrests, a death, parliamentary debates, corporate high drama; family feuding; multimillion-pound payoffs, the closure of a newspaper...and the climax: the 'most humble day' in the life of the most powerful media tycoon of this, or of any other, generation.

The Most Interesting Period in the Saga

But to me the most interesting period in the story, though it might not make such a good film, was the 18-month period following the *Guardian's* original revelation of the Gordon Taylor settlement – which blew apart News International's 'one rotten apple' defence in July 2009. It was interesting precisely because almost nothing happened. Not, you might think, a promising piece of cinema, except to the followers of nouvelle vague. But fascinating in what it said about Britain and the settlement so many people in public life had made, over two generations or more, with Rupert Murdoch.

Let's go back to 9 July 2009 and that Gordon Taylor revelation – which, we now know, had been the subject of so much internal discussion within NI since the previous year, though the executive chairman of News International, James Murdoch, seems to have been remarkable incurious about it. We broke it on the web on Wednesday evening, Thursday in print.

By the weekend the story was pretty much dead. The police conducted the quickest review in recent history – a few hours. News International came out with a statement saying that the *Guardian* had 'deliberately misled the British public'. Saturday's *Times* had Andy Hayman, the police assistant commissioner in charge of the original investigation, pouring cold water all over our disclosures. Sunday's *News of the World* carried a thunderous leader attacking the *Guardian* – and reprinting the Hayman article from *The Times*. Hayman insisted there were 'perhaps a handful' of victims of hacking and only a few hundred who had even been targeted. He specifically dismissed the notion that John Prescott might have been hacked.

These, in the light of what we now know, were astonishing positions for the police and Britain's largest private media company to be putting on the record. The police last week revised their score card of hacking targets to around 5,800 – including John Prescott. And we know now that Colin Myler, then editor of the *News of the World*, had been told what his lawyers thought of the *NoW's* rotten apple stance: 'fatal,' 'very perilous' and 'damning'. In fact, the QC's advice that Myler and team sought said that there was 'overwhelming evidence of the involvement of a number of senior…journalists in the illegal inquiries'.

The Story: Killed by the Police and Newspaper Company

So the story was almost killed by a combination of the police and a newspaper company – both institutions supposedly dedicated to dealing in the truth – saying things which were not true. The following Tuesday, Nick Davies and I appeared before the House of Commons select committee on culture, media and sport. It was a packed, standing room-only occasion: there was widely-held perception – bolstered, I suspect, by some NI black ops – that the committee would give the *Guardian*, not the *News of the World*, a hard time.

As it was, Nick Davies flourished hard copies of the 'for Neville' emails. The significance of them was immediately apparent. Andrew Sparrow, who has been covering parliament for a good many years, blogged: 'Wow! I've been covering Commons committee for 15 years and I've never heard such a dramatic opening statement.' You wouldn't have guessed it from the next days' newspapers, which barely bothered to cover the event, thus setting a tone for the next 18 months. A pattern had begun to develop.

In November 2009, the industry's regulator, the Press Complaints Commission, published its own report into our revelations and – the 'for Neville' email notwithstanding – found 'no new evidence' to suggest that anyone except the already-jailed reporter Clive Goodman had been involved in phone hacking. The report, now withdrawn, could not resist having a little jab at the *Guardian*, of all people.

Within days there came the news that the *News of the World* was being forced to pay the astonishing sum of £800,000 in damages to a former *News of the World* journalist who got on the wrong end of the bullying culture that an employment tribunal found existed under Andy Coulson. Coulson at that point was within six months of walking through the front door of 10 Downing Street. No paper other than the *Guardian* thought this record £800k award was news.

The following month the commissioner of police, Sir Paul Stephenson, came to see me to persuade me that Nick Davies was barking up the wrong tree. So, the following February, did his assistant commissioner, John Yates. Sir Paul was gracious enough later to say that he was glad I ignored his advice. At the end of February 2010 – an election now only 10 weeks away – came a story, which, when I first read it in an email from Nick Davies, pricked the hairs on the back of my neck.

When Coulson Hired a Corrupt Private Investigator

The story was that Coulson, while editor, had rehired a corrupt private investigator straight out of prison and that this man, Jonathan Rees, was currently on remand on suspicion of sticking an axe in the back of his former business partner's head (the case subsequently collapsed). Due to our media laws which prevent British papers from writing about people facing charges we could not use Rees's name, but we did run the story – referring only to 'Mr A'.

There was no follow-up. It was apparently not a story that the future Downing Street press secretary had been using the services of a known criminal now suspected of a notorious murder.

This was quite a moment for me. It did seem to me that there was an almost willful blindness in British police, press, regulatory and political circles to acknowledge what was becoming increasingly difficult to ignore. So I did two things. One was to lift the phone to Bill Keller, executive editor of *The New York Times*. He had none of the press restrictions that prevented us from telling the whole story. Furthermore, the *NYT's* involvement would bring a dispassionate pair of eyes to the affair. If we were overflowing the whole affair *The New York Times* would soon douse us with cold water. I also passed on the information about Coulson and Rees to Gordon Brown, Nick Clegg and David Cameron. Nothing happened.

The New York Times did publish a long and compelling story in September 2010 – after an exhaustive investigation of its own. It confirmed everything the *Guardian* had originally written, and added significant new findings of its own. The police reacted by treating the whistleblowers the paper uncovered as suspects. The Murdoch tabloids switched their support to Cameron the following month. By May, Cameron walked into Downing Street, Coulson at his side. The following month Murdoch launched his bid for full control of BSkyB.

I won't labour the full narrative of all the dogs that didn't bark during this period – and there were certainly notable exceptions in the press, broadcasters and MPs – but I hope you have the picture. All the forces in civil society that you would normally expect to be engaged in such a situation failed. What explains this pattern of behaviour?

Combination of Fear, Dominance and Immunity

The simplest explanation is a combination of fear, dominance and immunity. People were frightened of this very big, very powerful company and the man who ran it. And News International knew it. They had become the untouchables of British public life. Why fear? Well, this was a bad company to upset. It owned nearly 40 per cent of the national press as well as the controlling influence in a broadcaster sometimes as referred to as an 800lb gorilla. It owned the satellite platform and the EPG on which competitors were listed. It owned significant swaths of sports and movie rights.

It is a company intensely interested in its political muscle – an influence which politicians now readily admit they routinely courted because they felt they had no alternative. There became an unspoken reciprocity about the business and regulatory needs of Mr Murdoch and the political needs of anyone aspiring to gain, or stay in, office. Here are the echoes of the Jim Taylor machine in the 1930s Frank Capra film, *Mr Smith Goes to Washington*.

And on top of all this, there was – as we now know – a private intelligence operation. It was an intelligence operation which outsourced the dirtiest work to criminals and which, according to people in a position to know, had a formidable private investigation capability. Recently we have learned how anyone who crossed this company – whether they were MPs asking questions or lawyers filing suits – were likely to be put under surveillance themselves. Tom Watson MP was followed for five days. Mark Lewis and Charlotte Harris, two tenacious solicitors, were followed around, together with their children. The private eye doing this work says he was employed right up to July this year. It was claimed in questioning today that all the members of the culture, media and sport select committee had been placed under surveillance. We know a former culture secretary had her phone hacked.

Days before his death in July 2011 Sean Hoare, a former features journalist at the *NoW*, told *The New York Times* that editorial staff on the paper had the ability to track, as well as hack, their chosen victims – i.e. they could locate their targets to within yards. It cost £500. Here are the echoes of von Donnersmarck's 2006 film, *The Lives of Others*. Not because anyone is saying this was an organisation with the evil intent or far-reaching consequences of the Stasi but because it was using the same methods as state intelligence services and because the evidence is that, culturally, no one at the *News of the World* saw any problem in this kind of systemic intrusion into precisely that – the lives of others.

Company's own Intelligence Operation

So, just as people in public life sought the blessing or approval or this organisation, anyone this company decided to target was very vulnerable. Not only did the firm have the intelligence operation, it also had the means to publish any dirt it gathered to a mass audience. It had a formidable legal department which would defend any action and which constructed a public argument about why it was justifiable to invade privacy – up to and including the argument that it was commercially necessary

No wonder people were frightened of this company and may have decided not to challenge it. There are further echoes, inevitably, of films about the quixotic, sometimes cruel exercise of journalistic power in *Citizen Kane* and the *Sweet Smell of Success*. What does all this add up to? It speaks to one form of media exceptionalism. It tells you why media companies – of all the private forces and institutions in any country – need particular rules, which guarantee plurality and a level playing field when it comes to competition.

Just as it shouldn't have taken the Milly Dowler story to wake people to what was going on at the *NoW*, it shouldn't have needed Milly Dowler to wake MPs up to the issues at stake in the BSkyB deal. Ofcom is looking at this question, and it is part of Lord Justice Leveson's remit. But the public debate is muted – partly, I suspect, because the issues are technical and more complex. But if the laws are inadequate to the task it is, bluntly, time to change our laws and I hope MPs and peers spend as much time thinking about the issues of market dominance as they currently are about regulating the content and behaviour of the press.

The phone-hacking saga tells us things about privacy, as well. Firstly, it shows us that, in the wrong hands, there is sometimes a fine line between the exposure of private lives and blackmail. In several recent cases involving privacy injunctions the judges have actually used the word 'blackmail' about material being hawked around Fleet Street and its agents. They are not describing a literal criminal offence which the police should investigate. They are describing a trade-off between money for secrets, and/or money for silence of the sort that is familiar from blackmail cases.

Secondly, it teaches us how sickened people feel when their privacy is invaded. 'Violated' was the word used by the former *Sun* editor, Kelvin MacKenzie, when he looked at the pages which showed how his own phone messages had been intercepted. If you speak to other victims of the hacking they will tell you how deeply repulsive it was to think of a stranger listening into private communications with loved ones or family.

We write stories all the time attacking councils, corporations and governments for snooping or being careless with personal data. We understand 'privacy' in many other contexts. An Englishman's home is his castle and all that. But here was a newsroom blinded to the moral darkness of such intrusion when it came to their own behaviour. And, in that inability to turn a mirror on themselves, I doubt they are alone.

In the same breath as we, as journalists, expose the snooping of others we decry Article 8 of the Human Rights Act which insists that privacy is, indeed, a right for all to be balanced against other rights. Some journalists try to advance an argument that we, uniquely, have the right to disregard privacy when we choose to and that Article 10, which protects free speech, must always trump Article 8. I think that's a very slippery argument to make.

Let's acknowledge that this can also be a deeply political argument. There are many people who dislike and distrust any form of external intervention in the making and arbitration of our laws. They don't want Europe – or anything that smells of Europe – anywhere near our own parliament or courts. That's a perfectly valid view. But the backlash against Article 8 of the Human Rights Act needs to be read in that context as well – though it's not entirely clear to many what the abolitionists want to do about the European Convention of Human Rights, to which the UK is signed up as a condition of EU membership.

'Self Regulation' No Such Thing

What else did we learn from the phone-hacking saga? Well, talking of rules and codes, we discovered that the thing that we call 'self-regulation' in the press is no such thing. Whatever the original laudable ambitions for, and achievements of, the Press Complaints Commission the fact remained that it had no investigatory powers and no sanctions. No matter how much valuable work it did in terms of mediation and occasional arbitration, it was simply not up to the task of finding out what was going on in the newsrooms it was supposed to be regulating. I see that one of the first statements from Lord Hunt, now brought in to oversee the PCC, is that it is not a regulator. That's a welcome statement of what the *Guardian* has been saying for some years.

The PCC was lied to by News International. It said it was very cross about that, but did nothing about it. Under more considered leadership, the PCC might, when faced with the *Guardian's* allegations in July 2009, have simply said: 'We're not equipped to deal with this.' That would have exposed the powerlessness of the body, but it would at least have saved it from the folly of writing a worse-than-meaningless report which, as we wrote at the time, would fatally undermine the cause of self-regulation as represented by the PCC.

In the absence of anything that looked to the outside world like regulation, the rogue actions of, I hope, a few journalists, have landed the press as a whole with a series of inquiries which will last not months, but years, and which will, I suspect, be quite uncomfortable for all involved.

Many of my colleagues are very gloomy about all this. Some of the greatest advocates of transparency for others frown on what they see as washing dirty linen in public. But, by and large, I feel positive about what's happening. Here are a few reasons why:

1) The Leveson inquiry will provide a forum for the press to explain itself. There's a strand of media commentary that says we're facing an existential challenge, so therefore we should circle the wagons and repel all the nosey parkers who want to interfere.

It's true: the finances of the newspaper industry are in a pretty desperate state – hit by a combination of falling sales, declining advertising, rising costs and digital disruption. We could soon be facing the prospect of towns without newspapers. But it's better to talk about this – and the serious implications that flow from it – than hope people won't notice.

Wider Context of Decent Editorial Practices

2) Secondly, Leveson is an opportunity to put the behaviour of a relatively small number of journalists into a wider context of decent editorial practices. There are tens of thousands of journalists in the UK – broadcasters, the regional press, magazines, the trade press. Most of them would not have any idea how to hack a phone or hire a private detective, and 99 per cent of them don't go to work to dig into other people's sex lives. There's a danger that all the static and noise sometimes created around privacy is quite unrepresentative of what concerns the industry at large – just as the Church of England's obsession with gays and women sometimes drowns the valuable work and more fundamental teachings of the Church.

3) Thirdly, Leveson may well uncover uncomfortable truths about the way a number of journalists have worked in the past. That's true – and that's surely good, not bad? In what other sphere of public life do we think that transparency is an undesirable thing? With government or corporations – indeed, with any centres of institutional power – we generally believe that shining a light leads to good outcomes. Indeed, that's the central argument for the press as a public good: it's what we do all the time. So, we should have some confidence that good things will flow from holding the press up to scrutiny, however difficult it may be at times.

4) Finally, Leveson has already stimulated a debate and thinking about standards and journalism. His so-called teach-ins have brought together – for the first time in memory – all the national newspaper editors in one room. They have virtually all spoken and listened. The Editor of the *Daily Mail*, Paul Dacre, has already come up with two extremely interesting moves – a proposal on ombudsmen and the creation of his own corrections and clarifications column – which show an industry prepared to think positively and creatively about solutions.

So it's good to get many voices engaged. And to hear significant interventions from politicians and members of the judiciary, including the Lord Chief Justice, vigorously supporting the notion of a free and independent press. Who could have imagined our most senior judge quoting the scabrous 18th-century radical John Wilkes in aid of his argument? So a positive way of looking at Leveson is that it provides an opportunity for the industry to have a conversation with itself while also benefitting from the perspective and advice of others.

Let me chip in for the first time with a few thoughts on the debate. The first is about the most local form of regulation, which we started at the *Guardian* in 1997 – the readers' editor.

1. Readers' Editors

A character in *Pravda*, the 1985 Hare/Brenton play about a Commonwealth-born press baron (played by Anthony Hopkins) has a fictional journalist who comes out with the following line: "If every time we got something wrong we published a correction, then a newspaper would just be a footnote to yesterday's newspaper." The character adds: "A newspaper isn't just a scrap of paper, it's something people feel they have to trust. And if they can't trust it, why should they read it?"

The sentiment is a recognisable one. Many newspapers hate owning up to errors. Until recently there was an undoubtedly genuine feeling that if we confessed to our mistakes people would be less inclined to trust what we said.

But the truth, as all honest journalists know, is that newspapers are full of errors. Not just errors, but crude over-simplifications, mistakes of emphasis, contestable interpretations and things which should simply have been phrased differently. It seems silly to pretend otherwise. Journalism is an imperfect art – what Carl Bernstein likes to call the 'best obtainable version of the truth'. And yet many newspapers do persist in pretending they are largely infallible.

We decided to change all that back in 1997 when we appointed a readers' editor. We'd print their phone number in the paper every day and give them space independently to correct or clarify anything they felt we'd got wrong. To safeguard his or her position, I guaranteed in writing that I'd never interfere with anything they wrote and signed a contract saying they could only ever be sacked by the papers' owner, the Scott trust. In addition, I gave them a weekly column to address concerns raised by readers.

A few years later I wrote that this was the single most liberating act of my editorship. It freed me from dealing with stroppy callers; it cut the legal bills; it enabled reporters to immediately have a means of clarifying or correcting their mistakes; and it gave readers the sort of complaints service they regard as commonplace in their dealings with any other organisation. Having a readers' editor had led to a much more acceptance of the nature of the task we're all engaged on at the *Guardian*.

On a pragmatic level it seemed to have an air of inevitability. The *Guardian* is now read by more than 3 million people a day around the world: that's 3 million fact checkers – nearly all of them with access to social media networks on which they delight in pointing out things they disagree with or errors we've made. In addition, there are several media monitoring groups which scrutinise our content on a regular basis. In other words, if we get anything wrong, it will be exposed one way or another. Isn't it better to be seen to be doing it ourselves rather than to be evidently leaving material uncorrected while others do the job for us?

But a better argument is that it's just right. If journalists get things wrong there's an obligation on us to do something about it. It should be baked into the idea of journalism that the search for truth is helped by allowing others to add to, or clarify, or respond to one version of events.

And, precisely because it is, in human nature, so hard to admit error, it's generally better if someone other than the person ultimately responsible for the error, i.e. the editor, makes a dispassionate assessment.

Finally, there's a pragmatic dollop of self-interest that ought to make us adopt readers' editors and it's this: the more we can be shown to be taking responsibility for our own regulation, the less outsiders will seek to impose it on us.

What better way to resist interference – including by a PCC successor – than demonstrating that we take the responsibility of correction and clarification seriously?

I don't know how independent the *Mail's* readers' editor is – but Paul Dacre is absolutely right to start this and to have a fixed space everyday. That's crucially different from dropping in the odd correction on a random page when all other defences have failed.

The latter is a pretence that error in journalism is exceptional. The former accepts that it is routine. Which do you think is nearer to the truth? As the *Mail* says, its journalists produce 80,000 words a night in the newspaper alone and 'it is inevitable that mistakes do occur'.

So a good starting point for Lord Justice Leveson would be to make it a condition of belonging to a voluntary regulation regime that any newspaper over a certain size – say, 100 editorial staff – should employ, on a properly independent basis, a readers' editor to correct and clarify material promptly and prominently – and to be able to demonstrate this to the regulator.

That's a maximum of 1 per cent of editorial cost going towards the business of liaising with the readers, hearing their concerns, allowing a response and, where necessary, correcting the record which now lives permanently online.

My second suggestion is now considered commonplace, though it was dismissed for years. I'll state it anyway. We need …

2. A Regulator with Teeth

The PCC, as many of its critics never tire of saying, does many excellent things. It mediates well. It's free to complainants. Many of its adjudications are sensible and coherent. We should build on its work rather than junk it altogether.

But one question the Leveson inquiry is bound to ask is: 'How would a regulator handle a situation similar to the one the PCC faced in 2009?' – i.e. how could it behave like a proper regulator – with investigatory powers and sanctions – without being put on a statutory footing?

I suspect this was what Paul Dacre was hinting at when he suggested to the Leveson Inquiry that the time had come to appoint some sort of ombudsman with powers to investigate professional or ethical standards and to impose fines. He proposed a 'polluter pays' principle.

Here again, I agree with Paul Dacre. A useful example of a polluter being made to pay was the way in which the Independent Television Commission – the old regulator for ITV – reacted when, back in 1998, the *Guardian* published allegations about a programme on drug-running made by Carlton TV which included faked scenes. The ITC imposed a £2m fine after a thorough investigation, led by Michael Beloff QC and a former controller of editorial policy at the BBC. The corporate Affairs Director at Carlton at the time was someone called David Cameron.

Imagine, in July 2009, the PCC had called a leading QC and asked him/her to look at what had been going on at the *News of the World*. With powers to interview reporters and executives and forensically to examine the evidence – with NI paying the bill and with a £2m fine at the end.

It might not have got at everything – we can see how opaque such a devious media company can be – but the prospect of such an interrogation would have been a sobering thought for NI and would bear pretty heavily on the minds of all editors – so heavily that I suspect the services of the ombudsman would not often be in demand. The threat of his/her intervention – and there would need to be a suitable threshold of prima facie evidence – would be a real deterrent.

So, reader's editors to deal at the most local level with accuracy and other matters. Secondly, a regulator with teeth. What else could this regulator do?

Well, let's look at the list of people most journalists don't want to have a hand in deciding what we publish: the list would include the courts, politicians, anyone domiciled in Europe, and any lawyers acting on conditional fee arrangements. So we want something British, non-legalistic, free from anything that smacks of the state, and something that's cheap.

If that's the case, then doesn't logic suggest that we should be proposing to Lord Justice Leveson a new body which would offer a plausible and effective alternative to all these busybodies who are just dying to interfere.

3. PSMC: A One-Stop Shop

Let's stick an M (for mediation) in PCC. Maybe called it the Press Standards and Mediation Commission. It's now our own one-stop shop disputes resolution service so that people never had to go to law to resolve their differences with newspapers. It would be quick, responsive and cheap. We could even make this a carrot to tempt people into the fold of independent regulation – i.e. newspapers that signed up to PSMC would have clear advantages to newspapers that didn't.

Is it workable? Well, let's start with libel – and here it could be a positive advantage that parliament is currently discussion defamation reform, which could mean that Leveson could dovetail proposals with the excellent suggestions for overall reform which have come from Brian Mawhinney's joint committee and from such organisations as PEN and Index.

How might it work? The PSMC would employ a small permanent staff to deal with libel questions, and would have a panel of qualified and neutral mediators. The mediator could decide on meaning. S/he could rule on questions such as whether the piece was fair and accurate; whether it was an opinion or an allegation of fact; whether it was in the public interest; whether the subject of the article had a reasonable chance to respond and whether his/her response was included – i.e. the mediator, where appropriate, could go through the sorts of questions that crop up under a so-called Reynolds defence.

The mediator could rule on prominence and wording of any correction and apology and settle any issues of compensation. Most of the issues could be settled on paper. There would be no fees recoverable on either side, beyond the reasonable expenses of a claimant. A record of the discussions would be kept by the mediator. What's in it for claimants? It makes libel infinitely cheaper and simpler. What's in it for the press: the same. The quicker, cheaper resolution of the vast majority of defamation cases.

Of course, the mediation might fail. But, before any court action could be started, the trial judge would read the mediator's report of the attempts to settle. If a newspaper could be shown to have made reasonable and honest attempts to deal with the issue, that could be reflected in a cap on costs and/or damages. You could further and say that a reasonable offer of a correction and apology should be a complete defence to libel, subject only to the payment of damages.

Of course, the devil's in the detail and there would be much to work out if one were to think seriously about dovetailing the law of defamation with a new regulatory regime. But I think there's enough there to merit serious engagement.

So much for libel. But I described the PSMC as a one-stop shop. What about privacy? We are always hearing journalists deploring the use of the courts to create a backdoor privacy law. So can we go further and deal with privacy cases as well as libel?

Surely the logic is that we should try? But ,of course, we bump into the fact that, while there is a reasonable consensus about the iniquities of the libel law, there is much less agreement about the threat posed by a privacy law, or about the reasonable grounds for intruding on privacy. What are the difficulties? Well firstly we need to …

4. Agree on what We Mean by 'the Public Interest' – and Stick to it

I'm one of those who think the PCC's definition of the 'public interest' is actually pretty good. Until the PCC's report into phone hacking, I was happy to serve on the committee which revised it. Others think it's too prescriptive, old-fashioned, too obsessed with exposing iniquity, and too narrow.

But, whatever definition we come up with – and I'm all for expanding the group of people who help us get there beyond a small pool of editors – let's believe in it and be prepared to argue it. If we fight legal actions and mount campaigns over articles that even we don't pretend are in the public interest as we define it, aren't we inviting people to be cynical about our motives and our commitment to self-regulation?

Under the Human Rights Act, and at the request of the media by virtue of section 12 (4) inserted into the Act before it was passed, judges are obliged to pay special attention to this code. The evidence is that they do – especially when balancing article 8 (privacy) and 10 (freedom of expression). They will normally ask a newspaper whether they are saying that an article is in the public interest, as defined by the industry code. But, in the overwhelming majority of recent privacy injunction cases, the newspapers did not, in fact, argue that there was any public interest involved.

To which one might respond, what's a judge supposed to do? It's fashionable to blame one judge, Mr Justice Eady, for single-handedly creating a law of privacy in this country. But a moment of self-reflection might concede that, as an industry, we have sometimes done ourselves no favours by testing the state of the law with a series of really quite weak cases – so weak that very few have been appealed and in some of which the newspaper didn't even argue the merits of the case. There's simple pragmatism involved here.

Supposing we all can agree on a public interest defence – including the 99 per cent of journalists who don't write about other people's sex lives – then what would stop the PSMC getting involved in privacy as well as defamation? It's never been exactly clear what 'the industry' thinks of the idea of policing the boundaries of privacy itself. It's commonplace, as I say, to decry the judges trying to do it for us. So that suggests we should want to do so and that a one-stop shop that included privacy shouldn't be unthinkable.

Indeed, in May this year the chair of the PCC, Lady Buscombe, boasted that the PCC was already 'more active than judges in defending privacy'. She said: 'The PCC operates a pre-publication service that can work with editors to prevent intrusion before it happens.' The PCC director, Stephen Abell has said the same. But there are two challenges we would have to face up to:

- One is the question of prior restraint. Are we really capable of agreeing on, and resourcing, in a service which could prevent information from appearing because it believed it did not meet the public interest test of the code? It seems to be happening on an ad hoc basis already. Can we make it routine?

- Secondly, are we prepared for the PCMC to follow the general contours of the privacy jurisdiction as the courts have developed it?

The second is surely critical to persuading would-be claimants to use our one-stop shop over the courts. If it doesn't look as though we take privacy seriously – or if we diverge wildly from the results obtainable through law – then people will simply carry on using the courts. Why is this agreement over 'the public interest' so crucial? Because, in the end, the public interest, and how we argue it, is not only crucial to the sometimes arcane subject of privacy – it is crucial to every argument about the future of the press, the public good it delivers and why, in the most testing of economic times, it deserves to survive.

It also leads us beyond self regulation and into areas of the criminal law and the question of whether we can use this opportunity to lobby to rationalise the conflicting laws which now affect journalists, some of which enable journalists to plead the public interest, others of which don't – including new laws on bribery and the regulation of financial information.

The act of phone hacking has, since 2000, meant a compulsory jail sentence without any form of public interest defence. I'm the last person to defend phone hacking. But it's a little illogical that, for offences under section 55 of the Data Protection Act (which might involve even more serious breaches of privacy) there is a public interest defence. I'm not sure that makes much sense. Why don't we make the defences and penalties the same?

So – we've looked at how we could pre-empt a lot of external interference by coming up with effective regulation of our own: we'll get real about the public interest and we'll use a new consensus about the public interest to rationalise the defences available to journalists when faced with the criminal law. Finally, how can we use this opportunity to …

5. Learn from others

Anyone listening to some of the debate around issues facing the press would think we are the only ones grappling with difficult moral and ethical dilemmas. There's a streak of exceptionalism in some arguments – a belief that the press alone should not have to engage with universal issues.

Issues to do with privacy and intrusion are not unique to journalists: indeed, they are issues to which every citizen is becoming more and more attuned. The police, security services, public authorities, health services and private corporations are all working out the new rules of the game posed by technologies which have the potential to lay bare, store and analyse every aspect of our lives.

I would have loved George Orwell, who wrote his amazingly prescient novel, *Nineteen Eighty-Four*, in 1948, to have eavesdropped a conversation I had with a senior Google figure recently. He was musing about the potential of the Google face recognition software the company has evolved, whose effects are so far reaching the company can't quite yet decide what to do with it.

Essentially, the software can recognise and match a face to a name with any images sitting anywhere on the web, so long as one match has been made. What made this so troubling he said, is that digital spiders could then crawl the web and find every picture in the public domain and match it with an identity. So the moment one match is made, it would be possible to scan every street or crowd scene over several decades to see where a particular individual was. Link that to the sort of all-pervasive CCTV systems we have in this country and you have a formidable infrastructure – current, but also historical – for total surveillance.

Checklist of Criteria for Anyone Considering Invasions of Privacy

An interesting contribution to the debate about the rules the intelligence services might use was made by the former head of GCHQ, Sir David Omand, who recently drafted a checklist of criteria that anyone in his former trade contemplating invasions of privacy should ask themselves. I think they can equally usefully be asked by any journalist – indeed, we've incorporated a version of them in the *Guardian's* own code of practice. Here they are:

- There must be sufficient cause. What's the harm to individuals or families that might follow from intrusion?

- There must be integrity of motive – the intrusion must be justified in terms of the public good which would follow from publication.

- The methods used must be in proportion to the seriousness of story and its public interest, using the minimum possible intrusion.

- There must be proper authority – any intrusion must be authorised at a sufficiently senior level and with appropriate oversight.

- There must be a reasonable prospect of success: fishing expeditions are not justified.

What a good set of questions for journalists to ask themselves. What's more, the act of asking – if properly recorded at the time – would offer some sort of protection in the event of anyone, be it a regulator or a court, subsequently interrogating the behaviour. Some journalists are uneasy at this notion of keeping an audit trail of thinking, authority and pre-publication decision-making? But isn't that what we have got used to in using the so-called Reynolds principles for libel – laying a trail to show a court, if necessary, that certain steps of responsible journalism have been gone through before publication of matters of public interest?

So there are five modest bits of input into the debate that's arisen since the events of the summer. You'll notice the recurrence of two words that keep cropping up: 'public interest'. You can't avoid them – and we shouldn't want to. The public interest – the public good that results from what we do – is the main thing we have going for us as we make a public case – to the public – about the value of what we do. Sure, we can argue about the commercial need for papers to have enjoyable stories that people like to read. But, in the face of unprecedented financial, digital, legal and regulatory challenges and threats, we will always ultimately have to defend what we do on the basis of some notion of the public interest we serve.

The foundation of the PCC back in 1990 was a significant attempt to lash together news organisations with differing traditions and audiences around a common code on which we could all agree. You could argue that no one got very much out of it in a narrow sense. The *Financial Times* doesn't really need the PCC to make sure that it stays on the ethical straight and narrow. And the *Daily Star* showed just what it thought of the constant criticism by the PCC by walking out of it.

But there seemed to be an overriding imperative to agree a common professional and ethical code to which we would not merely pay lip service, but which would actually inform everything we do. Only by acting together could we repel the people who were looking for any excuse to tie our hands. That imperative is equally strong today. And a commonly agreed definition of the public interest has to be at the centre of all arguments about libel, privacy, confidence, data protection and regulation.

Current Fragility of the Industry
This is an incredibly anxious time for journalism. Anyone watching the recently released film, *Page One*, about *The New York Times*, will have picked up the everyday awareness within the newsroom that even one of the most powerful and professional newspapers in the world is clinging on to financial viability. So the film is about the current fragility of our industry. But it's also about the both the immense pace of transformation and the way the basics of journalism never change. For me, the most lifting moments are those that simply show journalists trying to get at the 'best obtainable version of the truth'. We see them asking questions, probing away at data. We eavesdrop earnest discussions in the newsroom about getting it as right as possible before they press the button to publish. And we see the power of a great newspaper as an institution.

Towards the end there's a sequence in which David Carr, the compellingly watchable media correspondent, is probing away at the circumstances behind the near-implosion of the Tribune company under its new owners, who seem to care little for the company's core journalistic traditions or mission.

At the end of all his digging Carr leans back and says something to the effect of, 'I've now done my job: this is where the institution kicks in.' Meaning: he, as a reporter, now depended on his editors to stand up to pressure, to publish and to defend his work. It's one of the reasons we need the fourth estate. To defend our Moscow correspondent when he is threatened by the Russian state. To get Ghaith Abdul Ahad out of jail when the Libyan government arrests him. To resist the police threats to prosecute Amelia Hill under the Official Secrets Act. To pay the £100k legal and accountancy bills to publish a 10-day series on tax avoidance. To allow Ian Cobain the time and resources to uncover, inch by inch, the story of Britain's apparent complicity in rendition and torture. To support Paul Lewis in his quest to get at the truth of the death of Ian Tomlinson and Jimmy Mubenga; or undercover policing; or the English riots. To give David Leigh the freedom and backing to investigate the illegal bribes paid by BAE or the toxic dumping tricks of Trafigura. To back David Conn as he remorselessly peels back the intersections where big money meets sport. To assemble the team that can make sense of the biggest trove of government, diplomatic and military secrets the world has ever seen – and to publish them comprehensibly and safely.

Brilliant reporters, with the backing of a solid, independent institution behind them. And then there was Nick Davies. There were several people in the summer who compared what he did with the phone-hacking story to what is still the text book case of how a newspaper can unearth and defend a story of overwhelming public interest – Watergate. Indeed, the comparison was made by Woodward and Bernstein themselves.

Nick Davies was threatened, lied to and ignored, but he did what good journalists do: tracked people down; won their confidence; verified what they told him; checked it with others; and, over time, painstakingly built up irrefutable evidence of what had gone on inside the *News of the World*. The eventual truth was revealed to the public, not by the police or parliament or the courts or any regulator. It was revealed by a reporter.

So, as we enter this period of reflection and investigation of the worst of what journalism can do, let's also keep in mind the best of what journalism can do. And that, for me, is a primary message for Leveson and the debate around hacking. Over the coming period we'll hear many uncomfortable truths about failed regulation, distorted priorities, illegal practices and a betrayal of the both the public and the public interest. But it's also a once-in-a-generation chance to celebrate great reporting, to think again about what journalism at its best can do and what it should be.

- This chapter draws together edited versions of Alan Rusbridger's contribution to the Leveson Inquiry on 16 November 2011 and his 2011 Orwell lecture at University College, London, on 10 November 2011 (see http://www.guardian.co.uk/media/2011/nov/10/phone-hacking-truth-alan-rusbridger-orwell)

Press 'Omerta': How newspapers' Failure to Report the Phone Hacking Scandal Exposed the Limitations of Media Accountability

Daniel Bennett and Judith Townend, in examining some of the reasons why the media went mum following the original convictions over the phone hacking scandal, argue: 'The vigour of journalism and healthy democratic debate is not merely dependent on the effective regulation of what is reported, it is also dependent on ensuring that harmful illegal activity is regarded as sufficiently "newsworthy" to be investigated and reported'

In April 2009, the *Guardian*'s special correspondent, Nick Davies, gave the House of Commons a preview of the media story of the decade. In evidence to the culture, media and sport select committee, he claimed there was 'a real will' on the part of the Press Complaints Commission (PCC) 'to avoid uncovering the truth about phone hacking' (Davies 2009a). The committee was probably not aware of the significance of Davies's observations. Chairman John Whittingdale told the investigative journalist that the committee had already considered the conviction of the *News of the World*'s royal reporter, Clive Goodman, and the private investigator Glenn Mulcaire for illegal voicemail interception in 2007. The committee 'did not want to revisit old ground too much'[1] (Whittingdale 2009).

But Davies had been working on the story since January 2008 and he believed there was far more to phone hacking at the *News of the World* than this investigation had revealed. Whittingdale's comment did not deter him. In July 2009, Davies broke an exclusive story that the chief executive of the Professional Footballers' Association, Gordon Taylor, had been paid £700,000 damages and costs in a secret deal with News International, the parent company of the *News of the World* (Davies 2009b). The claim? Taylor's voicemails had been unlawfully intercepted. The revelations blew open News International's repeated defence that phone hacking at the *News of the World* was limited to Clive Goodman, who had been portrayed as a 'rogue' journalist.

For the next two years, the *Guardian* continued to break stories about what was to become widely recognised as the 'phone hacking scandal' (*Guardian* 2006-11). According to political commentator Peter Oborne, phone hacking 'should have been one of the great stories of all time. It has almost everything – royalty, police corruption, Downing Street complicity, celebrities by the cartload, Fleet Street at its most evil and disgusting' (Oborne 2011). And yet the *Guardian*'s attention to the story was far greater than the minimal coverage offered by her UK competitors. In April 2010, Oborne observed: '[Nick] Davies's work…has gained no traction at all in the rest of Fleet Street, which operates under a system of omerta so strict that it would secure a nod of approbation from the heads of the big New York crime families' (Oborne 2010). The story finally received more significant coverage when former *News of the World* editor Andy Coulson was forced to resign as Downing Street director of communications in January 2011. Six months later, the *Guardian* revealed that the *News of the World* had intercepted and deleted the voicemails of murdered missing schoolgirl Milly Dowler. It was only at this point that a broad range of press titles deemed that phone hacking was a major scandal.

The media's silence on the issue (Bland 2011) has been noted by *Guardian* journalists (for instance, Wilby 2009; Greenslade 2011a) and it is not surprising that News International titles such as the *Sun*, *The Times* and *The Sunday Times* were reluctant to devote column inches to the troubles of their sister paper, the *News of the World*. The lack of coverage given to phone hacking from other tabloids might be explained by the fact that phone hacking could have been more widespread across Fleet Street (House of Commons 2010). We argue, however, that explanations for the non-reporting of the phone hacking scandal need to delve beyond simplistic, if valid, assertions of industry cover-up. In order to explain why the majority of national newspapers failed to regard phone hacking as newsworthy, it is necessary to unpick a tangled web of contributing factors. We explore competing professional, political and commercial interests; the failure of other organisations – particularly the Metropolitan Police – to investigate the matter thoroughly; and the intimidating power of News International.

How the Scandal was Reported

Despite significant revelations in July 2009 about the possible extent of phone hacking at the *News of the World*, coverage of the issue in the press was minimal. Exempting the *Guardian* and the *Observer*, a trawl of the articles published in the UK's major national press titles between 10 June 2006 and 10 November 2011 reveals a failure to report the phone hacking scandal in a sustained and systematic manner.[2]

The *Guardian* wrote at least 879 articles on the matter up to November 2011, far more than her daily broadsheet counterparts: the *Independent* wrote 489, the

Daily Telegraph 436, and *The Times* 332. Moreover many of these articles were written in 2011, long after the *Guardian*'s initial revelations in July 2009 and only after it was discovered that Milly Dowler's phone had been hacked in July 2011. A comparison at the end of 2010 demonstrates how little newsprint the story warranted before the major developments in 2011. Whereas the *Guardian* had written 237 articles, the *Independent* had 83, the *Daily Telegraph* 46, and *The Times* 43. Perhaps unsurprisingly, the tabloids gave the story barely minimal coverage. By the close of 2010, the *Daily Mail* and the *Mail on Sunday* had written 38 articles, the *Sun* 17, and the *Daily Mirror* and the *Sunday Mirror* a mere 11.

At various times between 2006 and 2011, aspects of the phone hacking story were simply not reported by British journalists. In the words of *Guardian* editor Alan Rusbridger, they were apparently 'blinded' to 'the significance of the issue' (Rusbridger 2011c). In November 2011, Rusbridger described how a former *News of the World* journalist was awarded £800,000 in 2009 for suffering 'what an employment tribunal regarded as a culture of bullying at the newspaper under its then editor, Andy Coulson' – a man who was subsequently employed by the Conservative Party (Rusbridger 2011c). This was not deemed newsworthy by any other news editor in the British press. In July 2011, Rusbridger wrote: 'There seemed to be some omerta principle at work that meant that not a single other national newspaper thought this could possibly be worth an inch of newsprint' (Rusbridger 2011a). He could have pointed to other significant editorial omissions.

It is not fair to say, however, that phone hacking was never mentioned in other newspapers until 2011, but simply tracking occurrences of the phrase 'phone hacking' does not reveal how the issue was reported. Exploring press articles in more detail shows that often journalists covered phone hacking in a minimal manner, reporting angles that undermined any basis for further investigation or attacking those who believed it deserved attention as a news story. The coverage of the House of Commons culture, media and sport select committee report in 2010 is an interesting example of how a major development was reported.

On 24 February, the committee published a 167-page report into press standards, privacy and libel which strongly criticised the *News of the World* and the extent of subsequent inquiries into phone hacking by both News International and the Press Complaints Commission. The committee believed it was 'inconceivable that no-one else at the *News of the World*, bar Clive Goodman, knew about the phone-hacking' (House of Commons 2010 par. 440). The MPs' report directly accused *News of the World* witnesses called by the inquiry of 'collective amnesia' and 'deliberate obfuscation' (ibid: pars 442; 495). For most newspapers, however, the committee's findings on phone hacking were not deemed particularly newsworthy.

On the day the report was published, readers of *The Times* would have needed to turn to page 15 for coverage of the committee's findings. The main 570-word article concerned the committee's conclusions on privacy and libel laws with no mention of phone hacking, which was covered in 244 words in a separate article. The *Daily Telegraph* had a similar focus. While the threat of 'libel tourism' and 'super-injunctions' on the freedom of the press warranted 1,361 words, only 333 words concerned phone hacking. Moreover, the article only documented the fact that the committee had not found any evidence that Andy Coulson was aware of phone hacking at the *News of the World* – the line also taken in the *Sun*'s 137 words on the report.

The *Daily Mail*'s readers were informed at relative length (873 words) that MPs were most concerned about a 'crackdown' on press freedom from privacy and libel laws, a perspective echoed in the *Express*. Unlike the *Express*, the *Daily Mail* did publish several sentences on the committee's concerns over press self-regulation, but the committee's phone hacking findings were only mentioned briefly in a separate box under the sub-heading: 'Tory Spin Chief Cleared'. The *Daily Mirror* did not mention the publication of the report.

The reporting of the committee's findings is a microcosm of the way the phone hacking scandal was consistently under-investigated and under-reported for a significant period of time between 2006 and 2010. But why were so many journalists and editors at a variety of different newspapers so reluctant to regard phone hacking at the *News of the World* as 'newsworthy'?

What Makes a Story 'Newsworthy'?

Ideally the 'newsworthiness' of a story is defined by its relevance to the public interest[3] and acts as a mechanism by which journalists 'objectively' select 'important' occurrences for publication from among any number of potentially newsworthy events (Molotch and Lester 1974: 105). In practice, the selection of news stories for publication has been shown to depend on a 'complex multifaceted gatekeeping process' (Clayman and Reisner 1998: 194) encompassing newsroom practices and routines (White 1964; Golding and Elliot 1979: 17; Gans 2004); journalists' access to 'newsworthy' information from their sources (Hall et al 1978; Fishman 1980; Schlesinger and Tumber 1994); the social organisation of the newsroom (Schudson 1989: 270-275); and the culture and commercial interests of the audience (McNair 2005: 28-29). The phone hacking scandal epitomised how a definition of 'newsworthiness' based on the public interest can be undermined by a combination of professional, political and commercial interests. Together they form an explanation for the press's collective redaction of developments in the phone hacking story until July 2011.

Not 'News' for the Newsroom and are the Public Interested?

Phone hacking was not stand out 'news' to the newsroom. Regardless of how far journalists attempt to establish the interests of their audience and the potential of the internet to transform gatekeeping (Robinson 2006; Bruns 2009), journalists still tend to publish stories which interest the newsroom. News appearing in newspapers is ultimately a consequence of reporters' and editors' decisions. If a story is 'not news' to the newsroom, a story is unlikely to become 'news' in the newspaper and it appears that the phone hacking of public figures was simply not regarded as sufficiently 'newsworthy' by newspaper journalists.

Johan Galtung and Mari Holmboe Ruge (1965: 67) argue that an event is more likely to become news if it is 'unexpected' within the context of what is 'culturally meaningful' and 'consonant with what is expected'. In February 2007, following the sentencing of Goodman and Mulcaire, *The Times*'s Dan Sabbagh suggested that the actions of Clive Goodman at the *News of the World* were not 'unexpected' nor unusual. Sabbagh said that from his own 'survey of reporters' the PCC should assume that 'the practice of paying private investigators to help to get into voicemails was widespread across Fleet Street' (Sabbagh 2007). The extent of phone hacking among national newspapers is not known, but the use of 'the dark arts' – a range of practices both legal and illegal – to obtain stories was apparently not uncommon even if it was often outsourced to private investigators.[4] In 2008, *Guardian* journalist Nick Davies devoted a chapter of his book *Flat Earth News* to the topic in which he claimed that the use of the 'dark arts' had been spreading since the 1980s and included 'blagging' confidential information, bribery of serving police officers, trawling dustbins and the use of Trojan horse viruses to access information on a target's hard drive (Davies 2008: 259-286).

As discussed below, not reporting the phone hacking scandal was, in part, a strategy of industry self-preservation, but also at play was the cultural socialisation of a norm of behaviour within the press that justified the use of the 'dark arts' as a way of holding power to account in the public interest. As Sabbagh noted, however, the remit for the adoption of these practices went further than exposing a risk of serious crime or national security issue, but was also justified to 'prevent hypocrisy in public life' (Sabbagh 2007). For the tabloid press, in particular, this included the personal lives of those who were interesting to the public – often celebrities. The normalisation of these practices within the press corps led to their diminishing significance as an issue that might be deemed 'unexpected' and thus 'newsworthy'.

It is perhaps, therefore, not surprising that newspaper editors felt that the internal practices of the media were also not of interest to the public and to their readers. Richard Wallace, editor of the *Daily Mirror*, claimed phone hacking was scarcely covered before July 2011 because it was a 'meeja story'. 'It's a very straightforward editorial decision…we didn't think our readers were interested in it. Frankly, they weren't' (Society of Editors 2011). Wallace might have been right, but the scarcity and tone of the coverage of phone hacking would have undoubtedly contributed to the perceived lack of interest from the public until 2011.

Not Deemed News by the Journalist's Official Sources

Phone hacking, however, was also not regarded as 'news' nor given credence by a number of others both within the wider media industry and those belonging to outside organisations. Although romantics cast the media in an adversarial relationship with 'official sources' of power, in practice various academic studies have demonstrated that journalists often rely on powerful 'official sources' of information for the news (Hall et al 1978; Fishman 1980: 52; Tuchman 1980: 81; Herman and Chomsky 1988: 18; Gans 2004: 116). If as Hall et al suggest, these sources act as 'primary definers' of news stories (Hall et al 1978: 57-59), then they hold considerable influence over journalists' understanding of 'newsworthiness'. In the case of phone hacking, the position of the PCC, the police and the Conservative Party towards phone hacking proved to be a significant barrier to reporting the scandal.

The PCC: An 'Old' Story

Investigations by the PCC into the phone hacking issue consistently turned up a lack of evidence. In 2007, a report on 'Subterfuge and Newsgathering' maintained that there was 'no evidence' that anybody other than Goodman and Mulcaire knew about phone hacking at the *News of the World* (PCC 2007). A subsequent PCC report, published in November 2009, was equally sceptical of the evidence of more widespread voicemail interception. Written as a response to the *Guardian*'s revelations in July 2009, the PCC's report maintained that the *Guardian* had only unearthed one new significant fact – that the *News of the World* had settled a legal action brought by the Chief Executive of the Professional Footballers' Association Gordon Taylor. The PCC might have concluded that this new information at least warranted more sustained investigation, not least because it was unlikely that Taylor's phone was being hacked at the request of Clive Goodman as part of his job as royal editor. Instead, the commission's report stated that the *Guardian*'s revelations 'did not quite live up to the dramatic billing they were initially given' (PCC 2009).

The PCC had seen 'no new evidence' that phone hacking was 'undertaken by others beyond Goodman and Mulcaire', nor 'evidence that *News of the World* executives knew about Goodman and Mulcaire's activities' (PCC 2009). For the PCC, the story also failed the journalistic tests of novelty and recentness – they regarded the information as 'old' or 'already in the public domain' and that if more extensive phone hacking had occurred it was not 'ongoing' (PCC 2009). The PCC's report was officially withdrawn on 6 July 2011 after it emerged that the phone of Milly Dowler had also been hacked in 2002.

The Metropolitan Police: 'No New Evidence'

The PCC board consists of former and present newspaper editors and does not have any legal powers to compel witnesses to provide evidence so it was not surprising that it failed to uncover the extent of the phone hacking scandal. Journalists would probably not have used the PCC's conclusions to judge the potential newsworthiness of a story, but they would usually listen to the Metropolitan Police – an organisation institutionally independent of the media industry with a range of investigative powers and regarded by journalists as an authoritative 'official source' of information.

The fact, therefore, that the Metropolitan Police repeatedly insisted that there was 'no new evidence' of more widespread phone hacking at the *News of the World* for eighteen months after the *Guardian*'s article in July 2009 was a strong disincentive for journalists considering further investigation into the story. The Metropolitan Police consistently maintained that their initial inquiry into phone hacking, which had resulted in the conviction of Goodman and Mulcaire, was extensive. In hindsight, it is clear that the initial police investigation was not sufficiently wide-ranging – and this contributed to the resignations of the Commissioner, Sir Paul Stephenson, and the Assistant Commissioner, John Yates.

The Metropolitan Police gave several reasons for its decision not to investigate phone hacking more thoroughly before the launch of Operation Weeting on 26 January 2011: lack of new evidence, the prospect of not securing successful prosecutions and the prioritisation of resources elsewhere (Metropolitan Police 2010; Yates 2011). It should also be noted, however, that there were a number of allegedly troubling links between the Metropolitan Police and the *News of the World*. Neil Wallis, a friend of John Yates, was employed as an advisor by the Metropolitan Police while Neville Thurlbeck, then *News of the World*'s Chief Reporter, was named as an alleged police informant in 2000, in a case unrelated to phone hacking (Harper 2011; Home affairs select committee 2011). More generally, a separate police inquiry – Operation Elveden – has been launched to investigate whether journalists are paying police officers for information.

The position of the police was used by the PCC and by News International as a key component of their own conclusions. News International chairman James Murdoch told the culture, media and sport select committee that he had relied on internal investigations and 'on the assertions and reassurances made publicly by the police, who had all the relevant information, that no new evidence was found, within 24 hours of the 2009 allegations...' (James Murdoch 2011). Moreover, the police's stance represented a significant stumbling block for journalists attempting to 'stand up' a story from an 'official source' through the journalistic ritual of 'triangulation' (Harrison 2006: 144-5). *The Times*'s editor, James Harding, for example, argued in a Society of Editors debate that one of the reasons why his newspaper had not followed up the *Guardian*'s coverage in July 2009 was the response of the police: 'On the day that it broke, the police came out later in that day and said there's nothing to see here. If you're calling and asking the question and the company says: "No, there's nothing to see here" and the police say: "No, there is nothing to see here"...that will inform the way in which reporters look at the story' (Society of Editors 2011).

The Conservative Party: Defending Andy Coulson
The Metropolitan Police was not willing to reopen their inquiry until January 2011, but the previous year the *Guardian*'s editor, Alan Rusbridger, had contacted *The New York Times*'s managing editor, Bill Keller, in an attempt 'to

stop the story from dying on its feet' (Rusbridger 2011a). The resulting *New York Times* investigation, published in September 2010, forced the Conservative Party to join the list of naysayers in defence of the Prime Minister's director of communications, Andy Coulson. Former *News of the World* journalist, Sean Hoare,[5] told *The New York Times* that his then-editor, Andy Coulson, had 'actively encouraged' him to hack messages when he was working at the newspaper. Coulson denied all knowledge of illegal activity. The allegation nevertheless sparked further coverage and discussion in the House of Commons forcing the Conservative Party and their coalition partners, the Liberal Democrats, to defend Andy Coulson's role in government. *The Times* claimed that 'senior Tory figures' had launched 'a co-ordinated campaign to close down the story' and quoted London Mayor Boris Johnson who described the concerns over phone hacking as 'codswallop' (Coates 2010).

The Fear of Speaking out against News International and the Media Industry

The Conservative Party's reluctance to draw attention to phone hacking could be attributed to the Coulson-connection and Prime Minister David Cameron's well-documented relationship with News International executives (Wright and Morris 2011). But why was the Labour Party so reticent to speak out? Peter Oborne believes that until the Milly Dowler voicemail revelations, the Labour leader Ed Miliband 'had made the pragmatic decision to ignore the phone-hacking story', 'explaining privately to confidants that he had no choice because the alternative would be "three years of hell" at the hands of the Murdoch press' (Oborne 2011). Labour had also been the governing party until 2010 and an overly critical stance of inaction over phone hacking would have invited criticism.

More generally, Oborne (ibid) argued that MPs were 'intimidated by the power of newspapers to expose and destroy them'. Reflecting on the scandal in 2011, Tom Watson MP felt that in the summer of 2009, 'every single MP I know thought the campaign [to expose phone hacking] was bordering on the insane. No one wanted to know. It was simply career suicide to challenge the powerful people that ran News International' (*Express & Star* 2011). In March 2011, Chris Bryant MP claimed that his colleagues had been warned off the story 'by a senior figure allied to Rupert Murdoch and a former executive of News International' (Bryant 2011). Details of News International's alleged surveillance of culture, media and sport select committee members are still emerging (Greenslade 2011b).

MPs were not the only group of people reluctant to take on News International and the media industry. According to the former senior investigating officer, Alexander Owens, the Information Commissioner's Office had discovered a 'Pandora's Box' of information at the house of private investigator, Steve Whittamore, including 17,500 entries in notebooks with requests for information from journalists. Owens claimed that despite the discovery of this paper trail, he was told by his line manager at the ICO that he was 'not to make any approach to any reporters or the press'. Owens said that the former deputy head of the ICO had told him that media groups were 'too big' to pursue (Owens 2011).

The failure to investigate and the scarcity of official condemnation from the PCC, the police, a number of MPs and the ICO helped keep the story out of the news: without powerful criticism by high-profile figures there was no fuel to add to the embers of the phone hacking fire.

Political Agendas and Commercial Rivalry

The vacuum of official independent denunciation of phone hacking and the lack of credence given to the story aided the development of the narrative that rather than being 'newsworthy', the phone hacking story was nothing more than a tool in the hands of people pursuing a politically motivated agenda (see Trelford 2011). For journalists, it was perhaps a more natural assumption that politics and business intrigue were responsible – narratives they constructed on a daily basis – rather than entertaining the possibility that their industry might actually be at fault.

Feeding on statements from News International and a number of politicians, journalists regularly reported that phone hacking was driven by a 'left-wing' or 'anti-Murdoch' campaign. In July 2009, Stephen Glover argued that phone hacking practices had already been exposed after the convictions of Goodman and Mulcaire. He portrayed a coalition of Labour MPs, the *Guardian* and the BBC taking 'pre-assigned positions' to 'imaginatively' repackage an 'old' story in the 'most sensational manner' (Glover 2009). In September 2010, the *Daily Mail* and *The Times* published several articles in response to *The New York Times*'s investigation which continued this theme, accusing Labour of a 'witch-hunt over phone hacking' (Coates 2010) and using the story as a 'stick with which to beat the hated Tory-Lib Dem coalition' (McKay 2010).

It was after the publication of a report into phone hacking, libel and privacy by the cross-party select committee in February 2010, however, that the line that the phone hacking story was politically motivated was most prevalent. The UK was just over two months away from a general election which contributed to a heightened sense that the phone hacking story was being re-visited for political advantage. The late insertion of a section on an £800,000 pay out to a sports reporter at the *News of the World* after 'persistent bullying' by Andy Coulson was seen as a particularly politically motivated move.

A Conservative Party spokesperson was quoted in the *Daily Telegraph* as saying the insertion was 'nothing more than a politically motivated attempt by the Labour members on the committee'. News International released a statement which claimed that 'certain members' of the culture, media and sport select committee were pursuing a 'party-political agenda' accusing them of 'innuendo, unwarranted inference and exaggeration'. Conservative MP Philip Davies, who was also a committee member, received widespread prominence for his critical comments of the last-minute insertion leading the *Sun* to portray the MPs' report as 'hijacked by Labour MPs for political gain' (Newton-Dunn 2010). Notably the Conservative MP chairing the committee, John Whittingdale, was not quoted in relation to phone hacking in the *Sun*, the *Daily Mail*, the *Daily Telegraph* nor *The Times*. Not only did Whittingdale's party allegiance not fit the media narrative, he was also willing to tell the BBC that the extent of phone hacking went 'very wide indeed' (see Robinson and Wintour 2010).

Accusations that political agendas were responsible for the over-reporting of the phone hacking story by the *Guardian* and *The New York Times* were interwoven with arguments that the coverage was driven by commercial rivalry. Rupert Murdoch, chief executive of News Corporation, believed:

> A lot of people had different agendas in trying to build this hysteria. All our competitors in this country formally announced a consortium to try and stop us. They caught us with dirty hands and they built the hysteria around it (Rupert Murdoch 2011).

But the theory Murdoch gave to parliament in July 2011 had long since found support from other quarters. Back in 2010, the *Daily Mail*'s Ephraim Hardcastle column had suggested that the BBC and the *Guardian* were running a 'warmed-up old story as a way of striking at media chief Rupert Murdoch', 'whom they fear and envy' (*Daily Mail* 2010). In January 2011, after the police had launched Operation Weeting, Dominic Lawson maintained that the *Guardian*'s business and political interests meant that unlike the police they had given phone hacking 'a primacy not obviously consonant with its significance in the battle against crime'. Speaking to the Society of Editors, *Times* Editor James Harding maintained that less coverage was given to phone hacking before 2011 partly because of the sense that when one news organisation reports on another 'there is an agenda there' (Society of Editors 2011). 'I think when that story broke in the *Guardian*, there was a tendency to see that.'

The New York Times's investigation in 2010 was also believed to have been commercially motivated. The *News of the World* responded to *The New York Times*'s coverage by taking the offensive and arguing that the latter's dedication of 'enormous resources over five months to investigating one of a rival group's newspapers' was a 'conflict of interest'. The *News of the World*'s managing editor, Bill Akass, even urged *The New York Times* to open an inquiry into whether *The Times*'s journalists had been in breach of their own 'ethical guidelines' (*New York Times* 2010). The *News of the World*'s line found a less forthright but nevertheless similar echo in *The Sunday Times*. Dominic Lawson implied that the reason *The New York Times* was investigating the story was because it was 'engaged in a ferocious circulation war with the *Wall Street Journal*, which is controlled by the same Rupert Murdoch to whom Andy Coulson ultimately reported when editing the *News of the World*' (Lawson 2010). In the United States, the *Wall Street Journal* urged its readers to 'see through the commercial and ideological motives of our competitor-critics' (*Wall Street Journal* 2011).

Conclusion: The End of Self-Regulation?

In July 2009, former *Sunday Times* editor Andrew Neil described the phone hacking scandal as 'one of the most significant media stories of modern times' (see Davies 2009) and yet until the beginning of 2011 the story received minimal attention in most media outlets. However much individual editors stress their independence, News International owned newspapers' aversion to covering the story is not difficult to comprehend: the legal, commercial and political stakes were high if additional allegations of phone hacking were made to stick. Some of the fallout – albeit affecting a small a piece of the Murdoch empire – has already occurred as a result: the collapse of the BSkyB deal; the closure of the 168-year-old *News of the World* newspaper; and further arrests of former News International staff.

It is also not surprising that the tabloid newspapers avoided investigating phone hacking at the *News of the World*. Allegations that illegal voicemail interception was widespread across Fleet Street have so far been denied. It is possible, however, that tabloids were wary of shining a light on the *News of the World* in case some of their own practices were subsequently interrogated. The failure to investigate or report the phone hacking scandal, however, was the consequence of a more complicated set of factors. We have traced a tangled web of overlapping personal, professional, political and commercial dynamics which meant many journalists and editors came to regard the phone hacking story as anything but 'newsworthy'.

For many journalists, the use of the 'dark arts' was not unusual. Their implementation was justified for a broad range of stories from those clearly with a 'public interest' to many other stories which were of interest to the public. Phone hacking was not 'news' to the newsroom and it was also deemed to be of little concern to the public how journalists obtained their stories. Critically, the failure of a variety of official sources of information including the PCC, the ICO, the police and members of the Conservative Party during 2010 to give credence to the story – particularly their public assurances that there was no new evidence of widespread phone hacking – discouraged journalists from further inquiry. It was therefore difficult to stand up the *Guardian*'s investigation independently without repeating Nick Davies' painstaking work.

Finally, the 'newsworthiness' of the story was attacked by representatives of News International and by other newspaper journalists who portrayed the *Guardian*'s story as part of a politically motivated 'left-wing' campaign or commercially interested 'anti-Murdoch' crusade regardless of any factual inconvenience in the construction of these narratives.

In an ideal world, newsworthiness acts as a considered accountability mechanism enabling journalists to select the most relevant stories for publication in the public interest for the benefit of democracy. The phone hacking scandal demonstrates that newspapers operating under a system of self regulation cannot be trusted as arbiters of newsworthiness in the public interest. The *News of the World*'s demise highlighted the problem of individual newspapers being allowed to self-regulate their journalism. The PCC demonstrated that it had no power to regulate the press and if the *Guardian*'s exposure of the phone hacking scandal is presented as evidence of an 'effective' system of press self-regulation, then it was shown to be worryingly dependent on their dogged pursuit of the story in the face of significant flak at various times from other news organisations, the PCC, the Metropolitan Police and the Conservative Party.

It was all too easy for the *Guardian*'s journalism to be attacked as a non-story driven solely by commercial rivalry and political agenda; a damning House of Commons committee report to be collectively ignored or condemned by the press; and for important civil legal actions to go unreported. Regulation of the UK press was effectively outsourced to the US in late 2010 as the *Guardian* rallied support for its story by calling in *The New York Times*. Moreover, evidence of serious illegal practice was not pursued by the ICO and in hindsight the Metropolitan Police's investigation into phone hacking was found to be inadequate. Journalists were able to break the law for substantial periods of time without sanction. Appropriate political and police attention was not given to the scandal until the newspapers decided phone hacking was, in fact, a front-page story – two years after Davies's scoop and long after many of the incidents of phone hacking had occurred. This is not a system of regulation we can rely on in the future.

By November 2011, the phone hacking scandal was being compared to Watergate (Bernstein 2011). The revelation in July that Milly Dowler's voicemail messages had been intercepted caused politicians and newspaper editors to treat phone hacking and the cover up as a national scandal. This triggered the Leveson Inquiry investigating the culture, ethics and practice of the press. The failure of vast sections of the media to treat the phone hacking scandal as 'newsworthy' before this point ought to have significant implications for the future of self-regulation of the press currently being explored by the Leveson Inquiry. The phone hacking scandal is not a lone example of blinkered reporting or, as Rusbridger put it, 'wilful blindness' (2011b). Stories about media malpractice are commonly given short shrift: the narrow reportage of the Information Commissioner's critical *What Price Privacy Now?* report,[6] for example, or even the selective reporting of the Leveson Inquiry itself (Greenslade 2011c).

The inclination for journalists not to regard a scandal within their own industry as 'newsworthy' is hardly surprising, but other stories might also be suppressed for a similar combination of professional, political and commercial interests – a fact that ought to be considered by Lord Justice Leveson's inquiry and other bodies considering the question of press regulation. The vigour of journalism and healthy democratic debate is not merely dependent on the effective regulation of what is reported, it is also dependent on ensuring that harmful illegal activity is regarded as sufficiently 'newsworthy' to be investigated and reported. A new system of regulation should not only end the abuse of self-regulation by the *News of the World*, it should also consider whether newspapers ought to be independently held to account for their editorial decisions regarding 'newsworthiness'.

Notes

[1] In reference to the Information Commissioner's Office Operation Motorman and Clive Goodman, jailed in 2007 for illegal interception of voicemail messages (ICO 2006a/2006b), covered in the culture, media and sport select committee's seventh report (House of Commons 2007)

[2] The Nexis® UK database was used to search national newspapers for the following terms in news articles between 1 July 2006 and 10 November 2011: ('phone tapping') or ('phone hacking') or ('voicemail interception') and ('news of the world'). The articles were filtered for 'moderate similarity' ensuring that most duplicates were discarded. Some duplicates may not have been filtered out and it is possible that articles relevant to phone hacking which did not satisfy the search terms were not counted. The data should, therefore, not be regarded as completely accurate in terms of unique numbers but the approach nevertheless provides an idea of the comparative weight of coverage given to phone hacking by each title

[3] As frequently pointed out, judges do not necessarily consider what is in the public interest to be the same as what the public finds interesting. See, for example, par. 147, Jameel & Ors v. *Wall Street Journal Europe* Sprl [2006] UKHL 44 (11 October 2006)

[4] National newspapers' use of private investigators is documented in the Information Commissioner's report, *What Price Privacy Now?* (ICO 2006b)

[5] Sean Hoare died in July 2011. In November 2011, an inquest found that he died of natural causes. He had used alcohol as 'a crutch' and 'was under stress because of interest generated by the breaking News International story', the coroner said (Davies 2011)

[6] In an editorial in August 2006, the *Guardian* described the first ICO report *What Price Privacy?* as a 'highly detailed, if little reported, document' about newspapers' use of private investigators. The second report, *What Price Privacy Now?* reflects on media coverage of its first report and notes: 'Coverage even in the broadsheets at the time of publication was limited. However, all broadsheets featured details of the report on their websites' (ICOb 2006: 10)

References

Bernstein, Carl (2011) Murdoch's Watergate? *Newsweek*, 9 July. Available online at http://www.thedailybeast.com/newsweek/2011/07/10/murdoch-s-watergate.html, accessed November 2011

Bland, Archie (2011) Anybody There? Why the UK's phone-hacking scandal met media silence, *Columbia Journalism Review*, May/June. Available online at http://www.cjr.org/feature/anybody_there.php?page=all, accessed November 2011

Bruns, Axel (2009) News Blogs and Citizen Journalism: New Directions for e-Journalism in Prasad, Kiran (ed.) *e-Journalism: New Media and News Media*, New Delhi: BR Publishing

Bryant, Chris (2011) House of Commons Adjournment debate, 10 March, Column 1171. Available online at http://www.publications.parliament.uk/pa/cm201011/cmhansrd/cm110310/debtext/1 10310-0004.htm, accessed November 2011

Clayman, Steven E. and Reisner, Ann (1998) Gatekeeping in Action: Editorial Conferences and Assessments of Newsworthiness, *American Sociological Review*, Vol. 63, April pp 178-199

Coates, Sam (2010) Labour witch-hunt over phone hacking, *Times*, 16 September

Daily Mail (2010) Ephraim Hardcastle, *Daily Mail*, 7 September

Davies, Caroline (2011) *NoW* reporter Sean Hoare died of liver disease, inquest hears, *Guardian*, 23 November. Available online at http://www.guardian.co.uk/media/2011/nov/23/sean-hoare-inquest-liver-disease, accessed November 2011

Davies, Nick (2008) *Flat Earth News*, London: Chatto and Windus

Davies, Nick (2009a) Uncorrected transcript of oral evidence, HC 275-vi, House of Commons, culture, media and sport committee, 21 April. Available online at http://www.publications.parliament.uk/pa/cm200809/cmselect/cmcumeds/uc275-vi/uc27502.htm, accessed November 2011

Davies, Nick (2009b) Murdoch papers paid £1m to gag phone-hacking victims, *Guardian*, 8 July. Available online at http://www.guardian.co.uk/media/2009/jul/08/murdoch-papers-phone-hacking, accessed November 2011

Express & *Star* (2011) Tom Watson reveals how the phone hacking scandal affected him, 17 November. Available online at http://www.expressandstar.com/news/2011/11/17/tom-watson-reveals-how-the-phone-hacking-scandal-affected-him/, accessed November 2011

Fishman, Mark (1980) *Manufacturing the News*, Austin: University of Texas Press

Galtung, Johan and Ruge, Mari Holmboe (1965) The Structure of Foreign News, *Journal of Peace Research*, Vol. 2, No. 1 pp 64-91

Gans, Herbert (2004) *Deciding What's News*, Evanston, Illinois: Northwestern University Press, second edition

Guardian (2006-11) Phone hacking archive. Available at http://www.*Guardian*.co.uk/media/phone-hacking, accessed November 2011

Glover, Stephen (2009) The BBC has conspired with the *Guardian* to heat up an old story and attack Murdoch, Independent, 13 July. Available online at http://www.independent.co.uk/news/media/opinion/stephen-glover/stephen-glover-the-bbc-has-conspired-with-the-Guardian-to-heat-up-an-old-story-and-attack-murdoch-1743193.html, accessed November 2011

Golding, Peter and Elliott, Philip (1979) *Making the News*, London: Longman

Greenslade, Roy (2011a) Doubting Don is so wrong about phone-hacking coverage, *Guardian*, 21 February. Available online at http://www.guardian.co.uk/media/greenslade/2011/feb/21/phone-hacking-newsoftheworld, accessed November 2011

Greenslade, Roy (2011b) Casting light on the *News of the World* shadowing of MPs, *Guardian*, 14 November. Available online at http://www.guardian.co.uk/media/greenslade/2011/nov/14/newsoftheworld-tom-watson, accessed November 2011

Greenslade, Roy (2011c) Leveson Inquiry: Embarrassed tabloids pass the buck in their coverage, *Guardian*, 26 November. Available online at http://www.guardian.co.uk/media/greenslade/2011/nov/26/national-newspapers-news-photography, accessed November 2011

Hall, Stuart et al. (1978) *Policing the Crisis: Mugging, the State, and Law and Order*, London: MacMillan

Harper, Tom (2011) *NoW* hacking suspect worked for the police as an 'informer', *Evening Standard*, 19 July. Available online at http://www.thisislondon.co.uk/standard/article-23971221-hacking-suspect-worked-as-police-informer.do, accessed November 2011

Harrison, Jackie (2006) *News*, London: Routledge

Herman, Edward S. and Chomsky, Noam (1988) *Manufacturing Consent: The Political Economy of the Mass Media*, New York: Pantheon

Home affairs committee (2011) Unauthorised tapping into or hacking of mobile communications, Examination of Witness (Question numbers 645-975). Available online at http://www.publications.parliament.uk/pa/cm201012/cmselect/cmhaff/907/11071902.htm, accessed November 2011

House of Commons (2007) *Culture, Media and Sport: Seventh Report*. Available online at http://www.publications.parliament.uk/pa/cm200607/cmselect/cmcumeds/375/37502.htm, accessed November 2011

House of Commons (2010) *Culture, Media and Sport: Second Report, Press standards, Privacy and Libel*. Available online at http://www.publications.parliament.uk/pa/cm200910/cmselect/cmcumeds/362/36202.htm, accessed November 2011

Information Commissioner's Office (2006a) *What Price Privacy?*

Information Commissioner's Office (2006b) *What Price Privacy Now?*

Jameel & Ors v. Wall Street Journal Europe Sprl [2006] UKHL 44, 11 October 2006. Available online at http://www.bailii.org/uk/cases/UKHL/2006/44.html, accessed November 2011

Lawson, Dominic (2010) Murky motives behind the phone hacking row, *Sunday Times*, 12 September

McKay, Peter (2010) Hague isn't Cameron's real worry, *Daily Mail*, 6 September

McNair, Brian (2005) What is Journalism? Hugo de Burgh (ed.) *Making Journalists*, London: Routledge pp 25-43

Metropolitan Police (2010) Press Statement, 24 February

Molotch, Harvey and Lester, Marilyn (1974) News as Purposive Behaviour: On the Strategic Use of Routine Events, Accidents, and Scandals, *American Sociological Review*, Vol. 39, No. 1 pp 101-112

Murdoch, James (2011) Culture, Media and Sport select committee, Uncorrected Transcript of Oral Evidence, Phone Hacking, 10 November. Available online at http://www.parliament.uk/documents/commons-committees/culture-media-sport/Uncorrected_transcript_CMSC_10_November_11_James_Murdoch.pdf, accessed November 2011

Murdoch, Rupert (2011) House of Commons Oral Evidence, Culture, Media And Sport committee, 19 July. Available online at http://www.parliament.uk/documents/commons-committees/culture-media-sport/Uncorrected_transcript_19_July_phone_hacking.pdf, accessed November 2011

Newton-Dunn, Tom (2010) Report on Press 'hijacked' by Labour MPs, *Sun*, 24 February. Available online at http://www.theSun.co.uk/sol/homepage/news/2866336/Key-Commons-report-on-Press-hijacked-by-Labour-MPs.html, accessed November 2011

New York Times (2010) Response From *News of the World*, *New York Times*, 1 September. Available online at http://documents.nytimes.com/response-from-news-of-the-world, accessed November 2011

Oborne, Peter (2010) Does David Cameron really need this tainted man beside him? *Guardian*, 4 April. Available online at http://www.guardian.co.uk/commentisfree/2010/apr/04/david-cameron-andy-coulson-election, accessed November 2011

Oborne, Peter (2011) What the Papers Won't Say, *Spectator*, 9 July. Available online at http://www.spectator.co.uk/essays/7075673/what-the-papers-wont-say.thtml, accessed November 2011

Owens, Alexander (2011) Oral evidence to Leveson Inquiry, 30 November. Available online at http://www.levesoninquiry.org.uk/wp-content/uploads/2011/11/Transcript-of-Afternoon-Hearing-30-November-2011.txt, accessed November 2011

Press Complaints Commission (2007) *Subterfuge and Newsgathering*. Available online at http://www.pcc.org.uk/assets/218/PCC_subterfuge_report.pdf, accessed November 2011

Press Complaints Commission (2009) *PCC Report on Phone Message Tapping Allegations*. Available online at http://www.pcc.org.uk/news/index.html?article=NjAyOA==>, accessed November 2011

Robinson, James and Wintour, Patrick (2010) *News of the World* phone hacking: Legal loophole to be closed, *Guardian*, 25 February. Available online at http://www.guardian.co.uk/media/2010/feb/25/phone-hacking-loophole, accessed November 2011

Robinson, Sue (2006) Gateway or Gatekeeping: The Institutionalisation of Online News in creating an altered technological authority, International Symposium on Online Journalism

Rusbridger, Alan (2011a) How We Broke the Murdoch Scandal, *Newsweek*, 17 July. Available online at http://www.thedailybeast.com/newsweek/2011/07/17/how-the-guardian-broke-the-news-of-the-world-hacking-scandal.html, accessed November 2011

Rusbridger, Alan (2011b) Hacking away at the truth: Alan Rusbridger's Orwell lecture, *Guardian*, 10 November. Available online at http://www.guardian.co.uk/media/2011/nov/10/phone-hacking-truth-alan-rusbridger-orwell, accessed November 2011

Rusbridger, Alan (2011c) Alan Rusbridger's statement to the Leveson Inquiry, *Guardian*, 16 November. Available online at http://www.guardian.co.uk/media/2011/nov/16/alan-rusbridger-statement-leveson-inquiry, accessed November 2011

Sabbagh, Dan (2007) Public lives and private eyes put in the spotlight, *Times*, 2 February

Schlesinger, Philip and Tumber, Howard (1994) *Reporting Crime: The Media Politics of Criminal Justice*, Oxford: Oxford University Press

Schudson, Michael (1989) The Sociology of News Production, *Media, Culture and Society*, Vol. 11, No. 3 pp 262-283

Society of Editors (2011) Conference video available at http://www.societyofeditors.co.uk/, accessed November 2011

Trelford, Donald (2011), For now, this 'scandal' is still light on evidence, *Independent*, 21 February. Available online at http://www.independent.co.uk/news/media/opinion/donald-trelford-for-now-this-scandal-is-still-light-on-evidence-2220685.html, accessed November 2011

Tuchman, Gaye (1980) *Making News: A Study in the Construction of Reality*, New York: the Free Press

Wall Street Journal (2011) News and Its Critics, 18 July. Available online at http://online.wsj.com/article/SB10001424052702303661904576451812776293184.html, accessed November 2011

White, David Manning (1964) The 'Gatekeeper': A Case Study in the Selection of News in Tumber, Howard (ed.) (1999) *News: A Reader*, Oxford: Oxford University Press pp 66-72

Whittingdale, John (2009) Uncorrected Transcript of Oral Evidence, HC 275-VI, House of Commons, culture, media and sport committee, 21 April. Available online at http://www.publications.parliament.uk/pa/cm200809/cmselect/cmcumeds/uc275-vi/uc27502.htm, accessed November 2011

Wilby, Peter (2009) The biggest media story in years – so why the silence? *Guardian*, 13 July. Available online at http://www.guardian.co.uk/media/2009/jul/13/news-of-the-world-phone-hacking, accessed November 2011

Wright, Oliver and Morris, Nigel (2011) Revealed: Cameron's 26 meetings in 15 months with Murdoch chiefs, *Independent*, 16 July. Available online at http://www.independent.co.uk/news/uk/politics/revealed-camerons-26-meetings-in-15-months-with-murdoch-chiefs-2314550.html, accessed November 2011

Yates, John (2011) Uncorrected Transcript Of Oral Evidence; Hc 903–I, Culture, Media and Sport Committee, 24 March. Available online at http://www.publications.parliament.uk/pa/cm201011/cmselect/cmcumeds/uc903-i/uc90301.htm, accessed November 2011

Notes on the contributors

Daniel Bennett is a PhD candidate in the War Studies Department at King's College, London. He is writing his thesis on the impact of blogging on the BBC's coverage of war and terrorism (2011). The project is funded by the Arts and Humanities Research Council in conjunction with the BBC College of Journalism. He writes Reporting War, a blog for the Frontline Club in London, which explores the use of new media to cover conflict.

Judith Townend is a doctoral candidate based at the Centre for Law, Justice and Journalism, City University London. Her research interests include privacy and defamation law, media ethics and journalistic processes. She has recently contributed to a number of publications, including the INFORRM media law blog, *Index on Censorship* and Guardian.co.uk. She studied social anthropology at the University of Cambridge before pursuing a career in digital journalism.

Beyond the Red Tops: Sensationalism and Ideology in Serious News

Hackgate is often represented as a triumph of investigative reporting – by the *Guardian*'s Nick Davies in particular. But Justin Schlosberg, focusing on the mainstream media's treatment of the WikiLeaks revelations, argues that the watchdog function of the serious media (including the *Guardian*) remains ultimately more spectacle than substance and more ideological than counter-hegemonic

Introduction

First exposed in the *Guardian*, the phenomenon of Hackgate may be read on one level as a victory for the serious press, and for British democracy at large. As much as it dealt a fatal blow to the *News of the World*, Hackgate seemed to underline the value of professional public interest journalism and its apparent health and vitality in certain sections of the media market. In particular, the story rose to headline dominance on the heels of a string of high-profile controversies exposing corruption and malpractice both at the heart and across the breadth of the British Establishment. Parliament, the Metropolitan Police, the Secret Intelligence Services, royal family and Ministry of Defence have all been on the back foot as a result of exposés in the last two years alone.

'Cablegate' – The *Guardian*-led news story constructed around the leaking of private US diplomatic cables by WikiLeaks in 2010 – epitomised this renewed watchdog confidence, as well as the capacity of broadsheets to influence the global news agenda. In spite of direct threats from the US government, and faced with the sharp end of a structural funding crisis affecting the news industry at large, WikiLeaks' mainstream media partners poured unprecedented resources into analysing and reporting on the leaks, laying bare the hidden duplicitous workings of Western international diplomacy.

This chapter examines coverage of the leaks during the first week of cable releases in November 2010 in two widely assumed mainstays of 'quality' journalism: public service broadcasting and the broadsheet press. Although very much the junior partners within the WikiLeaks informal pact, television outlets became crucial arbiters of salience in their framing and selection of the cable stories. The pact was widely touted as a new model of journalism, bringing order, analysis and responsibility to hacktivist-style journalism online; checking the gatekeeping power of professional journalists and dominant media groups; shining the light of publicity on public interest disclosures and giving a megaphone to whistleblowers; offsetting structural crisis by providing professional journalists with secure access to documentary material at minimal cost. But within a matter of months the holy pact between WikiLeaks and its Anglo-American press partners (the *Guardian* and *The New York Times*) had already ended in bitter acrimony and dispute.

On closer analysis, the performance of serious media in relation to the WikiLeaks cables reveals a troubling picture. Far from championing the whistleblowing cause, the strategy adopted by the mainstream media effectively delegitimised WikiLeaks, marginalised stories of significant public interest, and succumbed to the very whims of exclusivity and sensationalism which foreground the Hackgate scandal.

Above all, it resulted in an ideological filter which side-lined stories pointing to domestic political corruption of an acutely serious and pervasive nature: the subversion of accountability institutions. In particular, two cables highlighted apparent attempts by officials to mislead parliament over cluster bombs legislation and to undermine the on-going Iraq War Inquiry, both with a view to suppressing sensitive aspects of transatlantic military cooperation. These stories were distinct from the more headline-friendly controversies featuring charismatic personalities and easy-to-tell narratives. It is argued here that such stories, which call into question the credibility of due process and accountability mechanisms in liberal democracies, mark the boundaries of public debate and define the serious media's propaganda function.

The following analysis is based on quantitative analysis of media texts and supplemented by qualitative interviews with key journalists and sources. Since measuring public interest value is a notoriously difficult task, I rely predominantly on the discourse of journalists themselves to identify leaks of key significance and then assess the relative prominence they received in the coverage. But the analysis also rests on the assumptions that 1) stories revealing or alluding to corruption are of greater public import than those which centred on personal pen portraits or high society gossip; and 2) stories revealing or alluding to corruption at home were of greater public interest value than those concerning corruption abroad (Chomsky 1989).

The content analysis sample consisted of flagship terrestrial television news coverage, along with the *Guardian*'s print output, during the first week of cable releases. This was the moment in which WikiLeaks became a household name, with headline billing persisting throughout the week. The sample yielded around 80 minutes of focused reportage and studio discussion, along with over 20 thousand words of newspaper articles. With regard to the interview sample, it was considered necessary to solicit responses from a broad range of protagonists given the contesting narratives that have emerged in public discourse (Thorsen, Sreedharan et al. 2011).

These included eight television journalists, one former broadcast editor, three executives (including an in-house lawyer at the *Guardian*), four print journalists, two current and one former WikiLeaks associates, two current senior government press officers and a free speech advocate who has been publicly critical of Wikileaks. The case study culminates in a discussion of the implications of Cablegate in relation to Hackgate and unauthorised disclosure more broadly. It concludes that the watchdog function of the serious press is, not unlike their tabloid counterparts, ultimately more spectacle than substance, and more ideological than counter-hegemonic. Its implicit narrative celebrates accountability mechanisms and institutions, eschewing attention to their limitations and failures.

The Biggest Leak in History

In 2010, WikiLeaks secured what has been regularly touted as the 'biggest leak in history' (Leigh and Harding 2011). Allegedly stemming from a single source within the US military, the trove contained close to a million documents consisting of military intelligence reports from the front lines, as well as diplomatic cables spanning more than two decades. The alleged source was Private Bradley Manning, a junior military intelligence analyst stationed in Baghdad who was arrested in May 2010, having been reported to the authorities by a fellow 'hacker'. He was to spend the next ten months in solitary confinement under conditions that are currently the subject of a UN torture investigation[1]. But the arrest itself was to prove pivotal in ensuring that WikiLeaks became etched into the fabric of global public consciousness. It was after reading about Manning's arrest and the rumoured leaks that Nick Davies, of the *Guardian* – the journalist widely credited as the architect of Hackgate – approached Julian Assange in June 2010. Their subsequent negotiations formed the basis of a partnership between WikiLeaks and the mainstream media that gradually expanded to include *The New York Times, Der Speigel,* and *El Pais* amongst others.

Of the three sets of releases co-ordinated over a period of six months in 2010, the focus here is on the third – a climactic release of secret and confidential communications between the US State Department and its embassies around the world. This followed leaks of military intelligence reports from the wars in Afghanistan and Iraq consecutively. But it was the diplomatic cable releases that marked the peak of coverage intensity and the architects of all three releases were in no doubt as to its ultimate significance. According to Alan Rusbridger, editor of the *Guardian*:

> You could say the World Trade Centre was a bigger story, or the Iraq War. But in terms of a newspaper, where by the act of publication you unleash one story that is then talked about in every single corner of the globe, and

you are the only people who have got it, and you release it each day, this was unique (Leigh and Harding 2011: 199).

For some interview respondents, discrepancies in the balance of coverage and the muted impact of the cables were a function not of the content itself, but of its unimaginable scale. According to this narrative, even with the full weight of mainstream media resources, it was inevitable that important stories would get buried. According to Gavin McFadyen:

> You've got to understand the sheer scale of it. It was like going into a main library somewhere and saying which books are interesting? Well you have to start reading the books to know and there's just a vast amount of material. So it's very difficult I think to make choices other than on subjects we already know about so that you can interrogate the data looking for some stories on the banking crisis say, or something else that you had already had in mind but there might be a lot of material in there on subjects that you don't even know about. So that's part of the problem...You can also go back over some of the documents and realise there are stories in it that you didn't see the first time reading them...It was just the most gigantic mass of material, the most daunting pile you could imagine.

Clearly, the vast scale of the leak meant that extracting newsworthy material from it in the first place was a significant logistical and technical challenge. But it was a challenge that journalists overcame in several respects. Above all, the *Guardian* succeeded in uncovering material from which a wide range of stories covering radically different contexts and locales was produced. Indeed, in some ways the effort to extract news stories from the cables was too successful to the extent that there were too many, and they were too wide ranging for any to leave a meaningful imprint on the public consciousness. One recurring theme that emerged in analysis of interviews was the preponderance of responses that invoked memory loss in respect of the cable stories. In one illuminating interview, Dorothy Byrne, Head of Channel 4 News and Current Affairs, reflected on the importance and legacy of the cables:

> WikiLeaks revealed all sorts of very important information to the public across the world and anybody who says otherwise is just manifestly wrong. I find it bizarre that anybody would say that actually. Very strange. How could they think that it hadn't revealed anything?...Surely when we look back historically that will be what we will remember – we'll remember the important revelations.

But when asked to pinpoint any particular outstanding stories however, none could be recalled:

Oh god, to be honest I can't answer that question. I can't remember that far back so I'm not going to be of use to you…I would have to get it all out and look at it again. So I'm afraid I've got no answer to that question.

The inability to recall stand-out stories was a common admission amongst television journalists. The problem was encapsulated by Richard Watson, a journalist for BBC's *Newsnight* that covered the Iraq war logs extensively but was not directly involved in reporting on the cables: 'There were nuggets in there of real public interest stories. But unfortunately without going back to the archive I can't remember exactly which ones.'

Untold Stories

Amidst the avalanche, certain cables did emerge during the sample period which pointed to serious political corruption in the UK, particularly as regards military co-operation with the US. Two stories stand out in this respect. The first emerged on the third day of the cables and revealed that, according to the US ambassador in London, British officials had assured the US government that they had 'put measures in place' to protect US interests during the Iraq War Inquiry. The news value of this cable, both in terms of 'new information' and public interest weight was underlined by several journalists interviewed for this study. According to Carl Dinnen, reporter for the Channel 4 News, 'if somebody's potentially saying that they're capable of influencing an independent public inquiry into something as important as the Iraq War, that's hugely significant'.

Television journalists were asked during interviews to rank selected stories based on their news value. Seven out of the eight respondents ranked the above story as of equal or greater news value than the story regarding criticism of the UK war effort in Afghanistan by US and Afghan officials. Five of the respondents considered it to be headline material warranting extended analysis and investigation.

This contrasts sharply with the content sample analysed in which criticism of the UK war effort attracted more airtime than any other story during the first five days of coverage, despite only emerging on the penultimate day of the sample period. In stark contrast, the Iraq inquiry story was absent from all news reports and received only passing mention as a 'news in brief' piece on one edition within the sample.[2] This marginalisation was broadly reflective of the *Guardian's* coverage which featured the story only as a relatively minor 300-word article on page 12.[3]

The second story pointing to UK political corruption over military co-operation with the US emerged on day four of the coverage. It was based on a secret account of a meeting between British foreign office officials and their US counterparts in 2009. In it, UK officials are said to have suggested that a planned loophole in forthcoming legislation banning cluster bombs should be kept from parliament. Crucially, the loophole would allow US cluster bombs to be kept on British soil in the island territory of Diego Garcia. The cable paraphrases the Foreign Office official as saying:

> It would be better for the [US government] and [Her Majesty's Government] not to reach final agreement on this temporary agreement understanding until after the [cluster bomb bill] ratification process is completed in Parliament, so that they can tell Parliamentarians that they have requested the [US government] to remove its cluster munitions by 2013, without complicating/muddying the debate by having to indicate that this request is open to exceptions.[4]

The striking implication of this communiqué is that the US and UK governments had effectively colluded in an attempt to mislead parliament and undermine a crucial piece of human rights legislation. Once again however, the story was all but entirely absent from the television sample analysed, mentioned only briefly during a live two-way at 11pm on the BBC's second channel.[5] The topic was introduced by the anchor not as a story pointing to corruption, but rather 'confusion over what the former foreign secretary said about cluster bombs'.

Curiously, however, in this case marginalisation on television was not entirely reflective of the *Guardian*'s coverage which featured the story as a 900-word article on its front page.[6] The title also contrasted starkly from the anchor introduction on *Newsnight*:

> SECRET DEAL LET AMERICANS SIDESTEP CLUSTER BOMB BAN: Officials concealed from parliament how US is allowed to bring weapons on to British soil in defiance of treaty

Nevertheless, the edition as a whole was dominated by reports about Russian state corruption which dwarfed the cluster bombs story in both billing and word count. We are left with a picture of the British 'serious' news sector, consisting of the paper that brokered Cablegate and the core of public service television, as seemingly more concerned with diplomatic gossip and corruption in foreign governments than that within the British state. For all the resources and publicity that the mainstream media brought to bear on the cable releases, information arguably of the most acute British public interest remained confined to the side lines.

De-legitimising the Leaks

But what about the coverage which focused on WikiLeaks as an organisation, and Julian Assange as a figurehead? According to the data, this accounted for just under 40 per cent of all reporting airtime in the television sample. But the figure would be substantially higher if we were to take into account the live two-ways between anchor and correspondents where television journalists are most free to editorialise about the issues covered in reports. Few would argue that the questionable legitimacy of the leaks, and the nature of the leak facilitator, were valid and important public interest issues in their own right. According to Richard Watson of BBC's *Newsnight*:

> There was a tremendously big story behind the actual specific leak about who was Julian Assange, what was the organisation WikiLeaks, what role were they playing? It was almost as significant as the leaks themselves - the fact that we had an organisation here that was riding a coach and horses through previous protocol.

The legitimacy issue had been seized upon by US officials following the first set of releases – the Afghan war logs – in which WikiLeaks itself published more than 76, 000 documents, with comparatively little redaction (Brooke 2011). With the cable stories, WikiLeaks followed the *Guardian*'s lead both in terms of the cables published and in the redactions made. Nevertheless, questions of legitimacy remained pertinent particularly in respect of information that may have yielded little to no accountability value, but potentially damaged diplomatic progress towards peaceful resolution of conflict. Even information activists acknowledged that it was an issue which warranted public debate. Mikael Viborg is the owner of PQR, a Swedish web hosting company that has provided refuge for WikiLeaks under protection of the country's unrivalled free speech protection laws: 'The judgment should lie with the public, after the fact. The public should decide whether this was justified or not.'

But the important question here is whether contesting views were adequately represented in television news. In this respect, television news outlets overwhelmingly privileged official source definitions, perhaps most acutely revealed by the opening sentence of the BBC's first report on the cable leaks: 'Reckless and irresponsible - the White House condemns the website Wikileaks.'[7]

That the framing overwhelming endorsed official source positions was reflected in quantitative findings. Table 1 presents data showing the proportions of critical and supportive sources featured in reports (based on seconds of airtime).

Table 1 Comparing the prominence of sources critical and supportive of the leaks

	Bulletins	Analysis programmes	Early programmes	Late programmes	All
Supportive	12%	79%	14%	35%	27%
Critical	78%	11%	86%	65%	73%

Source: National film archives

In the data above there is one significant outlier which accounts for the relatively extreme inverse proportions shown in the Analysis column. This was a special report by Mark Urban on BBC's *Newsnight* which featured excerpts from an extended interview with David Leigh, of the *Guardian*. Not surprisingly, Leigh was supportive of the leaks which had provided the raw material for his stories. If we were to exclude this outlier from the data, the overall proportion of supportive sources would be just 12 per cent.

Outside of reports, the absence of a 'right of reply' approach to relaying official source views was striking. Consider for instance the following two-way response on a BBC news bulletin:

> Downing Street and the Foreign Office have both in strong terms condemned the publication of these secret messages not necessarily because of their contact but for the very fact that what started off as high level private communications has ended up being out there in public for all to see. They believe that governments do need to be able to communicate with each other in confidence and that governments internally should be able to have things that are private and keep them that way.

Though there is nothing intrinsically wrong with this statement on its own, the fact that it was not followed or preceded by any indication of a contrary view is clearly at odds with the BBC's commitment to impartiality. When reporters did on rare occasion reference alternative source views, they invariably did so in ways that subtly undermined them.

Why did journalists so brazenly abandon impartiality discipline when it came to the legitimacy debate? One plausible explanation is that the legitimacy debate was instinctively seen as an effective right to reply for official sources in response to the leaks themselves. If the majority of the reportage was focussed on the content of cables, the balance of live two-way exchanges was weighted significantly in favour of official source responses. But the problem was that officials by and large did not respond to the content of the leaks but simply attacked the legitimacy of the leak facilitator. In that sense, they effectively waived their right to reply. The attack on the legitimacy of WikiLeaks should have been presented as a distinct narrative with appropriate right to reply afforded to WikiLeaks and their supporters. Instead, official sources were allowed to effectively attack the source of the leaks as a defence against what the leaks revealed and proponents in favour of WikiLeaks were denied a platform.

The Serious News Scoop

One of the great paradoxes of the WikiLeaks story is that in order for the group to maximise ultimate exposure of its documents, it had to initially restrict supply. Herbert Snorasson was a WikiLeaks defector along with Daniel Domscheitt-Berg and the pair went on to found a new – as yet un-launched – leaking organisation. He put the paradox in these terms:

> It's a question of economics. The experience with WikiLeaks is that when the information is 'out there', it gets overlooked because of the risk of

being scooped. If there's an exclusivity period, you stand a much better chance of getting a media organisation to show interest in the material.

For Julian Assange, the ultimate goal is 'to increase perceived value to the point that journalists will invest time to produce quality stories'. The question then becomes: 'Which method should be employed to apportion material to those who are most likely to invest in it?'[8]

But the *Guardian* could not be described as a purely commercially-driven company. Indeed, according to its owners, the title is run on a non-profit basis.[9] The value of exclusivity must, therefore, be seen in a broader context than the pursuit of profit which takes into account the less tangible value derived from credibility branding and peer recognition. Though these may well provide an indirect boost to profitability, they also provide important justification for financial losses and hence, for cross-subsidy support. For the individual journalists and editors who negotiated the basis of exclusivity and had their names attached to the stories that came out, credibility and peer recognition were ends in themselves. Several journalists reflected in interviews on the careerist competitiveness between individuals that often underpins competition between outlets. Individualism within the press is more extensive than in broadcasting 'because broadcast journalists have to work in a team'. There is also, as Vaughan Smith, proprietor of the Frontline Club and supporter of Assange, pointed out, a relatively higher and growing proportion of newspaper journalists who work on a freelance basis. This includes Nick Davies, the journalist who brokered the WikiLeaks partnership for the *Guardian*.

But it was not just the *Guardian* and its journalists whose decisions were driven at least in part by a need for name association and recognition. According to Iain Overton, of the Bureau of Investigative Journalism, a branding battle developed between all multimedia partners:

> I remember that there was a real ding dong about the number of times we mentioned WikiLeaks on our web page and things like that. They wanted more mention and I was like, fine we can mention you a few more times if you want...They just wanted branding. But you can understand – everyone wants branding. The challenge is of course – when you're doing a multimedia collaboration – to work it so that people don't feel that they somehow are going second fiddle. Everyone always wants it to be 'in an investigation with etc'.

A Very British View of Corruption

This still leaves us with the problem of why UK-corruption stories were comprehensively marginalised, even from the analysis and late evening programmes. The problem is located not at the point of story extraction, but of selection and prioritisation. That the raw material for UK corruption stories was uncovered in the first week of release is evident simply and obviously in the fact that the stories did appear, albeit at the margins.

But organisational factors might be invoked on the basis that such a deluge of stories would inevitably create anomalies in the balance of coverage. Anomalies are by their nature not systematic and hence, not ideological. A system or model of ideological dominance could not depend on anomalies in view of their inherently random and unpredictable properties. We might consider the marginalisation of the Iraq Inquiry story to be one such anomaly. On a day in which the *Guardian* coverage was scheduled to give priority to cables emanating from Moscow, it is feasible that the Iraq Inquiry story was overlooked simply because eyeballs were focused elsewhere. This might explain why the controversy was buried on page 12 and why television news outlets, in deference to the *Guardian*'s agenda-leading role, paid it equally little attention.

But the marginalisation of the cluster bombs story is less easy to explain away as an anomaly simply because the *Guardian* gave it top billing. This suggests that television news outlets – elsewhere remaining faithful to the paper's priorities – in this case actively overlooked the story. Nor was this an isolated incident. Another case in point was a cable story which revealed that a Bangladeshi 'death squad' with an appalling human rights record was being trained by UK forces. The story ran on the *Guardian*'s front page on 22 December, long after the initial deluge of cable stories had subsided. But it was not picked up by any BBC or ITN television outlets, despite the day's agenda being relatively free of dominating headlines. In this context, it is worth considering a selection of news items which did make it on to the television news agenda, eclipsing the death squad story:

CYBER ATTACKS BY WIKILEAKS SUPPORTERS: QUESTIONS OVER SEVERITY[10]

ZARA PHILLIPS ANNOUNCES ENGAGEMENT TO MIKE TINDALL[11]

TESCO, SAINSBURY'S, ASDA & MORRISONS EXPANDING AT RATE NEVER SEEN BEFORE[12]

POPE TO BROADCAST CHRISTMAS MESSAGE TO THE BRITISH PEOPLE[13]

An alternative explanation for this marginalisation focuses on the issue of complexity and the relative constraints impinging on the broadcast medium. According to this view, complex stories involving detailed documents simply do not make good television. As Angus Fraser, China correspondent for ITV news, explained:

> Newspapers lend themselves more easily to large amounts of printed material. Putting that into a TV piece is very tricky in terms of what it looks like and whether the viewer could be subjected to what would essentially be page after page of graphicised text. It doesn't really lend itself to television where we deal with moving pictures.

But whilst this may be true of the bulletins, it is not in keeping with the approach taken by analysis programmes which are not only better adapted to cover complex controversies, but often prioritise them in a bid to distinguish their output from that of the bulletins. It was a point emphasised by Richard Watson, of *Newsnight*:

> We've got to be distinctive from other broadcasters, we've got to be distinctive from other newspapers where possible, and also the other news outlets like rolling news, *News at Ten* etc and the way that *Newsnight* does that is either through in depth analysis and discussion of stories, or it's with genuine exclusives and revelatory journalism.

Other journalists were at pains to stress that it is the issue of salience that matters most. For Kevin Marsh, former Editor of BBC Radio Four's *Today* programme, salience can and should transcend problems of both complexity and scale:

> The question you're always asking yourself when you're looking at anything is you know, 'where's the wow thing here?' And even in a very complex story like the cluster bombs story, which is fantastically complicated…but if I can see in a document like that, however complicated the story is, something that makes me go 'wow, right I can tell that story, I can make it mean something' and it makes my jaw drop then I would go for that.

Seen in this light, we might consider the cluster bombs story, and perhaps the Iraq inquiry story as well, to be lacking in the 'wow' factor which propels stories to the top of the news agenda. It is worth reiterating that although the *Guardian* featured the story on its front page, it was dwarfed by the Russian corruption story which dominated the edition. This suggests that there may have been simply insufficient news value in the actual detail of the controversy.

There was certainly a crucial distinction between the UK and Russian corruption stories in that the latter tended to focus on criminality whereas the former centred on subversion of accountability institutions. The cluster bombs story was in essence about an attempt to undermine parliament and the Iraq inquiry story was about the government exercising surreptitious influence over a supposedly independent public inquiry. There was no money laundering or contract killing and the central figures of the story were unknown bureaucrats. In many ways, they were reflective of the fact that institutional corruption was not, in relative terms, a particularly 'sexy' story to tell either on television or in print.

Conclusion
In sum, serious news coverage of Cablegate was ultimately contained by the omission of key public interest stories coupled with the failure of broadcasters to adequately challenge official source responses and in particular, their lack of engagement with allegations stemming from the leaks. This opened the door to

a vociferous and largely unquestioned attack on the legitimacy of WikiLeaks and unauthorised disclosure itself. It precipitated at least in one sense a spectacle of accountability, to the extent that it fed into a broader narrative of change amongst WikiLeaks supporters. The very aggression of official source responses was seen on one level as evidence of a game-change in the balance of informational power between citizens and elites. But the hollowness of official concerns began to surface in early 2011. According to one Reuters source, the US administration had publicly exaggerated the WikiLeaks threat in order to buttress its legal efforts against the group.[14]

This spectacle of accountability has profound implications for the aftermath of hackgate. The appearances of the Murdochs in front of Commons select committee for culture, media and sport have marked the peaks of coverage intensity across the serious/tabloid spectrum. They were tantamount to justice being 'seen to be done'. But it remains to be seen whether meaningful, substantive reform – the basis of true accountability – will manifest as a result of the phone hacking scandal.

Though the Leveson Inquiry into the ethics and practices of the press has set itself a wide ranging remit by any standards, the reaction of the British press has been to close ranks around the narrative that any significant change to the way the media is owned, structured or regulated is, in simple terms, bad news. Such *en masse* resistance does not bode well for the prospects of reform and is compounded by a framing which situates the problem in one particular sub-sector of the press, and in one particular rotten apple which was the former *News of the World*. The tacit implication of this framing is that the mainstays of serious, quality journalism are governed by a professional and credible commitment to serving the public interest above all else.

In contrast, this research has shown that both the *Guardian* and television news are prone to prioritising the wrong stories in public interest terms, at least as defined by journalists themselves. No doubt a degree of inevitable randomness played a part in coverage distortions during Cablegate. But the peculiar dynamics of exclusivity fostered an initial surge of stories which precipitated a good week 'to bury bad news' (including news emerging from the leaks themselves). There was also a tendency to select 'easier' stories from the point of view of both 'cultural congruence' (Entman 2004) and complexity.

Regardless of the causes of marginalisation, its effect was at least on one level ideological. The two stories which pointed to serious corruption 'at home' – subversion of accountability institutions – were marginalised in favour of diplomatic gossip and cables which illuminated corruption in foreign governments. Far from exposing crimes of the establishment, the strategy adopted by the serious news outlets ensured that they were left squarely in the shadows of the media spotlight.

Notes

[1] See
http://www.ohchr.org/en/NewsEvents/Pages/DisplayNews.aspx?NewsID=11231&LangID=E (accessed 17 August 2011). He has since been moved to a medium security prison where he is still awaiting trial at the time of writing.

[2] ITV *News at Ten*, 30 November 2010

[3] For the online version of the article see
http://www.guardian.co.uk/world/2010/nov/30/wikileaks-chilcot-iraq-war-inquiry?DCMP=EMC-thewrap08, accessed on 28 August 2011

[4] See http://www.guardian.co.uk/world/us-embassy-cables-documents/208206, accessed on 28 August 2011

[5] BBC *Newsnight*, 1 December 2010

[6] For the online version see http://www.guardian.co.uk/world/2010/dec/01/wikileaks-cables-cluster-bombs-britain?DCMP=EMC-thewrap08, accessed on 19 July 2011

[7] Bridget Kendall, BBC *One O'clock News*, 29 November 2010

[8] See http://www.wired.com/threatlevel/2008/08/wikileaks-aucti/, accessed on 29 August 2011

[9] See http://www.gmgplc.co.uk/the-scott-trust/, accessed 4 September 2011

[10] *Channel 4 News*, 22 December 2010

[11] ITV *News at Ten*, 22 December 2010

[12] BBC *One O'clock News*, 22 December 2010

[13] BBC *Ten O'clock News*, 22 December 2010

[14] See http://www.reuters.com/article/2011/01/18/wikileaks-damage-idUSN1816319120110118, accessed on 28 August 2011

References

Brooke, Heather (2011) *The Revolution will be digitised: Dispatches from the information war*, London: Random House.

Chomsky, Noam (1989) *Necessary Illusions: Thought Control in Democratic Societies*, Boston: South End Press.

Entman, Robert (2004) *Projections of Power: Framing News, Public Opinion, and US Foreign Policy*, Chicago: University of Chicago Press.

Leigh, David and Harding, Luke (2011), *WikiLeaks: Inside Julian Assange's War on Secrecy*, London: Guardian Books.

Thorsen, E. and Sreedharan, C. (2011) The media politics of Wikileaks: Public service or enemy of state? The Media Studies Conference, BFI, London.

Note on the contributor

Justin Schlosberg is a media activist, researcher and lecturer based at Goldsmiths, University of London. He is author of *Covering Crimes of the Establishment: Media Spectacles of Accountability*, forthcoming 2012 from Pluto Books.

Missing the Target and Spurning the Prize

Tim Luckhurst argues that the main question facing British policymakers is not how to prevent the hacking of telephones – nor even how to limit the political influence of an octogenarian media magnate who has already lost the confidence of several major shareholders. It is how to finance an ethical future

Stripped of the ideological dimensions that have given it such salience in parliament, the mainstream media and the blogosphere, the combination of events we know as Hackgate raises pressing questions about two issues of importance to the future of professional journalism: journalism ethics and journalism finance. This chapter argues that the financial crisis facing journalism is paramount. Without practical and enduring solutions to the profession's acute shortage of revenue and investment, the liberal-capitalist model upon which journalism's relationship with representative democracy depends will wither. Talking about ethics in a world with too few profitable, professional, independent news providers would be largely futile.

Ethics and Reporting

The ethical questions raised by the hacking of telephones belonging to celebrities, politicians and victims of crime include what should be enshrined in a code of ethics for reporters engaged in public interest journalism. Among the plainest lessons of Hackgate is that journalists under pressure circumnavigate rules-based systems. The BBC Editorial Guidelines, a fine set of ethical benchmarks for journalists, acknowledges candidly the key flaw in such detailed guidance. The Director General, Mark Thompson (2011), writes: 'In a perfect world the BBC Editorial Guidelines would consist of one sentence: use your own best judgment. No set of rules or guidelines can ever replace the need for producers, editors and managers to use the wisdom that comes from experience, commonsense and a clear set of editorial and ethical values...'

This chapter seeks to identify elements that might be included in a principles-based code of ethics applicable to all platforms in a multimedia environment. It does not pretend to be the first such attempt – both the BBC Editorial Guidelines and the newspaper and periodical industry's Code of Practice set out ethical guidelines to which journalists should conform – rather it attempts to steer Mark Thompson's 'best judgment'.

Phillips, Couldry and Freedman (2010) offer a trio of core journalism ethics for the multimedia age: accuracy, sincerity and hospitality. Accuracy and sincerity are established liberal values. To do Michael Schudson's 'things news can do for democracy' (2008: 11-27), journalists must make sure that what they say is not false and they must say what they actually believe. They are also relevant to investigation. To reveal information that is valuable to the public sphere, reporters must make every effort to ensure that their discoveries are true. They must report them sincerely, which in this context means completely, in context and without malice.

Absence of malice is crucial and it relates to the third part of the trio: hospitality. Philips, Couldry and Freedman (op cit) define this as the journalist's duty to take account of how what they do affects the conditions for dialogue between cultures and peoples. Stephen Ward (2010) advances a comparable ideal. He believes journalism should promote dialogue 'with liberal and humanitarian forms of thought from all and any cultures'.

Promoting such dialogue need not be reserved for global issues. It applies as neatly to domestic reporting and investigation. The *Guardian*'s exposures regarding Hackgate clearly promote dialogue with liberal and humanitarian forms of thought in that they invite compassion for innocent victims of hacking, encourage debate about the liberal purposes of journalism and promote the interests of the weak and vulnerable. But our acceptance of this principle should be subject to one caveat: to make complete sense, it requires a definition of liberalism as it should apply to journalism. An appropriate definition has existed since 1859 in John Stuart Mill's essay *On Liberty* – a core text for all interested in the purposes journalism serves in representative democracies and for students who wish to become journalists. Mill wrote that:

> The peculiar evil of silencing an expression of opinion is that it is robbing the human race: posterity as well as the existing generation; those who dissent from the opinion still more than those who hold it. If the opinion is right, they are deprived of the opportunity of exchanging error for truth: if wrong, they lose what is almost as great a benefit, the clearer perception and livelier impression of truth, produced by its collision with error.

A basic code for ethical reporting should encompass understanding that, while facts are sacred (accuracy), no opinion based upon them should be censored or silenced. Hospitality should work alongside the idea that we may disapprove of what a sincere journalist says but we should defend robustly their right to say it. While ethical journalism should always be wary of causing harm, it should not be as cautious about causing offence. As David Leigh (2006), investigations editor of the *Guardian*, explains: 'Investigative journalism is not a dinner party, particularly in a secretive country like ours where the privacy cards are stacked in favour of the rich and powerful.'

A code encompassing accuracy, sincerity and hospitality to liberal dialogue plainly does not condone the conduct of the *News of the World* journalists and hirelings who hacked Milly Dowler's mobile telephone. Hacking as a practice can accomplish accuracy, but that does not appear to have been the primary purpose of its extensive use by the *News of the World*. The newspaper did not always hack telephones to confirm or expand evidence acquired by conventional reporting. It appears to have engaged in widespread speculative hacking to gather information devoid of context which might then be presented as sensation. For these reasons its use of hacking – and any similar deployment by other titles – also fails the sincerity test and it is inhospitable. Sometimes it is a distortion of truth, the absence of which robs humanity of nothing worth possessing.

Accuracy, sincerity and hospitality are robust and valuable measures of journalism's worth, but they might be applied to entertaining, inconsequential reporting of the type that amuses without aspiring to Schudson's democratic purposes or attempting to speak truth to power. There can be no serious ethical objection to such journalism; ethical conduct can never become popular if it is defined as austere and sanctimonious, but a further test is required to set the ethical standard for public interest reporting and investigations. It is essentially the one John Birt and Peter Jay set out in a series of three articles published in *The Times* in 1974 condemning a 'bias against understanding' in television journalism and arguing for a 'mission to explain'. Birt would later refine these arguments to argue the case for 'significance'.

Significance, Hackgate and the 'Bias Against Understanding'

Birt defined significance in news broadcasting as the means by which explanation and analysis of public affairs would replace the 'bias against understanding'. Diligently applied to public interest reporting and investigation, it eliminates reductive narratives such as the 'He Said, She Said' formula – which Jay Rosen (2009) has condemned for producing false balance and leaving the reader clueless as to where truth lies.

Significance is relevant to the controversy over telephone hacking because, no matter how blatantly hacking fails other ethical tests, it is hard to demonstrate that the practice itself is intrinsically significant. Just as it can serve ethical or unethical journalism according to the purpose for which it is employed, hacking can also function as effectively in the service of trivial investigations as significant ones. The moral panic we have come to know as Hackgate often fails to distinguish between hacking as a mechanism for invading a celebrity's privacy and hacking to expose wrongdoing.

In the absence of a serious and consistent mission to explain, Hackgate has produced a bias against understanding. Britons have been invited to accept that telephone hacking is intrinsically threatening to ethical, public interest journalism when it isn't. Parliamentary and other informed opinion has focused hard on a problem that poses no great threat to the public sphere while ignoring the tyrannosaur in the nursery.

The Real Threat to Journalism

In September 2011, I wrote in *Times Higher Education* that the phone hacking scandal could hardly have been less well timed (Luckhurst 2011). Professional journalism's survival is threatened by the economic impact of digital technologies. The plurality and diversity of voice upon which representative democracy depends is in jeopardy. Needed urgently is debate about how well-resourced, professional newsgathering can be sustained. Instead, tired concerns about the ethics and ownership of popular newspapers are diverting attention from critical twenty-first century realities.

The hacking of Milly Dowler's mobile telephone generated a moral panic that was seized upon by a curious alliance of elite establishment and left-progressive opinion. At the same time it diverted attention from a crucial debate. That discussion, about whether professionally edited, fact-based journalism can continue to play the role of an estate in the multimedia age, will remain important after those responsible for phone hacking have been punished.

There is a crisis in journalism that has nothing to do with hacking and relates directly to the conduct of public affairs. It started with recognition that the internet has weakened the authority of large-scale professional media organisations and progressed to predictions that it will destroy it. Many thinkers in the field of journalism and media studies believe this and find it irresistible. They cherish the possibility that the power of big-media may be shattered by what laymen call blogging and they grace with the oxymoronic title 'citizen journalism'.

The essential difference between the two is that much blogging is an amateur activity carried out by people with no understanding of journalism's social purpose who operate with scant regard for facts (see, *inter alia*, Keen 2007: 16). Like the activists who, in the late eighteenth and early nineteenth centuries, published illegal newspapers seething with radical ideology, they prefer opinion to evidence. Liberated by broadband from a free market in which their ideas have no traction because too few find them interesting, they bleat – and tweet – wild rumours, half-truths and conspiracies.

That such freedom of expression is welcomed by people no editor would pay to provide copy is neither surprising nor objectionable. That it might replace professional journalism is troubling. As the news cycle accelerates, propelled by digital technology, the need for expert journalism that can distinguish fact from fiction and privilege objectivity over ideology grows too. Partnership with audiences is essential: they now possess the digital, mobile technology to send words, images and opinions to newsrooms at lightning speed. But they need professional journalists to sift and curate that information.

Citizens intrigued by events in Libya, Syria or Greece or interested in the death of Amy Winehouse do, certainly, pay attention to what is trending on Twitter. They take note also of peer-to-peer recommendations on Facebook and other social networking sites. But they do not rely on these horizontal communications to check facts. Once alerted by their friends, many of them follow links to reliable news sites curated by professional journalists.

Audiences have learned to follow this path from amateur information sharing to professional news reporting. They understand that professionally edited mass media has the authority and power to inform and enlighten. They appreciate that there can be a symbiotic relationship between social recommendation and fact-based, professional journalism. Regrettably, they do not yet understand that the expansion of online and social media is undermining the economic foundations upon which professional newsgathering rests.

Circulations Began to Decline – And they have not Stopped

News has never been more accessible or less well funded. A large chunk of blame lies with newspaper proprietors. When the internet was new they chose to offer free access online to editorial content for which they had always charged in their printed editions. Readers saw no compelling reason to pay for content they could read free on their computer screens. Circulations began to decline and they have not stopped. Audit Bureau of Circulations figures (2011) show that in September 2011 the 232,566 daily purchasers of the *Guardian* (down from 424,132 in October 2001 and from 278,129 in September 2010) were subsidising the reading habits of 2,613,405 daily unique users (2011) of Guardian Unlimited, that newspaper's free website. The *Guardian* demonstrated its editorial vigour by pursuing and breaking the telephone hacking story, but it may not survive to produce more such journalism. Indeed, the urgent importance of the financial crisis in journalism may be plainly understood through financial scrutiny of the newspaper that exposed Hackgate.

There is no space here to describe the intricate details of an investigation that has seen the Prime Minister's former Press Secretary, Andy Coulson, and the former Chief Executive of News International, Rebekah Brooks, arrested, occasioned the resignation of Sir Paul Stephenson as Commissioner of the Metropolitan Police and thrown open to parliamentary scrutiny the future of press regulation. Suffice it to say that Hackgate was exposed by a newspaper that may soon be bankrupt. Guardian News and Media, the company that runs the *Guardian*, lost £33 million in the year to March 2011 (This is London 2011). Andrew Miller, chief executive of Guardian News and Media's parent company, Guardian Media Group, has warned that the company could run out of cash in three years (Sabbagh 2011).

Despite this threat, the newspaper's team, led by reporters Nick Davies and Amelia Hill, seized on phone hacking to deliver an extended master class in ethical investigative reporting. It precipitated the crisis in which the *News of the World* was closed, James and Rupert Murdoch were obliged to appear before a parliamentary select committee, News Corporation's bid for BSkyB was abandoned and police, parliamentary and judicial inquiries were established.

The *Guardian*'s losses have reached peaks of £100,000 a day, but while its plight is desperate it is not unique. The *Independent* produces journalism consumed by 13,513,040 monthly unique users online from revenues generated mainly by 176,983 daily sales of its printed edition. It needs the generosity of Alexander Lebedev, its proprietor, as much as *The Times* (429,554 daily sales in September 2011, 678, 498 in October 2001) is kept alive by Rupert Murdoch's deep pockets and his commitment to news printed with ink on paper.

The link from newspapers teetering on the brink of insolvency to hacking is real. Tabloid circulations have been hammered too. The *News of the World* sold an average of 2,667,428 copies every Sunday in June 2011, the last month for which figures exist. In October 2001 it sold 4,104,227. Social networking, satellite television and video games have all taken time once allocated to newspaper consumption. But declining circulation made competition ruthless. And, when circulation wars are intense, journalists often break rules to win market share.

That is the context in which hacking occurred. Comparable pressures helped to generate atrocious journalism in the era of Beaverbrook and Rothermere, Britain's original press barons. Even in the glory days of Fleet Street's red-top tabloids, when Freddie Starr ate hamsters and profits flowed, the urge to beat rivals with attention-grabbing scoops produced excesses. As mobile telephones became ubiquitous in the early 1990s, it did not take unscrupulous journalists long to recognise their potential.

By 1997, when I became a broadsheet newspaper executive, few editors did not know that it was possible to hack a mobile telephone's message box. When it first became controversial I had the process explained to me by a colleague who had never worked for News Corporation. We did not need or use such tricks at the *Scotsman*, but we knew they could be performed. It is ideologically appealing to elite progressives to imagine that such criminality occurred only at newspapers owned by Rupert Murdoch, but it is not true. We know that the *Guardian*'s own David Leigh once hacked a mobile phone. In 2006 Leigh (2006) wrote: 'I, too, once listened to the mobile phone messages of a corrupt arms company executive – the crime similar to that for which Goodman now faces the prospect of jail. The trick was a simple one: the businessman in question had inadvertently left his pin code on a print-out and all that was needed was to dial straight into his voicemail.'

Response to Hackgate Informed by Ideology and Self-Interest

Speculative hacking is deplorable, but only marginally more so than the glee with which it has been seized upon by politicians, elite liberal newspapers and several broadcasters. Their attitude is informed by ideology and self-interest and, sometimes, intensified by jealousy. Some members of both Houses of Parliament despise journalists for revealing the details of their expense accounts.

Editors of near-bankrupt quality newspapers, of which the *Guardian* is probably closest to economic extinction, hate them for their populism and profitability.

Into their toxic embrace walked the late, lamented *News of the World*, plaything of Rupert Murdoch, the man the left loves to loathe. I think *The Simpsons* ridicule him best. The episode in which Fox is a drag race sponsor, along with Amalgamated Pornography, Kingpin Malt Liquor, Laramie Cigarettes and Cop Stopper Exploding Bullets is fun. So is the one in which a Fox telethon spokesperson says: 'Sure, Fox makes a fortune from advertising but it's still not enough,' and 'So, if you don't want to see crude, low-brow programming disappear from the airwaves please call now' (Peterson 2011).

But, for some in parliament and beyond, satire can never beat sanctimony. So, while the revelation that News Corporation hirelings tapped Milly Dowler's telephone appalled ethical journalists, MPs and ideologically hostile journalists barely tried to conceal their joy. Celebrities with grudges to bear and secrets to conceal did not try. For Hugh Grant, ill-chosen celebrity front man for the Hacked Off Campaign, the disgrace of the Screws is manna. He is liberated from any obligation to distinguish between illegal conduct and reporting liable to embarrass him. So are Max Mosley and other C-listers who imagine the discomfort they have suffered at the hands of the red-tops is a constitutional issue.

Robust discussion about whether hacking might ever be in the public interest would be interesting. The answer is plain: David Leigh was right; there are circumstances in which a reporter gaining access to private telephone messages can be morally and ethically justified. If it exposes crime or serious impropriety; if it protects public health and safety; if it prevents the public from being misled by an action or statement made by a powerful individual or organisation, then editors should be allowed to sanction it. The Regulation of Investigatory Powers Act 2000 – which first made phone hacking a criminal offence – should be amended to permit such action in the public interest.

But such reform would not reverse closures of newspapers or redundancies among journalists. It could not secure the future health of the vibrant, commercial press that held Eden to account over Suez, revealed the truth about Thalidomide and brought down John Profumo. It could not keep the *Guardian* fit and free to expose 'the scandal of tax-dodgers with private jets pretending to live in Monaco, but still working four days a week in a London office' (Leigh 2007) as the excellent David Leigh has done. It would not fund the meticulous investigation through which the *Guardian* exposed hacking.

It is hard to persuade the British electorate to think about the processes whereby the news that informs their democracy is gathered and distributed. Privacy law, libel tourism and an increasingly stretched law of contempt have barely raised a murmur despite the efforts of editors to publicise their woes. The closest the general public usually gets to thinking about the cost of journalism is when they pay the BBC licence fee. Despite that, there are many Britons who will complain about a pay wall at *The Times* and still believe that BBC journalism is free despite the annual disappearance from their bank accounts of Auntie's £145.50 levy. It is worth every penny, but free it is not. Nor is any journalism of quality.

I welcome Lord Justice Leveson's Inquiry into press ethics and practices in relation to the public, politicians and police. It is an appropriate response to a profoundly troubling episode in public life. It is essential that operations Weeting and Elveden (the Metropolitan Police investigations into telephone hacking and alleged payments to police) be pursued thoroughly. But when each of these appropriate reactions to egregious conduct is complete, journalism's core crisis will remain. The pressing question that deserves more thought than hacking is how to fund expensive investigative, foreign and public interest reporting in the multimedia age.

Matt Drudge's decade-old predictions that, in the internet age, 'every citizen can be a reporter, can take on the powers that be' and that the net 'gives as much voice to a 13-year-old computer geek...as to a CEO or Speaker of the House' (see Hargreaves 2005: 132-133) is daily exposed as naïve. Most loners with computers lack the skills and ethics to gather and report news. A minority who do not, including some who provide a valuable critique of mainstream news values, face the same difficulties their predecessors in the era of print struggled to overcome: they lack the resources to achieve scale, resist legal pressure and speak truth to power at a volume power cannot ignore.

Crucial Role of the Non-Corporate Media

Keeble (2011) emphasises the crucial role played by the non-corporate media in the development of alternative journalism. It also spawned journalists such as Robespierre, who regarded his ideological opponents as criminals and insisted that, 'We must rule by iron those who cannot be ruled by justice.' Similarly brutal populism is common online, not because it represents majority opinion but because the net permits free expression of prejudice. Unaccompanied by a large-scale, professional news industry informed by ethical values, the chaotic anarchy of the internet may disappoint us by nurturing a new generation of zealots.

Before Hackgate, a consensus was beginning to emerge among professional journalists and analysts of journalism that networked individuals and traditional media would learn to work together in the public interest. Citizens with information would help professional reporters to do a better job of keeping the powerful honest and accountable to the people they serve. Professional journalists, working within robust ethical guidelines would fulfil their duties and offer the engaged citizens of the 21st century what Eric Hobsbawm called 'an explanatory narrative adequate to its complexities' (see Holden 2002).

Since the emergence of representative democracy in economically liberal nation states, professional journalism has served the public sphere well. It has helped citizens to engage in critical debate about the practices of government and state. It has exposed wrongdoing, helped to keep power honest and advanced the case of reform. It has defended democracy and civil rights. When every celebrity has changed the default settings on their mobile phone, the challenge of ensuring that good journalism can continue to perform these duties will remain urgent.

The internet can make this possible. It allows reporters to work collaboratively with their audiences and gives them access to an unprecedented range of data and sources. But the multimedia skills required to nurture, fertilise and reap such collaborative journalism do not come cheap. They demand the backing of profitable newsrooms sufficiently wealthy to maintain independence from government and informed by ethical values: newsrooms such as the ones maintained by several great British newspapers that are alarmingly close to collapse.

John Kampfner (2011), Chief Executive of *Index on Censorship*, recently made a powerful case against treating hacking as the biggest problem confronting journalism in an article for *Media Guardian*. Kampfner argued that modern 'journalism is too weak, not too strong'. He advised Lord Justice Leveson to 'prevent wrongdoing without killing an already sickly patient' and he pointed out – via comparisons with continental European systems of media regulation – that state intervention in the activities of a free press very rarely serves the public interest. I would add that it may, of course, serve the ideological purposes of those who believe the state can be a magnanimous leviathan.

Lord Judge, the Lord Chief Justice (2011), added his voice to this rising murmur of support for a raucous and unencumbered free press in his keynote speech to a human rights law conference in London. He pointed out that an independent press will, from time to time, behave with 'scandalous cruelty and unfairness' but on the same day another part of it will expose scandal and hold power to account. Lord Judge concluded that the public value of the second role is priceless. He warned that, whatever means of regulation are designed to reduce the occasions of unacceptable behaviour by elements of the press, 'they must not simultaneously, even if accidentally, diminish or dilute the ability and power of the press to reveal and highlight true public scandals or misconduct'.

How Lord Leveson and the legislature that appointed him can avoid 'diminishing or diluting' that ability in a market in which the most ethical news providers are all loss making is difficult to predict. Easier to perceive is the excellence, reach and impact of professional journalism produced in the arena of foreign news while Hackgate was unfolding.

Ethical Foreign Coverage

Sambrook (2010: 99) identifies three key roles for professional foreign affairs journalists in the multimedia era. He argues that they should provide three core services:

- coverage of breaking news and live events;
- deep specialist niche content with analysis and expertise;
- the aggregation and verification of other sources of information.

While Hackgate and its aftermath were powerful presences on the domestic news agenda, British consumers of professional journalism were provided with extensive reporting of that other great phenomenon of 2011, the so-called 'Arab Spring'. Examples in that coverage illustrate that the ability to serve Sambrook's purposes exists and is already being deployed. These examples meet the ethical tests of accuracy, sincerity and hospitality to liberal dialogue. They are also significant.

1) Coverage of Breaking News

Speed and commercial reward do not ethical journalism make, but beyond the adrenaline-fuelled enthusiasm of those involved and the technological allure of portable BGAN satellite links, some of the journalism Sky News produced in Libya has confirmed the enduring ethical value of eye witness reporting in the multimedia age. Chief Correspondent Stuart Ramsay's fever always to be first did not just bring live pictures of fighting to our homes and iPads (Ramsay 2011). It delivered evidence of the murder of prisoners by pro-regime troops at a military compound south east of Tripoli.

However, as the BBC's Jon Leyne (2011: 42) observes in his chapter for *Mirage in the Desert? Reporting the Arab Spring*, 'It's not just a question of journalists scripting a live action Hollywood action movie. Without intelligent analysis and explanation, the viewers, listeners and readers would soon grow bored of the spectacle.' British viewers, listeners and readers have been well served in this regard.

2) Specialist Content with Analysis and Expertise

On Thursday 20 October, the *Guardian* published in print and online Angelique Chrisafis's feature describing the post-euphoric reality of life in Sidi Bouzid, the small town in Tunisia's interior where Mohammed Bouazizi, the Gavrilo Princip of the 'Arab Spring', killed himself on 17 December 2010. Chrisafis (2011) reported the violence and squalor created and experienced by a desperate generation of educated and skilled Tunisians who believe they have no chance of obtaining work. The accompanying analysis by Ian Black (2011) described the dangers of 'presenting Tunisian politics as a zero-sum game, with a Westernised and technocratic liberal elite worrying about the economy, versus Islamists with a hidden agenda on the other'. Here was work that met my ethical tests.

As compelling was BBC correspondent Gabriel Gatehouse's determined attempt to hold to account those Libyan fighters who imagined that a new democratic era for their country might properly begin with the brutal and summary killing of Colonel Gaddafi. Gatehouse recognised that the dictator's death might offend the rule of law and the principles of due process and civil liberty upon which representative democracy depends. He began to ask how a democratic future can be built upon conduct that rejects democratic values. (BBC News, 7 and 8 November 2011). His work on radio, television and online ticked my ethical boxes.

3) Aggregation and Verification of Other Sources of Information

The curatorial role journalism must perfect if it is to provide valuable service in the era of horizontally connected citizens was performed to expose the hoax we now know as the 'Gay Girl in Damascus'. Daniel Bennett (2011), a PhD candidate in the War Studies Department at King's College, London, has described this process in another excellent chapter for *Mirage in the Desert?, Reporting the Arab Spring*. Bennett demonstrates that traditional journalists deploying traditional tools would not have exposed Tom McMaster – the postgraduate student at Edinburgh University who invented Amina Araf, a.k.a. the fictional 'Gay Girl in Damascus'. Partnership between old and new models of journalism performed the task. By exposing the false and allowing us to recognise the 'authentic voices' seeking political change this curatorial partnership served ethical purposes admirably.

From the Arab Spring to Hacking

While the future shape of excellent public interest journalism is emerging all around – and journalists are worrying desperately about how it will be financed. Lord Justice Leveson is exploring the relics of a discredited past. His work may be useful – an effective, independent replacement for the PCC would be good for journalism but its work will matter most in the event that populist tabloids are the best funded survivors of journalism's economic crisis. Since the closure of the *News of the World*, these are the titles most directly engaged in the popular, celebrity journalism that millions of Britons continue to purchase with alacrity.

I reject Hugh Grant's view (Kampfner 2011) that the famous have every right to determine when and how their private lives should remain private. John Kampfner (2011) is right: the main difference between a celebrity who profits from their private life and one who complains about intrusion *is* that the former has a better agent. Many stories the public are interested in are insignificant, but there is nothing hospitable in the view that popular journalism must be restricted and newspaper profits further undermined. It oozes arrogance and condescension in the service of a cause – restraining the tabloid press – which the internet has rendered redundant.

Lord Leveson's attention is concentrated on problems the solution of which will not nurture ethical journalism. There is a fair amount of it about – and it is beginning to make excellent use of new technologies to deliver accuracy and sincerity, hospitality and significance. The real crisis facing ethical professional journalism is that it is commissioned and published almost exclusively by newspapers and broadcasters that are losing money or dependent on subsidy.

The prize is discernible. We can have excellent coverage of breaking news and live events. We can have deep specialist analysis and expert curation. These services can be supplied ethically to issues of significance at home as well as abroad. But how such work is to be funded if profitable, popular journalism cannot be deployed to subsidise it remains a mystery.

Professional journalists can benefit from a clear set of ethical guidelines, but they already know how to provide excellent service to the public sphere. Their work this year has demonstrated that. The question facing British policymakers is not how to prevent the hacking of telephones – or even how to limit the political influence of an octogenarian media magnate who has already lost the confidence of several major shareholders. It is how to finance an ethical future.

References

Audit Bureau of Circulations (2011) Newspaper circulations. Available online at www.guardian.co.uk/media/abcs, accessed on 8 November 2011. Daily unique user figures for newspaper websites cited in this chapter are for June 2011. Available online at www.guardian.co.uk/media/2011/jul/28/abce-june-mail-online?INTCCMP=SRH, accessed on 8 November 2011

BBC News (2011) Libyan Forces Capture Gaddafi, 7 November. Available online at www.bbc.co.uk/news/world-middle-east-15385955, accessed on 7 November 2011

BBC News (2011) Muammar Gaddafi: How He Died. Available online at www.bbc.co.uk/news/world-africa-15390980, accessed on 8 November 2011

Bennett, Daniel (2011) A 'Gay Girl in Damascus': the Mirage of the 'Authentic Voice' and the Future of Journalism, Mair, John and Keeble, Richard Lance (eds) *Mirage in the Desert? Reporting the Arab Spring*, Bury St Edmunds, Abramis Academic pp 187-195

Black, Ian (2011) Failure Could Begin 'Arab Autumn', *Guardian*, 20 October p.19

Chrisafis, Angelique (2011) The Revolution Is Unfinished. Daily Life Has Changed, But for the Worse, *Guardian*, 20 October pp 18-19

Grant, Hugh (2011) Speech at Liberal Democrat Conference, 18 September 2011 cited in

Hargreaves, Ian (2005) *Journalism: A Very Short Introduction*, Oxford: Oxford University Press pp 132-133

Holden, Anthony (2002) Reporting the Reporters: Review of People's Witness by Fred Inglis, the *Observer*, 5 May. Available online at www.guardian.co.uk/education/2002/may/05/highereducationnews, accessed on 7 November 2011

Judge, Lord Justice (2011) Speech on press regulation – full text. Available online at www.guardian.co.uk/media/2011/oct/19/lord-chief-justice-press-regulation, accessed on 8 November 2011

Kampfner, John (2011) Leveson Throws Media's Future in the Air – But Where Will It Land?, *Guardian*, 3 October p. 30

Keeble, Richard (2011) How Alternative Media Provide the Crucial Critique of the Mainstream. Available online at www.medialens.org/index.php?option=com_content&view=article&id=38:how-alternative-media-provide-the-crucial-critique-of-the-mainstream&catid=1:alerts&Itemid=9, accessed on 7 November 2011

Keen, Andrew (2007) *The Cult of the Amateur*, Boston: Nicholas Brealey

Leigh, David (2006) Scandal on Tap, *Guardian*, 4 December. Available online at www.guardian.co.uk/media/2006/dec/04/mondaymediasection, accessed on 7 November 2011

Leigh, David (2007) Are Reporters Doomed?, *Guardian*, 12 November. Available online at www.co.uk/media/2007/nov/12/mondaymediasection.pressandpublishing3, accessed on 7 November 2011

Leyne, Jon (2011) The Reverberating Echo Chamber – Beyond the Spectacle, Mair, John and Keeble, Richard (eds) *Mirage in the Desert? Reporting the 'Arab Spring'*, Bury St Edmunds: Abramis.pp 40-43

Luckhurst, Tim (2011) Black and White and Dead All Over, *Times Higher Education*, 8 September pp 38-43

Mill, John Stuart (1859) *On Liberty*, Acton, H. B. (ed.) (1972) *Utilitarianism, On Liberty and Considerations on Representative Government: J.S. Mill*, London: J.M. Dent & Sons Ltd, first published in Everyman's Library 1910, this edition pp 65-170

Peterson, Brian (2011) Swipes at Fox on the *Simpsons*. Available online at www.snpp.com/guides/foxswipe.html, accessed on 7 November 2011

Phillips, Angela, Couldry, Nick and Freedman, Des (2010) An Ethical Deficit? Accountability, Norms and the Material Conditions of Contemporary Journalism, Fenton, Natalie (ed.) *New Media Old News*, London: Sage

Ramsay, Stuart (2011) Their Skeletons Were Still Smouldering. Available online at http://news.sky.com/home/world-news/article/16058092, accessed on 7 November 2011

Rosen, Jay (2009) He Said, She Said Journalism: Lame Formula in the Land of the Active User. Available online at http://archive.pressthink.org/2009/04/12/he said_shesaid.html, accessed on 7 November 2011

Sabbagh, Dan (2011) *Guardian* and *Observer* to adopt 'digital first' strategy. Available online at http://www.guardian.co.uk/media/2011/jun/16/guardian-observer-digital-first-strategy, accessed on 11 November 2011

Sambrook, Richard (2010) *Are Foreign Correspondents Redundant?* Oxford: Reuters Institute for the Study of Journalism

Schudson, Michael (2008) *Why Democracies Need an Unlovable Press*, Cambridge: Polity Press

Kelly, John (2009) *Red Kayaks and Hidden Gold: the Rise, Challenges and Values of Citizen Journalism*, Oxford: Reuters Institute for the Study of Journalism

This is London (2011) Available online at http://www.thisislondon.co.uk/markets/article-23963174-loss-making-guardian-risks-all-on-digital-first.do, accessed on 4 November 2011

Thompson, Mark (2011) Director General's introduction to the BBC Editorial Guidelines. Available online at www.bbc.co.uk/editorialguidelines, accessed on 8 November 2011

Ward, Stephen (2010) *Global Journalism Ethics*, Montreal: McGill-Queen's University Press

Note on the contributor
Tim Luckhurst is Professor of Journalism at the University of Kent. Parts of this chapter have previously appeared in *Times Higher Education*.

Section D. Ethics: 'That's a county east of London innit?' (attributed to Kelvin MacKenzie, former Editor of the *Sun*)

John Mair

Lord Leveson's Inquiry is into the culture, practices and *ethics* of the press. Ethics the way journalists behave or misbehave – is at the heart of the whole phone hacking saga and scandal. Is it ethical, if not legal, to hack the mobile phone of a 'target' – celebrity or not? Is it then 'ethical' then to use that information in a published story? What exactly does 'ethics' mean in the morality free zone that plainly too many tabloid newsrooms have become? Is ethics really 'a county east of London' as famed former *Sun* Editor Kelvin MacKenzie is reported to have said when asked about them.

But, in any case, what are journalistic ethics, how are they taught, how are they imbibed in newsrooms and how are they subverted or destroyed by the culture of a newsroom or news organisation?

John Mair, chair of the Institute of Communication Ethics (which organised the conference from which this text emerged), points out the similarity between the hit television reality show TOWIE: The Only Way is Essex, and the phone hacking drama unravelling before our eyes at the Levinson Inquiry. He looks at the lessons to be learned from Hackgate: TOWIE (not) and salutes the qualities of the good investigative journalism by Nick Davies, of the *Guardian* which brought it all to light.

Eamonn O'Neill is a very experienced investigative journalist in print, radio and television over many decades. He now teaches it to journalism students in Scotland. His contribution looks at some of the short cuts which he has had to take to get a 'result' but in the public interest.

Jackie Newton and Sallyanne Duncan examine one particular act which tests journalism ethics – the 'death knock' on a deceased person's relatives, friends and/or colleagues to get hold of photographs. Short cuts were not unknown there. These have become easier with social media such as Facebook and their treasures troves behind thin electronic walls. Yet Newton and Duncan worry that protection or regulation of this facet may not help free journalism

In another piece examining 'death knocks' and related issues, Glenda Cooper looks at how the internet, and especially Facebook, can be used ethically (or not so) by journalists today. The 'death knock' does not have to happen on a front door. She looks at some of the damage which can be caused by this easy – and lazy – journalism.

The internet is at best morally confusing, at worst a jungle. Anything goes. Sean Dodson lays out some basic guidelines – currently missing from any codes – for journalists using online material

Is unethical behaviour inevitable and unavoidable? Should journalists be allowed *not* to cover a story they find unethical or distasteful? Should they be allowed a 'conscience clause'? Tony Harcup, author of *The Ethical Journalist* (Sage, 2007) argues that any 'conscience clause' will not heal all of journalism's ills. He sees it is a fairly modest proposal. But, he stresses: 'Given the ethical vacuum that appears to have been created in certain newsrooms by the almost totally unconstrained management prerogative that followed Rupert Murdoch's victory at Wapping in 1986, isn't it time we gave it a try?'

Finally, asks Chris Frost, should we not acknowledge the National Union of Journalists' central role in setting the moral framework in the workplace? Ethical standards will improve when journalists are allowed to belong to their union without fear of reprisals, argues Frost, chair of the NUJ's Ethics Council. Fear, he says, has prevented many journalists from speaking out about phone hacking and other 'dark arts'.

So, is the Only Way for the Future Ethics?

TOWIE: The Only Way is (Not) Ethics?

Hackgate and Leveson have become the autumn's must-see viewing for the chattering classes, according to John Mair who takes a critical peep at all the sensational goings-on. But at least, he says, it all proves something useful: good, investigative journalism works!

TOWIE: The Only Way is Essex has been the 'structured reality' (whatever that is) television Hit of 2011. It follows a group of Essex wannabes as they go about their bizarre daily lives. TOWIE (Not): The Only Way Is (Not) Ethics has been the chattering classes' hit of 2011. This follows a seemingly amoral group of journalists, their editors and proprietors through an ethical and legal minefield on phone hacking, much of it live on television. It has well earned the moniker Hackgate and looks likely to end up in the criminal courts and maybe prison for some of the TOWIE (Not) has beens.

TOWIE (Not) has so much drama that it has put any reality show, structured or not, to shame. This serial takes place in parliamentary committee rooms, the High Court in the Strand and, soon, in a series of magistrate and higher courts. The major act has so far gone on for six months publicly but the events about which they talk stretch back over a decade. It will run and run...

The Whole World is Watching...

Prelude: Picture the scene. One of the main streets of a tropical paradise and the land of my birth: Guyana. An Old Colonial Club. Mid morning in the Tropics. I am riveted to my laptop and a live feed of an old man and a young buck testifying to a British parliamentary select committee. Why? Because today, 19 July 2011, 80-year-old Rupert Murdoch, the most powerful media magnate of our time, and his 39-year-old son and (then) presumed heir James are giving evidence to the House of Commons culture, media and sport select committee hearing on phone hacking. The whole world is watching, even in Guyana.

Rupert is playing the old man who cannot comprehend and is full of remorse (but with a young wife and several *consigliere* behind to support him) whilst James

('Mr USA MBA') is playing the know-it-all and interpreter for the old codger. But they simply do not or if they do they are not telling it. This is un-missable wall-to-wall viewing even in the tropical heat.

Five months later. A cold day in Oxfordshire. Same laptop. Same huge interest. 29 November 2011. Paul McMullan, the former Deputy Features Editor of Murdoch's *News of the World* is giving oral evidence to the Leveson Inquiry on the culture, practice and ethics of the press. That will sit for at least a year and will, without doubt, change British journalism forever. McMullan is a caricature of the tabloid journalist. The hack's nightmare. You can almost picture him in the long raincoat and trilby with a 'PRESS' card tucked in. He has retired from journalism to another trade – he runs a pub in Dover.

McMullan's evidence is jaw dropping. He admits when on the *News of the World* to breaching people's privacy as a matter of course, harassing them and more. In his world view – and he says also of his fellow tabloid hacks – 'Privacy is for paedophiles'. This, too, is unmissable viewing. Hackgate and Leveson have become the autumn's must-see viewing for the chattering classes. This breaks through to popular culture too when 'ordinary people' such as the parents of Milly Dowler and Madeleine McCann and cult figures such as J. K. 'Harry Potter' Rowling and Hugh Grant tell of being the hunted – not the hunter.

Hackgate has pulled the Murdoch media empire (the biggest in Britain) apart at the seams this year. It could yet lead to its downfall. What started as a small bush fire – *News of the World* royal editor Clive Goodman and his private detective friend Glenn 'Trigger' Mulcaire having their collars felt and being detained at Her Majesty's pleasure in 2007 for hacking illegally into the phones of the royal family and others – could become the forest fire that consumes the latter day Citizen Kane. That one 'rogue reporter' (as News International kept telling the world) became several rogue reporters and eventually a whole rogue newsroom in the *News of the World*.

Several Bin Bags of Documents left Unturned

Back in 2009, the Metropolitan Police investigated and found nothing much of concern, though they left several bin bags full of documents unturned. A smart firm of lawyers – Harbottle and Lewis – was brought in to give the organisation, quickly and cheaply, a clean bill of health and they did. No surprise there. The Press Complaints Commission, the so-called self regulator of the British press, 'investigated' and also found nothing. That was when the *Guardian* first broke the story to much Fleet Street indifference and even derision. Things then looked good for News Int. and the Murdochs. They had escaped the ethical noose.

Yet it took just one journalist – Nick Davies, of the *Guardian*, and his *uber*-supportive Editor Alan Rusbridger – to keep digging despite all setbacks and those throwing cold water on the story to blow the cover of the Murdochs and News International. The 'rogue' reporter was a 'rogue newspaper'. That closed.

It was a triumph of investigative journalism. The few hacked by NI in 2007 became nearly 6,000 in late 2011.

The smoking gun that turned Hackgate from a chattering classes' story to a national scandal was the discovery that the *News of the World* had commissioned the hacking of the phone of murdered, but then merely missing, teenager Milly Dowler in 2002. That gave false hope to her parents and may have hampered the police search for her killer. The line in the journalistic ethical sand, already slight amongst Britain's 'red tops', had been firmly crossed The 'News and Screws' was now a pariah paper and a rapid advertiser boycott (helped, it must be said, by a benevolent Twitter tribe) forced the Murdochs to close it down within four days after 168 proud years of existence.

Within two weeks the Chief Executive Officer of News International, Rebekah Brooks, was forced to fall on her sword. So too the Metropolitan Police Commissioner, Sir Paul Stephenson (his case not helped by his having taking a huge hotel gift from a friend) one of his Assistant Commissioners John Yates (the man who had shown a lack of curiosity over eleven black bags of evidence in 2009) and so also the Chair of the PCC, Baroness Buscombe.

Murdochs Dragged Kicking and Screaming to Select Committee

The Murdochs, *père et fils*, were dragged kicking and screaming to that July Commons committee where Rupert's *faux* senility, a pretend pie and wife Wendy Deng's right hand saved their bacon at least for another day. The Drama seemed to be reaching a *denouement*. It wasn't. The Commons culture committee had more hearings; so too did at least two other parliamentary select committees and Lord Leveson set up his judicial inquiry into culture and ethics. That opened with a couple of barnstorming seminars to focus his Lordship and his panel of advisers then properly and under oath in the august setting of the Royal Courts of Justice in the Strand. Leveson has proved to be a Pandora's Box of revelations about tabloid practices and tabloid mores in modern Britain,

What are the ethical lessons to be drawn from this Eton mess of a scandal? Firstly, some journalists have few ethics when it comes to getting a story. If you need to hack a mobile phone, you do or get a 'tec' to do it for you and on an industrial scale if needs be. That is just part of the armoury that includes 'blagging' (using deceit to obtain somebody's private details, health records, bank records, whatever) and more.

McMullan's Leveson appearance and his *tour d'horizon* of the twisted moral compass of tabloid hacks should be played to all first year wannabe journos at university as the antipathy of what we might expect.

Secondly, the *News of the World* editors know or knew what was happening even if they pretended to look the other way. Clive Goodman, the original 'rogue reporter', revealed this in his 2007 resignation letter to Les Hinton, then CEO of News International in Britain (a former *consigliere* who was forced to resign after 52 years serving 'Rupe' because of Hackgate). Dissembling about that knowledge does not cut the mustard for long. Rebekah Brooks was 'on holiday' when Milly Dowler's phone was hacked, Andy Coulson, Goodman's editor, saw no evil or says he did not. Coulson, unbelievably as it seems now, less than a year later, was the Prime Minister's chief official spokesman until January 2011 when reality caught up with him.

David Yelland, the former editor of Murdoch's *Sun*, who worked with Brooks and Coulson at NI, told a Coventry Conversations audience in December 2010 that it was inconceivable that the editor did not know about the £100,000 plus a year paid to Glenn Mulcaire. Anything more than £1000 would have to be signed off by 'someone in deep carpet land. It would be impossible for anyone at News International to not know what was going on'. Further down the newspaper food chain Darren Parkin, Editor of the *Coventry Telegraph*, told another Coventry Conversations audience in 2010/2011: 'As Editor I know every cough and spit in my newsroom.' Plainly, Coulson was deaf as well as blind when it came to phone hacking.

A Culture of Phone Hacking at *NoW*

Secondly, one 'rogue reporter' cannot operate in isolation or without support. Goodman was part of a culture of phone hacking at the *News of the World*. The truth of that is now becoming clear as more and more associated with the scandal (or the parallel but so far largely unreported one of 'bungs' to policemen) are having their collars felt by the re-invigorated Metropolitan Police investigation. As of 7 December 2011, 18 people have been arrested and bailed to appear at a later date.

But is the *News of the World* newsroom like an isolation ward in the Murdoch Empire? The only one with the 'hacking' disease? Is the *Sun* newsroom next door pure as the driven snow? Are the other Murdoch tabloid newsrooms round the world clean and uncontaminated? Almost certainly not. My hunch is that the Empire is rotten to the core driven by the ethics of Rupert Murdoch, sheer competition and the need to make big profits.

Thirdly, press self regulation in the UK is as dead in the water as a wooden duck in an MP's pond. Dead and buried. It was always a nonsense for the editors to regulate themselves delivering an odd slap here and there to little avail. The fig leaf of lay members of the PCC was always just that. You cannot be the judge and jury in the modern world. Broadcasters in Britain are subject to the rigours of the law, so why should the press not be? The newspapers have drunk their last drink in the last chance saloon. The 2011 Society of Editors conference examined Hackgate and the PCC from every which way and concluded that the best posture to take was an ostrich one. Denial and tinkering with the PCC was the order of the day. This simply will not wash. Lord Justice Leveson will be the lever for change there.

Fourthly, the police and the press are too often in bed with each other aided by greased palms and other favours. It appears to reach right to the top. Sir Paul Stephenson even went to warn off the *Guardian* on the phone hacking story. News International .executives went in and out of a revolving door at Scotland

Yard – allegedly with pockets full of gold. That had to stop and will stop. Some investigative journalism may suffer as a result but it is a small price to pay.

Fifthly, politicians need also to get out of the beds of the press barons and lose their fear of their power. Murdoch had ready access – even if he went in by the back door – to No. 10 Downing Street under the last three Prime Ministers: Blair, Brown and Cameron. The access nexus was more informal too.

The Murdoch/Cameron 'Chippie' set

The Murdoch tribe cultivated Cameron in his Chipping Norton country lair. The 'Chippie' set over the Christmas 2010 period grew to resemble the 'Cliveden set' eighty years earlier. The Murdochs, Freuds, Brooks and Camerons were continually hopping in and out of each other's dining rooms in the North Oxfordshire countryside. It was unhealthy and much under-reported at the time. David Cameron says he took a self-denying ordinance and never had any 'inappropriate' conversations with his News International/News Corporation hosts.

Their attempt to take over the rest of the very profitable Sky Television they did not already own – launched when they spotted a favourable political wind after the 2010 election of the Conservative/Liberal Democrat Coalition – came literally within hours of succeeding and was only derailed by the explosion of Hackgate in July 2011. It was a close call and one that should never occur again. Politicians are elected, media baronies are not. That division of power should be well policed.

Last, good journalism works! Nick Davies (and Alan Rusbridger) of the *Guardian*, did not give up for two years and more. Davies did what good, hard working hacks do – he dug, dug and dug and ignored the noises off, however powerful the voices. Some journalists have an ethical frame and they will be determined to get to the truth, however uncomfortable for them. The *Guardian* is already being garlanded with newspaper/media industry awards. Deservedly.

Murdoch may fall

The end of this particular drama is a long way off. Leveson Part One is six months off reporting. That will undoubtedly be followed by legislation on regulation. The criminal charges have yet to be heard in the magistrates courts of London. There's a long road between them and freedom or not for the nearly two score defendants. Then, Leveson goes into Part Two of his investigation on the practices in that *News of the World* newsroom.

The biggest lesson from all of this is simple. In newspapers, as in the world, The Only Way *is* Ethics: TOWIE. That is the reality, structured or not.

Investigative Journalism and its Relationship to the Hacking Scandal – Confessions of an (Ethical) Investigative Journalist

Eamonn O'Neill reflects on the limits and restrictions under which he has worked on investigations for the UK print and broadcast media over the last two decades and how it relates to the hacking scandal

Introduction

In choosing projects to reflect on for this chapter, I have tried to be mindful of the fact that not all readers will be familiar with the professional world inhabited by journalists who specialise in investigations. Therefore, I begin with a brief, if also philosophical, job description based on the 22 years which I have worked in this genre of journalism. A definition of what constitutes 'investigative journalism' is also briefly mentioned here, as much to remind ourselves of where the qualitative bar should be set, as opposed to where it is often to be found.

Four examples of cases I have worked on for various platforms are cited here. These are chosen to illustrate how solid investigations can be carried out with comprehensive legal oversight which does not restrict or inhibit robust investigative practices. On at least two occasions I explain how I may have breached the law (or at least bent it) in the name of hard-hitting journalism. In all examples, pushing at the boundaries (e.g. going undercover) was not my first option but actually my *last*. The examples explain the processes I underwent for newspapers, glossy-magazines, newspaper magazines and national broadcasters.

I have not chosen the examples which show me in the best light simply because I know there are plenty of colleagues out there who could testify to my many mistakes down the years. Instead, I have selected the examples I felt throw light on the oversight current regulation and guidelines which exist in our profession. I do not intend to examine in minute detail the laws governing the

196

media in the UK, since I know there are colleagues better-qualified than me who can a far better job. Instead, with an eye on my university-teaching role and academic-responsibilities, I intend to explain and analyse what it is like to undertake difficult and high-profile investigations within the recent past when at times, I was fully aware less-scrupulous members of the press were also on the hunt for headlines connected to exactly the same topics I was working on.

What Constitutes Investigative Journalism?

Robert Greene, the late and much-missed former editor of the US's *Newsday* magazine, had a major hand in defining investigative journalism as being the fruit of the journalist's own labours; something which someone in power wanted to stop becoming public; and which resulted in a story that had some kind of measurable impact at reader-level and perhaps even within a legal context too. Later, this three-point definition was more or less adopted by the University of Missouri-based Investigative Reporters and Editors (IRE) organisation, the preeminent body in the US for all reporters specialising in this kind of journalism. It is also a definition which I have absorbed and applied to the academic and practical work carried out by students who study on the MSc in Investigative Journalism at the University of Strathclyde where I am its Course Director.

Add to that Carl (Watergate) Bernstein's insight that 'all reporting should be the search for the best obtainable version of the truth' and you have probably the finest and clearest statements of intent relating to investigations. Bernstein, in particular, deserves credit for distilling into a single sentence the notion that reporters will report a fact and a connected analysis on a Monday, only to revise both the following day, whilst still maintaining the gap between the two versions was not a negative reflection on the journalist involved.

American authors Ettema and Glasser also add an interesting dimension to the debate when they claim that investigative journalists were also what they rather grandly termed 'custodians of conscience'.[1] They elaborate on this concept and explain:

> In this way investigative journalists are the custodians of public conscience. To think of journalists in this way, however, is not to suppose that they can, all on their own, repair systemic breakdowns or clean up institutional disorder…They are not the guardians of some superior moral knowledge. Rather, these journalists hold the means to report and disseminate stories that can engage the public's sense of right and wrong. These journalists are, in other words, custodians of exactly what we imagine conscience to be: a morally engaged voice.

More recently on this side of the Atlantic, the *Guardian's* editor Alan Rusbridger stated in his submission to the Leveson Inquiry that:

> We meet at a time when, for the first time since the Enlightenment, it's possible to imagine societies – towns, cities, and even countries – without

any agreed or verifiable forms of the truth. As journalists we would like it
to be self-evident that what we do is as crucial to democracy as a clean
water supply or a fire service. That surveys show that this is not a widely
held view ought to be a matter for self-reflection. Since Watergate
journalists often like to cite big campaigning investigations to demonstrate
why what we do matters. It's we, the free press, who exposed phone-
hacking, MPs' expenses, illegal rendition, the truth about the death of Ian
Tomlinson, match-fixing in sport, World Cup votes for sale, chicanery in
the arms trade, cash for questions and so on. This work of investigation is,
indeed, vital evidence of the importance of the free press. As vital is the
institutional muscle of the press that stands behind a reporter engaged in
this kind of work.[2]

Some may regard these aims, definitions, analysis and editorial beliefs, as
being a load of old sanctimonious tosh which goes against the scrappy nature of
the British press's historical roots. Yet to do so would be to miss the point that
'investigative journalism' in the US has been taken far more seriously, been
codified and taught at university level in a way which leaves its British
counterparts in the dust. Only in very recent years has the UK begun to offer
separate awards for this kind of journalism and engaged in both serious study
and teaching within a university setting of its theories and practices.

Additionally, given the cooperation in recent years between the likes of the
Guardian with *The New York Times*, in the case of the WikiLeaks story, it is clear
that from the 'insider' accounts of both parties, shared values for this kind of
investigative reporting were much in evidence and was something the readers on
both sides of the Atlantic benefited from. In other words when it comes to
investigative journalism it is important to look at both the US and UK and then
take a deep, Zen-like breath.

A key difference which cannot be ignored, of course, is the First Amendment
to the US Constitution, part of its Bill of Rights, which states: 'Congress shall
make no law respecting an establishment of religion, or prohibiting the free
exercise thereof; or abridging the freedom of speech, or of the press…' Such an
astonishing and farsighted clause ensured fertile conditions for investigative
journalism in the modern-era whilst also contextually reminding its practitioners
that the founding fathers regarded their work as serious, important and above
all, part of the country's continuing national story. They recognised that creating
the legal conditions for a separate and free press, ensured constant surveillance
of the state and federal institutions and the public officials who worked inside
them. In that sense they were recognising their own frailty and weaknesses and f

State control over the British media has not existed since the end of the 17th
century, the last time when journalists were expected to be licensed in some
shape or form in order to practise their craft and profession. In the four
centuries since then, the industry (a rather cohesive term than is merited for a
messy group of outlets and even messier collection of individuals) has slowly but

surely blotted its own copy-book in terms of self-regulation until the standing of a 'journalist' as a career choice has probably never been lower. Unfortunately, the constant and erroneous referring of tabloid hacking practices as part of their 'investigations' has also damaged a genre of journalism I have worked in and valued immensely in the process.

Professional Perspective

During successive interviews I did for radio across the summer of 2011, I found myself having to defend 'investigative journalism' whenever the subject of illegal tabloid hacking activities was raised. I found this odd but not entirely surprising. I also heard other colleagues far more articulate and eloquent than me, face the same onslaught. In my designated role as so-called 'expert' on investigative journalism, I had to repeatedly explain to bewildered researchers, producers and presenters that I knew little more than they did about the nasty predominately-tabloid practices which were being unearthed during this timeframe. I explained I had only encountered the tabloid sector a handful of times over the two decades-plus I'd been carrying out investigations for the print and broadcast media across the UK. They seemed taken aback by this answer, sometimes barely concealing their scepticism, assuming that all investigative journalists met regularly in some shady watering-hole and swapped tips whilst telling appalling tales of terrible deeds.

I had to disabuse them of this scenario and explain I had heard rumours of the illegal practices investigative reporters got up to for tabloid paymasters. When pressed I told them I had only direct experience twice of tabloid techniques: Firstly, in the early 1990s when a tabloid reporter from a daily newspaper warned me off investigating a strange tale involving abuse in psychiatric facilities with a threat that my Channel 4 project would be scooped by his better-funded (i.e. he told me he had contracted private detectives) story anyway; Secondly, when I was contracted to *Esquire* magazine in the 1990s and became suspicious when a Sunday tabloid scooped me several times on a range of off-diary investigations I had been working on.

The latter example led me to seriously consider whether someone at the magazine had accessed or stolen my copy and was feeding its findings to a tabloid for a fee and allowing them to contact the subject of the investigations, contacting them for comment, thus giving them the space to form a defence against my allegations and generate more stories on the same topic.[3] I still suspect this but cannot prove it. However, another more sinister explanation was also suggested to me by colleagues, namely that my own phone was hacked for information.[4]

During the interviews in the summer of 2011 I was met, on at least one rather awkward exchange, with sheer incredulity regarding my claims that I did not know such appalling breaches of ethics was occurring and for not agreeing it simply *must* be happening across the entire print media in the UK.[5] The assumption was that *all* investigations of any merit or weight must involve something illegal or at the very least shady. I want to illustrate in this chapter how four investigations I have carried out during my career managed to fulfil the criteria for this genre set out earlier but were also all legal.

Professional Context of Investigations

The central reason for beginning this chapter with definitions and explanations for the existence of investigative journalism was to contextualise the practice within an intellectual, legal, professional-ethics and moral universe.[6] This was to place my own ethical-framework against this backdrop and to begin to challenge the thesis that the most effective investigations can only be carried out when media laws are explicitly broken. I disagree with this argument and counter with the thesis that solid investigations can, for the most part, be carried out within existing legal and professional laws and guidelines. Does this mean the laws and guidelines are perfect? No, far from it. Is this a reason to go out and break them? Of course not. Should we periodically test their limits? Always.

This position means I have from time to time, pushed at and occasionally straddled or breached, such ethical lines-in-the-sand. However, throughout each example which follows it should be borne in mind I was settled in the sincere belief that *if* I was running a red light then, like an ambulance, I did so because I felt was serving a greater good along the lines Ettema and Glasser have described earlier. The four examples are:

a) The Tax Trap

Channel 4 – *The Tax Trap* (1992): This production for the *Scottish Eye* investigative strand (described to me by one veteran producer as '*Dispatches* with a Sporran') involved me having to assume the undercover identity of a specialist tax accountant. The premise of the investigation was that several Scottish companies were being heavily ripped-off by the Inland Revenue (IR) because they dealt in cash and were open to accusations of fiddling their books. A genuine specialist accountant explained to the production team that he had witnessed the IR reaching deals with his clients based on spurious calculations.

I, therefore, participated in a meeting which I secretly taped via a hidden microphone, which allowed me to capture IR employees more or less admitting in this closed session, that they plucked figures from thin air (albeit based on their calculations about what the individual in question *may* owe). Scottish Television engaged lawyers at the earliest stages of this project. They expressed the central fear that entrapment could be an issue. I rehearsed my fake identity with colleagues for several hours in the days preceding the operation. The lawyers also needed convincing that the whole project was in the public interest. Only after allowing them to see the research and case studies we'd assembled did they finally agree to this.

To add another layer of legal complexity, we had filmed two IR employees as part of the project whilst they were doing their jobs. These were decent officers going about their business, under the misapprehension they were being filmed for a Channel 4 'fly on the wall' series. In fact we were investigating the very practices they represented. All of this raised the public-interest standard to a very high level. Again, legal scrutiny and consultation with the network took place at the highest levels. This allowed us to defend ourselves when the inevitable backlash occurred.[7] This felt worthwhile because it represented a challenge to the power of the tax system in the UK and illustrated how the small businessman was sometimes battered into submission simply because they were slipshod – but not criminal – in their filing practices.

b) Hospital Investigation

The Scotsman – Hospital Investigation (2002): This investigation required clearance from the publication's lawyers before and after the project had been completed and before publication. In particular, there was concern about me entering the hospital with a source in the undercover guise of a member of staff. It was agreed that the risk was worth the 'public interest' pay-off. In the event, the result was better than could have been predicted. It turned out the £1m water filtration system was broken and had been 'repaired' by using an old, oil-stained fire hose attached by Duct-tape from the water-supply, thus bypassing the state-of-the-art filtration system which sat there like a redundant shiny hulk, to the main hospital pipe which ran the water to ill patients and was used for everything from dialysis to hand-washing.

The claims of negligence were so serious that I instituted the 'two-source' rule for everything which I printed. This meant I had multiple sources supporting others, each source not being aware who the other was. I also ensured that fair comment was received in good time for publication. In the event, several staff members were, I was told, either moved or sacked from their positions after publication.

c) MI5 Spy Investigation

Esquire magazine – MI5 Spy Investigation (2000): A complex and difficult investigation, in which I set myself the challenge of investigating not what ex-MI5 man David Shayler had been claiming in the press (notably the *Daily Mail* which bought his story for around £20k) but *who* he was before and during his MI5 life. This meant contacting former fellow-student peers at Dundee University; a former teacher (who had been deliberately misquoted by MI5 spin-doctors); and the spy's own family and friends. The British-end of the project was straightforward but I was shocked to discover that most colleagues in the press swallowed the misinformation the MI5 people were openly peddling in London to me and others.

Instead, I decided to investigate everything on my own terms and soon found out that Shayler's biography was of a bright young man who liked the limelight but was also loyal and clever. If his recruiters had any doubts about him then they had ample opportunity to weed him out from the beginning of the tortuous MI5 recruitment process. He had been selected via an advertisement with a Samuel Beckett quotation and interviewed by a 're-tread' (i.e. retired spook who is contracted in to interview new recruits) who, according to my sources, often look askance at the generation beneath them. Yet an MI5 source admitted to me off-the-record that they had been trying to snag interesting and off-beat characters from the 'middle-classes' who represented the next generation of intelligence officers protecting the country.

Thus in Shayler, they got precisely what they were looking for. I was granted access to him by his girlfriend Annie Machon (another ex-spy) and she, in turn, made sure his family and friends spoke to me as well. The level of access I was afforded was exemplified by the fact his parents in Beaconsfield, Buckinghamshire, not only chatted to me frankly for hours but actually allowed me to see his bedroom and rummage around his bookshelf. I was determined to build up a full, rounded portrait of this man and explain to readers why I thought he had thrown it all away and divulged national secrets. Editors at *Esquire* took legal advice and passed this on to me, especially regarding whether or not I would *by proxy* be accused of breaking the Official Secrets Act, since senior figures in on the political stage in the UK had labelled Shayler an out-and-out traitor. It was agreed I would not seek any more state secrets from him but would seek to measure and grasp his motivations.

The most difficult part for me personally was physically meeting his girlfriend in London (she was not restricted from travelling) and Shayler himself in Paris. In London, I met Machon near the BBC in Regent Street in a hotel and was immediately aware (with her expert 'watcher-aware' training) I was under surveillance. This meant being spied on by two spies in the hotel itself, and followed by them outside as we took a taxi (the preferred MI5 mode of transport to lose anyone in London). In Paris, when I tracked down and met a jumpy but exceedingly likeable Shayler, things got even worse. The on-the-run spy was being tailed by the French domestic secret service (*Direction Centrale des Renseignements Généraux* or Central Directorate of General Intelligence), the UK's MI6 (Secret Intelligence Service), some Americans from their CIA and, almost comically, a lone Libyan who trailed in everyone's wake like a forlorn, spurned lover.

The sheer number and range of intelligence operatives watching the UK ex-spy morning, noon and night, was clear evidence to me he had obviously spilled some valuable beans. (It would have been funny had it not been so worrying, especially when I spotted several of them trailing us down a tiny street called Rue St. Sulpice, all clearly visible in the street's short 100 yard stretch and all desperately trying to look nonchalant). Moreover, when I accidentally and surreptitiously happened to witness my Left Bank hotel room being raided by French intelligence officers, it was clear that I was treading on delicate ground. The central ethical factor in my relationship with Shayler was that I refused to pay him anything (not that he asked for it) for his involvement with my assignment. I also was not trying to make 'friends' with him. Nor did I deliberately try to get drunk with him to pump him for new secrets.

Instead, I challenged the core allegation being punted by the MI5 PR people that he was a busted-flush and rogue agent who had used guile and

Machiavellian cunning to sneak through the recruitment process. In fact, the more I checked him out, the clearer it was that he had worked hard, been open and straight, allowed him and his family to be fully-vetted and during his time in the service had been a decent, if frustrated, agent. My first-draft ran to a ridiculous 8,000 words until my editor Philip Watson, culled it to a manageable 6,000 words. Lawyers for the magazine legalled it from start to finish and came back to me numerous times. It was line-edited and fact-checked to within an inch of its life. To make matters even more bizarre, by the time we had reached the editing stage, I was taking satellite calls whilst staying in – I am not making this up – 'Goldeneye' the holiday villa of Ian Fleming, author James Bond, where he had written all 14 of the spy thrillers in Jamaica. It was a suitably melodramatically and corny location to deal in state secrets and suburban realities.

d) Robert Brown/Miscarriage of Justice Victim
STV/Channel 4/BBC/*Guardian*/*Scotsman*/Herald – Robert Brown/Miscarriage of Justice Victim (1993-2005): This investigation went through many phases over the 13 years I investigated it in print and broadcast media. The central hurdle was balancing my responsibilities as a journalist with the fact that some of the information I was constantly uncovering was of evidential value to his defence/appeal legal team. This is not a new dilemma. During the investigation into the Birmingham Six case by Chris Mullin, former investigative journalist for *World in Action* and ex-Labour MP and Blair government minister, I have since learned from their lawyer, Gareth Pierce, that they often disagreed about timing and tactics. What works for a journalist does not always work for a lawyer.

This rule applied to the Robert Brown case and I had to balance my role as a reporter with the increasing realisation I genuinely believed this man's innocence. Brown was convicted in Manchester in 1977 for the murder of a 56-year-old single woman named Annie Walsh who lived alone. From day-one he maintained his innocence yet, inexplicably at the time, he had signed a confession after being arrested. He was sentenced to life and thrown into the black hole of the UK's Cat A prison system. I came across the case in late 1991 when my boss at Scottish TV, ex-shipyard worker and Granada veteran, Gus Macdonald, sent the case file to me. He, in turn, had been alerted to it by an old shipyard pal and instead of ignoring the plea, he passed it on with the handwritten advice: 'Eamonn, this certainly looks like a stitch up.' I investigated it for the next 13 years. Legally, it was a nasty case to tackle: No funding; no support from a media organisation for a decent length of time except in the endgame when BBC Scotland came aboard; no constant legal support to protect my investigations. This meant that different media outlets had different demands: Print were obsessed with documents; Broadcast were obsessed with not allowing me to personally interview subjects because it was felt I had become too much of a campaigning figure. (I always maintained 'I had not crossed the line but it had crossed me.') At several stages sympathetic individuals in the Home Office risked their careers to pass me documents protected by the Official Secrets Act. I risked prosecution by accepting and using them but felt the 'red-light' (see above) rule applied inasmuch as a greater good was served by breaking the law than by respecting it, something Ettema and Glasser would understand.

In that sense I was technically on the wrong side of the law, but on the right side of my professional ethical value system. As the day of the appeal approached I contacted two key witnesses: firstly, a female who had claimed Brown had been near the locus of the murder on the day the victim died; secondly, a retired Home Office scientists whose notes, I believed, had been altered by others after they left his desk in order to frame Brown. I wrote, telephoned and eventually visited the former. She would not answer her door. I left myself open to harassment charges by my repeated and focused attempts but felt my actions were justified since a man was serving his 26th year in jail partly because of her testimony. (When Brown was finally exonerated, the first call I received on the steps of the Court of Appeal in London was from this woman suddenly wanting to change her story and give me a version supporting Brown – later when I took her up on her offer, she reverted to her original stance of ignoring me.)

I had difficulty tracing the latter scientist but when I did call him, found a hesitant but honest man. He was reluctant to go on-the-record but eventually agreed. Later he retracted this. I suspect someone had monitored my calls or possibly my interviewee had sought legal advice from a lawyer or his former Home Office employees, and this had scared him off. Again, my repeated and energetic efforts to pin him down could be open to misinterpretation as harassment. Once again, I felt the circumstances merited it.

My final ethical dilemma involved the central figure to the entire Brown drama, a corrupt retired Detective Inspector from Greater Manchester Police called Jack Picton Butler, who lived in the Roe Cross Green area of the city. He had beaten and framed the then 19-year-old Brown into signing a demonstrably false confession to murder, an act which robbed Brown of a quarter of a century of his life and the victim's family of seeing the right man convicted. The original 1977 jury did not know that Butler was already under investigation for corruption when they accepted his testimony at Brown's trial. In 2002, he would be named in Brown's successful appeal as the key individual whose subsequent 1983 conviction for corruption and perjury meant the original 1977 Crown case was holed below the water line. I had tracked him from day-one but finally decided to 'doorstep' him in 2005.

In the intervening two and a half years since Brown wrongful conviction was overturned I had repeatedly sent him letters and logged calls to his home in an effort to get him 'on-the-record'. Lawyers from *The Herald* in Glasgow and BBC Scotland, both of whom contracted me on a freelance basis, advised me to approach him via telephone and in writing before trying for a face-to-face meeting. I sourced his location quite easily via the UK Electoral Roll which was available for a small fee online. In the case of the BBC, he was monitored by them under the usual strict Producer's Guidelines. I did not play a role in this process.

Later, I did attempt to confront him for the *Herald*; however this was unsuccessful but still revealing. He refused to answer the door and instead his wife shouted abuse at me and a photographer. Later that day as I waited at a discreet distance inside my car, he called me on my private mobile number to announce: 'I am not in here...' which ranks as one of the more strange excuses for not speaking to a reporter I have come across. The article complete with his non-interview, appeared in print a week later and was subsequently honoured in three separate national and international awards.[8] No legal blowback from former DI Butler ever surfaced. The entire project was conducted, from start to finish, within the current broadcast and print media, legal framework and guidelines. I did not feel restricted or that the power of the story was diminished in any way, shape or form.

Conclusions

As someone who has worked for decades in investigations at pretty-much the highest levels in the UK, I believe that one overriding factor guides my work: I one day may end up in the dock defending the value of what I have done. That reality means that I believe – wholeheartedly – that the best investigative journalism sometimes, as Bob Greene stated, can change the law or at least test it. In such a state, it is incumbent upon us as journalists to be aware of that as we go about the business of gathering our information.

Is there an exception to that? Yes, of course, if you are in the business of short-term headlines and profit-above-all-else then there might be a warped justification for cutting corners, shinning drainpipes, raiding bins, stalking targets, using disproportionate surveillance and breaching human rights, left, right and centre.

If that's your game, then you are not a member of the profession I hold dear. It's deeply unfashionable to say that journalism should have a moral and social-justice underpinning but as the work of Ettema and Glasser, and even Woodward and Bernstein has shown, that is the rock we built our house on. For those that reject that, then there is another place to rent down the road. It's the place Murdoch built, where anything went, where nothing except the bottom-line and the headline was sacred, and where the pain of a Sunday 'Make-the-Facts-Fit-the-Headline' approach was washed away by the high-of-the-hit and something no one worried about until Tuesday.

Real investigative journalists in the UK envy the US' First Amendment and acknowledge the landmark status of Watergate, but also like the fact that we have our own roots, traditions and triumphs (e.g. *The Sunday* Times' Insight Team on the Thalidomide scandal was historic and rightly-applauded globally). We also understand why the UK press aspires to be self-regulated even after the Hackgate mess. That's what we aim for – but we still acknowledge this system might be failing and falling short. We don't particularly look forward to meetings with lawyers, but neither do we sprint in the opposite direction or pay for hired-guns to tell us what we want to hear. We know limits exist, but we are willing to throw a punch at them when it counts. All laws exist in a state of flux and we are content in the knowledge that sometimes the greater-good is served by challenging them. Therefore, if a corrupt politician is felled by a fake-fax to a Parisian luxury hotel, then that's a price worth paying. But hacking the mobile phone of a teenage murder victim and misleading a wounded family is simply cowardly and hiring detectives on an industrial scale to chase celebrities is cynical and wasteful.

Since the era of W. T. Stead (editor of *Pall Mall Gazette* 1883-1889), who put his liberty on the line to unearth the sordid child-prostitution activities of upper-class Victorian societies, there have been individuals in the UK willing to risk all to hold a mirror up to contemporary society in the hope progressive and positive change which benefits all will occur. This is not a legacy we mess with, nor is it a tradition we like to dress up in fake sheik clothes for the headline-equivalent of a jolly jape and a laugh down the pub with the 'hacks' afterwards.

It is to the UK's investigative journalism community's everlasting credit that the editor of the *Guardian*, and one of his reporters, followed in Stead's footsteps on the matter of illegal tabloid hacking. They alone stand tall in this whole grisly mess, they walked the talk when others in the media cowered and sneered, whilst lawyers worked into the night trying to thwart them, proving that great investigative journalism does exist in the UK and is willing to confront those that others fear.

So before anyone starts saying the hacking scandal means British investigative journalism is on its knees and was partly to blame for the stink, remember that it was the noble actions of one section of the industry which threw much-needed light on the seedy actions of another. If that sounds pious, self-righteous or self-aggrandising then may I suggest, in the immortal words of that brave, lone-reporter, a true 'custodian of conscience', Nick Davies: 'Let dog eat dog...'

Notes

[1] See *The Reporter's Craft as Moral Discourse, Custodians of Conscience: Investigative Journalism and Public Virtue* by James S. Ettema and Theodore L. Glasser (New York: Columbia University Press, 1998) pp 3-4

[2] Rusbridger Alan, The Importance of a Free Press, *Guardian*, 6 October 2011. Available online at http://www.guardian.co.uk/media/2011/oct/06/importance-free-press-alan-rusbridger, accessed on 28 November 2011

[3] At the time of writing, (December 2011) I have corresponded with officers from the 2011 Operation Weeting investigation by the Met and have been told in writing (a) There is currently no evidence my phone(s) was/were hacked; (b) However, they agree that on the face of it, I am correct in assuming someone had intercepted my research

[4] To date, the detectives at the Met have not been able to confirm this but they are actively dealing with my inquiries. I remain sceptical about whether I was hacked and

suspect that I my articles were accessed during the production phase and distributed then pre-production

[5] When this particular interview took place I refrained from mentioning to listeners that my interrogator was a paid columnist for the Murdoch owned *Sun* newspaper in Scotland.

[6] Unlike a former senior colleague at Scottish Television in the 1990s who preferred to refer constantly to investigations as 'Hey-ho it's only rock and roll', meaning their only inherent value was their occasional sensationalist aspects. Anything deeper merited the ultimate put-down as being either 'worthy' or 'pointy-heady'

[7] The programme was followed up by *The Sunday Times* Insight Team investigating the issue. This led to criticism being registered by the Inland Revenue via No 10 Downing Street. The then MD of STV, Gus Macdonald, defended my investigation in what was termed 'robust' fashion

[8] The British Press Awards; Paul Foot Award; Investigative Reporters and Editors Awards (USA) – 2005.

Note on the author

Dr Eamonn O'Neill is a Lecturer in Journalism and Course Director of the MSc in Investigative Journalism at the University of Strathclyde, Glasgow. Over a career spanning 22 years, he has been honoured for his investigative journalism in both broadcast and print in the British Press Awards, BAFTAs and the Paul Foot Award. In 2008, he became the first British recipient of an Investigative Reporters and Editors Award (Special category – Tom Renner Award) in one of the USA's premier peer-judged honours for his work investigating miscarriages of justice. In 2010 and 2011, he received honours in the Strathclyde Excellence in Teaching Awards following nominations by students. He is currently producing/presenting a new BBC Radio Scotland series O'Neill Investigates. He is married and has twin sons.

Hacking into tragedy: Exploring the Ethics of Death Reporting in the Social Media Age

The general debate about press ethics in the reporting of death and tragedy is being fuelled by exceptional cases rather than the norm – and could well do harm by resulting in further 'protection' through regulation when informed access would be far more helpful, according to Jackie Newton and Sallyanne Duncan

On 4 July 2011, the Metropolitan Police revealed that Millie Dowler's phone had been hacked during the investigation into her disappearance. This transgression against a murdered teenage girl ignited the phone hacking scandal in the public imagination, causing the closure of a profitable, popular Sunday newspaper and bringing Rupert Murdoch to a London hotel room to issue a 'sincere and humble' apology to the Dowler family. While the phone-hacking of politicians, sportsmen, celebrities and even members of the Royal family had seemed serious, scandalous but perhaps surmountable for News International, this was a step too far.

The closure came about because certain journalists and a private investigator on the title had broken one of the few taboos of privacy left in the social media age; they had committed a criminal act against a murder victim and further damaged her grieving family. As Kieran, Morrison and Svennevig (2000) have demonstrated, the right to privacy is not viewed by the public as an absolute. Some people have a greater right to it than others, and the bereaved, usually thrust into the media spotlight by tragedy, are top of that list.

While no-one could deny the venality and criminality of the hacking of Millie Dowler's phone, the fall-out from it has the potential to skew attitudes towards every area of contact between the media and the tragically bereaved. This scandal puts the intrusive behaviour of a small minority of the national press in the spotlight, with protection of the victims seen as the correct moral and ethical response, particularly as stories emerge about other potential victims: survivors and bereaved families of the 7/7 bombing; relatives of service personnel killed in Afghanistan. This study, however, suggests that more protection or regulation is not the answer to developing the fragile relationship between reporters and the newsworthy bereaved. In short, it could result in further conflict rather than mutual understanding.

The concern is that:

1. many more families feel excluded from reports of their relatives' deaths than feel intruded on. A number of families in this study had been prepared by the police for intense media interest in the death of their loved one. When it did not arrive, or when their loved one's death was ignored or covered briefly without contact with the family, they felt 'let down'. One mother of a murder victim said this perceived lack of interest added a further layer of hurt to her bereavement. 'It was as if my son's death counted for nothing';

2. families also perceive a 'hierarchy of victims' and believe the agenda is set by *cause célèbres* who may have had a different experience of the press than the 'ordinary' family (Newton 2011);

3. journalists are more negative about the death knock (interview with the bereaved following a tragedy) than its recipients are, and are more likely to consider it morally and ethically dubious (Duncan and Newton 2010).

It is also important to acknowledge that the majority of encounters between journalists and the bereaved happen in the regions where there is a stronger level of accountability between reporter and subject. Regional journalists generally have a heightened awareness of the effect of their reporting on those involved in their stories and their community. For many, the phone-hacking scandal has already had an unfair impact on the way they are perceived by potential interviewees. One regional editor said: 'In the current climate their view of the press will be formed by national headlines so they think we're all totally without morals and awful human beings.'

Paul Dacre, Editor-in-Chief of the *Mail* group titles, endorsed this notion when he told the Leveson Inquiry that there were thousands of 'decent journalists in the UK who don't hack phones' and in some cases in the regions, 'work for a pittance' because 'they passionately believe that their papers give voice to the voiceless' (Leveson 2011: 1). They may, however, be expected to use social media to access material without the knowledge of bereaved relatives and friends. Although this action is legal some people, particularly those at the centre of sensitive stories, might view it as being similar to hacking. The phone messages of Milly Dowler, Rose Gentle and other traumatised families were intercepted at a time of intense anxiety, without their consent. Equally, images taken from the social media sites of those who took their own lives in Bridgend in 2008 were also intercepted at a time of intense anxiety, again without their consent. The phone hacking episode was clearly illegal but lifting from social media is a much more ambivalent act.

The risk is that the fallout from the hacking scandal and Leveson could make journalists more likely to avoid bereaved families and turn to social networking sites (SNS) in order to write death knock stories. Will it lead to more social media 'hacking' where journalists use material without the bereaved's consent? Paradoxically, will this act be more intrusive than the much-maligned 'death knock' which at the very least can offer an opportunity for the family to have a voice within the story? To find answers to these questions we consulted 49 reporters from the regional press and six editors or senior journalists who had news-room responsibilities about using social media in death knock stories. We also conducted 24 interviews with bereaved groups and families. Their comments were illuminating and went a long way to dispelling the myth that all journalists are uncaring, unprincipled hacks and that all bereaved families want to be left alone.

Modern Day Death Knocks

The death knock remains an important journalistic activity in the digital age. Reporters from our study believe it is a key part of the news process, offers the potential for good quality human interest stories, and can be a platform to warn others of dangers in society. The therapeutic value of assisting the bereaved relatives to pay tribute to their loved one and the community's entitlement to be informed of events in their area are also identified by journalists as a significant validation for undertaking this form of traumatic reporting. These instincts were borne out by many of the family members interviewed, with one 'expert' witness, a bereaved parent who now counsels others, saying: 'To me there's always a story behind the headlines and if that story is told in a proper manner with compassion and accuracy between the person with the pen and the person telling the story I think it's a good marriage. It's a good thing to do because it can also help families being able to talk about their loved one.'

But there is an emotional cost to the journalist, particularly those who are inexperienced at dealing with grieving family members. Therefore, it could be assumed that given the ready supply of emotive quotes, personal details and pictures available from social networking sites it would seem that potentially journalists could get the necessary components of a death knock story without having to put themselves through a stressful visit to the family. It may require them to enter an ethical grey area that shares some characteristics with phone hacking but enables them to avoid direct contact with the bereaved. Some publications which have encouraged this approach have found themselves subject to the scrutiny of the UK Press Complaints Commission (see PCC cases, Miss Sharon Clarke v Maidenhead Advertiser, 24.11.2011; A Couple v The *Guardian* and the *Daily Mail*, Report 73; Katie Butcher v *East Grinstead Observer*, Report 76; Ms Rebecca Smisson v the *Sun*, Report 77; and Ms Allie Catt v MK News, Report 78; also see PCC *Briefing Note on the Reporting of Suicide* 2009a).

However, their contraventions appear to be exceptions rather than the rule. The research for this chapter showed that the surveyed reporters did not appear to merely take comments and pictures from these sites as a matter of course. Instead, it was evident they used them to source those who knew the deceased or to read tributes for research purposes, with the aim of gaining access to the family. However, as one digital editor noted this should be the starting point. He said: 'It can help with the initial contact if you are saying to them: "We've seen all these great comments on Facebook. Would you mind if we used them?"'

All the journalists in the study recognised the importance of interviewing the family and none would shirk from this task, despite the apparent pressures such interviews place on them, and their potential to cause often unintentional harm to their interviewees. Using the deceased's profile was deemed to be a last resort when all other attempts to speak to close relatives had failed, or as a means of adding to the story, rather than an easy dodge for the journalist. One local newspaper reporter said:

> Approaching the family is the most uncomfortable, awkward and difficult task...however inevitable and unavoidable...Headlines in the paper may often be the first 'real' encounter the bereaved family experience from the tragedy at hand. Sensational headlines become the brutal reality before they themselves have come to terms with their loss. However, relying on friends (when you are unaware of their relationship to the deceased), as opposed to the family, could give a tainted, prejudiced and misconstrued view of the subject.

A regional newspaper reporter added: 'As a reporter your aim is to produce a story and if this can only be done by using information from a social networking site then that is what you do. I would still make every effort to contact the family concerned by phone or via a death knock.'

Paradoxically, respondents had mixed views about the quality of information and quotes they got from friends, whether in interviews or taking comments from the sites. Most thought SNS-sourced quotes were not as good or much the same as they get from interviewing those close to the deceased. None thought they were better and all of them would prefer to visit the family. One evening newspaper reporter said:

> The quotes from speaking to a family in person are always better. You build up more of a rapport, better conversation and trust. More always comes out of face-to-face interviews than phone/email etc.

A local radio journalist highlighted news production reasons for seeking an interview with the bereaved. She said: 'It [a social media-sourced quote] is not as good. It's a bit different for me because I'm a radio broadcaster, so ideally we need the face-to-face interview. Quotes from social networks are a last resort, but they do help.' Another regional journalist appeared to favour using social media-sourced quotes: 'It depends. A lot of the time you get just as good quotes from a SNS because people are happier to say how they feel when they write it than saying it to someone.' Also, adolescents, in particular, may find that sharing their feelings on a SNS with their friends allows them to express their grief more easily than in a face-to-face situation (Roberts 2004).

By selecting relatively non-controversial comments from those who have no familial connection to the deceased, but whose relationship may have been equally as intense, the journalists appear to make a measured choice to avoid causing offence to the immediate relatives, and for the most part this tactic appears to be valid, as few families had specific complaints about the use of SNS. However, many of the relatives interviewed were concerned about unauthorised use of social media material in a more general sense. Two interviewees worried that it may lead to less direct contact with the family, and one woman whose brother had been murdered felt that reporters rely too much on social media and sometimes fail to check the accuracy of information. 'They'll look around on Facebook and Twitter and some of that stuff is just lies. Then the poor family has to answer all these questions about stuff that didn't happen.' Others had taken the decision to tell their story themselves through tributes on the websites of support groups, fulfilling a need to find a public context for their loss (Gibson 2001; Griffith 2004). Although they were happy for that material to reach a wider audience, they still felt they should be given warning if it was to appear in the mainstream media.

A significant area of contention appears to be the use of material that is in the public domain. Journalists mostly believe that this is freely available for them to use whilst the public take a different view. Generally, journalists said they did not think that it was intrusive to use comments from a deceased's site if the profile is set to public, stating that the individual has chosen to publish details of their life on the internet. One daily newspaper journalist described it as 'a virtual version of taking comments from cards and flowers at the scene'.

This argument highlights the murky waters of ethical decision-making. The key issues here are context, control and consent – the context in which the information is used, the level of control that the relatives of the deceased have over the material that is used, and whether the journalist has received consent from the family for the publication of the material.

Context

In terms of context, the deceased may well have chosen to keep their site public but it is unlikely they gave much thought to it being accessed by anyone other than their friends and family, whereas tributes left at the scene of a death are placed there in the accepted recognition that they are likely to be read by others. Research by Ipsos MORI for the PCC found that 78 per cent of adults aged 16-64 who are members of a social networking site said they would change information they publish about themselves if they thought the material would later be reproduced by mainstream media. Within that age bracket 35 per cent said they did not think before posting information that third parties might use it without their consent (Press Complaints Commission 2009b). So if a reporter was to use material from their social media site would they consider that hacking? This journalist highlighted the dilemma.

> Tricky...I suppose, strictly speaking, it is not intrusive, because everyone can adjust their privacy settings on SNSs to block people they don't know. They are in the public domain. [I'm] Unsure about the morality question though. It certainly made me feel uncomfortable. I think a lot of people who use SNSs don't realise the implications of publishing their personal details, thoughts and pictures on the internet – they don't read through the terms and conditions of SNSs when they sign up to them and perhaps have a limited understanding of the web.

As noted in the reporter's quotation above, people often fail to think through the consequences of publishing personal information on their SNS and in these circumstances it can be argued that there is a duty on the journalist who is consciously using the information in a manner which is different from its intended purpose to at least consider the implications of wider publication for those concerned. Some of the respondents appeared to do this but struggled to reconcile their own anxieties with their duty to the job, recognising that 'journalism by definition is intrusive'. One journalist from a news agency said: 'I have no choice – this is our job, to be nosey – and if it is a question of you getting a story or a rival it's always better to have tried yourself and to be told to neff off than not to try at all and have no show in the next day's papers.'

There seemed to be a perception amongst the reporters who participated in this research that by leaving a site as public facing and thus in the public domain, individuals had less justification to claim intrusion and therefore they were 'fair game'. But as Singer notes: 'The key ethical issue here involves disclosure, of both presence and intent' (Friend and Singer 2007: 87). It is also about exposure. Even if the information available on the person's profile is in the public domain it is protected to a certain extent because it is not 'efficiently accessible' to a wider audience who may be unaware of its existence (boyd 2008: 15). The information's reach is limited and thus it benefits from micro exposure. However, by including it in a news story which could be syndicated throughout the world the journalist provides a platform for macro exposure.

Generally, though, the reporters were sensitive to the family's pain, stating that they respect their wishes regarding material taken from a site, particularly photographs. However, one daily newspaper reporter raised another ethical difficulty, assessing the authenticity of the material. 'I do think it is intrusive and I think that people have a more outrageous version of themselves on these sites. I think that it does not always reflect that person and the best way of writing a story in this situation is to speak to relatives firsthand.'

Control

By believing in the value of interviewing the family the surveyed journalists enable the relatives to maintain a level of control over the story, something that is important to the bereaved, which may be denied to them when material is taken predominantly from the deceased's SNS, unless of course the journalist seeks consent from the family to reproduce quotes and pictures. One evening newspaper reporter said: 'I think most people would prefer we actually door-stepped them in person – that way they can choose how much or how little they want to say.'

Many families expect to be contacted and may even be prepared by the police for media attention (Newton 2011). If they do not receive any, they can feel snubbed and are more likely to feel resentful about any subsequent story that is carried. A former news editor who was interviewed for this study said: 'I've taken calls on the newsdesk from people who have complained that their family tragedy didn't receive coverage. It's very hard. What do you say? Your story wasn't tragic enough?'

Many people have a reasonable expectation that their local paper will cover the death of their loved one in a sensitive manner and that they will be given a role in that coverage. As a long-serving news editor in the North West was fond of saying: after a tragic death families in Liverpool expect 'the undertaker, the priest, and the *Liverpool Echo*'. Managing such expectations can be difficult in the current situation where fewer journalists are doing more and more work. However, when a tragedy is newsworthy these observations demonstrate that there is a need for the loss to be acknowledged and for the family to be part of the tribute article. One senior editor described this as being 'part of the memorabilia, as important as the hymn sheet at the funeral'.

Control is an important concept for the families at this time. As Coté and Simpson (2000: 94) point out, reporters are very aware of their role and task, but the interviewee has 'just lost control of his world'. Having a journalist turn up in person and deal honestly and sympathetically with the story is preferable to the SNS alternative, which tends to alienate the families from the account of the death. One bereaved relative said she would always advise families to participate in the story: 'I would say speak to the press, but always, always ask them to understand the pain you are going through.' However, there is a limit to the amount of control a family can expect to have and journalists must be clear about this.

Not all death knock stories will result in glowing tributes. In many there is a complicating factor such as an element of criminality which the families may not be happy with, or some ambivalence caused by counter claims about the nature of the tragic event. It is understandable that in these circumstances journalists would be less happy about contacting the family because of the anticipated response and would perhaps be more reliant on social media. However, 'expert' interviewees, that is those who have been bereaved by tragedy themselves and gone on to support or campaign for others, all said that contact with the family was perhaps even more important in these circumstances. One said:

> When things are going to come out anyway, it's allowing the family to put their side of it. Supposing little Johnny was dealing drugs, or had been killed because he was stealing to pay for his drug habit. The family are going to be devastated about that anyway, so what I would say is that they should come in on the human side about their loss. It could be about how he got into drugs, how this devastated the family, and how it has cost him his life.

Consent

Some people who have experienced journalists taking material from their site or those of friends or family could view reporters' actions in this situation as stealing part of an individual's identity because they have lost control over its use, and perhaps as a result the intrusion they experience can seem heightened. The PCC states: 'Using pictures supplied by friends or from social networking sites, without the close family's consent, can cause unintentional distress' (Press Complaints Commission 2009b: 17).

Equally, emotional harm could be caused by the journalist when relatives view material from their loved one's SNS which they were unaware existed or did not expect to be given wider publication and which they had not given their permission to be reproduced. One evening newspaper reporter highlighted this dilemma: 'The thornier issue arises when [the] family are unaware their loved one's picture is going to appear in the paper, and it may cause further shock or distress at what is already a difficult time. I have still done this, however, usually to meet expectations of tabloid news or picture desks. However, the prepared response is that it was in the public domain.'

This occurred in the coverage of the Bridgend suicides where relatives felt they had no control over the use of the images. The PCC reported: 'Each time there was a new death, republication made it difficult to move the grieving process on' (Press Complaints Commission, 2009b: 16). However, the journalists in this research seemed to be aware that when using comments or pictures from a deceased's SNS without the family's knowledge they could be intruding into their grief and shock. In turn, they demonstrated a strong ethical perspective by mostly stating that they were concerned about using such material and the consequences of doing so. One evening newspaper reporter said: 'I did on occasions struggle with this, and find a clear yes or no on a doorstep preferable to the grey area of consent assumed by virtue of online publishing.' Another evening newspaper reporter said: 'Yes, it is undoubtedly an intrusion to do this without their knowledge, but I used this process because of the pressure of deadlines, newspaper policy, and the awareness that other media outlets would do the same whether we did or not.'

It was evident from the reporters' responses that they employ self-control in their use of SNS material by choosing comments that are less personal and reflect well on the deceased. They also seem to distinguish between pictures and comments, considering the use of pictures to be more sensitive and therefore something that they should seek consent for, whereas they take the view that publishing comments, particularly tributes, to a wider audience can be beneficial to the family.

In an interview for this study a senior editor said the question of whether or not to use pictures from social media sites to illustrate stories of death and tragedy was the most common dilemma reporters brought to him. He said there were three key issues: the privacy settings on the site, the appropriateness of any picture likely to be used, and the consent of the family. Journalists on his newspapers would always try to gain consent from the families for the use of such pictures to comply with PCC guidelines, he said. Even if full consent could not be gained, the very act of contacting the family gave them some warning that a story with a picture was likely to appear. 'Essentially you have to make sure that it is an appropriate picture. If someone was drunk or pulling faces then clearly that is not appropriate and would be a breach of clause 5... [of the PCC code of practice] because it is not a sensitive use.'

One of the digital editors interviewed agreed, saying that he would never sanction the use from social media of a sensitive picture, for example of a child who had been killed, without consent from the family. However, a regional TV producer was less concerned about consent in such circumstances. 'If, for example, someone is killed in an incident considered newsworthy we will check if they have a Facebook site and lift the pictures. But is there any difference between that and knocking on doors to try to find a picture or trawling through school albums etc?'

Conclusions

Many encounters between journalists and the newsworthy bereaved are anticipated and positive – particularly in the regions. It was disappointing then, that the Leveson Inquiry decided to work on the view that there is, or should be, little difference in approach or ethics between journalists working in the tabloid or broadsheet, national or regional press. It is also concerning that the 'headline atrocity' – the hacking of Millie Dowler's phone – should be cited as evidence of the need for more regulation of the press, when the families and journalists interviewed as part of this research are themselves far more concerned with reaching a degree of mutual understanding and finding ways to lessen the stress of the death knock interview and other similar encounters on both families and journalists. Journalists' lack of confidence and distress in approaching the bereaved has been well documented (Keeble 2009; Castle 1999). It could be argued that reporters need more encouragement to include the bereaved in stories about their relatives' deaths, rather than further regulations which could provide them with 'ethical' reasons to avoid that family.

During this study it became apparent that members of these groups of bereaved families were excluding themselves from research interviews with the authors because they had not had any bad experiences of the press. The assumption was that in discussing the behaviour of the media, good news was no news. This adds to concerns that the general debate about press ethics in the reporting of death and tragedy is being fuelled by exceptional cases rather than the norm – and could well do harm by resulting in further 'protection' through regulation when informed access would be far more helpful.

That informed access should be based on the three principles of context, control and consent, thus providing journalists and the bereaved with a route to navigate their way through this emotionally testing situation. Indeed, the journalists in this study seemed well aware of their ethical responsibilities when dealing with the bereaved and do appear to reflect critically on their use of social media material. It is encouraging to note that they would always contact the family where possible, enabling the relatives to place the story in an informed context where they can give their consent to the use of sensitive material and where they have a level of control over the content. For these journalists using social media is not a substitute for interviewing grieving relatives.

However, they do appear to adopt a fair game attitude about making use of public domain material and access to it is given as a justification for intrusion. That said, the type of information and images the reporters choose to use appear to be non-controversial and sensitively treated. In this regard they are demonstrating an element of self-control. Nevertheless, there is a more complex ethical question here about the nature of intrusion. Because a profile is open to public inspection does not negate the intrusion that might be felt by close relatives at its use, even though their loved one may have willingly participated in making it public on their site. It is within this tricky difference in perception that comparisons to hacking can occur, giving rise to feelings of personal hurt, invasion, anger and disgust.

The result is confusion between the public and the journalist about what constitutes 'hacking' of social media. Some reporters are concerned about the context of using material that was not intended for wider publication and wrestled with the perennial dilemma in reporting sensitive stories of duty to their job and causing harm to the relatives. If nothing else, this proves that they are reflective practitioners, not merely news processors. Harm lies in journalists adopting a 'fair game' attitude merely because material is in the public domain. This does not take account of its intended purpose nor the fact that many people either fail to understand or ignore the implications of setting their site as public facing. It is not sufficient to place the onus on the individual, who may have had very limited encounters with the media before the death of their loved one. As boyd notes: 'Social convergence requires people to handle disparate audiences simultaneously without a social script. While social convergence allows information to be spread more efficiently, this is not always what people desire. As with other forms of convergence, control is lost with social convergence' (boyd 2008: 18).

When journalists make information from a profile or wall of a deceased that is already public more public then they turn private individuals into public figures through their death. If they are going to avoid accusations of hacking by social media, then they need to handle the reporting situation with extreme care by entering into an ethical contract with the bereaved. Protection or regulation is not the answer when what the bereaved wish is to actively participate in stories about their loved ones.

References

boyd, Danah (2008) Facebook's Privacy Trainwreck: Exposure, Invasion, and Social Convergence, *Convergence*, Vol. 14, No. 1 pp 13-20

Castle, Phillip (1999) Journalism and Trauma: Proposals for Change, *Asia Pacific Media Educator*, No. 7 pp 143-150

Coté, William and Simpson, Roger (2000) *Covering Violence: An Ethical Guide to Reporting about Victims and Trauma*, New York: Columbia University Press

Duncan, Sallyanne and Newton, Jackie (2010) How do you feel? Preparing Novice Reporters for the Death Knock. *Journalism Practice*, Vol. 4, No. 4 pp 439-453

Gibson, Margaret (2001) Death and Mourning in Technologically Mediated Culture, *Health Sociology Review*, Vol. 15, No. 5 pp 415-424

Griffith, John (2004) Private Grief, Public Kindness, *Insight Magazine*, Winter p. 37

Keeble, Richard (2009) *Ethics for Journalists*, London: Routledge, second edition.

Kieran, Matthew, Morrison, David E. and Svennevig, Michael (2000) Privacy, the public and journalism : Towards an analytic framework, *Journalism*, Vol. 1, No. 2 pp 145-169

Leveson Inquiry, Seminar 3 on *Supporting a free press and higher standards – Approaches to Regulation*. Evidence from Paul Dacre. Available online at

http://www.levesoninquiry.org.uk/wp-content/uploads/2011/11/Paul-Dacre.pdf , accessed 21 November 2011

Newton, Jackie (2011) The knock at the door: Considering bereaved families' varying responses to news media intrusion, *Ethical Space*, Vol. 8, Nos 3/4 pp 7-13

Press Complaints Commission (2009a) *Briefing Note on the Reporting of Suicide*. Available online at http://www.pcc.org.uk/news/index.html?article+NTU4MQ==, accessed on 27 October 2011

Press Complaints Commission. Complaint Cases, Report 73, A Couple v *Guardian* and the *Daily Mail*. Available online at http://www.pcc.org.uk/news/index.html?article=NDA5NAw==, accessed on 27 October 2011

Press Complaints Commission. Complaint Cases, Report 76, Katie Butcher v *East Grinstead Observer*. Available online at http://www.pcc.org.uk/news/index.html?article=NDg4NAg==, accessed on 27 October 2011

Press Complaints Commission. Complaint Cases, Report 77, Ms Rebecca Smisson v *Sun*. Available online at http://www.pcc.org.uk/news/index.html?article=NTly4Mw==, accessed on 27 October 2011

Press Complaints Commission. Complaint Cases, Report 78, Ms Allie Catt v *MK News*. Available online at http://www.pcc.org.uk/news/index.html?article=NTQ44NA==, accessed on 27 October 2011

Press Complaints Commission. Complaint Cases, Miss Sharon Clark v *Maidenhead Advertiser*, published 24.11.2011. Available online at http://www.pcc.org.uk/cases/adjudicated.html?article=NzQ4MA==, accessed on 26 November 2011

Press Complaints Commission, (2009b) *08 The Review*. Available online at http://www.pcc.org.uk, accessed on 27 October 2011

Roberts, Pamela (2004) The Living and the Dead: Community in the Virtual Cemetery, *OMEGA*, Vol. 49 No. 1 pp 57-56

Singer, Jane B. (2007) Ethics and the Law, Friend, Cecilia and Singer, Jane, *Online Journalism Ethics*, Armonk, New York, M.E. Sharpe pp 80-114

Note on the contributors

Jackie Newton is a Senior Lecturer in journalism at Liverpool John Moores University. She has 30 years' experience as a print journalist, carrying out her first death knock at the age of 17, and going on to doorstep bereaved relatives for regional newspapers and as a freelance for tabloid national newspapers. She has also worked on journalism education initiatives with Support after Murder and Manslaughter Merseyside. She has published on bereaved families' varying responses to news media intrusion and with Dr Sallyanne Duncan on preparing novice reporters for the death knock.

Dr Sallyanne Duncan is Programme Director of the MLitt Journalism programme at the University of Strathclyde, Glasgow, Scotland. Her research interests focus on the reporting of events involving trauma, bereavement or anxiety, particularly concerning the individual family. She has published on narrative styles in death reporting, ethical issues in reporting women asylum seekers' stories, codes of ethics for bloggers, and with Jackie Newton on preparing novice journalists for the death knock. Her doctoral thesis examined the pressures placed on, and the processes undertaken by, journalists who cover intrusive stories such as large-scale disasters, and more commonly, personal traumatic experiences.

Facing up to the Ethical Issues surrounding Facebook Use

Glenda Cooper asks if the increasing use of social networking sites as the first port of call when a story breaks – to find photographs, information about people's lives, frank views they may have expressed – is the other end of a (very long) continuum to phone hacking?

L ife as a nurse in the NHS can be tough: long hours, difficult patients, stressful jobs. It's no wonder that a young nurse called Rebecca Leighton looked forward to her nights out; as she put it herself she was a 'happy-go-lucky kinda gal, loves the wkend if im not workin and having a laugh with the people i call friends for a reason [sic]'[1]. Like thousands if not millions of other twentysomethings she posted pictures of herself on Facebook at parties – some pouting for the camera, others with arms thrown around her fiancée pulling silly faces, one swigging straight from a bottle of wine.

But Leighton never thought to protect her privacy settings on the social networking site; so when in 2011 there were unexplained deaths at the hospital she worked at – Stepping Hill, near Manchester – and she was initially questioned and then charged with contaminating saline bags with insulin, her unguarded words and comments flew straight into the wider public domain via the newspapers.

What could she complain about? Unlike celebrities such as J. K. Rowling, Steve Coogan and Hugh Grant – and families such as the McCanns and the Dowlers – who have told the Leveson Inquiry in detail about how they were bugged, stalked and hacked, Leighton had put all this private detail into the public domain herself. Phone hacking is illegal. The state of mind that allowed journalists to use such a device routinely, with not even a cursory pretence that it was in the public interest, ended up reducing the subjects of stories to objects, and those who had sometimes only the most tenuous of links to them forming what columnist Joan Smith called 'collateral damage'.[2]

But is the increasing use of social networking sites as the first port of call when a story breaks – to find photographs, information about people's lives, frank views they may have expressed – the other end of a (very long) continuum to phone hacking? Such sites have proved an invaluable short cut for hard pressed desks and reporters, both broadsheet and tabloid, trying to find information at short notice. But what ethical questions does plundering webpages without permission of their originators raise in modern day journalism?

While there can be no comparison between phone hacking and use of such sites – one illegal and intruding on completely private messages, it is worth considering this: there were 800 phone hacking victims at latest estimate.[3] As of July 2011, there are 29.9m Facebook accounts in the UK.[4] What kind of journalism are we getting if every part of your life is only a mouseclick away from being splashed across the front page of a national paper?

'The irony is that tabloids are obsessed with writing about "people",' says Smith, 'yet they forget that those they are writing about are people. They turn them into two dimensional figures.'[5]

'It's Always Bad Weather in my Memory'

When a crime or a tragedy occurred in the (mythic) old days, as a hack to get your hands on that coveted photo album, to delve deep into a person's private life, to get that key detail to raise your story from the mundane to the compelling, it would involve some legwork on the ground (either from yourself, or if you worked for a rich enough paper, a substitute rookie or agency reporter) performing those journalistic rites of passage: the doorstep and the deathknock. These shorthand terms refer to the practices of waiting outside someone's house for a comment, or trying to persuade a grieving family to talk about the deceased.

Apart from a few – such as Wensley Clarkson who recounts in *Tabloid Tricks*,[6] vivid tales of camping out anywhere from Cecil Parkinson's front door to the home of a couple who had both undergone a sex change at the *Sunday Mirror* and *Mail on Sunday* – most journalists recall such experiences with a shudder. 'I hated [deathknocks]. To do them, I found I had to get myself into a dark place on a par with the family – as best I could,' says one former *Sun* journalist.[7] 'I will never forget the look of disgust on the man's face when I asked whether he'd like to comment on camera after his daughter's suicide,' adds a freelance television reporter.[8] 'In my memory it is always bad weather when I had to do doorsteps or deathknocks – whether that was the case or just the miserable feeling that you associate with having to knock on a door in those situations,' recalls one former local journalist who now works as a national newspaper news editor. 'Nobody ever tells you what to do apart from a general remark to "just be careful not to be insensitive" – you're just left hanging.'[9]

Those who get sent to do such stories are often, ironically the youngest and least experienced reporters for local papers or agencies. Not just because this is a job that no one else wants to do, but because they are seen as more likely to get the story. 'As a news desk you try to send people with empathy,' says the news editor (ibid). 'You may have very good reporters but they may not be so good on a human level. We would often send young journalists [on doorsteps and deathknocks] because they would seem less threatening than a grizzled old hack, and people might be more likely to talk to them.'

'I turned up outside the house of the sister of two young men killed in the construction of the Channel Tunnel,' recalls the former *Sun* journalist of his first deathknock for his local paper.

> It was in the heart of Kent's former mining community and my paper had been against the mining strike. The snapper, a veteran of many years standing, refused to get out of the car because he knew we would be abused. I knocked and they opened the door and the family dog escaped. It was one of those painfully prosaic moments in the midst of a human tragedy as I and the sister, in her slippers, ran around trying to contain the barking dog. I don't remember the details, other than I was too scared to be dishonest or artful and I, therefore, probably came across honestly. I got the full biographical details and a good story…From then on I was always sent on death knocks.

While the positive side was that he felt that he could almost act as a counsellor for people who wanted to talk, there was a darker side: 'I was doing this for my own ends. I would get round this by trying to be clear that I was there for the paper and that they should only tell me what they wanted – if they wanted. But I am never sure that the relationship was transparent. Could they really know their own mind?'

'A Reporter has let Themselves Down Badly if they don't do a Facebook search'

Over the past decade, the growth of social networking sites changed all this. Today Facebook, Twitter, MySpace, Bebo – even in what now seems the prehistoric Friends Reunited – have all been plundered for words and images in the past decade. Any 'collect' [a family photograph from the past] that you see in a newspaper these days is likely to have come from Facebook. As Paul Fievez, a former night picture editor recently blogged:

> Within seconds of a story breaking, news and picture desks are all assigning reporters, photographers and picture researchers to log-in to Facebook, Twitter, Linked-In, Friends Reunited. All of the other social networks and personal web-sites are Googled and scoured for pictures and information. If there is a live web-cam, pictures are grabbed and frequently published without any regard to copyright. Likewise, any images on the social sites and personal blogs or web-sites of anyone involved are all also grabbed before anyone has a chance to close the site down, and are then published, syndicated, used on television, re-published or broadcast repeatedly.[10]

The view of most journalists is that of veteran *Guardian* investigative reporter David Leigh – if you put something in the public domain then it's fair game. As he said in an interview in 2009: 'If you want to put stuff about yourself up in the public domain…and people can make what use of it they like. I don't see any point in complaining about it. If you don't want the information out there, don't put it out there.'[11]

The news editor agrees: 'As a news editor I would expect my reporters to find pictures on Facebook – a reporter has let themselves down badly if they don't do the Facebook search.'

Yet when Kevin Marsh was Editor-in-Chief of the BBC College of Journalism, he noted that there was a fundamental disconnect between how journalists and users saw social networking sites. 'There's no doubt most teenagers don't think when they post to Facebook they don't think it is public…they see it as a public private space. It's like a conversation in the pub — it's in a public space, but not everyone and their uncle can eavesdrop.'[12]

That misunderstanding between private and public tripped up not only Leighton, but another twentysomething girl, Amanda Knox, convicted and then cleared on appeal of the murder of the British student, Meredith Kercher. Knox proved gold dust for journalists looking for colour with her nickname 'FoxyKnoxy' – that she put on her MySpace page, where she had also posted short stories that involved a drugging and rape scenario of a young girl, and a picture of herself posing with a gun. A YouTube video of her drunk at university also emerged, all fodder for articles such as the *Daily Mail*'s exposé of 7 November 2007: 'FoxyKnoxy: Inside the Twisted World of Flatmate Suspected of Meredith's Murder.'[13]. Invasion of privacy? If so, like Leighton, Knox had effectively invaded her own.

Regulators and Social Networking Sites: Publish at your own Risk

The reality was, however, that women such as Knox and Leighton had probably never considered that their unguarded photographs and comments would have a wider circulation than friends and acquaintances. 'Foxy Knoxy was a nickname actually to do with Amanda Knox's style of playing soccer, but the way it was used caused immense damage to her in the early part of the trial,' says Smith. 'She was portrayed as a sexually voracious woman and during her appeal the prosecutor even called her a witch.'

With Rebecca Leighton, there were plenty of candid photographs on Facebook which played up to the party girl image the media wanted. 'We used a Facebook picture because there was no official one released and no snatched one,' says Neal Keeling who led the *Manchester Evening* News's team and which has broken many of the significant developments in the case. 'In contrast, national papers like the *Mail* added in all sorts of comments based on her Facebook wall. That kind of approach is shortcut journalism: "We can't get the family or friends to speak so we'll nick stuff off Facebook."'[14]

Yet most journalists will instinctively side with Leigh: if you don't want it used, don't publish. And in many cases so far, the Press Complaints Commission has agreed: for those who willingly put material in the public domain, even if intending it only for a small audience, they run the risk the mainstream media will utilise it, if the public interest argument can be put forward. Even if a person has attempted to protect their photographs/comments from general view by privacy settings, that does not mean they cannot be used according to the PCC. For example, the *People* reported comments made by John Hayter, a serving police officer on his Facebook and Friends Reunited pages after the controversial death of Ian Tomlinson at the G20 protests in April 2009: 'I see my lot have murdered someone again. Oh well, shit happens.'[15] His profiles on these sites were not publicly accessible, but the PCC ruled in Goble v *People* 2009 there was a clear public interest in seeing how serving police officers viewed Tomlinson's death.

Equally there are some stories where the use of networking sites is clearly unethical. For example, a story in the *Sunday Express* claimed survivors of the Dunblane massacre, now turning 18, had 'shamed' the memory of the deceased with 'foul-mouthed boasts about sex, brawls and drink-fuelled antics' posted on their social networking sites. The newspaper justified its decision to publish on the basis that the boys' identities had been made public in 1996 when the shooting happened. The PCC warned, however, that the boys had been out of the spotlight for 13 years and concluded: 'Even if the images were available freely online, the way they were used – when there was no particular reason for the boys to be in the news – represented a fundamental failure to respect their private lives.'[16] As Pam Dix, of the group Disaster Action, which supports the bereaved and survivors of disasters, says, this goes way beyond notions of privacy:

> We would consider this kind of usage to have a detrimental impact on the emotional and, indeed, potentially the mental health of those whose information has been trawled and used. The notion that 16-year-olds are fair game, in a way that children are not, is also something that needs to be addressed (as per Charlotte Church's evidence to the [Leveson] Inquiry).[17]

And Marsh recalled at the time of Benazir Bhutto's murder, he became aware of another phenomenon because Bhutto's son Bilawal was at college with Marsh's son:

> There were hundreds of false Facebook and My Space sites 'set up by Bilawal' to try to get information or photographs. They were set up by journalists saying things like 'I've lost all my photos of my mates, can you repost them'. I can't think of the real life equivalent of that. It's like breaking into someone's house and stealing their photo album.[18]

Those cases may seem clear-cut. But what about the case of Toby Rundle – an Oxford undergraduate found hanged who earlier had set up a MySpace page which included the question: 'Who I'd like to meet – God, just to ask him what I'd done wrong'? It was, his mother said, after his sudden death, a spoof page and it should not have been used by journalists as it gave the wrong impression of her son. But the PCC ruled: 'One of the hazards of posting information online is that it can remain permanently and publicly accessible, and that a degree of control is lost once it is uploaded.'

Or what about the experience of teenager Charlotte Noble, this time in a case looked at by Ofcom? After her father was killed in an aircrash, UTV used a picture of Charlotte on Facebook, although her mother's privacy settings were 'strict'. Because UTV said they had obtained the photograph through someone who was a friend of Mrs Noble's on Facebook, Ofcom took the view that because Mrs Noble had placed the photograph on Facebook – a social networking site – and granted her 'friends' access to it, the privacy of the photograph was significantly compromised.[19]

Pushing Open an Ajar Door

Some media organisations are becoming increasingly aware that smash-and-grab raids on personal data on the internet raise difficult questions. Recent stories to prove problematic have included images of Ian Redmond, the bridegroom killed in a shark attack in the Seychelles, and victims of the M5 crash that were taken from Facebook. Elisabeth Ribbans, managing editor of the *Guardian*, argues that, while it can be acceptable for the media group to use information sourced this way, there should be a a clear public interest in doing so and the argument that something is already 'out there' is very nuanced one. When Redmond was killed in August 2011, the *Guardian* newsdesk held off publishing the Facebook photograph of the Redmonds' wedding that many other new organisations were using, and felt they should seek guidance from the family. Ribbans says:

> We contacted the Foreign Office to see if [Ian's widow] Gemma Redmond had expressed any views on the use of that picture; they weren't aware of any views and it seemed we were the only news organisation to have approached them about it. They asked Gemma on our behalf and she provided an image of the couple on their honeymoon with specific permission for the *Guardian* to use it. As a result we were able to proceed comfortably with a sensitive story. It was definitely the right thing to do in this particular case.[20]

The BBC has also updated its guidelines on how use of material from social networking sites should be used. It comments:

> Whilst some in the media might argue that, once an individual has begun a declarative lifestyle…they cannot expect to be able to set limits on that, people making content for the BBC should ask themselves whether a door that is only ajar can justifiably be pushed further open by the media….And it should be considered that the use of social media content by the BBC often brings that content to a much wider public than a personal website

or social media page that would only be found with very specific search criteria.[21]

However, others argue that there is a fundamental misunderstanding often by (older) journalists about how many younger people understand privacy, Marsh's previous comments notwithstanding. As the news editor says:

> BBC guidelines risk making people more squeamish than they need to be – not realising that kids are different. There's a real age divide in how bothered people are about privacy. Look at the phenomenon of tribute pages that spring up on Facebook for example after someone dies, and what kids write publicly about – with the expectation this is going to be used. The parents of those kids would probably not want those feelings or thoughts expressed in public in the same way.

And Leigh raises the valid point that for many, the discussion journalists should be having does not concern privacy on the internet when it comes to using such pictures, but one of money:

> If you put a picture up, are you authorising people to copy your picture? You give away the information, but do you give away the right to reproduce the picture? If you put a picture of yourself drunk or sober on Facebook and some broadcaster wants to purloin it, that's because it's got a commercial value to them and you should have the rights over whether willing to sell it or not..

Yet in privacy terms, there may be more restrictions out there than journalists fully realize. While most of the discussion around privacy has related to celebrities (e.g. the Douglas case,[22] concerning the wedding pictures of Michael Douglas and Catherine Zeta Jones), the 2004 victory of Naomi Campbell over the *Mirror* after they printed pictures of her coming out of Narcotics Anonymous[23] and the case of von Hannover[24] (in which the European Court of Human Rights ruled respect for the private life of Princess Caroline of Monaco had been breached by photographs of her shopping or on holiday in public places) one case for journalists to ponder may be the 2003 case of Peck v UK..[25]

Geoffrey Peck was a man suffering from depression when late at night he took a knife and went to Brentford High Street where he tried to slit his wrists. The council had installed CCTV, and when an operator saw what was happening, they called the police and summoned medical help. To show the usefulness CCTV could have, the council later released both still photographs and short clips to local newspapers and TV.

But the ECHR found that releasing these photographs and films without Peck's consent and without assurances his identity would be masked infringed his right to privacy under Article 8 (the right to privacy). He was in public but he was not involved in a public event or a public figure. He might have expected to be spotted by a passerby but not to have the image published and broadcast to thousands.

The court ruled that the fact that the footage was taken whilst Mr Peck was in a public street did not exclude it from being regarded as a private situation, and giving footage to the media meant it was viewed far more widely than Mr Peck could possibly have foreseen. Those media organisations who push open an ajar door could potentially find themselves on the wrong side of the law as a result.

'If I were a patient, I'd want answers'

Rebecca Leighton's name was almost inevitably prefixed with the words 'party-loving', thanks to such Facebook comments as 'Bad bad day follow(ed) by wine is a must', or 'Oh what will tonight bring…drunken nurses'. After charges concerning the contamination of the saline were dropped and Leighton was released, she reflected on how she had been portrayed by the media. 'I was just out with my friends having a good time. Everybody I know does that. I've not done anything different to what anyone else would, you know a 27-year-old girl, that goes out with her friends,' she tried to explain.[26]

It may be difficult to sympathise with Leighton, who has since been sacked from Stepping Hill for stealing tramadol. But that does not make her a murderer – nor does it mean her whole life is up for grabs.

Of course, the old-style doorstep should not be sentimentalised; witness the treatment of *'Allo 'Allo* actor Gorden Kaye back in 1990.[27] Yet the former *Sun* journalist is clear about what he would feel like relying on Facebook alone for similar stories to Leighton:

> I would be telling myself that it was 'ok' because the pictures were in the public domain. But I know I'd be conning myself….To speak to and for real people means you have to meet them and feel what they feel…How can I translate the true pain and emotions of a family if I rely on a picture and some stylized words that capture a moment in time from Twitter or Facebook? Also, there is nothing to hold me to account other than my conscience and, under pressure from a Fleet St editor, a conscience is a luxury most hacks can't easily afford.

And Joan Smith, who interviewed several survivors of the Yorkshire Ripper face-to-face and spent a week after the London Iranian embassy siege of 1980 with the embassy caretaker to reconstruct the event, believes that using technology in this way gives journalists 'a lot of control'. 'You become a silent watcher. It's an immensely powerful role and easy to forget the public interest justification,' she says. 'There is a huge disconnect between people putting stuff about themselves on web pages, thinking they're talking to their friends and not realising they are a potential source for journalists.'

As for Rebecca Leighton, after the early coverage she ended up initially being refused bail for her own protection, and after her release ended up living with her parents. She claims she feels now that she can't walk down the street on her own because she feels so scared.

Most importantly, Neal Keeling, of the *MEN*, also feels in the furore over use of Leighton's Facebook page a vital part of the story has also been missed, one that only his team are still pursuing: 'The charges have been dropped against Rebecca Leighton. So who was responsible – someone who still works at the hospital? A bank nurse?' he asks. 'The media got obsessed with their angel of death story and have not investigated fully. If I was a patient I'd want answers.'

Notes

[1] Becki Leighton's Facebook page
https://www.facebook.com/profile.php?id=533118996, accessed on 27 November 2011

[2] Smith, Joan (2011) I was targeted as collateral damage, *Guardian*, 22 November 2011 Available online at
http://www.guardian.co.uk/media/video/2011/nov/22/joan-smith-collateral-damage-phone-hacking-video, accessed on 13 December 2011

[3] O'Carroll, Lisa (2011) Phone hacking victims to number 800, *Guardian*, 10 December 2011. Available online at
http://www.guardian.co.uk/media/2011/dec/10/phone-hacking-victims-800, accessed on 13 December 2011

[4] Arthur, Charles (2011) Facebook grow slows for a second month, *Guardian*, 13 June 2011 Available online at
http://www.guardian.co.uk/technology/2011/jun/13/facebook-growth-slows-for-second-month, accessed on 13 December 2011

[5] Interview via telephone, November 2011

[6] Clarkson, Wensley (2011) Tabloid Tricks. Available online at
http://www.wensleyclarkson.com/, accessed on 13 December 2011

[7] Interview, London, 28 November 2011

[8] Telephone interview, 30 November 2011

[9] Phone interview, 30 Nov 2011

[10] Fievez, Paul (2011) Borrowed photos (2) Gentlemanranters. Available online at http://gentlemenranters.com/page_325.html#pf220, accessed on 30 November 2011

[11] Whittle, Stephen and Cooper, Glenda (2009) *Privacy Probity and Public Interest*, Oxfrod: Reuters Institute for the Study of Journalism

[12] Whittle and Cooper op cit

[13] Fernandez, Colin and Hale, Beth (2007) Foxy Knowy: Inside the twisted world of flatmate suspected of Meredith's murder, *Daily Mail*, 6 November 2007. Available online at http://www.dailymail.co.uk/news/article-

492092/Foxy-Knoxy-Inside-twisted-world-flatmate-suspected-Merediths-murder.html, accessed on 13 December 2011

[14] Interview via telephone, 4 December 2011

[15] Nelmes, Amy (2009) My lot have murdered someone again, *People*, 26 April. Available online at http://www.people.co.uk/news/uk-world-news/2009/04/26/my-lot-have-murdered-someone-again-s-happens-93463-21308828/, accessed on 29 November 2011

[16] Mullan, Weir, Campbell v Scottish Sunday Express 2009. Adjudication available online at http://www.pcc.org.uk/news/index.html?article=NTc5Mw, accessed on 13 December 2011

[17] Via email, 29 November 2011

[18] Whittle and Cooper op cit

[19] See Ofcom Broadcast Bulletin 189 12 September 2011. Available online at http://stakeholders.ofcom.org.uk/binaries/enforcement/broadcast-bulletins/obb189/obb189.pdf, accessed on 13 December 2011

[20] Via email, 28 November 2011

[21] BBC *Editorial Guidelines*: Pictures from Social Media Sites. Available online at http://www.bbc.co.uk/editorialguidelines/page/guidance-social-media-pictures, accessed on 30 November 2011

[22] Douglas v Hello! [2005] EWCA Civ 595

[23] Campbell v Mirror Group Newspapers [2004] UKHL 22

[24] Von Hannover v Germany [2004] ECHR

[25] Peck v United Kingdom [2003] EMLR 15

[26] Interview with Rebecca Leighton, *This Morning* ITV, 19 September 2011. Available online at http://www.itv.com/thismorning/life/innocent-saline-nurse-rebecca-leighton/, accessed oon 13 December 2011

[27] Kaye, well known for his role as Rene Artois in the comedy series *'Allo 'Allo*, had sustained serious head injuries in a car accident in January 1990: while in hospital, he was 'interviewed' by a *Sunday Sport* journalist. Kaye failed in his attempt to stop the *Sunday Sport* publishing the 'interview'

Note on the contributor
Glenda Cooper was the 14th Guardian Research Fellow at Nuffield College, Oxford, and former visiting fellow at the Reuters Institute for the Study of Journalism. She is currently a PhD student at City University looking at user-generated content and the reporting of disasters. She has worked as a staff correspondent for the BBC, Channel 4 News Radio, the *Independent*, *Daily Mail*, *Daily Telegraph* and the *Washington Post*.

Improving Integrity Online: Towards a Code of Conduct for Journalism on the Internet

Sean Dodson lays out some basic guidelines – currently missing from the codes – for journalists using online material

The reputation of journalism is in a bad way. A number of high profile scandals have eroded public trust in journalism while recent polls suggest that the decline of trust in journalism is more pronounced than even that of politicians (Kellner 2011).

The Leveson Inquiry is looking into the extent of improper conduct within News International – and beyond – but although the scope of its remit is wide, it cannot hope to address the entirety of the structural transformation required in the media since the deregulation of the 1980s (Chapman and Kinsey 2008).

Sociologists such and Castells (1996) have characterised the change since deregulation as 'the rise of the network society' in which the growth of telecommunications and computer networks have reshaped the industrialised world and created 'a new global paradigm' (Volkmer 2003).

The rise of the network society, particularly the growth of the internet, is disrupting the way newspapers and broadcasters work. The growth of telecommunications and computer networks has created an abundance of new methods of distribution. Moreover, the internet has become the 'go-to point' for journalists to source their contacts and stories (Krotoski 2011), as well as providing a new way in which the reader and the writer relate (Fortunati 2009).

But when we examine the behaviour of journalists, and particularly their codes of conduct, we can see that their ethical standards have failed to keep pace with technological change. For example, research indicates that readers are increasingly concerned with the issue of online news credibility (ibid) and yet a stress on the accuracy of online sources is yet to be integrated into existing codes.

The point of codes of ethics is to help gain public trust. And yet, in a recent survey, 58 per cent of adults in the UK said the phone hacking scandal has had a negative effect on their perception of UK newspapers, while 51 per cent said that the scandal had made them less trusting of all British news organisations (Bazilian 2011). It follows that for the media to remain credible it must be trusted by its readers, viewers and users. In other words, it needs to behave – and be seen to behave – with integrity. A number of scandals in recent years: the appalling treatment of the McCann family, the hacking of Millie Dowler's mobile phone along with the blatant plagiarism of high profile journalists such as Johann Hari, of the *Independent,* have all become visible examples of journalists lacking personal and professional integrity. Of course integrity, in itself, is a virtue. It is defined by the *Oxford English Dictionary* as 'soundness of moral principle; the character of uncorrupted virtue, esp. in relation to truth and fair dealing; uprightness, honesty, sincerity'.

The moot point is whether integrity can ever be inculcated by an external organisation and then embodied in an ethical code of practice. Can a set of guidelines or principles be developed to help journalists behave with more integrity? As noted by Luckhurst (2011) any set of codes of ethics for journalists needs to be based on principles rather than rules. Furthermore, journalists are rightfully wary of accepting legislation that has the threat of curtailing their freedom of expression. But then again, all newsrooms have a list of written and unwritten 'rules' about how to behave both inside and outside the office.

What we need to do to improve journalistic standards is help codify the best practice from those newsrooms and organise them into a set of universal guidelines for all journalists working on and from the internet.

Furthermore, the absence of a code to define the new practices that have been presented by the internet could partly explain how and why the internet is also causing a sense of 'professional discomfort' (Cassidy 2007) among journalists and creating a need to reassess professional roles. Print and online journalists 'differ in the evaluation of credibility of online news' and although journalists' acceptance of the internet as a 'source of credible information is evolving' perhaps because of the 'incorporation in the professional ideology of traditional journalists of the norms and values of online journalism' (ibid).

The ethics of journalism, therefore, seem to be changing but a close examination of the existing codes reveal that few of these changes have yet to be addressed.

NUJ and PCC Codes

The oldest code in the UK is the National Union of Journalists (NUJ) Code of Practice which has existed in various forms since 1936. It is seen as a reliable code (Chapman and Nuttall 2011) adopted by working journalists working either online, offline or on-air. The NUJ code is remarkable for both its scope and its brevity. Journalists have a guide to their entire range of professional behaviour in just 336 words. The NUJ code was updated as recently as 16 September 2011 but it makes no mention of the internet. Indeed, although the code has been adapted many times in recent years, there is nothing in the language of the code that could not have been there when it was first written.

While the NUJ Code of Conduct is aimed mainly at journalists, the code of the Press Complaints Commission is more often referred to as the 'editor's code'. Compared to the concise NUJ code, the PCC code weighs in at a relatively verbose 1,640 words (PCC 2011). If the NUJ code deals in general ethics, leaving interpretation to journalist's common sense, the PCC code deals much more in specifics. But like the NUJ code, the PCC code makes no specific reference to the internet. Nor does it make any reference to the online domain. The PCC code does mention 'digital communications' (in clause 3.1, Privacy) and then again (clause 10.1) with regard to 'clandestine devices and subterfuge'.

> The press must not seek to obtain or publish material acquired by using hidden cameras or clandestine listening devices; or by intercepting private or mobile telephone calls, messages or emails; or by the unauthorised removal of documents or photographs; or by accessing digitally-held private information without consent.

BBC's *Editorial Guidelines*

Any study of ethical codes must refer to the BBC and its detailed *Editorial Guidelines*. Indeed, the BBC is rated as the world's largest traditional media organisation on the internet (Alexa, 2010). Its *Editorial Guidelines* span 75,000 words yet 'internet' is mentioned only 13 times. More commonly is 'online' with more than 250 mentions in the latest version from July 2011.

Thus clause 3.4.24 stresses that, for news, the BBC considers itself 'a permanent public record' and that its journalists need to be aware of the permanency of the content they post online. So, the *Guidelines* advise on how often web pages should be updated and how they need to be date-stamped.

Six Dominant Themes of the *Guidelines*

Six dominant themes emerge in the *Guidelines* relating to online journalism: transparency, hyperlinking, online subterfuge, privacy, accuracy and user-generated content.

Transparency

The BBC now expects its journalists to be transparent about the 'nature and provenance' of online content instructing them to 'identify who has created it' (1.2.10). Seeking contributors from chat rooms, message board or social networking group, for example, now requires the permission of the editor. It also makes a further pledge (3.1) to 'validate the authenticity of documentary evidence and digital material'. Moreover, BBC journalists are also expected to (3.4.3/3.4.4) uphold a higher standard of accuracy. Email contacts must be vetted on the phone, user-generated content should be handled with scepticism.

Hyperlinking

Journalists are advised to link only to sites believed to be accurate (3.4.15). External links must be within the law and must 'not breach the BBC *Editorial Guidelines* on harm and offence. Moreover 3.4.15 advises that links from BBC Online to third party websites should lead to sites which are 'factually accurate'. A further clause, 4.4.10, states that where BBC online sites covering 'controversial subjects' offer links to external sites, 'we should ensure that the information on those external sites, represents a reasonable range of views'.

Subterfuge

The *Guidelines* advise that 'anyone actively intervening to steer the course of an online discussion for a BBC purpose, without revealing their link to the BBC, must be acting in the public interest' (6.3.9).

Privacy

The BBC also has specific guidelines for handling material gleaned from social media. Clause 7.4.8 advises that 'although material, especially pictures and videos, on third party social media and other websites where the public have ready access may be considered to have been placed in the public domain, re-use by the BBC will usually bring it to a much wider audience'. Journalists are advised to consider the impact of re-use, particularly when in connection with tragic or distressing events. There are also copyright considerations. Moreover, since material from social media is 'considered to be in the public domain' all re-use needs to be considered carefully in relation tragic or distressing event, especially in times of armed conflict or war.

Accuracy

The *Guidelines* specifically refer to the growing use of user-generated content (3.4.3/3.4.4). Journalists are advised to not automatically assume that the material is accurate and should take reasonable steps to seek verification. Special care is needed over lobby groups. 'We should carefully scrutinise and...corroborate eyewitness accounts submitted by email before using them, for example, by talking to eyewitnesses on the phone. We should ensure that user generated content is clearly identified as such.' Another clause dealing with the accuracy of online content is 3.4.22, which advises that 'when a material change is made to an item of content, the change should normally be indicated to users unless, for example, there are legal or editorial reasons not to do so'.

User-generated content

The *Guidelines* advise (11.4.4) that 'in times of conflict, there are special sensitivities, for example about the security of operational military plans'. Thus, journalists are advised to avoid naming casualties until next of kin have been informed, and handling unsubstantiated rumours.

> This applies, particularly, to user-generated content when users normally expect their material to be published as soon as it is sent to us. At such

times, we may publish additional guidelines to the effect that we will concentrate comment and debate about the conflict in a limited number of spaces, with additional hosting and moderation, to maintain a full debate we will be prepared to switch to pre-moderation if necessary.

Lord Patten on BBC Editorial Independence

Significantly, the chairman of the BBC Trust, Lord Patten, in a speech to the Society of Editors' annual conference (Hill 2011) highlighted both the importance of the editorial independence at the corporation and the constraints on its investigative powers in this way:

> As a publicly funded broadcaster whose output is so directly intrusive, there are some areas where we ought to be particularly careful in our journalism or even decline to follow where newspapers or online journalism may properly lead.

The phone hacking scandal is arguably the biggest political story in the UK of recent years (Oborne 2011) yet the BBC (with the exception of Richard Watson, of *Newsnight*) has been conspicuous in its failure to investigate it – with other media (most notably the *Guardian*, Channel 4 News and *The New York Times*) setting the pace.

Other Responses – Here and Abroad

Other professions are drawing up codes of conduct to deal with the challenges of the network society. The British Medical Association (BMA), for instance, recently published *Using Social Media: Practical and Ethical Guidance for Doctors and Medical Students*. While the paper does not go quite as far to say that social media is bad for your health, it does suggest that doctors need to be careful in their dealings with the internet, recommending care in setting their own privacy settings and advising them on declaring conflicts of interest.

A code being drafted by the European Journalism Centre in Maastricht (Hudson 2010) is also seeking to expand the definition of journalist to include bloggers.

In the US, both *The New York Times* and the *Los Angeles Times* publish their code of ethics, and surprisingly perhaps, given the level of detail contained in both, neither makes specific reference to the internet. But in West Virginia, the guidelines of the more modest title, the *Roanoke Times*, include specific policies on confirming information gathered online via 'offline' sources; managing personal comments and profiles on social networks (echoing that of the BMA) and defining good hyperlinking practice when promoting content. The guidelines add (see *Roanoke Times* News Standards and Policies 2011):

> Staffers should realise that comments they post online, whether on personal web sites or other non-newspaper sites, about stories they have covered or other newsroom matters can affect perceptions of their

credibility and the newspaper's credibility as well, and they should exercise good judgment in making these comments.

On the use of social media, they comment:

It is the journalist's job to consider the variety and diversity of sources used for stories, and the same applies to sources found on social networking sites. Consider if finding sources this way leads you to a predominance of people of a certain race, ethnicity, political persuasion, belief system, world view, age or income (ibid; see also Oliver 2009).

As the Space between Public and Private Spheres Diminishes

One of the most complex issues facing the media today relates to the breaking down of the distinctions between the public and private spheres (see, for instance, Gerstein 1978 and Sennett 1977). Material from social networking sites is seen by its users as intimate and the PCC is receiving a growing number of complaints from users who feel their intimacy has been invaded by the press (PCC).

Most recently Lucy Gamble, a former prefect at Cheltenham Girls School, and now a student at Cambridge University, complained that her personal information on Facebook had been used by the *Daily Mail* to portray her as 'a good girl gone bad' (PCC 2011a). While the PCC found that its code had not been breached, the *Mail* did agree to remove the offending article from its database.

Another young student, Stephen Nutt, son of Professor David Nutt, the former government drugs advisor, found pictures he had posted on Facebook splashed across the pages of the *Sun*. His crime: to be drunk at a teenage party and to have had a picture taken of him smoking a roll-up. The *Sun* insinuated that the cigarette in question was a marijuana joint (Nutt says it was not). Again, the PCC found that the code had not been breached, but the *Sun* agreed to remove it from its database (PCC 2011b).

The *Daily Telegraph, Sunday Mirror,* and the *People* have all been admonished for raiding intimate information from social networking sites (PCC 2009, 2010) And the *Hull Daily Mail* has been caught using bogus Facebook pages on stories that were not deemed to be in the public interest (PCC 2010c).

In each of the instances, the PCC has ruled that its code has not been breached, although it has arranged for the offending image or article to be removed. This suggests that there is a tacit understanding that the current code is inadequate. Indeed, although the use of social networking websites has yet to be codified, the PCC is using precedence to bring its code up to date. Significantly, when serving police officer John Hayter found himself in the public eye after some unwise comments on Facebook over the death of Ian Tomlinson during the London G20 protests in April 2009, the PCC, in its ruling, commented:

The commission has recently made clear that it can be acceptable in some circumstances for the press to publish information taken from social networking websites, even when the material is originally intended for a small group of acquaintances and not publicly accessible. However, this will generally be only in cases where the public interest overrides the individual's right to privacy (PCC 2009).

And when the *Peterborough Evening Telegraph* took pictures of a young boy Tyler Whelan from Facebook after his tragic death, the PCC ruled that its code had been broken only in relation to the treatment of children, not the appropriation of the image (PCC. 2011b)

Internet Hoaxes

Journalists also need to learn how to trust material they gather on the internet. Recently Dobrica Ćosić fell victim to an internet hoax with the state-run Serbian television announcing wrongly that Ćosić had been awarded the Nobel Prize for Literature (Gustini 2011). The hoax was repeated by a various news organisations (including the *Guardian*) because journalists failed to check. A simple search of the Alexa Page ranking system would have shown that the site at http://www.nobelprizeliterature.org/ was a hoax. Or again, the Associated Press (AP) could have avoided falling for a fake press release which claimed that GE (General Electric) would repay the US government the $3.8 billion in unpaid taxes. The fake press release, titled 'GE Responds to Public Outcry – Will Donate Entire $3.2 Billion Tax Refund to Help Offset Cuts and Save American Jobs' was posted at a site called http://www.genewscenters.com/ (Weisenthal 2011). Again a rudimentary search into the site's page rank would have exposed the hoax.

Conclusion: The Codes Need Updating

According to Damian Tambini, of the London School of Economics, applying 'the old ethical standards in competition with blogs and social media…may simply be commercial suicide. But to let standards slip will lead to irresponsible journalism, and to the public questioning the legal and other privileges that are enjoyed by journalists' (Beckett 2010).

So by synthesising best practice from the BBC, the European Journalism Centre and the *Roanoke Times* we can begin to sketch out the contours of a future code. It could stress these guidelines:

1. Link to only what is accurate.

2. Scrutinise online contacts.

3. Be honest about provenance.

4. Recognise the intimate sphere and respect it where possible.

5. Learn to value and distinguish social capital online.

6. Conduct yourself with the same level of integrity online as you would be expected to in the real world.

References

Alexa (2011) Alexa top sites. Available at http://www.alexa.com/topsites, accessed on 20 December 2011

Bazilian (2011) Survey Shows Hacking Scandal's Effect on Media Credibility, UK. and US. view news outlets differently, Adweek, available at http://www.adweek.com/news/press/publishers-challenge-audience-report-137182, accessed on 20 December 2011

BBC (2011) About the BBC. Available online at ttp://www.bbc.co.uk/aboutthebbc/purpose/what.shtm, accessed on 1 October 2011

BBC *Editorial Guidelines* (2010) Available online at http://downloads.bbc.co.uk/guidelines/editorialguidelines/pdfs/Editorial_Guidelines_in_full.pdf, accessed on 25 October 2011

Beckett, Charlie (2010) Media Ethics in the New Media Landscape, London School of Economics and Political Science Polis blog. Available online at http://blogs.lse.ac.uk/polis/2010/09/14/media-ethics-in-the-new-media-landscape-new-paper/, accessed on 20 December 2011

British Medical Association (2011) Using social media: practical and ethical guidance for doctors and medical students. Available online at http://www.bma.org.uk/images/socialmediaguidancemay2011_tcm41-206859.pdf , accessed on 10 November 2011

Cassidy, William P (2007) *Online news credibility: An examination of the perceptions of newspaper journalists, Journal of Computer-Mediated Communication*, Vol. 12, No. 2 pp 478-498

Castells, Manuel (1996) *The Rise of the Network Society,* Blackwell: London

Chapman, Jane and Nuttall, Nick (2011) *Journalism Today: A Themed History*, Blackwell: London

Chapman, Jane. Kinsey, Marie (2008) *Broadcast journalism: A critical introduction*, London, Taylor and Francis

Fortunati, Leopoldina (2009) The influence of the internet on European journalism, *Journal of Computer-Mediated Communication*, Vol. 14, No. 4 pp 928-963

Gerstein, Robert (1978) Intimacy and Privacy, *Ethics*, October, Chicago: University of Chicago Press pp 76-81.

Gustini Ray (2011) Serbia's Dobrica Cosic Did Not Win the Nobel Prize for Literature, the *Atlantic.* Available online at http://www.theatlanticwire.com/entertainment/2011/10/sebrian-author-dobrica-cosic-did-not-win-nobel-literature/43425, accessed on 20 December 2011

Hill, Amelia (2011) BBC unable to investigate hacking, says Patten, 14 November, *Guardian.* Available online at: http://www.guardian.co.uk/media/2011/nov/13/bbc-political-bias-lord-patten, accessed on 25 October 2011

Krotoski, Aleks (2011) What effect has the internet had on journalism? *Observer*, 20 February. Available online at: http://www.guardian.co.uk/technology/2011/feb/20/what-effect-internet-on-journalism, accessed on 10 November 2011

LA Times (2007) *Ethics Guidelines.* Available online at http://latimesblogs.latimes.com/readers/2007/07/los-angeles-tim.html, accessed on 10 November 2011

Hudson, Howard (2010) *Media Coverage Ethics for a Changing Media Landscape*, European Journalism Centre. Available online at http://www.ejc.net/magazine/article/media_coverage_ethics_for_a_changing_media_l andscape/, accessed on 10 November 2011

Kellner, Peter (2011) Number cruncher: A matter of trust, *Prospect*, No. 175, September

New York Times Company Policy on Ethics in Journalism. Available online at: http://www.nytco.com/press/ethics.html, accessed on 10 November 2011

Luckhurst, Tim (2011) Paper at Institute of Communication Ethics Annual Conference, Foreign Press Association, London, 28 October

NUJ code of conduct (2011) Available online at http://media.gn.apc.org/nujcode.html, accessed on 10 November 2011

PCC code of practice (2011). Available online at http://www.pcc.org.uk/cop/practice.html, accessed on 10 November 2011

PCC (2011a) Mr Callum Chaplin on behalf of Ms Lucy Gamble. Available online at: http://www.pcc.org.uk/news/index.html?article=NzIwMw==, accessed on 10 November 2011

PCC (2011b) Resolved cases: Mr Stephen Nutt. Available online at: http://www.pcc.org.uk/case/resolved.html?article=NjExOQ==, accessed on 10 November 2011

PCC (2010a) Complainant Name: Mr Neil Pizey. Press Complaints Commission. Available online at http://www.pcc.org.uk/news/index.html?article=Njg0Mg==, accessed on 20 December 2011

PCC (2010b) Complainant Name: Lucy Phillips. Press Complaints Commission. Available online at http://www.pcc.org.uk/news/index.html?article=NjU5MA==, accessed on 20 December 2011

PCC (2010c) Complainant Name:Mr Paul Smith. Press Complaints Comission. Available online at http://www.pcc.org.uk/news/index.html?article=NjU0Mg==, accessed on 20 December 2011

PCC (2009) Complainant Name: Phyllis Goble. Available online at http://www.pcc.org.uk/news/index.html?article=NjA4MQ==, accessed on 20 December 2011

PCC (2009) News: Complainant Name: Phyllis Goble. Press Complaints Commission. Available online at http://www.pcc.org.uk/news/index.html?article=NjA4MQ== , accessed on 10 November 2011

PCC (2011a) News: Complainant Name: Shaun Harrison. Press Complaints Commission. Available online at http://www.pcc.org.uk/news/index.html?article=NzI3Nw==, accessed on 10 November 2011

PCC (2011b) Press Complaints Commission. Available online at http://www.pcc.org.uk/news/index.html?article=NzI3Nw==, accessed on 20 December 2011

Roanoke Times (2011) News Standards and Policies. Available online at
http://www.roanoke.com/newsservices/wb/xp-59614, accessed on 10 November 2011

Sennett, Richard (1977) *The Fall of Public Man*, London: Faber

Kiousis, S (2001) Public Trust or Mistrust? Perceptions of Media Credibility in the
Information Age, *Mass Communication and Society*, Vol. 4, No. 4 pp 381-403

Volkmer, Ingrid (2003) The global network society and the global public sphere,
Development, Vol. 46, No. 1 pp 9-16 quoted in Chapman, Jane and Kinsey, Marie (2008)
Broadcast journalism: A critical introduction, Routledge: London p 54

Weisenthal, Joe (2011) Falls For Hoax Press Release Saying That GE Will Repay
Government $3.8 Billion Tax Break, Business Insider, the Business Insider. Available
online at http://articles.businessinsider.com/2011-04-13/news/30029965_1_tax-
refund-tax-havens-tax-avoidance#ixzz1h6DyY3Af, accessed on 20 December 2011

Note on the contributor

Sean Dodson is the leader of the undergraduate journalism course at Leeds Metropolitan
University. He is also a journalist who has been covering the social uses of technology
for the *Guardian, Wired, Design Week, Press Gazette*, the *South China Morning Post* and the
Melbourne Age. He is currently researching a doctorate on the internet of things.

Standing up for Standards: Could a 'Conscience Clause' Protect Ethical Journalism?

A 'conscience clause' will not heal all of journalism's ills. It is a fairly modest proposal, suggests Tony Harcup. But, he stresses: 'Given the ethical vacuum that appears to have been created in certain newsrooms by the almost totally unconstrained management prerogative that followed Rupert Murdoch's victory at Wapping in 1986, isn't it time we gave it a try?'

When the National Union of Journalists (NUJ) began to talk seriously in the early years of the twenty-first century about the need for a 'conscience clause' to protect any journalist ordered to act unethically, the union was reviving a concern it had first expressed some seven decades before. Back in 1931, the NUJ had appealed to newspaper proprietors and editors alike to refrain from instructing staff to use 'distasteful and unseemly' methods of covering stories or getting pictures, and the union went on to promise 'to treat the case of a member who was dismissed for refusing to carry out instructions repugnant to his sense of decency, as one of victimisation, i.e. to maintain him while getting fresh employment' (Mansfield 1936: 372). Shortly afterwards the NUJ established its code of ethical conduct for journalists, becoming the first body in the UK to do so; a good half century before national newspaper editors gathered in the backroom of the 'last chance saloon' to write their own code (Bundock 1957: 128-129; Cole and Harcup 2010: 125-126).

Journalists Complain of Coming Under Pressure

Twice, in 2001 and 2004, journalists working for the *Daily Express* reported their own newspaper to the organisation that had emerged from that lock-in at the last chance saloon: the Press Complaints Commission (PCC). This was in the days when the Express Group deigned to consent to 'self-regulation' and take part in the PCC's procedures. Members of the newspaper's editorial staff were

240

prompted to take such unusual action by an unrelenting – and, for many of them, frankly embarrassing - series of front-page splashes such as 'ASYLUM: WE'RE BEING INVADED'; '1.6 MILLION GYPSIES READY TO FLOOD IN – BRITAIN HERE WE COME'; and 'WE CAN'T COPE WITH HUGE GYPSY INVASION'. When some journalists complained that they felt under pressure to produce stories to fit a pre-conceived editorial line thought to reflect readers' prejudices, the issue was added to the agenda of what was to have been a routine bread-and-butter gathering of the NUJ chapel at Express Newspapers. An unusually crowded meeting of *Express* journalists went on to pass the following motion:

> This chapel is concerned that *Express* journalists are coming under pressure to write anti-Gypsy articles. We call for a letter to be sent to the Press Complaints Commission reminding it of the need to protect journalists who are unwilling to write racist articles which are contrary to the National Union of Journalists' code of conduct (quoted in Ponsford 2004).

In effect, *Express* journalists were appealing to the PCC for protection against their line managers, although the paper's editor later insisted: 'I have never forced anyone to write anything' (quoted in Snoddy 2006).

The union wrote to the PCC asking it to insert a 'conscience clause' into its editors' code of practice, whereby journalists who refused unethical assignments would be protected from disciplinary action or dismissal over such a refusal. The *Express* journalists' workplace representative (Mother of Chapel or MoC) at the time was Michelle Stanistreet who, when interviewed not long afterwards for my book *The Ethical Journalist*, explained that the journalists' plea had been rejected in peremptory fashion without any investigation: 'We wrote to them asking for a conscience clause, but they said that journalists don't come under such pressure, so there is no need for one, and it's just a matter between the employer and the employee' (quoted in Harcup 2007: 123).

That uncompromising, almost uncomprehending, stance was reiterated when a PCC representative told an ethics conference around the same time: 'It is not our job to become involved in disputes between employers and their staff' (quoted in Bayley and Macaskill 2004: 17). Perhaps not, but the idea of a conscience clause was to help provide a mechanism for ethical journalism to prevail without it necessarily leading to a dispute, whereas the absence of a clause left all the power in the hands of the employer.

The NUJ managed to gain some modest support elsewhere for its conscience clause idea. MPs on the Commons culture, media and sport select committee concluded in 2003 (in one of what has seemed like an incessant series of reports on press standards and self-regulation over the past decade): 'An additional element of the [PCC] code should be that journalists are enabled to refuse an assignment on the grounds that it breaches the code and, if necessary, refer the matter to the commission without prejudice' (CMS 2003). The suggestion promptly sank, with seemingly the only trace of it being a sympathetic editorial in the *British Journalism Review* arguing that 'the introduction of a conscience clause into the Press Complaints Commission code of conduct would be a welcome improvement, not only to reporters' working lives but also to the standards of newspapers in general', as it would give reporters and photographers at least some defence against the 'rogue bosses' who sometimes send them out on 'shameful assignments' (Hagerty 2003: 4).

Empowering journalists to improve standards

Undeterred, the NUJ took the initiative and in 2005 its national executive came up with model wording for such a clause: 'A journalist has the right to refuse assignments or be identified as the author of editorial which would break the letter and spirit of the code. No journalist can be disciplined or suffer detriment to their career for asserting his/her rights to act according to the code' (Gopsill and Neale 2007: 255). After lengthy debate within branches, chapels, the NUJ's elected ethics council and full annual delegate meeting, the following clause duly became enshrined in the NUJ's own code of conduct, which forms part of the union's rulebook: 'The NUJ believes a journalist has the right to refuse an assignment or be identified as the author of editorial that would break the letter or spirit of the code. The NUJ will fully support any journalist disciplined for asserting her/his right to act according to the code' (NUJ 2010: 22). The union's President in 2005-6, Tim Lezard, declared: 'It's vital for us to have a say in our work. The conscience clause isn't about muzzling the media, it's about empowering our members and improving industry standards' (quoted in Gopsill and Neale 2007: 255).

And there the matter lay until the summer of 2011 when the *Guardian*'s revelations about Milly Dowler's phone having been hacked by a private investigator working for the *News of the World* became the tipping point in the Hackgate scandal. Questions of journalistic ethics were back on the political agenda and, amidst all the talk of phone hacking on an industrial scale, followed by the Murdochs' summary closure of the so-called *News of the Screws*, the thought began to occur: would all this have happened if journalists there had been empowered to speak out about dodgy practices? Indeed, could it possibly have been more than coincidence that the scandal had occurred in a workplace from which independent trade unions had in effect been banished?

Journalist Paul Foot had long ago warned that the sort of cowed and subservient atmosphere found within too many newsrooms following the Wapping dispute of the 1980s would prove fatal for journalistic standards, because active NUJ chapels within newsrooms provide a vital forum in which 'journalists can collect and discuss their common problems, free from the management hierarchy. A recognised trade union adds to the spirit of independence inside a newspaper which is so crucial to successful investigative journalism' (Foot 2000: 86). Of course, as a committed trade unionist and one-time editor of *Socialist Worker*, he would say that, wouldn't he? But does that automatically invalidate his point?

There will always be members of the awkward squad such as Foot who will speak out and stand up for themselves and for their colleagues; journalists such as Michelle Stanistreet, who as MoC was prepared to say 'Boo!' to *Express* owner Richard Desmond, or the legendary James Cameron, who voted with his feet rather than stay and moan about the ethics of his job in the manner of a 'rueful whore' (Cameron 1968: 84). There are other examples of journalists taking Cameron's route of principled escape, as when Katy Weitz left a job on the *Sun* in 2003 because of what she saw as her paper's apparent bloodlust for the Iraq war (*Press Gazette* 2003), when technology columnist David Hewson quit *The Sunday Times* in 2005 because he felt it was being too uncritical of the new technology business (Ponsford 2005), and most recently when Richard Peppiatt left the *Daily Star*, accusing it of 'making the facts fit the story, because the story is almost pre-defined' (Peppiatt 2011a).

And then, on extremely rare occasions, journalists have taken a more collective stand over an ethical issue, as when NUJ members at the *Oxford Mail* walked out for a day to defend a photographer disciplined for refusing to snatch a picture of a disabled five-year-old outside school, following appeals by the child's mother for an end to media attention (McIntyre 2004).

Are we Sure we Should be Doing This?

And what of awkward squad stalwart Nick Davies, who – if anyone does – surely personifies the journalistic independence of spirit that the late Paul Foot was talking about? Along with his *Guardian* colleagues, Davies kept returning to the phone hacking story long after less awkward journalists began echoing the line put out by that unholy trinity of News International, the Metropolitan Police and the PCC: that it was a dead horse being flogged for no purpose. Whilst we might hope that every journalist embodies the bravery and/or stroppiness of a Foot, a Cameron or a Davies, it isn't necessarily going to be the case. Nor should journalistic standards depend solely on the presence of such outspoken individuals within a workplace.

In my experience the vast majority of journalists want to do a decent job and not to be ashamed of their craft. That is why many believe that a 'conscience clause' along the lines proposed by the NUJ – and now supported by the International Federation of Journalists (IFJ 2010), the Trades Union Congress (*Journalist* 2011), and phone hacking victims' lawyer Mark Lewis (Slattery 2011) – might redress the balance slightly and help create a climate within newsrooms whereby, just occasionally, a senior, middling or even lowly journalist might feel able to ask: 'Hang on a minute, are we sure we should be doing this?'

After all, many journalists now have adherence to the editors' code written into their contracts of employment, notwithstanding the fact that – unlike the NUJ code which is the result of discussion and agreement via the union's democratic structures – ordinary journalists below the rank of editor have no say in how the PCC code is drafted, amended or implemented. That being the case, surely the least they ought to be able to expect is that they might be defended if they put their head on the chopping block by telling their boss: 'What you are instructing me to do goes against the code, is unethical, and I will not do it.' Even with a conscience clause in place, such action is likely to be rare indeed. Frivolous recourse to playing the conscience card would be discouraged by the inescapable reality that using it in such a way would hardly be likely to improve anyone's career prospects in a highly competitive industry.

However, editors and proprietors might have reason to be grudgingly grateful if an ethical intervention were to save them from themselves; as in 2006 when a group of *Daily Star* journalists forced a rethink about the wisdom of the newspaper running a spoof version of a supposed Islamic *Daily Fatwa*, which claimed to demonstrate 'how Britain's fave newspaper would look under Muslim rule', promising a 'page three burka babes picture special' and offering a 'free beard for every bomber' (Burrell 2006). Only after news of the journalists' opposition was passed up the editorial chain via the NUJ was the page pulled at the last minute. 'It was as if a light had suddenly come on and they saw what they were doing,' said Father of Chapel Steve Usher. 'The guys who raised it did the company a huge favour' (quoted in *Journalist* 2006). Media commentator Stephen Glover (2006) agreed that owner Desmond 'should be grateful to have been saved by a bunch of NUJ rebels'.

Viewing Events through a Different Window
If the amicable withdrawal of that offending page before it had been printed was an example of the interests of staff and proprietor being one and the same, the norm is that their interests do not necessarily align so neatly. As journalist and journalism teacher Angela Phillips argued in evidence to yet another parliamentary inquiry into the media:

> In debates about ethics the role of the ordinary journalist is too often subsumed within that of the editors and proprietors as though those people who work for the news media always have exactly the same interests, and the same power to protect their interests, as do those who employ and direct them. This fundamental error applies to the teaching of ethics on journalism courses in colleges and universities just as much as it has always applied to the policy makers who have attempted to legislate or regulate the media. The reality is that journalists are what Bourdieu refers to as 'weakly autonomous'...As individuals, their autonomy is circumscribed by a steeply hierarchical employment structure, with an editor at the top who is under constant pressure to chase audience ratings or circulation (Phillips 2008).

Within this context, it is worth noting that Hackgate took place within a highly pressurised, constrained and hierarchical newsroom, whereas the journalist who did the most to expose it, Nick Davies, enjoys an unusually autonomous working relationship with his own newspaper. It would, of course, be simplistic to deduce from this that an obsequious newsroom is an ethical accident waiting to happen whereas relative journalistic autonomy produces more ethical journalism – and we should not forget that highbrow newsrooms have also produced unethical journalism, as attested to by the cases of Johann Hari at the *Independent* (Milmo 2011) and Jayson Blair at *The New York Times* (Mnookin 2005) – but could there not be at least an element of truth in such a deduction? True, not all journalists will be able to work as far behind the frontline of the commercial circulation war as Davies has been able to in recent years, but that is all the more reason to offer such journalists some element of ethical protection.

It might be that Lord Justice Leveson is more open to such an argument than have been newspaper proprietors to date, judging by the fact that in reversing his earlier decision to refuse the NUJ 'core participant' status at his inquiry, he seemed to acknowledge that the union represented views from the newsroom floor that might be different from the views of those traditionally allowed to speak on behalf of what is typically termed *the industry*. 'I see considerable force in the submission that, through its members, the NUJ does provide a different window on the issues with which the inquiry is concerned and, just as important, is able to access evidence on the issues of culture, practice and ethics which the inquiry might not otherwise be able to obtain,' he said in his ruling (Leveson 2011: 3).

Would a Conscience Clause Work?

The NUJ – under the leadership of former *Express* MoC Michelle Stanistreet, who in 2011 became the union's General Secretary – has used its presence at the Leveson Inquiry to once again raise the issue of a conscience clause. Given the climate created by Hackgate it is possible that the NUJ may now be pushing at a door that, if not exactly open, might be unlocked. Or at least less heavily bolted to keep it out. That being so, it is worth asking whether adding such a clause to journalists' codes of practice could help to protect ethical journalism. The short answer is that we will never know unless we try it; the slightly longer answer is that the evidence points towards a qualified yes.

It is not that a conscience clause would be a magic solution to what are perceived as journalism's ethical shortcomings; it is not that all citizens nor indeed all journalists would necessarily agree on what those shortcomings might be; and it is not that such a clause would eliminate the grey areas of interpretation that are often where the real choices are made. Such a clause would be very unlikely to be 'top of mind' for the vast majority of journalists the vast majority of the time, and the chances are that it would be used very, very rarely if ever. But – and this certainly is a big but – its mere existence could help contribute to a healthier workplace culture within newsrooms in which questions can sometimes be asked and objections can occasionally be voiced without the foot soldiers of journalism (lowly reporters and photographers) fearing a verbal onslaught at best and being shown the door at worst. The Leveson Inquiry heard evidence from Richard Peppiatt (2011b) that he would have been 'laughed out the door' of his newspaper if he had tried to use the editors' code to raise an ethical issue at work, adding: 'The spectre of being "let go" at any moment is a powerful deterrent against sticking your head above the trench if you disagree with something that is occurring.' As Michelle Stanistreet told the inquiry:

> It's not journalists who develop and foster the culture in any one newspaper group. In any workplace, where does the power reside? Not at the bottom, where the majority work to get the job done. It's at the top. In journalism, the reality is that there's often a stark expectation from on high: deliver the goods, get the job done, bring in the story, whatever the means. If you don't, well the consequences are often simple and clinically brutal (Stanistreet 2011).

Editors and proprietors might fear that empowering journalists even in such a mild way as envisaged in a conscience clause could result in routine and unacceptable editorial interference by employees or their representatives. The historical record does not support such fears. Even when the NUJ was at its strongest and able to negotiate closed shop agreements – or 'clothes shops', as one Leveson transcription had it, perhaps in a sign of the times (Merrill 2011: 87) – it only rarely attempted to use its influence on editorial matters. Yet, as Foot asserted, the mere existence of an independent forum within a workplace has the potential to contribute towards a more ethical climate. Research into ethical interventions by journalists working on six provincial newspapers in the north of England and the English Midlands discovered just three modest instances over the years, one of which involved staff objecting politely to the compilation by their newsdesk of an internal league table of 'death knocks'. One journalist explained:

> [S]taff were rated on their performance during death knocks. For example, a full story and collect-pics was worth, say, ten points and a total knockback zero points…Bearing in mind the editor is a member of the PCC, the chapel raised this issue. We were told it was only a bit of fun organised by the reporters themselves. However, immediately after chapel intervention the scheme was abandoned and the Death League tables taken down from offices (quoted in Harcup 2002: 110).

As with the *Daily Fatwa*, it is perhaps another example of line managers being saved from themselves by a quiet word from below. The above study, from 2002, concluded:

> Without a collective voice and collective confidence, control of the ethics of journalism will remain largely in the hands of editors and proprietors, with individual journalists being left with little choice but to do what they are told or resign – conditions of production hardly conducive to a journalism that contributes to a well-informed citizenry… [J]ournalistic

ethics cannot be divorced from everyday economic realities such as understaffing, job insecurity, casualised labour, bullying and unconstrained management prerogative (ibid: 112).

Events in the decade since have done nothing to challenge that conclusion. Quite the reverse, in fact. The Leveson Inquiry heard allegations that a culture of bullying at the *News of the World* may have been one factor in the creation of a climate of fear and silence where ethical malpractice may have been concerned. In contrast, a workplace in which ethical concerns can be discussed by journalists both informally and formally if felt necessary, on either an individual or collective basis, can surely only be good for journalism and ethics alike. Isn't the essence of journalism supposed to be about asking questions?

That was a lesson learned the hard way during an earlier newspaper scandal, Jayson Blair's long-running plagiarism at *The New York Times*, after which journalists were promised by their editor: 'The cure for what has ailed us is called journalism. The only way to communicate is to speak up in an atmosphere where outspokenness is...never penalised' (quoted in Mnookin 2005: 213). Asking questions about journalistic practice can only be a positive thing for ethics, even when it is an uncomfortable process, and journalists ought to be allowed to ask such questions occasionally, just as those of us involved in journalism education ought to welcome students who question conventional wisdom.

A conscience clause as proposed by the NUJ, offering journalists some form of contractual protection, might be one small step in the direction of making such questioning more possible for more journalists than it has been in recent years. Such a clause could be added to the existing PCC editors' code or to the code of any successor body that emerges post-Leveson and, while we are at it, why not to the Ofcom Broadcasting Code, the BBC *Editorial Guidelines*, and to the internal codes of those news organisations that issue their own? Precisely how it would be framed, worded and enforced would clearly require careful thought. However, it might be that the precise details could turn out to be of less significance than the symbolic value of such a clause because, even if it were to be rarely invoked, knowledge of its existence could help to empower journalists. Such knowledge could provoke a moment of reflection by any or all involved in the editorial process and that moment could turn out to have been a crucial one. You never know, such a pause for reflection might just be enough to prevent the next distasteful, unseemly or repugnant outrage at source before any damage is done either to the target or to journalism. It might facilitate the nipping in the bud of what could have grown into unethical journalism, before anyone is harmed, before it becomes a crisis, before judges and lawyers are once again brought in to pick through journalism's dirty laundry basket in public.

A conscience clause will not heal all of journalism's ills. It is a fairly modest proposal, addressing just one element of the complex relationship between ethics and journalism. But, given the ethical vacuum that appears to have been created in certain newsrooms by the almost totally unconstrained management prerogative that followed Rupert Murdoch's victory at Wapping in 1986, isn't it time we gave it a try?

Note

This chapter is an extended version of Tony Harcup's submission to the Leveson Inquiry and draws on ideas discussed in more depth in his book *The Ethical Journalist*.

References

Bayley, Ros and Hilary Macaskill (2004) *Journalism and Public Trust*, London: NUJ

Bundock, Clement J (1957) *The National Union of Journalists: A Jubilee History*, Oxford: Oxford University Press for the NUJ

Burrell, Ian (2006) Newsroom Revolt forces *Star* to drop its 'Daily Fatwa' spoof, *Independent*, 19 October

Cameron, James (1968) *Point of Departure*, London: Readers Union

CMS (2003) House of Commons Culture, Media and Sport Select Committee Fifth Report. Available online at http://www.publications.parliament.uk/pa/cm200203/cmselect/cmcumeds/458/45804.htm, accessed on 11 Nov 2011

Cole, Peter and Tony Harcup (2010) *Newspaper Journalism*, London: Sage

Foot, Paul (2000) *Articles of Resistance*, London: Bookmarks

Glover, Stephen (2006) What on earth was the *Daily Star* thinking of?, *Independent*, 23 October

Gopsill, Tim and Neale, Greg (2007) *Journalists: A Hundred years of the National Union of Journalists*, London: Profile

Hagerty, Bill (2003) Editorial: A Matter of Conscience, *British Journalism Review*, Vol. 14, No. 3 pp 3-5

Harcup, Tony (2007) *The Ethical Journalist*, London: Sage

Harcup, Tony (2002) Journalists and ethics: The quest for a collective voice, *Journalism Studies*, Vol. 3, No. 1 pp 101-114

IFJ (2010) *Calling to Account*, International Federation of Journalists. Available online at http://www.ifj.org/assets/docs/172/085/6bd06ac-f8c3855.pdf, accessed on 11 November 2011

Journalist (2011) Unions back conscience clause for journalists, October/November

Journalist (2006) Star chapel stops gross Muslim slur, November/December

Mansfield F. J. (1936) *The Complete Journalist: A Study of the Principles and Practice of Newspaper-making*, London, Sir Isaac Pitman and Sons

McIntyre, Peter (2004) An example to so many, *Journalist*, November/December

Merrill Legal Solutions (2011) 6 October seminars transcript. Available online at http://www.levesoninquiry.org.uk/wp-content/uploads/2011/11/leveson061011amd1.doc, accessed on 15 November 2011

Milmo, Cahal (2011) *Independent* columnist apologises for plagiarism, *Independent*, 15 September

Mnookin, Seth (2005) *Hard News: Twenty-one Brutal Months at The New York Times and How they Changed the American media*, New York: Random House

NUJ (2010) NUJ Rules 2010. Available online at http://www.nuj.org.uk/innerPagenuj.html?docid=182, accessed on 8 November 2011

Peppiatt, Richard (2011a) What is the day-to-day Effect of Competitive Pressures on Working Journalists? Presentation to the Leveson Inquiry on 6 October 2011. Available online at http://www.levesoninquiry.org.uk/news-and-events/events/competitive-pressures-on-the-press-and-the-impact-on-journalism/, accessed on 14 Nov 2011

Peppiatt, Richard (2011b) Witness Statement. Available online at http://www.levesoninquiry.org.uk/wp-content/uploads/2011/11/Witness-Statement-of-Richard-Peppiatt.pdf, accessed 29 November 2011

Phillips, Angela (2008) Memorandum to the House of Lords Communications Committee. Available online at http://www.publications.parliament.uk/pa/ld200708/ldselect/ldcomuni/122/122we13.htm, accessed on 11 November 2011

Ponsford, Dominic (2004) *Express* staff call in PCC over anti-Gypsy articles, *Press Gazette*, 30 January

Ponsford, Dominic (2005) Columnist quits after row, *Press Gazette*, 19 August

Press Gazette (2003) *Sun* writer quits over 'pro-war bias', *Press Gazette*, 28 March

Slattery, Jon (2011) Investigate how a NI private investigator became an NUJ member, the union's leadership is told, 15 November 2011. Available online at http://jonslattery.blogspot.com/2011/11/investigate-how-ni-private-investigator.html, accessed 15 November 2011

Snoddy, Raymond (2006) A mountain to climb for Hill, *Independent*, 20 February

Stanistreet, Michelle (2011) NUJ submission to Leveson inquiry, available online at http://www.nuj.org.uk/innerPagenuj.html?docid=2310, accessed on 16 November 2011

Note on the contributor

Tony Harcup began working in journalism in the late 1970s as a staff and freelance journalist for media ranging from small local weekly publications to national newspapers and magazines, both alternative and mainstream. Since the late 1990s he has worked in journalism education and is currently a senior lecturer at the University of Sheffield. He is the author of *The Ethical Journalist* (Sage 2007), *Journalism: Principles and Practice* (Sage 2009), and *Newspaper Journalism* (Sage 2010, with Peter Cole); his next book will be *Alternative Journalism, Alternative Voices* (Routledge, forthcoming).

Ethics and the newsroom culture

Ethical standards will improve when journalists are allowed to belong to their union without fear of reprisals, argues Chris Frost, academic and chair of the NUJ's Ethics Council. Fear, he says, has prevented many journalists from speaking out about phone hacking and other 'dark arts'

Despite the clear public anger over the Hackgate revelations and the barely disguised glee of politicians who have been terrified of the power of the tabloids for decades, there has not been an immediate call for press closures, restrictions on press freedom or an immediate start to strict regulation. The public is concerned, but is willing to wait and see what evidence is presented before deciding how much the press should be limited in the future. Perhaps, depressingly, it is just further evidence of the influence the newspaper industry can wield despite falling circulations.

The tabloids may not be giving more coverage to the saga than they need, but that seems hardly significant in the present climate. The Leveson Inquiry is playing to the gallery with celebrity following celebrity to spout shocking and potentially damaging revelation. Witness after witness is delivering devastating uppercuts to the press condemning it for its callous, criminal and bullying ways.

But we should not get confused into thinking this is all about journalistic morality. Most journalists are clear that the practices being exposed by Leveson were wrong; all accept they were illegal. This is not a failure of journalistic ethics, it is instead about a toxic, polluting newsroom culture that not only allowed, but actively encouraged outright criminality in pursuit of greater profits; a polluting culture because it was gradually spreading its poison as the norm of journalistic behaviour throughout the UK industry.

Amidst the accusations of Leveson, it is important to remember that many journalists in this country, nearly all of them probably, are reasonably honest and ethical. Despite the ethical pollution of News International and other tabloids, they are generally determined to do a good job. In difficult circumstances for small salaries and limited job security, they labour away trying to compose stories that are readable, entertaining and significant. They differ little from most workers in whatever industry you choose. They want to do a good job but they want to keep that job, especially in tough economic times, and there lies a major part of the problem.

Leveson and What Went Wrong

Lord Justice Leveson is being asked to examine the culture, practices and ethics of the media; and the relationship of the press with the public, police and politicians. The key to this is the culture of the press, because on this hangs all the other elements. Ethics and practice are dependent on the culture in a newsroom and the culture of those working as journalists.

Crucially, the Leveson Inquiry was triggered by the revelations that phone hacking was not the work of a single rogue reporter (as News International had insisted following the conviction of Clive Goodman for phone hacking in 2007), even though this was no surprise to those working in the industry or those close to it. Nor was it a surprise that journalists were engaged in other illegal and unethical activities such as intrusion, computer hacking, bullying and intimidation. Even the PCC must have been uneasily aware that this was all happening just beyond its gaze, whatever it might have told parliament. The culture, media and sport select committee reported in February 2010:

> Evidence we have seen makes it inconceivable that no-one else at the *News of the World*, bar Clive Goodman, knew about the phone-hacking...We cannot believe that the newspaper's newsroom was so out of control for this to be the case. The idea that Clive Goodman was a 'rogue reporter' acting alone is also directly contradicted by the Judge who presided at the Goodman and Mulcaire trial...Despite this, there was no further investigation of who those 'others' might be and we are concerned at the readiness of all of those involved: News International, the police and the PCC to leave Mr Goodman as the sole scapegoat without carrying out a full investigation at the time. The newspaper's enquiries were far from 'full' or 'rigorous', as we – and the PCC – had been assured. Throughout our inquiry, too, we have been struck by the collective amnesia afflicting witnesses from the *News of the World* (House of Commons 2010: 101).

The point is not just that journalists were phone hacking, nor even that newsrooms knew they were phone hacking and did not prevent or condemn it but that newsrooms and journalists were practising and condoning widespread criminal acts – from phone hacking, to computer hacking to stealing documents, rooting through rubbish bins as well as routinely telling lies, fabricating stories, threatening people and inventing quotes. The toxic culture that had become accepted as the norm was one where journalists felt intimidated into doing what was required of them and where editors did not challenge what their reporters were up to either because they were scared about what they would learn, or because they knew all too well how these desirable but morally questionable stories were obtained.

History of Ethical Behaviour in the Newsroom

Journalists and the public are divided both between and amongst themselves about whether the phone hacking scandal has exposed a press that has got worse in recent years, or a press that merely behaves badly in a different way. There are even some who, despite having very little evidence, suggest things are getting better. Paul Dacre, chair of the editors' code committee that draws up the Code of Practice which the Press Complaints Commission uses for its adjudications, told the Leveson Inquiry there were several myths surrounding the PCC:

> Myth One is that the conduct of the press has deteriorated over the years. Let me assure you the British press is vastly better behaved and disciplined than when I started in newspapers in the seventies. Then much of its behaviour was outrageous. It was not uncommon for reporters to steal photographs from homes. Blatant subterfuge was commonly used. There were no restraints on invasions of privacy. Harassment was the rule rather than the exception (Dacre 2011).

This sparked some instant retorts from old hands. Some, such as media commentator and journalism professor Roy Greenslade, and the Society of Editor's director, Bob Satchwell, felt ethical standards had overall definitely improved since the 1960s. Others were less convinced. Website www.Gentlemenranters.com called for evidence and received several responses belittling the claims. Alan Hart, a staff reporter for the *News of the World* from 1971 to 2000, wrote about Dacre's accusations about stealing pictures from the homes of victim's relatives:

> I had always assumed them to be apocryphal. How could it be otherwise? The danger of the theft being noticed while the snapper was still in the house would have been enormous. And if the photographer made good his escape with the stolen photo, his larceny would have been obvious when the photo appeared in his newspaper. Either way it would surely have led to a complaint and the danger of being sacked. It seems extraordinary to me that journalists of the stature of Paul Dacre and Bob Satchwell should take these old scribes' tales seriously. I was a staff reporter on a weekly, an evening and, ultimately, a national tabloid, and never once saw or heard of it actually happening (Hart 2011).

Another former reporter, John Rodgers, of Fleet Street News Agency, told Ranters:

> I never found it necessary to physically take a print without consent. Sweet talking usually did the trick. If that didn't work, the promise of money often did. If I had the opportunity, I would always look at the back of prints for the name and address of the photographer. Should the owner

not part with the print, I would then approach the photographer. (Rodgers 2011)

Even Roy Greenslade, in the same edition, admitted:

Well, I concede that I've no personal knowledge of picture theft though I recall hearing about it many times in the past. It isn't something the culprits are likely to admit nowadays (Greenslade 2011).

Revel Barker, a long-experienced journalist, speculates in the same edition that maybe it was all sparked by a fictional scene from a sixties film *The Angry Silence* written by Bryan Forbes who plays the part of a reporter in the film. Art imitating life, or vice versa? (Barker 2011).

But many members of the public and celebrities giving evidence to Leveson are equally certain that ethical standards have declined. *Daily Star* reporter Richard Peppiatt quit his job after finding he could no longer stomach the type of stories he was asked to write.

National Union of Journalists General Secretary Michelle Stanistreet told Leveson in the NUJ's opening statement that in the early years of the new millenium some journalists at the *Daily Express* when she was then a chapel representative felt so strongly about the newspaper's coverage of asylum seekers that they were considering leaving (Stanistreet 2011). The chapel at the *Express* even complained about their own newspaper to the PCC in 2001 (Gopsill and Neale 2007: 254).

The jury will always be out on whether ethical standards have improved. There is no way to carry out meaningful research to measures ethical news gathering over a forty-year period. The PCC and its supporters claim standards have improved because it suits their purpose. Equally, old hands are pleased to claim they worked hard and played hard, but always stayed just on the right side of legal and ethical – well, just about.

Journalism Training and Education

If standards have improved, it is likely that the major developments in the training and education of journalists over the past 25 years have had something to do with it. Journalism training has undergone some quite dramatic changes over the past 40 years or so. Until the early sixties, virtually all journalism training in the UK was done in and by newspapers with broadcasters relying on recruiting former newspaper journalists until they started training schemes of their own in the 1970s. Training courses for new staff on newspapers were largely limited to block or day release sessions in the local college teaching media law, public administration and shorthand. Such training as there was in ethics was on the job, learning from one's seniors.

Since the early 1980s, the growth of undergraduate courses and the development of masters programmes combining theory and practice and the consequent expansion in the number of university journalism departments has done the most to advance thinking about ethics, initially in the educational establishments but spilling out on to the job. A three or four-year degree course allows the time required to develop students' thinking about ethics and prime their questioning of standards in journalism alongside all the other elements of a good journalism course.

The tradition on the one-year diploma or NCTJ courses was for a practical approach with limited time for ethics. A detailed knowledge of media law was taught, but was presented as being a barrier to reporting and therefore as something to be worked around. The Press Complaints Commission and broadcast codes were taught as they became available but this wasn't until the early nineties. This limited approach to ethics teaching led many students to believe that ethical problems were rare and involved lengthy debate instead of being pervasive, often requiring instant decision against deadline.

There were few journalism textbooks even by the 1990s that spoke much of ethics; a typical example of a popular journalism textbook of the seventies, eighties and nineties is *Practical Newspaper Reporting* by Geoffrey Harris and David Spark, first written in 1966 for the NCTJ with a second edition in 1993 (Harris and Spark 1993). This mentioned the fledgling PCC and the new editors' Code of Practice in a total of just two and a half pages.

This soon changed with the explosion of undergraduate degrees in the UK with authors of journalism ethics textbooks such as Matthew Kierans (ed) (1998), Colin Shaw (1999), David Berry (ed), Chris Frost, Claude-Jean Betrand, Tom O'Malley, and Clive Soley, (all in 2000), Raphael Cohen-Almagor, (in 2001), Karen Sanders (2003), Valerie Alia (2004) Harcup (2005), Richard Keeble (2009).

All of this, together with the more visible PCC and Ofcom, has meant a better appreciation of the need for a socially responsible journalism, even if this has not been necessarily reflected in certain newsrooms.

The Balance of Newsroom Power – and the Fear Factor

The development of ethics education is one of the important elements that feeds into how newsroom culture works. The other is changing balance of power between newspaper management and journalists over the period of the past 20 to 30 years. Thatcherism marked an era in which the Conservative government was determined to reduce the power of trade unions. Print unions in the newspaper industry had been very powerful from the end of the Second World War through to the late 1980s. The changing economic pattern of the early 1980s, the recession and the determination of the Thatcher government to destroy the power of the unions led many newspaper proprietors to reverse this claiming union power had become too oppressive. However, with the move to new technology in the middle eighties, including the dramatic News International dispute (Harcup 2002: 105) negotiations were held between unions and newspaper managements to introduce new technology . But as journalists came increasingly to input their stories directly by computer, many of the traditional jobs of the typesetter were phased out. For a few months power shifted from the printers' unions to the journalists' union, the NUJ, but this lasted only long enough to negotiate decent settlements for the move to new technology.

After that, throughout the late eighties, newspaper managements moved swiftly to ensure the NUJ did not take over the mantle left vacant by the National Graphical Association. The Newspaper Society forced the ending of the national agreement in provincial newspapers and derecognition and personal contracts became the norm in individual workplaces. By the early to mid-nineties there were few recognised chapels left in the industry and many journalists now on personal contracts felt excluded from union activity. This led to the climate of 'fear, obsequiousness and conformism within newsrooms' (Foot 1991 cited in Keeble 2001: 6) that is still pervasive in the industry.

Although the NUJ managed to renegotiate recognition in many workplaces through the early years of the new century, fear of losing one's job or damaging career prospects has remained a constant worry for many journalists. In fact, bullying and intimidation became such a problem that the NUJ launched a 'Stop Bullying' campaign in 2008 (see NUJ 2008). NUJ General Secretary Michelle Stanistreet reported to Leveson in the NUJ's opening statement:

> At the heart of any newspaper culture is the editor – what he or she says goes. For anyone who's worked in a newsroom, the concept of an editor who didn't know just what their troops were getting up to is laughable. Editors rule the roost. They set the tone – not just in the editorial line of their newspapers but in the way that the newsroom operates. What's accepted, what's not; the tone of an editorial conference; whether bullying – sadly commonplace – goes unchecked; the dispensing of praise or the nature of the inevitable roasting when the goods aren't delivered (Stanistreet 2011).

This fear has prevented many journalists from speaking out about phone hacking and other 'dark arts'. The time when journalists could work collectively to right ethical problems has largely gone. Even the NUJ Ethic's Council became concerned about holding disciplinary hearings that might have the effect of breaking fragile chapels rather than exposing poor behaviour and most complaints about NUJ members breaching the Code of Conduct were ended with the council trying to encourage good behaviour rather than punishing bad practice.

This change had followed the concerns of many members about the union's policing activity. In the union's 1988 annual report, joint chairs Pat Healy and Marc Wadsworth complained: 'Uncharitable critics, who totally misrepresented our role, cast us as the union's thought police. Some went further in the debate about our existence and crudely posed the argument as one of Code of Conduct versus the Closed Shop' (NUJ 1988 p. 32).

The Ethics Council that year received 132 complaints, 25 of them going to formal hearings. The figures for 2010 show three complaints with no formal hearings. This is mainly because of a rule change preventing all but NUJ members complaining about breaches of the code and not surprisingly, union members rarely want to bring complaints against other members.

Before the break-up of chapels in the 1980s and 90s there had been some limited evidence of collective action over ethical issues and Harcup (2002: 108) points to several cases where chapels came together collectively over ethical issues. The *Guardian* chapel, for instance, secured a correction from an unwilling editor after the newspaper wrongly labelled a striking miner as a strke breaker. Examples of collective action over ethical issues in this century are severely limited. The *Newcastle Evening Chronicle* ended the practice of keeping a league table of reporters' performance on death knocks after a challenge by the chapel (ibid: 110). In another example, the *Express* joint chapel took action to complain to the PCC about its own paper's coverage of asylum seekers as NUJ general secretary Michelle Stansistreet told the Leveson Inquiry in the NUJ's opening statement:

> In September 2001, when I was one of three NUJ chapel reps at Express Newspapers, we took the unprecedented step of making a complaint to the Press Complaints Commission about the reporting of the *Daily Express*'s coverage of asylum seekers. Some journalists at the title, particularly those directly involved in the coverage, felt so upset and angry about the racist tone of the Express's coverage, and so powerless to individually do anything about it, that they were considering leaving their jobs. The NUJ chapel met and issued a public statement about the 'hate stirring' front page headlines – one of which was ASYLUM SEEKERS RUN FOR YOUR LIVES – and what we felt to be editorial interference from the proprietor (Stanistreet 2011).

The report goes on to mention the *Daily Star* chapel demanding the removal of a spoof page 'the *Daily* Fatwah' and succeeding.

Robert Jay QC, counsel to the inquiry, also questioned whether the newsroom culture was all it should be in his opening statement to the inquiry:

> Part of the mitigation advanced on Goodman's behalf before Mr Justice Gross was that his job was on the line and that he was under constant pressure to come up with new and tantalising stories. These pressures led him to cut corners and to indulge in what might be described as a lazy form of journalism, rather than using traditional, fairer and more time-consuming methods. The cult of celebrity and the quest for this sort of salacious morsel which might, at best, form the basis for an exclusive story is part of the wider picture because it encourages journalists to yield to the temptation to peer into secret worlds if the technology exists to allow them to do so. Further, if the prevalent *zeitgeist* is that no limits exist because as a matter of principle, the celebrity's life is altogether in the public domain,

then any ethical constraints on such behaviours are much diminished (Jay 2011)

The Cult of Celebrity and Leveson

Celebrities need to offer the public an insight into their private lives in order to build a relationship that brings them the fans they crave. Often they, or their agent, will develop a character, a virtual representation of themselves for public consumption. Journalists attempt to see past this character, this hypocrisy, to the real person, because that is what readers want. It is also what editors want and it is they who have the real power. Alastair Campbell, Tony Blair's former communications director and a former tabloid journalist, was only too well aware of this as he told Leveson:

> Mr Peppiatt came over as something of a lone voice, but I believe his voice carried more weight and moral authority than the editors. There are many more who feel and think as he does. But they are badly paid – casual shift reporters earn little more than they did when I was in Fleet Street thirty years ago – they are under massive pressure, and they know that if they step out of line, the bosses on their six and seven figure salaries can find plenty of cheap young replacements elsewhere (Campbell 2011).

John Dale, a columnist for *Press Gazette*, reporting on the Leveson Inquiry, also pointed to the difficulties faced by many journalists: Tabloid reporters who refused to break the law sometimes found themselves being sneered at, derided and accused of being 'not macho enough' (Dale 2011: 20). He paints a picture of split newsrooms where many young and vulnerable entrants broke the law while some of the more senior veterans of Fleet Street were prepared to risk their career and stand up to pressures from management.

Campbell also attacked editors, accusing them of not doing their jobs properly:

> It is also my belief that most editors do not challenge their journalists, even when the story is proven to be wrong. There was a considerable furore recently when it was revealed that the *Independent* columnist, Johann Hari, took quotes from other people's books and interviews and made them part of his own. There was a similar furore over the broadcaster Alan Yentob pretending to have been in interviews which were actually done by a producer or researcher. Yet I am not aware of a single case where a story based on anonymous quotes has, on being shown to be wrong, led to a reporter being disciplined or the paper acknowledging the possibility of invention (Campbell op cit).

The dominance of the PCC by publishers (who provide the funding) and editors (code committee and commissioners) has also been seriously damaging to newsroom culture. This exclusion of working journalists from ethical decision-making (not a practice mirrored in countries such as Sweden, Holland or Norway whose journalistic cultures are more widely respected) has led to journalists seeing themselves entirely as employees and not responsible for their journalistic morals; just there to do a job as they are instructed.

Impact of the Decline of Trade Union Power on Ethical Standards

The weakening of trade unions through the eighties and nineties meant that journalists were less likely to take on such issues collectively and that ethical debates, involving the entire workforce, essential to any trade or profession involved in the moral approach to their duties were denigrated by editors and publishers. For instance, although the culture media and sport select committee identified in 2003 that journalists should be protected in the workplace if they refused to carry out an assignment they believed breached the code of practice, the Society of Editors opposed this saying editors should be solely responsible for workplace ethics. The PCC refused to get involved saying this was an employment issue.

> We heard persuasive arguments from PressWise and the NUJ that the writing of the Code into journalists' contracts of employment should be backed up by either representation on the Code Committee or a conscience clause in the Code or both...We recommend that the Code Committee, Pressbof and the Commission, consider the following in relation to the Code of Conduct....An additional element of the Code should be that journalists are enabled to refuse an assignment on the grounds that it breaches the Code and, if necessary, refer the matter to the Commission without prejudice (House of Commons 2003: 28).

The Future

Clearly ethical standards will only improve with a strengthening of internal regulation of the newsroom, as Robert Jay QC stressed to the inquiry:

> ...a range of internal checks and balancing, including the following: rule books, codes of practice, clearly spelt out obligations in employment contracts, training and internal seminars, proper involvement of and oversight by in-house legal advisers, proper accounting systems for approving expensive payments, in particular cash payments to sources, risk management systems and proper whistleblowing policies. The evidence submitted to the inquiry demonstrates a wide range of corporate governance systems within the industry, from the virtually non-existent on the one hand to the extremely detailed on the other (Jay op cit).

He went on to say that some witnesses had pointed out that these were no substitute for journalists being trusted to use their own moral intuition. And he stressed that this could only work if pressure was not placed on them to deviate from this path: 'This rather assumes that their moral compasses are pointing in the right direction in the first place and the pressures do not exist to cause that compass needle to want to deviate from the right direction' (ibid).

These points are crucial to the future of a free but responsible press. Firstly, the education of trainees needs to be taken more seriously by the industry. Most journalism lecturers are aware of the double standard that sees them teaching ethics they know are too often derided by news editors once the trainee starts work.

Secondly, editors should be entirely and solely legally responsible for all that goes in their papers, as is the case in many papers elsewhere in Europe. This would at a stroke ensure that they would go to some lengths to ensure they know what is going on in their newspapers and that no illegal activity was being carried out. But it is not just editors who need to be involved. The view put around by the PCC and the Society of Editors that editors are the sole arbiters of ethics has been shown to be very damaging. Either editors such as Andy Coulson and Rebekah Brooks knew what was going on in their newsrooms (and so are legally responsible), or they did not know: in which case there was no moral leadership just illegality compounded by smokescreens. Journalists also need to be involved in the day-to-day ethical practices of a newsroom if we are to improve ethical standards of journalistic practice in the UK.

Finally, there are the two other key, linked elements underpinning bad practice identified earlier: weakened unions and the fear of losing one's job. No journalists should be afraid that they will lose their job if they are doing it properly: identifying good stories, sourcing them and gathering evidence in a rigorous but legal way and then writing them in a way that will attract and hold readers.

Journalists should be able to belong to their union without fear of reprisals so that they can join professional debates about standards and ethics within their branch, chapel and the wider union as well as support each other's moral behaviour collectively in the work place. Their union should represent these journalists on the new press standards body so that there is a voice of the working journalist represented amongst those of the public, editors and proprietors. Journalists should also be able to refuse an assignment they believe will be unethical or involve unethical or illegal activity to achieve and receive protection by law from dismissal and, as far as is possible, from detriment to their career. Only when a newsroom is free from unreasonable fear and when editors are legally responsible for their papers and journalists believe themselves responsible for their own actions will we be able to see a general application of acceptable standards.

References

Barker, Revel (2011) Available online at
http://www.gentlemenranters.com/page_324.html#ahsupp219, accessed on 12 December 2011

Campbell, Alastair (2011) Final Version of Submission to Leveson Inquiry. Available online at http://www.alastaircampbell.org/blog/2011/11/30/final-version-of-submission-to-leveson-inquiry, accessed on 17 November 2011

Dacre, Paul (2011) Speech at the Leveson Inquiry: Full Text. Available online at http://www.guardian.co.uk/media/2011/oct/12/paul-dacre-leveson-speech, accessed on 27 November 2011

Dale, John (2011) *Press Gazette*, 1 October p. 20. Available online at www.pressgazette.co.uk

Foot, Paul (1991) Strenuous liberty…a nervous revival, *British Journalism Review*, Vol. 2, No. 4 pp 5-8

Frost, Chris (2011) *Journalism Ethics and Regulation*, London: Pearson Education, third edition

Frost, Chris (2010), *Reporting for Journalists*, London: Routledge, second edition

Gopsill, Tim and Neale, Greg (2007) Journalists: 100 years of the NUJ London: Profile Books

Guardian (2011) *Richard Peppiatt's letter to Daily Star proprietor Richard Desmond*(http://www.guardian.co.uk/media/2011/mar/04/daily-star-reporter-letter-full (accessed 12/12/11)

Greenslade, Roy (2011) Available online at http://www.gentlemenranters.com/page_324.html#ahsupp219, accessed on 12 December 2011

Harcup, Tony (2002): Journalists and Ethics: The Quest for a Collective Voice, *Journalism Studies*, Vol. 3, No. 1 pp 101-114

Harris, Geoffrey and Spark, David (1993) *Practical Newspaper Reporting*, Oxford: Focal Press, second edition

Hart, Alan (2011) Available online at http://www.gentlemenranters.com/page_324.html#ahsupp219, accessed on 12 December 2011

House of Commons (2003) Culture, Media and Sport Committee: *Privacy and Media Intrusion: Fifth Report of Session 2002-3*. Available online at http://www.publications.parliament.uk/pa/cm200203/cmselect/cmcumeds/458/458.pdf, accessed on 27 November 2011

House of Commons (2010) Culture, Media and Sport Committee: *Press Standards, Privacy and Libel Second Report of Session 2009–10 Volume I* London: Stationary Office

Jay, Robert (2011) Speech at Leveson Inquiry: Full Text. Available online at http://www.levesoninquiry.org.uk/wp-content/uploads/2011/11/Transcript-of-Morning-Hearing-14-November-2011.pdf, accessed on 27 November 2011

Keeble, Richard (2001) *Ethics for Journalists*, London: Routledge, first edition

Keeble, Richard (2009) *Ethics for Journalists*, London: Routledge, second edition

NUJ (2008) Available online at http://www.nuj.org.uk/innerPagenuj.html?docid=858&string=bullying, accessed on 1 November 2011

NUJ (1988) Annual Report London: NUJ

Rodgers, John (2011) Available online at http://www.gentlemenranters.com/page_324.html#ahsupp219, accessed on 12 December 2012

Stanistreet, Michelle (2011) Available online at
http://www.nuj.org.uk/innerPagenuj.html?docid=2310, accessed 12 December 2012

Note on the contributor

Professor Chris Frost is Head of Journalism at Liverpool John Moores University. He is the author of *Journalism Ethics and Regulation* (Pearson Education 2011, third edition), *Reporting for Journalist* (Routledge 2010, second edition) and *Designing for Newspapers and Magazines* (Routledge 2011, second edition). He is also chair of the NUJ's Ethics Council, a former President of the NUJ and Treasurer of the Association for Journalism Education.

Section E. Hacks and Cops: Men in (and out) of Uniform

John Mair

They both sup from the same cesspit of human misery at times. Journalists/'hacks' and policemen/'cops' share more in common than they like to admit. Both are (or should be) curious; both are (or should be) suspicious; both are (or should be) seekers after truth (whatever that is); both are (or should be) interested in bringing wrong doers to heel; both are (or should be) giving power to the powerless; both are (or should be) constantly questioning the powerful; both are (or should be) mischief-makers if need be; both are (or should be) interested in results.

The hack/cop nexus is closer than we think. The days of the cub reporter reading the custody sergeant's charge book upside down in the station for free information may have gone to be replaced by the recorded police press office message even if that recording is a live person – but the relationship is still real and still close.

Many many stories come from police sources and not just for the declining number of crime correspondents in the newspapers. Policemen know things that journalists want to find out and publish. Sometimes vice versa. This author once had to remind a Swansea detective inspector of the division of labour when he asked me in a police canteen if I knew: 'Who murdered Danny Dyke?' I did not, nor was it my job to.

But has the odd pint with a police source in a dark bar or cup of tea in the canteen been replaced by something more formal and maybe corrupt? Put simply, is money now changing hands on too regular a basis these days between hacks and cops...

The Metropolitan Police now appear to have finally woken from their Rip Van Winkle slumber on the phone hacking scandal. They are now (December 2011) running three investigations:

- Operation Weeting on illegal phone hacking and possible perversion of the course of justice which restarted in January 2011. So far 18 people have been arrested and bailed as a result of that as of 7 December 2011.Charges may follow in March 2012;

- Operation Elveden, on police/press relationships and possible corrupt practices, has made eight arrests as of 21 December 2011;

- Operation Tuleta into possible computer hacking and invasion of privacy at News International – with just one arrest to date.

Since July 2011, both Metropolitan Police Commissioner Sir Paul Stephenson and Assistant Commissioner John Yates have fallen on their ceremonial swords. More could follow…

In this section, Ben McConville and Kate Smith take a close look at the perhaps unhealthy compact between hacks and cops that grew up around the Murdoch press and ask whether 'crossing the thin blue line' is healthy both for democracy or for a free press.

John Tulloch elegantly delves into the history of the relationship and examines Charles Dickens and others for clues. The hack/cop is far from new so long as they sup from the same cesspit they will always need each other like two drunken men. If the current phone hacking scandal and regulatory changes it generates leads to the lifting up the drawbridges around the police stations and fewer leaks or tips, then that could lead to fewer good stories and maybe an impoverished popular press.

Crossing the Thin Blue Line

The too-close relationship between the press and the police has been highlighted in the Hackgate scandal. Ben McConville and Kate Smith examine what circumstances allowed this to happen and the implications for democracy and a free press

Introduction

In March 2003, the then-Editor of the *Sun*, Rebekah Wade (later Brooks), made the most startling admission to the UK's House of Commons media, culture and sport select committee. The tabloid had paid serving police officers for stories. Hildy Johnson, the wily editor in Ben Hecht and Charles MacArthur's celebrated play, *The Front Page* (1928), would have been proud. The announcement was not made with any sense of shame, more one of a glib 'of course we do'. How else would Britain's biggest selling daily tabloid get stories?

It was a perfunctory response from a media executive who saw no moral dilemma or problem with the idea of paying and, therefore, corrupting a police officer. It also revealed wider arrogance within some sections of the British media, a journalistic arrogance noted by Watergate reporter Carl Bernstein in terms of a failure to 'engage in self-reflective scrutiny where their social obligations are concerned' (cited in Allan 2007: 194).

It took some years for this comment to foment in the Westminster village, but by the time Rupert Murdoch closed down the *News of the World* in the summer of 2011 over the phone hacking scandal, the closeness of the relationship between News International and the Metropolitan Police was laid bare. It was clear that relations had become too close. As the phone hacking scandal engulfed News International, senior officers in the Metropolitan Police were dragged in. Commissioner Sir Paul Stephenson resigned his post in July 2011 after it was revealed that former *News of the World* editor Neil Wallis had been paid public relations fees for a contract with the Met Police. Assistant Commissioner John Yates resigned, but was later cleared of misconduct by the Independent Police Complaints Commission, amid allegations of helping to secure a job at Scotland Yard for Wallis's child. The accusation of corruption was enough for some to fall on their swords.

Debates around press freedom in Western liberal democracies often centre on the relationship between the journalists, owners and politicians, (see Curran 2002: 79) but this chapter will look at an overlooked but vital linkage; the media's relationship with another centre of power, the police. It will analyse this relationship in terms of the liberal pluralist position and the study of newsroom practices. It will assess if it is possible for the press and the police to come to a new understanding in a post hacking-scandal environment.

"Fancy lunch?" The Celebrity Sphere Meets the Political Sphere

The comment by Wade in 2003 was quickly 'corrected' by Andy Coulson, then-Editor of the *News of the World* and subsequently David Cameron's spin doctor, who claimed both he and Wade had acted 'within the law'. Otherwise it passed almost unnoticed and they seemed to get away with it.

As tabloid editors in Murdoch's empire, Coulson and Wade wielded a huge amount of power. Coulson resigned as editor of the *News of the World* after the phone hacking scandal emerged in 2007. Royal reporter Clive Goodman and private investigator Glenn Mulcaire were jailed for hacking into messages of three members of the British royal family and five other public figures. This included the interception of messages at Prince Charles's London residence Clarence House and a revelation that Prince William had strained a tendon in his knee. News International dismissed the scandal as the work of one 'rogue' reporter. Coulson was soon rehabilitated and appointed head of press for Prime Minster David Cameron who assured the public everyone deserved a second chance.

There was no doubt that News International felt the loss of Coulson, who had graduated through the ranks of the company. First by editing the showbusiness column Bizarre, then on to the editor's chair of a newspaper, a route preceded by Piers Morgan, who himself went on to edit the *Daily Mirror*. A number of theorists including Bourdieu (1998) and Franklin (1997) have pointed out that in the tabloidisation of news, politics and economic coverage had been replaced by sports and stars and you could add to this latterly reality TV coverage. In essence principled and serious journalism was replaced by celebritised infotainment (see Allan op cit: 203), hard news replaced by soft news. Franklin (1997: 7) noted the rise of infotainment as 'evident in both print and broadcast media, to retreat from investigative journalism and the reporting of hard news to the preferred territory of "softer" or "lighter" stories'.

At News International the training ground for tabloid editors had recently become the showbusiness column. This part of the newspaper is the embodiment of Franklin's 'newszak' where light stories were designed to entertain and were often just the fictional narratives of public relations specialists. Tabloid journalists are often portrayed as arch manipulators, as many are, but they are also manipulated themselves by public relations specialists while those who work in showbusiness columns are among the most manipulated journalists in a tabloid newspaper. They often run with public relations material over a real story: newszak over news. They construct stories around PR stunts and photographs, or 'pseudo events' as set out in the classic description of public relations by Daniel Boorstin (1992).

Chris Atkins' documentary *Starsuckers* (2009) demonstrated how easy it is to manipulate the showbusiness desks of the tabloids, which seem happy to take outrageous stories about celebrities at face value without fact-checking or triangulation. The practices of showbusiness journalists are such that they form relationships with the contacts they need, be they stars, booking agents or public relations executives. They operate in the celebrity sphere, which can be characterised as a 'meso-public sphere' as set out by John Keane (1995: 1-22) in response to Jurgen Habermas's idea of the public sphere. Habermas (1961/1989), in his seminal analysis of the public sphere, argued that the commercialisation of mass communication networks has reduced 'rational critical debate' to cultural consumption in which active citizens became mere consumers.

The celebrity sphere is quite separate from the political sphere and engenders a sense of place in and among the stars, often placing the journalist on an equal footing with their quarry. This is evidenced in the Bizarre column where Coulson, Piers Morgan and *Sun* Editor Dominic Mohan were often pictured alongside stars, actors and musicians as the newspaper attempted to accord them celebrity journalist status. As a result of this positioning and despite the manifest manipulation by public relations executives, the emerging celebrity journalist tended to go along with the hype and believe they have gained a new status.

Once they were promoted to the editor's chair they continued to operate as though they were still in the celebrity sphere and not the political sphere. Tabloidisation meant that the content and nature of their publications was dominated not by politics but by celebrity stories. This is not to suggest they were naïve in any way, it was possibly more a sign of arrogance. They were culturally prepared and journalistically trained for a different sphere. The *modus operandi* of the celebrity sphere is to do lunch and get close, if not friendly, with the subjects of stories. Yates confirmed to MPs that he had lunched with News International executives on a number of occasions. While these may have been perfectly innocent meetings with legitimate media and journalist contacts, it is clear that in the context of the phone hacking scandal and the admission of serving officers, that it looked bad to the wider audience.

The Journalism Crisis Deepens

British journalism was already in crisis before the phone hacking scandal as circulations plummeted and newsroom staff levels diminished. In the decades since the late 1960s the tabloidisation of the press brought the public sphere in Britain to the point where political discourse had become muck-raking and slanging matches. The *Sun*'s headlines such as the 1992 General Election story:

'It was the *Sun* what won it' and the backing of Tony Blair in 1997 gave the impression that Murdoch's newspaper empire was the kingmaker of British politics.

Even if the reality was more that Murdoch's newspapers tended to fall in line with the likely winners of an election, the net result was a reduction in the quality of political debate in some sections of the British media. The content of the British media had become dominated by infotainment, celebrity culture and content reduced to bite-sized nuggets about football stars and reality TV. Bourdieu (1998) pointed out that on news channels in France and around the world 'talk show chatter' had replaced discourse. In his excoriating analysis of news culture, he pointed to the depoliticisation of politics to the level of anecdote and scandal. Bourdieu asserts that this meant newspapers had to 'smooth the edges' (ibid: 44) so not to offend, and led to a concentration on stars and sport over politics and economics.

News anchors such as Bill O'Reilly and Glenn Beck on Murdoch's Fox News have a combative style of debating and discourse which often descends into neo-liberal rants around domestic and foreign policy. During the 2008 Presidential Election campaign this often manifested itself in attacks on the frontrunner Barack Obama who was often portrayed in a negative light around his Muslim ancestry by news networks including NBC (see NBC 2008).

So celebrity journalists could move into celebritised politics and editorships seamlessly, applying the same skills to the political world as they did so successfully with their former roles. This strategy of schmoozing rather than remaining objectively without fear or favour also worked for other institutions, including the police.

Previous studies on the crisis in British journalism have focused on declining sales, but in the wake of the phone hacking scandal and journalism's relationship with the police, the notion of journalism's social responsibilities has come to the fore. The Leveson Inquiry has looked at some of the operational aspects of this such as the hacking of Milly Dowler's mobile phone while the murdered schoolgirl was still missing or the hacking of phones belonging to relatives of the London bombings of July 2005. These were manifestations of the massive slump in standards in some areas of the British media, but what had caused this to happen?

The newsroom culture in some of the British media is one where bullying is prevalent, perhaps even encouraged, and journalists live under the constant threat of the Sword of Damocles of losing their contract, job or even being greylisted. The dynamic is such that dubious behaviour becomes commonplace. This not only applies to phone-hacking, but also the conduct and nature of relationships around all newsroom practice, including how to deal with the police. So, even though paying police officers for stories or paying operatives for information obtained from the police computer is clearly illegal and immoral, if senior executives are doing it or allow it, then by custom and convention more junior staff follow suit. It is legitimised by becoming the norm.

The Malcolm Tucker Factor

The rise of the arrogant streak in British journalism coincided with greater control and manipulation by spin doctors and public relations material. In the years since New Labour came to power in 1997, there has been a blurring of the lines between the media and the major institutions of the state and a large rise in the number of special advisors. According to the BBC there were 38 special advisors working for John Major's Conservative government in 1996 at a cost to the taxpayer of £1.8m. By 2004 the number peaked at 84 and in 2009 there were 74, at a cost of £5.9m (see BBC 2010). The political sphere, political discourse and the machinations of government had become dominated by partisan advisors working in the interest of political parties rather than the state.

While the foul-mouthed character Malcolm Tucker (in the acclaimed BBC comedy, *The Thick of It*) might be an exaggerated spoof of Alastair Campbell (Tony Blair's spin doctor), the rise of spin machines started to chip away at public life in the UK. In the US, freedom of speech is enshrined in the constitution and there is a system of press conferences for politicians and civil servants from the president down. However, in the UK with its unwritten constitution, political journalists have to take part in the archaic institution of the political lobby system at Westminster to gain access to political elites. Lobby reporters at Westminster deal not only with civil servants or press officers but with special advisors who are well versed in 'the dark arts' of proactive media control. Campbell was proud to describe himself as a 'control freak' and typified the bruising, pugilistic nature of the new breed. His proactive, rapid response brand of news management spread throughout Whitehall. Dissenting journalists were swept aside by a mixture of aggressive spin and shutting out of the flow of information.

Over at Scotland Yard the number of press officers in 2011 totalled 45. The Metropolitan Police's Head of Communications Dick Fedorcio told the Commons select committee in July 2011 that 10 of those in the press team were former *News of the World* reporters (see BBC 2011). The traditional relationship between the press and police had been underpinned by healthy mutual suspicion and forged on the understanding that at a very basic level they needed each other. It became clear during the July 2011 select committee hearings that News International and the Metropolitan Police had a close relationship to the point where staff and it can only be assumed, their work practices, had become interchangeable.

The Police as Lobbyists

Brian McNair (1998), in assessing the impact of public relations and political pressure on journalism, said that all manner of non-party organisations can make 'meaningful and effective' interventions. From terrorist organisations to trade unions, businesses and lobby groups, all can use public relations techniques to 'shape news, manage opinion and, ultimately, influence government decision making' (ibid: 153). While McNair looked at environmental pressure groups such as Greenpeace and its public relations tussles with businesses such as Shell, it is equally applicable to the police. Dealing with crime and the funding of the police has become a major issue since the 1970s and sophisticated police lobbying have grown around issues such as the number of police on the streets and reduction of crime figures.

During the years of Tony Blair's premiership the interests of the government and police became more aligned. Former Commissioner Sir Ian Blair became a supporter of government policies which resulted in a massive increase in funding for the police and its initiatives – from street patrols to new strategies on gun crime, youth crime, gangs and drugs culture. Police numbers in England and Wales peaked at about 142,151 in 2009, up by 15,000 on 1998, according to the Centre for Crime and Justice Studies (2010).

The media's power to manipulate public opinion helps manufacture consent and maintain the dominant ideology of the times. This need not only be consent for the governing elite, justifying a war or support for an economic programme of swingeing cuts. This can also be consent for the cost, strategies and practices of policing. During the Blair years, New Labour took on the Tories' mantle of being tough on crime. The number of officers on the beat increased and police expenditure increased by 50 per cent in real terms from £9.83 billion in 1998/1998 to £14.55 billion in 2008/2009 (Centre for Crime and Justice Studies op cit). The right-wing press, News International and Associated Newspapers titles in particular, become cheerleaders for this new era of zero tolerance policing.

Nick Davies (2008) sets out a scenario of falling media revenues and cuts in the number of reporters in the media coupled with the rise of PR machines as a reason for the weakening of the power of the press. In his theory of the 'news factory' (ibid: 47) Davies claims longer hours, higher workloads and the feeding of news from PR sources ('churnalism') had led to a press unable to carry out its basic watchdog functions. Throughout the 1990s and early 2000s relations between the media, government and police were far from harmonious, although there was broad consensus around issues of crime and policing. Aeron Davis (2007) in his analysis of the mediation of power assesses the nature of inter-elite conflict and power points out, 'inter-elite conflict and negotiations are as important for sustaining elite power bases as elite attempts at influencing mass media and opinion' (ibid: 55). As a result, journalists and elites form part of the same 'elite discourse networks'.

What about the Public Interest?
Debates on the freedom of the press in society tend to revolve mostly around state and private media ownership within models of Western liberal pluralism and press freedom. As James Curran concludes in his work on media and power, a media system in the UK has grown 'which is controlled neither by market nor state' (Curran 2002: 247). If the British media is to carry out a watchdog function, it cannot do this while getting too close to the police. It

must be free to criticise and condemn as well as praise and condone. Likewise the police need distance from the media in order to ensure that judicial process is done and is seen to be done. All the more so when some in the media are engaged in criminal activities.

Conclusion: Towards a New Dynamic of Regulation

Should there be formal rules or regulations on the links between press and police? A police force that is a powerful lobby organisation can be damaging to political process, yet it is now a political actor with a strong public relations function. The media, on the other hand, need to be free to criticise and hold accountable the police without prejudice.

However, the myriad ways in which both institutions interact may render any formalised rules unworkable. Rules on how senior executives interact around meetings may be useful, but in terms of operational duties it is complicated. The police and press already have a number of conventions around incidents such as missing children and major breaking stories. On crime stories there is the Contempt of Court Act 1981 which underpins the rules of engagement. The reality of the day-to-day operations of the police and the media is that they do need to have a close functioning relationship.

This understanding is enshrined in the daily contact between reporters and police officers in the local and regional media in the UK. The very act of police calls, where reporters visit police stations to find out the stories on their patch, is the bedrock of British journalism and police practice. This formalised and yet non-compulsory meeting occurs across the country on a daily basis, with no rules of engagement, rather a moment when individuals find their way into a relationship of trust and mutual understanding. Its formality means ensures an arms-length relationship can be established and both parties negotiate their way to a firm understanding that there are lines that should not be crossed. Rather than introduce a raft of potentially unworkable rules which only resonate with and respond to the popular demand of the moment, the police and press could both do with going back to the old school, arms length understanding of the roles of each institution within a democracy.

Meanwhile, at time of writing (December 2011), these issues are coming under the spotlight at the Leveson Inquiry. Former British Army intelligence officer Ian Hurst, who claimed his computer was hacked by journalists, told the inquiry in November 2011 that he believed the Met Police had covered up journalistic abuses and claimed corruption in the force at the 'highest level'. Hurst said Scotland Yard had 'let society down' and added: 'That is exactly what you are dealing with here ladies and gentlemen – corruption.'

References

Allan, S. (2007) *News Culture*, Maidenhead: Open University Press, second edition

BBC (2010) The Hidden World of Special Advisers, 2 September. Available online at http://www.bbc.co.uk/news/uk-politics-11165381, accessed on 12 December 2011

BBC (2011) Phone hacking: 'Humbled' Murdoch rejects blame, 20 July. Available online at http://www.bbc.co.uk/news/uk-politics-14195259, accessed on 12 December 2011

Boorstin, D. (1992) *The Image: A guide to Pseudo Events in America*, New York: Vintage

Bourdieu (1998) *On Television and Journalism*, translation by P.P. Ferguson, London: Pluto

Davies, N. (2008) *Flat Earth News*, London: Chatto & Windus

Davis, A. (2007) *The Mediation of Power. A Critical Introduction*, London: Routledge

Centre for Crime and Justice Studies, King's College London, (2010). Available online at http://www.kcl.ac.uk/news/news_details.php?news_id=1361&year=2010, accessed 14 December 2011

Curran, J. (2002) *Media and Power*, London: Routledge

Franklin, B. (1997) *Newszak and News Media*, London: Hodder

Habermas, J. (1989) *The Structural Transformation of the Public Sphere*, translated by Burger, T. with Lawrence, F., Cambridge, MA: MIT Press

Keane, J. (1995) Structural transformations of the public sphere, *The Communication Review*, Vol.1 No. 1 pp 1-22

McNair, B. (1998) *The Sociology of Journalism*, London: Arnold

NBC (2008) Channel 4 LA, 15 August. Available online at http://www.youtube.com/watch?v=BRk2yV080t4, accessed 14 December 2011

Note on the contributors

Ben McConville is a principal lecturer in journalism at Northumbria University. He is also a contributor to the Associated Press news agency and former deputy news editor of the *Scotsman*. Kate Smith is a lecturer in journalism at Edinburgh Napier University and a freelance writer and journalist.

Oiling a Very Special Relationship: Journalists, Bribery and the Detective Police

John Tulloch critically examines the history of the relationship between journalists and the police and wonders whether current efforts to stamp out payments between hacks and cops could lead to the death of popular journalism

'No one pays like the *News of the World* do.'
(attributed to the private eye Jonathan Rees, Davies 2011)

'20 per cent of the Met [force] has taken backhanders from tabloid hacks.'
(Paul McMullan talking to Hugh Grant, *New Statesman*, 2011)

'Police investigating allegations of illegal payments to officers by journalists arrested a 48-year-old man today. The man, believed to be a journalist, was arrested at about 10.30am at an address outside London in connection with allegations of corruption and was taken to a south west London police station'
(*Press Gazette*, 4 November 2011)

Introduction

This chapter explores aspects of the early history of relations between London-based journalists and London's police from the origins of the Metropolitan Police in 1829 with the aim of providing a historical context within which the present crisis can be placed. It analyses the reasons for the development of a uniquely close relationship on the basis of a set of permanent, mutual needs, despite recurrent attempts to regulate and control police-press communications.

Apart from the issues of 'corruption' raised by the monetary relationship between police and press, the changing nature of the needs of the popular press for a regular supply of crime-related stories and ready access to victims and perpetrators, are balanced against the requirements of the police for positive publicity in its political struggle for resources, and the public interest in a timely flow of information about crime.

Law and Order News: the Seminal Text

Steve Chibnall's classic book *Law and Order News*, published in 1977, has been highly influential for a generation in setting a frame within which British police-press relations could be viewed. (Chiball 1977b, and see Chibnall 1975a and b, 1977a, 1980, 1980, 1981). Crudely summarised, this frame was that instances of the payment of police sources have been comparatively minor and that payment is only part, and a small part, of the rich spectrum of police/press relations – and mainly used, Chibnall observes, by less experienced reporters, 'on the fringe of a specialisation' without the right contacts:

> I was told of one such journalist who was obliged to take a bottle of whisky with him every time he visited a policeman: A second complained 'I'm in a moral dilemma – I will not pay policemen for information (athough I'm prepared to buy them a beer or a meal) and I do not have the regular contacts which most crime reporters have. So what do you do when you want information? Well, the best sources are either bent policemen who want money for stories, of disgruntled policemen who don't usually want payment' (Chibnall 1977b: 149-50).

In a brilliantly suggestive scenario, Chibnall describes a pattern in which friendship and trust links between journalists and police officers are 'characterised by exchange' (ibid: 152). Journalists and police are in a trading relationship in which intangible invisible goods such as friendship, sociability, information, gossip and the reinforcement of mutual esteem counts for more than cash:

> The most obvious exchange resource the journalist has at his disposal is money. But, although direct payment of certain types of sources is recognised as legitimate, it is generally considered as inappropriate (although not unknown) method of getting information from the police. It is far too crass and unsubtle and defines the reporter/source relationship as one of business rather than friendship. The offer of food and drink, on the other hand, carries connotations of sociability rather than commerce or corruption…other, more powerful exchange resources…derive from [the reporter's] position within an organisation offering the possibility of instant communication with the public (ibid: 153-154).

The Process of 'Assimilation'

Over time, Chibnall argues, this leads to a process of 'assimilation' – police officer and journalist bond and begin to reflect each other.

Overall this is a comforting picture of human sociability. It confirms a human side of the police and of the journalist, where mutual manipulation is softened by friendship. But this essentially sentimental picture is called into question by the *News of the World* revelations, as another one of journalism's sustaining myths. Two conclusions might be drawn:

1. That the comforting myth was in part true, and there has simply been a major change in the relationship between the media and the police in the last 30 years. Specifically, we might point to the rise of the modern private investigations industry, worth £250 million a year (Milmo et al 2011) and acting as an intermediary by means of which this relationship, like many others under capitalism, can be outsourced. We might add some observations about extraordinarily rich or desperate newspapers in ferocious competition. This is broadly the conclusion of Nick Davies, who argues that 'there has always been a little dirty places, a little illegal stuff going on in the shadows of Fleet Street' (Davies 2008: 266) but confesses 'it's never easy to look back…and see how the germ first started'.

He locates the origins 'in the old days' some time before the 1970s, when 'crime reporters regularly bunged cash bribes to serving police officers in order to procure information'. Davies argues that the new regime at Scotland Yard inaugurated by Sir Robert Mark 'crushed the old corruption in the mid 1970s' but that by the early 1980s newspapers had established a new way to bribe police officers through the mechanism of private investigators (ibid: 267). Davies's succinct account is echoed in the rambling, surreal testimony of the former *News of the World* journalist Paul McMullan before the Leveson Inquiry. When asked if police officers were prepared to accept money in return for information, he said:

> Yeah, not as much as they did in the 1980s, but now I think it would be very difficult to offer a policeman pretty much anything for anything. But certainly, as – well, the 70s was a notoriously corrupt time, but then it got stamped on and got progressively harder to get information from the police unless it was in an official way (Leveson Inquiry 2011).

2. But one might draw a contrary conclusion: that something has been missed, and/or not much talked about, in descriptions of the history of crime journalism, and that 'assimilation' was often on the basis of a mutually profitable relationship between police and journalists. Of the industrial scale of the operation by the late 90s there is no doubt. Davies relates that, in March 2003

> …the Information Commissioner's Office raided the home in New Milton, Hants, of a private investigator named Steve Whittamore and seized a mass of paperwork which turned out to be a detailed record of more than 13,000 requests from newspapers and magazines for Whittamore to obtain

confidential information, many of them potentially in breach of the law. Several staff from the *Guardian's* sister paper, the *Observer*, were among Whittamore's customers (Davies 2011).

Estimates vary widely as to the number of Metropolitan Police officers and detectives the *News of the Screws* may have had on its books by the time its 168-year career was brought to a tragic halt in July 2011. The revelation of industrial scale bribery confirms the suspicion that journalists paying the police for information is now deeply rooted in the culture of the British popular press. But was it ever thus?

Crime News at the Birth of the Popular Press in the UK

Few things are more tedious than the historian's reflex of 'nothing new…' But it can be argued that this goes back to the birth of the popular press and that we simply have no reliable evidence to assess its scale. What can be stated is that crime news was one of the basic staples in the rise of the press in the early nineteenth century, along with gambling, sexual scandal and sport. Along with sport and scandal, crime was commodified.

The *Newgate Calendars* of the late 18th century, full of bloody murders and last dying speeches on the scaffold, blazed the way, and were the most popular and profitable publications of their day. Newspapers created a rough and ready form of 'soft' social regulation to which the early police played a 'hard' role. Dickens refers disparagingly to the 'Old Bow-street Police' and their propensity to hang around with Grub Street denizens:

> We think there was a vast amount of humbug about these worthies. Apart from many of them being men of indifferent character, and far too much in the habit of consorting with thieves and the like, they never lost a public occasion of jobbing and trading in mystery and making the most of themselves. Continually puffed besides by incompetent magistrates anxious to conceal their own deficiencies, and *hand-in-glove with the penny-a-liners of that time*, they became a sort of superstition (Dickens 1850 in Slater 1997: 266, my italics).

The Bow Street office was finally disbanded in 1838 (Metropolitan Police 2011). Dickens himself played a significant role in the rise of the modern British police, and his enthusiastic promotion of the new Metropolitan Police, and the creation of the Detective department in 1842 (ibid), directly parallels the creation of the modern popular press (see Collins, 1965; Shpayer-Makov, 2010).

The prime exponent of this popular press was to become the *News of the World*, from its start in 1843, but it joined a host of weekly popular newspapers, such as Robert Bell's *Penny Dispatch* (1841) and Edward Lloyd's *Penny Sunday Times and People's Police Gazette* (1840), in shocking crime news, and a diet specialising in 'seductions, rapes, murders and any other sort of horror' (Morison 1932: 242). Until the advent of Alfred Harmsworth and the rise of the popular daily newspaper of the 1890s, this was the largest and economically most buoyant part of the British press, organised on a prototype of the factory lines that 50 years later would become commonplace.

Given its size and profitability, it is at least plausible that paying, as well as wining and dining police officers and detectives for tips, was fundamental to this culture of Victorian popular journalism, but these papers – particularly Robert Bell's – were also frequently prepared to attack the newly established police as well as the church 'and anything else established' (ibid: 242).

This was not just a working class market. The middle-class magazine *Household Words*, which Dickens started in March 1850, fished in the same waters with somewhat different motives and featured a substantial number of articles on the police, many concentrated in the first issues and focusing on the work of detectives. Although the evidence is slight, it is highly likely that Dickens made discreet payments to favourite police officers, as well as publicly hosting parties for detectives in his offices (Dickens 1850). This was not difficult for, as Philip Collins points out, the *entire* Detective Department for the metropolis consisted of a mere two inspectors and six sergeants (ibid, 205-6). He wrote stories for his magazines based on the use of his police contacts, edited and rewrote police articles by his contributors, and accompanied police raids into the East End. In an age that was very suspicious of the organised state, he functioned as a one-man propagandist for the new police force and the new 'science' of detection.

Dickens' Hero-worshipping of the Men in Blue

This campaign involved a high degree of selective perception and contemporaries criticised what appeared to be a hero-worshipping tendency – most unlike Dickens – that seemed to take him over when he got near a detective or an imperturbable man in blue. 'The imperturbability of the British policeman was soon, indeed, part of the national mythology' (Collins 1964: 203) and actively promoted by Dickens from *The Old Curiosity Shop* of 1840 onwards. Other critics, such as Humphrey House in his classic book *The Dickens World* (1942), puts it down to his authoritarian tendencies and his obsession with neatness and precision, and – House was writing in the Freudian-ravaged 1930s – his anality. Untidy criminality needed to be sorted out and his articles about night tours with the police and the detective parties in his office, House says, 'show a kind of clerical satisfaction in the functioning of a well-run organisation' (ibid: 202).

The account has considerable explanatory power, although it ignores a fundamental source of the detective – author love-in – for Dickens and for other journalists. This is the fundamental congruence of their respective crafts, well summarised by Haia Shpayer-Makov:

> To a great extent, the activity of Victorian and Edwardian detectives was similar and, increasingly they were expected to do similar things. The essence of their work relied on investigation – on the act of probing and exposing…both developed the skills of taking evidence, interviewing witnesses and, on the basis of scattered pieces of information, constructing

a narrative, often explaining a burning or puzzling issue. Their professional status depended on their ability to perform these tasks repeatedly and successfully (Shpayer-Makov 2009).

Payment of course was, by its nature, covert. One of the most celebrated policemen of the Victorian age, Inspector Charles Frederick Field (1805-1874), chief of the detective branch from 1846, owed his prominence to Dickens. Field was well-known as the 'model' of Bucket in *Bleak House* (serialised March 1852-September 1853) which conferred on him a form of early stardom, although Dickens appeared to deny this in a letter to *The Times* in September 1853 (Collins ibid: 206-7). After Field retired in December 1852 and opened a private inquiry bureau, Dickens is reported to have subscribed £300 to a testimonial (a sizeable sum equivalent to about £8000 today), although there is some dispute about this.[1] (See Collins ibid, n.35: 341)

Other evidence of payments is a bit scarce. As an editor Dickens was tight with money in his payment of contributors to *Household Words* (Buckler 1951: 1180). However, in a letter to his chief sub editor W. H. Wills in April 1851 setting out his plan for another police article that became 'The Metropolitan Protectives' (*Household Words* 1851) he wrote:

> Any of the Scotland Yard people will do it, I should think; if our friend by any accident should not be there, I will go into it. If they should recommend any other station house as better for the purpose, or would think it better for us to go to more than one under the guidance of some trustworthy man, *of course we will pay any man and do as they recommend*. But I think one topping station-house would be best (Stone op cit: 253-254, my italics).

Over this period, the Metropolitan Police avoided major scandals (Collins 1964: 200) but acquired an unsavory reputation for corruption and incompetence in the 1870s after Dickens's death. From its origins the question of 'perks' was a live issue, although four out of five of the men dismissed were sacked for drink related offences (Emsley 1991: 221). Recurrent efforts were made to control the use of perks at various points in the 19th century. Indeed, ferocious attacks by the press on police venality and incompetence were a feature of the late Victorian scene – particularly marked during the outbreak of murders in the East End in the 1880s attributed to 'Jack the Ripper' (Cobb 1956: chapter 16). Conan Doyle's limited Inspector Lestrade, 'one little sallow rat-faced, dark-eyed fellow', sprang from the fertile ground of a stack of press cuttings (Doyle 1887). Payments to policemen only became comprehensively illegal with the passing of the Prevention of Corruption Act in 1901, and it was made an offence for a police officer to receive payment and for someone to make one, in the context of recent increases in police pay and allowances (Robertson 2011). According to Chibnall, a major reason for the reluctant establishment of the Scotland Yard press office in 1919 was 'fears about unauthorised leaks produced by reporters bribing officers' (Chibnall 1979).

Cosy Culture between Crime Correspondents and the Cops – Then and Now

By that time a cosy and, to some extent, self-regulating culture had arisen between a corps of Fleet Street crime correspondents and the police in which each side needed each other – the police used the press for publicity, to get a result, to fight for better resources and advance their careers. Journalists relied on police tip-offs to get the latest information, access to victims and lurid details to dress up stories. Copious amounts of alcohol in a number of well-established London watering holes oiled the relationship. But references to money payments in journalist's memoirs are sparse. Hints remain. Consider the guarded references of Frederick Higginbottom – a noted *Pall Mall Gazette* journalist – in his memoirs:

> Go back to notorious murder mysteries of the eighties of last century...Every one was written up by expert reporters in touch with the police, and each of them provided sensations for months. The police used the Press then, as they do now, and they gave away information *freely* if it helped them to trace a missing suspect (Higginbottom 1934: 15, my italics).

Now a host of accounts have begun appearing in the press testifying to the ubiquity of this culture. For example, Duncan Campbell observes:

> It has *always* been known, by both police and the press, that some officers will trade information for money. Victims of crime or tragedy are often amazed at the speed with which the media arrive in the wake of the emergency services. Now they know why (Campbell 2009, my italics).

A 'veteran journalist' in the *Camden New Journal* claims:

> I CANNOT see why such unforgiving looks were given to Rebeccah [sic] Brooks, chief executive of News International, for telling a Commons committee that journalists paid police officers for stories – or words to that effect. Journalists of another generation would know that it was *common practice* to pay policemen for stories. When I worked on a west London weekly, too far back in time to date in this column, I would drop in to the local cop shop and if a story given by an officer was sold on to a national or London evening, the proceeds would be shared. Today, this would be considered a corrupt practice, I suppose, but it shades into insignificance compared with what is fundamentally wrong with many journalists (*Camden New Journal* 2011, my italics).

As the *Telegraph* observes:

> Payments by journalists to police officers have a long history. One long-retired crime correspondent recalls having a list of officers to whom he

would regularly send a £5 note 'wrapped in a plain WH Smith envelope'. 'I'd never use office stationery and I'd use a different typewriter each week so it couldn't be traced,' he said. 'I never felt I was bribing them but of course I was. But then these weren't just tips they were giving me,' he said with professional relish. 'These were stories that could go straight into the paper. What I liked best was when they told me the story before they'd even told Scotland Yard' (Born 2003).

However, Chester Stern, a former crime correspondent at the *Daily Mail* and *Mail on Sunday* with 20 years' experience, told the *Telegraph* in the same story that the paying of police officers is much less pervasive than many think:

'Yes it goes on but it is very much the exception rather than the rule,' he said. Stern said that during 20 years on the crime beat he was happy to wine and dine police contacts but drew the line at giving them cash. 'Ninety per cent of the information you need can be got through legitimate means' (ibid).

The researcher of Victorian journalistic morals finds real difficulties in uncovering a covert culture whose basis was cash – the beauty of cash, of course, lies in its being untraceable. Modern prosecutors, with many more tools at their command, still face great difficulties, as was shown in the trial of Neville Thurlbeck in 2000.

Mr Thurlbeck was cleared of allegations that he paid a Detective Constable Farmer to supply information on people whose details were kept on confidential police computer records. The prosecution alleged that Farmer made scores of police computer checks on people's criminal records for him and cited 36 stories in the *News of the World* allegedly containing information supplied by him, including:

...a Labour MP with a conviction for committing an obscene act; an alleged threat to the Queen from stalkers; a story about a man said to be involved with the mass murderer Rosemary West; and a priest with convictions for sex offences. He said the recorded outgoings of Det. Con. Farmer and his wife dropped between the start of 1997 and mid-1998, suggesting he had an alternative source of cash (Farmer 2000).

Conclusion

But does this expensive pursuit of information brokers and allegedly corrupt police officers serve the wider public interest? Most of it is likely to be very hard to prove and the former Metropolitan Police chief, Brian Paddick, argues that there is 'absolutely no point' in attempting to investigate whether journalists were paying police officers: 'If these claims are true' he says, 'then it is most likely officers were paid in cash and there is no way of proving it' (Channel 4 News 2011). One might observe that this seems to discount a careful auditing of gold bath taps against the ostensible income of the officer.

A final point to ponder: could efforts to stamp out payments between hacks and cops lead to the death of popular journalism? Optimistic estimates are that as many as 140 Mirror Group journalists may face criminal charges for phone hacking, bribery and associated crimes. As Guido Fawkes (Paul Staines) dramatically claims:

> The idea that this crisis is only about News International is fanciful...In short every major newsroom in the land has used illegal techniques to obtain information. We are on the verge of criminalising hundreds of journalists (Fawkes 2011).

So here's an interesting ethical conundrum. Freedom of the press may require us to argue for a tolerable level of corruption to enable crime to be reported, especially the crimes of the powerful, in the wider public interest. It doesn't lend itself to transparency, or ethical puritanism, and it doesn't exactly meet any Kantian test – mild corruption of the police by journalists might, indeed, lead to highway extortion for imaginary driving offences, as happens in Russia and the ex-Soviet republics. But it may be a price worth paying.

References

Born, Matthew (2003) Paying the police: Newspapers have a lot of form, *Daily Telegraph* 14 March. Available online at http://www.telegraph.co.uk/news/uknews/1424573/Paying-the-police-newspapers-have-a-lot-of-form.html, accessed on 17 October 2011

Buckler, William E. (1951) Dickens the Paymaster, *PMLA*, Vol. 66, No. 6 December pp 1177-1180

Camden New Journal (2011) Paying police for news stories isn't the malaise of modern journalism, 26 May 2011. Available online at http://www.camdennewjournal.com/paying-police-news-stories-isn't-malaise-modern-journalism, accessed on 17 October 2011

Campbell, Duncan (2009) The man in the mac: A life in crime reporting, *Guardian*, 5 September. Available online at http://www.guardian.co.uk/uk/2009/sep/05/crime-reporting-duncan-campbell, accessed on 17 October 2011

Campbell, Duncan (2011) Now the painful task of cleaning up the Metropolitan police begins, *Guardian*, 8 July. Available online at http://www.guardian.co.uk/commentisfree/2011/jul/08/metropolitan-police-paul-stephenson, accessed on 17 October 2011

Channel 4 News (2011) Police 'cash for info' probe 'pointless' –Brian Paddick, 15 April. Available online at http://www.channel4.com/news/reporters-paying-police-probe-pointless-says-paddick, accessed on 19 October 2011

Chibnall, Steve (1975a) The crime reporter, *Sociology*, Vol 9, No. 1 pp 49-66

Chibnall, Steve (1975b) The Police and the Press, Brown J. and Howes G. (eds) *The Police and the Community*, Farnborough: Saxon House

Chibnall, Steve (1977a) Worlds Apart: Notes on the Social reality of corruption, *British Journal of Sociology*, 28 (June 1977): 138-54. (with Peter Saunders)

Chibnall, Steve (1977b) *Law and Order News: Crime Reporting in the British Press*, London: Tavistock

Chibnall, Steve (1979)The wooing of the fourth estate: The Metropolitan Police and the news media 1970-1976, Holdaway S. (ed.) *British Police*, London: Edward Arnold:135-149

Chibnall, Steve (1980) Chronicles of the gallows: A social history of crime reporting', Christian H. (ed.) The Sociology of the News Media, *Sociological Review Monograph*, Vol. 29 pp 179-217

Chibnall, Steve (1981) The Crime Reporter, Cohen, S. and Young J. (eds) *The Manufacture of News: Mass Media and Social Problems*, London: Constable, second edition

Cobb, Belton (1956) *Critical Years at the Yard*, London: Faber and Faber

Collins, Philip (1965) Dickens *and Crime*, London: Macmillan, second edition

Davies, Nick (2008) *Flat Earth News*, London: Chatto and Windus.

Davies, Nick (2011) Jonathan Rees: Private investigator who ran empire of tabloid corruption, *Guardian* 11 March Available online at http://www.guardian.co.uk/media/2011/mar/11/jonathan-rees-private-investigator-tabloid, accessed on 17 October 2011

Dickens, Charles (1850) A Detective Police Party, *Household Words*, 27 July and 10 August

Dickens, Charles (1851) On Duty with Inspector Field, *Household Words*, 14 June

Doyle, Sir Arthur Conan (1887) *A Study in Scarlet*, Chapter 2 The Science of Deduction. Available online at http://www.gutenberg.org/files/244/244-h/244-h.htm, accessed on 1 December 2011

Emsley, Clive (1991) *The English Police: A Political and Social History*, New York: St Martins; London: Harvester Wheatsheaf

Farmer, Brian (2000) Tabloid journalist cleared of paying police officer for stories, *Independent*, 21 July. Available online at http://www.independent.co.uk/news/media/tabloid-journalist-cleared-of-paying-police-officer-for-stories-707398.html, accessed on 20 October 2011

Fawkes, Guido (2011) We are on the verge of killing popular journalism, 16 July. Available online at http://order-order.com/2011/07/16/we-are-on-the-verge-of-killing-popular-journalism/ accessed on 3 December 2011

Grant, Hugh (2011) The bugger, bugged, *New Statesman*, 12 April. Available online at http://www.newstatesman.com/newspapers/2011/04/phone-yeah-cameron-murdoch, accessed on 20 November 2011.

Higginbottom, Frederick J. (1934) *The Vivid Life: A Journalist's Career*, London: Simpkin Marshall

House, Humphry (1942) *The Dickens World*, London: Oxford University Press; second edition 1965 OUP paperback

Mawby, Rob C. (2010) Chibnall Revisited. Crime Reporters, the Police and Law and Order News, *British Journal of Criminology*, Vol. 50 pp 1060-1076

Milmo, Cahal, Brown, Jonathan and Blake, Matt (2011) Beyond the law, private eyes who do the dirty work for journalists, *Independent*, 13 July. Available online at http://www.independent.co.uk/news/media/press/beyond-the-law-private-eyes-who-do-the-dirty-work-for-journalists-2312702.html, accessed on 27 October 2011

Morison, Stanley (1932) *The English Newspaper*, Cambridge: Cambridge University Press

Robertson, Geoffrey (2011) *News of the World: A* newspaper is gone, but an inquiry is as urgent as ever, *Guardian*, 8 July. Available online at http://www.guardian.co.uk/profile/geoffreyrobertson, accessed on 25 October 2011

Shpayer-Makov, Haia (2009) Journalists and Police Detectives in Victorian and Edwardian England: An Uneasy Reciprocal Relationship, *Journal of Social History*, Vol. 42. No. 4 pp 963-987. Project MUSE, 1 July. 2011. Available online at http://muse.jhu.edu/

Shpayer-Makov, Haia (2010) From menace to celebrity: The English police detective and the press, c.1842–1914, *Journal of Historical Research* Volume, Vol. 83, No. 222 pp 672–692, November. Article first published online: 21 December 2009

Shpayer-Makov, Haia (2002), *The Making of a Policeman: a Social History of a Labour Force in Metropolitan London,1829-1914*, Aldershot, England, and Burlington Vt., USA: Ashgate Publishing

Stern, Chester (2010) The *News of the* World's special relationship with the police, *Guardian*, 6 September 2010. Available online at http://www.guardian.co.uk/commentisfree/2010/sep/06/news-of-the-world-special-police-relationship, accessed on 25 October 2011

Stone, Harry (1969) *The Uncollected Writing of Charles Dickens, Household Words 1850-1859*, Vol. 1, London: Allen Lane

Websites

Leveson Inquiry: http://www.levesoninquiry.org.uk

Transcript of testimony of Paul McMullan. Available online at

http://www.levesoninquiry.org.uk/wp-content/uploads/2011/11/Transcript-of-Afternoon-Hearing-29-November-2011.txt , accessed on 10 December 2011

Metropolitan Police 2011: History of the Metropolitan Police – Timeline. Available online at http://www.met.police.uk/history/timeline_index.htm, accessed on 27 October 2011

Witness statement of Nick Davies to Leveson Inquiry. Available online at http://www.levesoninquiry.org.uk/wp-content/uploads/2011/11/Witness-Statement-of-Nick-Davies.pdf, accessed on 10 December 2011

Note
[1] For Field, see http://www.ric.edu/faculty/rpotter/chasfield.html, accessed on 25 October 2011

Note on the contributor
John Tulloch is Professor of Journalism and Head of the School of Journalism, Lincoln University. He is co-director of the Centre for Journalism Research (CRJ). Previously (1995-2003) he was Head of the Department of Journalism and Mass Communication, University of Westminster. Edited books include *Tabloid Tales* (2000) (edited with Colin Sparks) *Peace Journalism, War and Conflict Resolution* (2010) (edited with Richard Lance

Keeble and Florian Zollmann), and *Global Literary Journalism* (edited with Richard Lance Keeble), forthcoming 2012. He has also written recently on extraordinary rendition and on the journalism of Charles Dickens, Gitta Sereny and Gordon Burn.

Section F: Dead Duck: Is Statutory Regulation the Answer?

Richard Lance Keeble

At the heart of British journalism lies the principle of self regulation and the celebration of the 'free press'. Our democracy is supposedly the fruit of centuries of struggle for freedom of expression (Winston 2005) with the mass-selling press which emerged in the second half of the nineteenth century free from direct government and political controls seen as the culmination of this process.

Media self regulation is built around the promotion of ethical codes. Yet these provoke a range of responses from journalists (see Nordenstreng 1997). Some regard them as vehicles of professionalisation, as a means of professional education, as instruments of consciousness-raising and as deliberate attempts by journalists to regulate the media and ward off legislation restricting their activities still further.

Significantly the first codes emerged in the first decade of the last century in Poland and the United States as part of more general moves towards professionalisation. In Europe, such codes were adopted gradually after World War One (in Sweden, France and the UK), immediately after World War Two (Italy, Belgium) and around the late 1960s and 1970s (Spain, Portugal). In America, many newspapers have their own customised codes, watched over by an ombudsman (they are mostly men). And US research suggests that journalists on newspapers with ombudsman are more likely to exercise 'ethical caution' in their work (see Wilkins and Coleman 2005: 112).

A contrasting response stresses the role of codes as mere rhetorical devices to preserve special privileges such as access to the powerful and camouflage hypocrisy. Codes can also fulfil important public relations functions. As Chris Frost suggests (2007: 248): 'They are often introduced to reassure the public that a profession has standards of practice and to imply, at least, that professionals who transgress those standards will be disciplined. Many professions and trades have raced to introduce codes of practice over the past few years in the light of rising consumer consciousness.'

The most important self regulatory codes are operated by the NUJ (www.nuj.org) and the Press Complaints Commission (www.pcc.org). In contrast, broadcasting is regulated by the Office of Communications (Ofcom) which was set up by legislation. Its code, introduced in July 2005, is a weighty document – its 10 sections have as many as 28 clauses in some cases. If a breach of the code is found, Ofcom can impose a fine, revoke a licence or forbid a repeat of a programme. In addition, the BBC also regulates its own performance through issuing detailed guidelines to producers (accessible at www.bbc.co.uk/guidleines/editorialguidelines/).

And that's not the end of media regulation in the UK: there's the Teenage Magazine Advisory Panel, set up by the Periodical Publishers Association (www.ppa.co.uk) after MPs expressed concern over the allegedly explicit sexual content of teenage magazines in 1996. In January 2000, the Internet Service providers set up the Internet Watch Foundation (see www.iwf.org.uk) as an industry-funded, self-regulatory body aiming to remove child pornography from UK-administered web servers. And the Brussels-based International Federation of Journalists has its own succinct Declaration of Principles on the Conduct of Journalists. Some may argue that the British media are far too regulated already!

Hackgate throws Spotlight on Codes

The eruption of the Hackgate scandal has certainly thrown the spotlight on the performance of the various regulatory bodies – and the effectiveness of their codes. Firstly in this section Steven Barnett argues that the press needs to learn from its broadcasting cousins on how best to regulate its activities. Thus he proposes a new, beefed up regulator with a range of new powers including:

- to initiate thorough investigations into allegations of malpractice;
- to impose effective and proportionate sanctions, including the right to prompt corrections with equal prominence;
- to impose punitive fines where breaches are deliberate and/or reckless;
- an independent ombudsman;
- to accommodate – in confidence – the complaints of individual journalists about unethical practices in their workplace.

He concludes: 'For the sake of journalism's integrity, and for the sake of those who are still clamouring at the doors of university of departments to learn the craft and the principles of journalism, we must ensure that the British press learns from the history and reputation of British television.'

In the next chapter, Stewart Purvis argues that no journalist in their right senses, whatever the pressures on them, would now hack a phone or pay a police officer. Put more bluntly, it's the fear of getting caught. And if that's one of the legacies for post-Hackgate journalism it might just turn out to be one of the most effective, he concludes.

Phil Harding, as the former BBC Controller of Editorial Policy, wrote the BBC's *Editorial Guidelines* and was involved in many contentious decisions on what sort of journalism qualifies as being in the 'public interest'. Here he argues that it is vital for those who care about the future of good journalism and its proper role in a civic society to take the lead in defining the 'public interest'. And he warns: 'If we don't, the substantial risk is that others will do it for us and they could be people who know little and care even less about the future of journalism.'

Damian Paul Carney, Principal Lecturer in Law at the University of Portsmouth, is a qualified barrister who has published extensively on media law. Here he proposes the setting up of a new regulatory body for the press providing strong remedies for complainants, better internal controls on ethics and complaints – and enough independence from government and industry to appease the general public.

Barry Turner dares to question the questions being asked at the Leveson Inquiry. For instance, why focus on media ethics when the hacking hacks have clearly broken the law?

The principles of a democratic and accountable media
It might be worth pointing out that the Leveson Inquiry is distinctly (and predictably) UK-centric when, in fact, the experiences of media councils elsewhere could be drawn on to inform the discussions. Many critics argue, for instance, that in Britain, management and editorial functions have become too closely intertwined. In some countries steps have been taken to prevent such developments. In Holland, for example, newspaper companies have introduced statutes into their collective labour agreements separating the interests of the editor and management. Thus, if journalists object to any particular assignment they can raise the issue with an editorial council which also has a say in any merger or sale plans and on advertising matters. In Germany some newspapers have agreed understandings with staffers giving then a voice in editorial decisions and in the editor-in-chief's selection.

Similarly, the code to which the Norwegian Editors' Association and National Association of Norwegian Newspapers are signatories (drafted on 1953 and revised in 1973) entitles editors to:

> free and independent leadership of the editorial department and editorial work and full freedom to shape the opinions of the paper even if they in single maters are not shared by the publisher or board…The editor must never allow himself/herself to be influenced to advocate opinions that are not in accord with the editors' own conviction (cited in Bromley 2000: 113).

Editorial staff are also given considerable powers to challenge intervention by proprietors. Publishers who have tampered with editorial decisions have found themselves without an editorial staff; in one case a newspaper went bankrupt when its staff quit following the publishers' order to remove an article about his family business. The strength of journalistic support for the code and for editorial autonomy has tended to reduce the potentially negative impacts for ownership concentration (Keeble 2009: 86-87).

This section ends, then, appropriately focusing the debate on the principles of a democratic and accountable media. The Coordinating Committee for Media Reform, an umbrella organisation of advocacy groups, academics and individuals campaigning for meaningful reform of the UK media, argues that a system which monitors and challenges unaccountable formations of media power, encourages significant new news initiatives, fosters more public involvement and holds unacceptable journalistic practices to account is the least we deserve.

References

Bromley, Michael (2000) The Manufacture of News, Berry, David (ed.) *Ethics and Media Culture: Practices and Representations*, Oxford: Focal Press pp 111-131

Frost, Chris (2007) *Journalism Ethics and Regulation*, Harlow: Pearson Education

Keeble, Richard (2009) *Ethics for Journalists*, London: Routledge, second edition

Nordenstreng, Kaarle (1997) *Reports on Media Ethics in Europe*, Tampere, Finland: University of Tampere, Department of Journalism and Mass Communication

Wilkins, Lee and Coleman, Renita (2005) *The Moral Media: How Journalists Reason about Ethics*, Mahwah, NJ, Lawrence Erlbaum Associates

Winston, Brian (2005) *Messages: Free Expression, Media and the West from Gutenberg to Google*, London: Routledge

Why the Press must Learn from the History and Reputation of British Television

On the basis of holding corporate power accountable to the public interest, Steven Barnett proposes a number of principles which a new regulatory system for the press should embrace

'While there are thousands of journalists checking facts and running stories past eagle-eyed lawyers, there is a pack of hacks who act with a thuggish disregard for the law. They have become that corrupt power in the land that many of us entered the trade to hold to account.'[1]

Thus Allison Pearson, with characteristic elegance, summed up the two greatest ironies emerging from the phone-hacking scandal: first that the very Fourth Estate on whom we rely to 'speak truth to power' and keep democracy honest had themselves become the last bastion of unaccountability; and second that the behaviour of a very small – but very powerful – minority was infecting the reputational standing and professionalism of the vast majority of dedicated hacks. Indeed, the web of deceit extended well beyond phone hacking to corrosive and malicious newsroom practices which smacked more of calculated bullying than a fearless desire to expose corruption or wrongdoing.

Journalism and Accuracy: Theory versus Practice

Forget, for the moment, about the thorny issue of privacy versus free speech, of disputed definitions around the public interest, and those grey areas around celebrity revelations which have become part of Leveson's staple diet. Let us concentrate on one of the most basic articles of journalistic faith: truth-telling. There is really no ambiguity there: the 'truth' may not always be easily divined, and even after several sources have been cross-checked there can be room for interpretation. But the responsibility of journalism to seek after accuracy and the *best version* of the truth should not be questionable. Indeed, the Press Complaints Commission – whose reputation has been justifiably trashed by the events of the last few years – is crystal clear on the issue of accuracy which is proudly set out as the very first rule of the Editors' code of practice:

> 1 i.) The press must take care not to publish inaccurate, misleading or distorted information, including pictures.

We could not wish for a clearer recitation of the first article of journalistic faith. Moreover, just to underline the importance of journalistic integrity, the very next subsection describes the remedy:

> 1 ii) A significant inaccuracy, misleading statement or distortion once recognised must be corrected, promptly and with due prominence, and – where appropriate – an apology published. In cases involving the commission, prominence should be agreed with the PCC in advance.

Now let's examine some of the evidence which emerged as the victims of egregious press behaviour took to the stands and recited the catalogue of deliberate, reckless, often malicious and sometimes vindictive lies which were published in British newspapers for the gratification of readers. There was Sienna Miller who described her attendance at a party for sick children where, when one child pretended to shoot her with a gun, she rolled around on the floor playing dead. Someone took a picture on their mobile phone, which ended up in the *Daily Mirror* as a story about Miller being disgracefully drunk at a children's party.

There was Charlotte Church whose example of fabricated nonsense came not from the distant past but from the *Sunday People* of 6 November 2011, just one week before the formal evidence sessions of the Leveson Inquiry were due to begin: a front-page story – complete with photograph and quotes from Church and her partner – which detailed how she had drunkenly proposed to her fiancé while singing at a karaoke bar. In fact, the photograph had been taken in 2007, the quotes had been concocted, and at the time of the 'proposal, she had actually been performing in a different bar in a different town in front of a large public audience'. And, of course, the internet not only globalises the lies within hours, but makes them permanent – within 36 hours, this particular tale had been picked up and recycled by 70 outlets around the world presenting it as fact. The apology which subsequently appeared in the *People* – and the *Sun* and the *Daily Mail* which had slavishly repeated the story the following day – is unlikely to have been republished in 70 other jurisdictions.

Outrage over Brutal Treatment meted out to Ordinary People

If we are less willing to feel sympathy for celebrities whose lives are routinely misreported (perhaps seeing it as a tolerable downside to the fame and fortune which accompanies success), we should certainly be outraged by the similarly cavalier and brutal treatment meted out to ordinary people who have become victims of extraordinary events. How could any civilised person justify the newspaper headlines which greeted the McCanns within a few weeks of their daughter being abducted in Portugal, including allegations that they had sold their daughter for money or were hiding her body in a freezer? There can be no conceivable justification for the campaign of vilification, innuendo and straightforward lies which confronted two parents desperate to find their kidnapped daughter. Equally appalling was the coverage in virtually every tabloid newspaper of Christopher Jefferies, a perfectly ordinary and law-abiding landlord, portrayed by lazy journalists as a weird and eccentric suspect capable of murdering Joanna Yeates. No doubt off-the-record briefings by the local police contributed to the denigration, but the temptation of sensationalist headlines during a slow news cycle was too much for a tabloid culture in which accuracy had long ago been sacrificed on the altar of speed and profitability.

Even those who have not become entangled in extraordinary events outside their control have found themselves embroiled in this shameless culture of victimisation. Before phone-hacking and Leveson exposed the seamier side of journalism, an almost unnoticed blogger had told her tale of blatant *Daily Mail* distortion. Juliet Shaw was a PR consultant and jobbing journalist who innocently responded to the newspaper's call for interviews with people who had left the city for a life in the country. She invited a *Mail* interviewer into her home, found herself being interrogated about her sex life, and ended up the subject of a double-page spread which so grotesquely distorted her private and personal life that she became a laughing stock in her own community. It was an article that broke every rule of decent journalism, and yet still this single mother had to fight for two years against the intimidating tactics of the *Mail*'s corporate machine before they finally agreed to a small financial settlement – and still without the apology which the editors' code supposedly demanded and which she really craved.[2]

These are examples of flagrant and cynical breaches of the PCC code in which individuals are targeted. On the receiving end are real people whose lives are turned upside down – in some cases traumatised – by reckless journalistic practices within a profession which for too long has believed itself to be beyond accountability, and in a few cases even above the law.

Casualties of Deliberate Misrepresentation

But there are other casualties of this kind of deliberate misrepresentation, especially those minority groups which are targeted by newspapers pursuing a particularly vicious and aggressive agenda to portray them in a negative light. In the spotlight, invariably, are those on welfare ('feckless scroungers', 'benefit cheats'), asylum seekers, and increasingly Muslims. Within a regulatory system which is only prepared to entertain named complainants, the routine and systematic libelling of minority groups goes unpunished. Richard Peppiatt gave the Leveson Inquiry a disturbing insight into the mentality of the *Daily* Star's corporate and editorial philosophy while he was there:

> Much more insidious was when this same philosophy was applied to stories involving Muslims and immigrants, when yet again a top down

pressure to unearth stories which fitted within a certain narrative (immigrants are taking over, Muslims are a threat to security) led to casual and systemic distortion.[3]

And beyond the individuals and groups which suffer from these corporately directed distortions, there is a broader problem around presentation of information that might assist readers in understanding matters of immediate political interest. Arguments around the importance of a diverse and vibrant press often focus on its contribution to an informed democracy, and the poverty of public understanding that might follow from a failing press. This becomes a more difficult argument to sustain when examining some of the deliberate misrepresentations featured in the news columns of, in particular, tabloid newspapers which follow a clear political line.

Thus, in recent debates about pension reform and the public sector demonstrations which followed, readers of the *Daily Mail* and the *Sun* read 'news' stories about gold-plated public sector pensions and the urgent need to rebalance the rewards of private versus public sector employment. Readers of the *Daily Mirror* were more likely to read stories about the impact of pension reforms on low-paid nurses and teachers. None of these readers were likely to emerge any better informed about the political and context for the proposals, the economic rationale, or alternative proposals. These blurred edges between fact and comment were illustrated graphically (and amusingly) in Alastair Campbell's evidence to Leveson when analysing the dominant approach of most British newspapers' approach to Europe in its news pages:

> At various times, readers of these and other newspapers may have read that 'Europe' or 'Brussels' or the 'EU superstate' has banned, or is intending to ban: kilts, curries,, mushy peas, paper rounds, Caerphilly cheese, charity shops, bulldogs, bent sausages and cucumbers, the British Army, lollipop ladies, British loaves, British made lavatories…In addition, if the Eurosceptic press is to be believed, Britain is going to be forced to unite as a single country with France, Church schools are being forced to hire atheist teachers, Scotch whisky is being classified as an inflammable liquid, British soldiers must take orders in French, the price of chips is being raised by Brussels, Europe is insisting on one size fits all condoms, new laws are being proposed on how to climb a ladder, it will be a criminal offence to criticise Europe, Number 10 must fly the European flag, and finally, Europe is brainwashing our children with pro-European propaganda.[4]

It is, perhaps, scarcely surprising, in the face of such an overwhelming burden of 'evidence' about absurd European restrictions on British everyday life, that most British people are opposed to Britain joining the European currency and further European integration. It is perfectly possible that such Euroscepticism is an integral part of British culture and that the newspapers' fanciful inventions simply reinforce existing prejudices. Even if true, it remains axiomatic that democracy is better served by voters and citizens being offered news stories which bear some relation to reality.

Protecting Journalists and Changing the Newsroom Culture

For those of us who are journalism educators, these fabrications and flights of fancy are especially frustrating because they are a grotesque contradiction of everything we attempt to convey to students and – even worse – of the professional ambitions for journalism which most students willingly embrace. In my experience, aspiring journalists do not start their university courses with a burning desire to hide in bushes with long-lens cameras, entrap celebrities by offering them lines of cocaine, fabricate interviews, invent stories about bogus asylum seekers and benefit scroungers, or blag confidential information about the relatives of terrorism victims. Every aspiring journalist I have taught starts with a measure of idealism about wanting to make a useful contribution to knowledge, understanding, and even democracy. It is newsroom cultures which turn them into something less than their idealised vision.

Something happens, therefore, within those newsrooms which turn the journalists who know and respect editorial codes of conduct to the privacy invaders and fabricators who have featured during Leveson. And it has become increasingly clear, at least from those brave enough to speak out, that this culture emanates from senior editorial and corporate figures, driven primarily by commercial objectives which have scant regard for any notion of professional ethics. Moreover, it is also clear that there is no protective framework for those who wish to cling to some notion of journalistic idealism, and that the regulatory system was held in private contempt. Peppiatt, again, revealed the ethical vacuum and permanent sense of professional insecurity in which journalists at the *Daily Star* worked:

> It seemed to me that reporters' employment contracts were structured specifically to limit the possibility of any ethical protest. Many, including myself, were on casual contracts, which is to say they can be terminated at anytime. The spectre of being 'let go' at any moment is a powerful deterrent against sticking your head above the trench if you disagree with something that is occurring. Even if someone was bold enough to complain, no channel existed for employees to raise concerns about ethical or journalistic practices. My feeling was certainly that the further up the chain of command you went the less, not more, concern over newsroom behaviour existed.[5]

Much the same point about relentless commercial pressure and the consequences for professional practice was made by Sharon Marshall whose book published in 2010 detailed her experience of working for ten years on seven different tabloid titles:

Hacks are pushed by deadlines, pushed to fill the paper, pressured as they face relentless daily push to deliver, whilst all the time being challenged by younger, cheaper shifters coming up through the ranks who are desperate to steal their jobs. On newspapers you not only compete against the rest of Fleet Street, but bosses would frequently put a desperate young journalist and an older staffer on the same story and set them in competition against each other. Add to that the constant threat of redundancy as circulations fall and staffing levels decrease each year, so newspapers can survive.[6]

Anarchy in the Newsroom

Reinforcing this sense of newsroom anarchy has been an overarching lack of accountability to any set of rules or appropriate behaviour which might have provided a brake to some of the journalistic excesses which are now a matter of record. Should any of these hard-pressed tabloid hacks have summoned up the courage (or stupidity) to wave the Press Complaints Commission code in front of their news editors, the reaction would most likely have been incomprehension (or possibly fury). While tabloid editors have attempted to convince both Lord Justice Leveson and the public at large that they lived in fear of adverse adjudications from the PCC, rather more revealing evidence about the attitude of proprietors was revealed by Piers Morgan from his time as *News of the World* editor. Having been the subject of an upheld complaint to the PCC in May 1995 for publishing intrusive photos of Earl Spencer's wife, Morgan was subjected to the PCC's 'ultimate sanction': a referral to the offending newspaper's proprietor. Having been publicly rebuked by Murdoch, Morgan found his private reaction rather different:

> 'I'm sorry about all that press complaining thingamajig', [Murdoch] said, to my astonishment. He definitely used the word 'sorry'. And it was clear by his failure to even remember the name of the Press Complaints Commission that he doesn't really give a toss about it. 'We had to deal with it the way we did or they'd have all been banging on about a privacy law again and we don't need that right now. Anyway, it's done now. How are you going to sell me more papers?'[7]

It is difficult to think of a more eloquent indictment of the PCC's toothless and ineffectual nature, and it is scarcely surprising that those journalists who might have sought protection for their own interpretation of ethical behaviour have felt vulnerable. It is even less surprising that those whose professional consciences were untroubled by the stories they were asked to pursue were given such little cause for self-reflection that newsroom practices emerged which were unthinkable elsewhere. In Sharon Marshall's words again: 'There is a feeling of invincibility in the newsroom, as it seeks out and prints each story, and if no one's there to check it, things can start getting out of control.'[8]

One of the most frequently heard arguments in opposition to any greater regulatory scrutiny of the press is the risk or fear of 'state' interference with free expression. This would have greater force were it not for the fact that another branch of British journalism provides a genuinely protective framework both for ethical editorial practices and for independence from any inappropriate political pressure. Broadcast journalism offers some clear points of departure for a new regulatory settlement that could transform the tabloid newsroom culture and liberate good journalism while eliminating the worst.

Lessons from Television

Despite the rise of the internet, television remains the public's most important source of national and international news. As surveys consistently testify, it is also the most trusted: my own research three years ago, long before the phone-hacking scandal, showed that over half the UK population felt they could trust television journalists (nearly two thirds for the BBC) compared to 43 per cent for broadsheet newspaper journalists, and just 15 per cent for tabloid journalists.[9] These results are not surprising because Britain's television journalism has a reputation – internationally as well as at home – for being robust, independent, ethical and accurate. It is the product of both institutional evolution and thoughtful regulation, and demonstrates that a sensibly constructed, responsibly implemented and genuinely independent regulatory regime can actually promote high journalistic standards rather than restrain them.

If regulation 'chills' television journalism, how does one explain the information and investigation records down the years of programmes such as *Panorama, World in Action, This Week, Dispatches,* and *Unreported World,* as well as news analysis programmes such as *Newsnight, Channel 4 News* and the *Today* programme? While ITV's appetite for this kind of journalism may have dimmed in recent years, both the BBC and Channel 4 – each in their different ways subject to statutory regulation – have continued to support and invest in journalism which holds governments, public authorities, corporations and powerful individuals to account. Ironically, ITV's reduction in peak time current affairs is directly attributable to the relaxation rather than tightening of regulatory requirements.[10] During the second half of 2011, while the Leveson Inquiry was hearing from the victims and perpetrators of wholesale press irresponsibility, a number of television reporters and editors were attesting to a House of Lords select committee about their ability to conduct fearless and independent investigative journalism within a statutory regime.[11]

It is also a framework which ensures that effective sanctions are imposed when standards are breached. Carlton Television was punished in 1998 for its award-winning documentary *The Connection* which purported to show how drugs were routinely smuggled into the UK from Columbia. When large parts of the programme were exposed by the *Guardian* as faked, Carlton were obliged to broadcast a peak-time apology and were subjected to an unprecedented £2 million fine by the Independent Television Commission which described the programme as 'a wholesale breach of trust between programme makers and viewers'. The message was unequivocal: such practices are unacceptable newsroom practice, and sanctions will be punitive.[12]

This is categorically not an argument for statutory regulation of the press, for the imposition of impartiality rules on the press, or for licensing of newspapers. It is, however, a comparison which helps us to understand that an independent regulatory framework can not only protect but actively promote the kind of accessible, information-rich, and watchdog journalism which most professionals wish to practise and on which democracy thrives. Neither licensing nor frontline statutory regulation such as Ofcom are necessary for proper implementation of the PCC code, nor for instilling in our newspapers the kinds of newsroom practices that are routine in broadcasting. What is essential, however, is that any self-regulatory system incorporates the kinds of investigatory powers, punitive sanctions and protection for the public that have produced a television journalism culture which takes its professional codes of conduct seriously. As I explain below, this will require self-regulation to be supported by a backstop, independent body with the democratic legitimacy of parliament.

Freedom of Speech and the Public Interest

Our broadcasting environment therefore provides empirical evidence that journalistic freedom is not impaired by an effective regulator with teeth, but there is also a more subtle philosophical argument centred around notions of corporate power and accountability. It has been most eloquently advanced by the Cambridge philosopher Onora O'Neill who made the distinction in her 2002 Reith lectures between 'individual' free speech and 'corporate' free speech, and warned that we were 'perilously close to a world in which media conglomerates act as if they too had unrestricted rights of free expression'.[13]

Baroness O'Neill elaborated on this theme in a lecture in November 2011 when she distinguished between individual self-expression and the speech of powerful organisations: 'the communication of the powerful can shape and influence, improve and damage others' lives, and in democracies we have long since taken steps to regulate the communication of most powerful organisations'. Crucially, however, she drew a distinction between regulating media *content*, which was not acceptable, and regulating media *process* which was both acceptable and desirable as a means of ensuring transparency for audiences as well as accountability of the powerful.[14] Regulating the *process* by which fairness, accuracy, respect for privacy, and redress for journalistic malpractice are properly implemented by the press need entail no constraint on newspapers' freedom to publish.

Integral to this idea is a developed concept of protecting and promoting journalism 'in the public interest', a framework which should be determined by parliament. It need not be prescriptive and, like all laws, would inevitably require interpretation and refinement through the courts. Importantly, however, it would enshrine the fundamental importance of journalism's watchdog function, and could therefore serve to *liberate* rather than restrict the very journalism which apologists for self-regulation suggest would be endangered. A statutory definition might therefore safeguard the absolute right to publication in the case of:

- exposing wrongdoing, injustice or incompetence amongst private or public officials in positions of responsibility, including abuses of public office;
- protecting the public from potential danger;
- preventing the public from being misled either by erroneous statements or by the hypocrisy of those attempting to create a false image of themselves;
- revealing information which fulfils a democratic role in advancing a better understanding of important issues or assists the public to come to electoral or other decisions of clear democratic importance.

A democratically agreed public interest framework could then be extended to legitimise other journalistic techniques which are currently not protected – not just phone-hacking itself, but robust defences for the new Bribery Act and the current Official Secrets Act. The corollary would be less or no protection for trivial, inaccurate or intrusive journalism which caused distress or harm with no genuine public interest justification. The argument of some newspaper editors – that law is being made by 'unaccountable, unelected and invisible judges' – would, of course, have less purchase if a public interest framework were enshrined in law.

Principles for a New Approach to Regulation

Taking together the relevant lessons that can be adapted from our broadcasting framework, and the principle of holding corporate power accountable to the public interest, it is possible to articulate a number of principles which a new regulatory system should embrace. These would include (though not be confined to):

- power to initiate thorough investigations into allegations of malpractice, including misreporting or misrepresentation of groups as well as individuals;
- effective and proportionate sanctions, including the right to prompt corrections with equal prominence;
- power to impose punitive fines where breaches are deliberate and/or reckless;
- an independent ombudsman;
- a means to accommodate – in confidence – the complaints of individual journalists about unethical practices in their workplace;
- severe financial penalties (for example, addition of VAT) for those publications which refused to participate in the new system: there may also be a case for compelling membership in the case of publications with very large circulations;

- an assumption in favour of prior notification for stories involving privacy, with protection afforded to newspapers on the public interest grounds outlined above;

- an individual Standards Executive, with seniority at board level, to be nominated by each publication, with an obligation to monitor newsroom behaviour, to act as a conduit for informal editorial advice, and to be accountable to the Ombudsman in responding to investigations or complaints;

- audit requirements: a clear record of advice sought and obtained from the nominated editorial adviser for any journalistic investigation that might involve a code breach.

The last point is particularly important because it is standard practice within broadcasting, and would guarantee that a record of ethical considerations within a publication is available if necessary for inspection. The audit trail should clearly be understood as two separate stages: first, permission to breach guidelines on the basis of *prima facie* evidence (to guard against fishing expeditions); and second, for permission to publish on the grounds that the public interest defence has been satisfied. This point was made by Steve Hewlett, on the basis of a long and successful career as a television journalist, writing about the procedures in television when a journalist proposes to invade someone's privacy:

> Stage one requires the journalist to convince their editor that sufficient *prima facie* evidence exists about the activities of an individual or company or whatever to justify the intrusion...Once the material has been gathered, a further approval to use it, based on what, if anything, has been discovered...must be obtained. This might sound bureaucratic but it creates a paper trail for decision making, and forces proper consideration of the issues.[15]

Implementation Devolved to an Independent Body

Ideally, implementation of these new regulatory principles should be devolved to an independent body selected from within the industry (including working journalists): an active self-regulator *of* the press but not in thrall to it. The Irish Press Council has been mooted as a good working model of how this body might be constituted. Crucially, however, self-regulation alone will not work. In the fallout from the phone-hacking revelations and the manifest failure of the PCC to deal with journalistic malpractice, there was a growing clamour from the industry that the PCC was, in fact, never designed as a self-regulatory system. These apologists for continued self-regulation had apparently forgotten the recommendations of the original Calcutt report in 1990, set up after equally flagrant breaches of ethical standards in the 1980s, and Sir David Calcutt's conclusions when he reviewed the new system of self-regulation in 1993:

> The Press Complaints Commission is not, in my view, an effective regulator of the press. The commission has not been set up in a way, and is

not operating a code of practice, which enables it to command not only press but also public confidence.[16]

It will be therefore be necessary to introduce a backstop body given powers by Parliament that invests self-regulation with real teeth and creates proper accountability. Without such a body, it will not be possible to levy fines or to ensure that an Ombudsman is genuinely independent from the industry. In order to regain public trust – and to ensure that powerful corporate interests are not allowed to dictate the terms of regulation – such reserve statutory powers will be essential. An analogous model might be the Solicitors Regulation Authority, a self-regulatory body which has the power to impose unlimited fines and is backed in law by an independent Legal Services Board. It is conceivable that Ofcom might perform this task, as long as the frontline regulatory tasks are performed by a body derived from the industry.

It is important to remember that, for the reasons given earlier, the vast majority of working journalists would also welcome a new framework which genuinely protects fairness, integrity and high ethical standards. Those who oppose radical reform – as opposed to reform which tinkers around the edges but essentially leave the press alone to put their own house in order – are drawn mostly from the large corporations who have overseen (and in some cases clearly encouraged) some of the most offensive and appalling transgressions of ethical codes in British journalism history. Despite their protestations to the contrary, it is not a free press which these corporations are desperate to protect but their own power and profitability at the expense of those they target. For the sake of journalism's integrity, and for the sake of those who are still clamouring at the doors of university of departments to learn the craft and the principles of journalism, we must ensure that the British press learns from the history and reputation of British television.

Notes

[1]Allison Pearson, Leveson Inquiry: Phone hackers are sick vultures that prey on the vulnerable, *Daily Telegraph*, 24 November 2011

[2]The full story can be found on the following blog, dated 31 January 2011. Available online at http://nosleeptilbrooklands.blogspot.com/2011/01/true-story-of-daily-mail-lies-guest.html, accessed on 1 December 2011

[3]Richard Peppiatt, evidence to Leveson Inquiry, published 29 November 2011. Available online at http://www.levesoninquiry.org.uk/evidence/?witness=richard-peppiatt , accessed on 1 December 2011

[4]Alastair Campbell, evidence to Leveson Inquiry, published 30 November 2011, Available online at http://www.levesoninquiry.org.uk/evidence/?witness=alastair-campbell, accessed on 1 December 2011

[5]Peppiatt, evidence to Leveson op cit

[6]Sharon Marshall, 2010, *Tabloid Girl*. London: Sphere Books p. 255

[7]Piers Morgan, 2005, *The Insider*, London: Ebury Press p. 82

[8]Marshall op cit, p. 236

[9]Steven Barnett, On the Road to Self-Destruction, *British Journalism Review*, Vol 19, No. 2, 2008 pp 5-13

[10]This is the theme of my recently published book, which traces the context for and emergence of Britain's global reputation for high quality, independent television journalism: Steven Barnett, *The Rise and Fall of Television Journalism*, Bloomsbury Academic, 2011

[11]The Lords select committee on communications initiated an inquiry into investigative journalism, for which I acted as specialist adviser. Those giving evidence from television included Dorothy Byrne, Head of News and Current Affairs at Channel 4; Ian Squires, Controller of Current Affairs and News at ITV; Tom Giles, editor of *Panorama* and its long-standing reporter John Ware; and independent producers Ray Fitzwalter, Roger Bolton, and Roger Graef. Available online at http://www.parliament.uk/business/committees/committees-a-z/lords-select/communications-committee/inquiries/the-future-of-investigative-journalism/, accessed on 1 December 2011

[12]The full story can be found in Raymond Fitzwalter, *The Dream that Died: The rise and Fall of ITV*, Leicester, Matador Publishing, 2008 pp 202-203

[13]Onora O'Neill, *A Question of Trust: The BBC Reith Lectures 2002*, Cambridge: Cambridge University Press, 2002 pp 93-94

[14]Onora O'Neill, The Rights of Journalism and the Needs of Audiences, Lecture to the Reuters Institute for the Study of Journalism, 21 November 2011

[15]Steve Hewlett, PCC2 can learn a lot about privacy from TV, *British Journalism Review*, Vol. 22, No. 4, December 2011 pp 23-25

[16]Sir David Calcutt QC, *Review of Press Self-Regulation*, Department of National Heritage, January 1993, London: HMSO, Cm 2135 p. 41 par 5.26

Note on the contributor

Steven Barnett is Professor of Communications at the University of Westminster, specialising in media policy, regulation, journalism and press ethics. For the last four years, he has acted as specialist adviser to the House of Lords select committee on communications on a number of parliamentary inquiries, and in December 2011 he was called to give evidence to the Leveson Inquiry. He sits on the editorial board of the *British Journalism Review* and writes frequently for the national and specialist press. He is the author or co-author of a number of books, of which the most recent *The Rise and Fall of Television Journalism* was published by Bloomsbury Academic in November 2011.

Journalism After Hackgate

No journalist in their right senses, whatever the pressures on them, would now hack a phone or pay a police officer. Put more bluntly, it's the fear of getting caught. And if that's one of the legacies for post-Hackgate journalism it might just turn out to be one of the most effective, argues Stewart Purvis

It is a sad symbol of the predictability of our trade that by appending the suffix 'gate' to a word we signal to the reader, viewer or listener that a story has become a scandal. Watergate, which begat a whole load of new 'gates', remember was the office building in Washington where, in 1972, burglars working for the Republican Party broke into the headquarters of their Democrat rivals – and so began a sequence of events that led to the resignation of President Nixon.

According to Wikipedia's guide to the list of scandals with the suffix 'gate' (who writes these things?) there have been more than 100 'gates' so far. Some were significant political events. Others were front-page royal scandals such as the 'Squidygate' and 'Camillagate' tapes. And there are many that frankly one struggles to remember what they were about.

So what will the lasting legacy of Hackgate be for journalism? Will there be lasting effects or will it be consigned to the lower league tables of scandals along with 'hotcoffeegate', 'brothelgate' and 'nipplegate'? As I write (November 2011) Hackgate is far from over. The police investigations continue. Nobody other than Glenn Mulcaire and Clive Goodman has yet been tried and sentenced. We still don't know when James Murdoch was told that the scandal went much wider inside News International.

A Progress Report

The Commons committee questioning him hasn't finished its work yet. The inquiry into hacking and a whole series of inter-related issues is still in its early days. We don't know what the implications will be for the Communications Act which is due in the later stages of this parliament. So the best time to judge the full legacy of Hackgate and where it is on the scale from Watergate to

'Hotcoffeegate' is probably around 2015. So here's a progress report, a very interim report back .

2011 has been a year that whenever the word 'journalism' is used, the word 'regulation' is never far behind. I have been particularly interested as one of the few senior journalists who has also been a senior regulator. After three decades in daily journalism, I spent three years as the content regulator at Ofcom. A kind of poacher turned gatekeeper.

As a journalist, I have been involved at some point in some role in the production of BBC Radio News, ITN News on ITV, Channel Four News, Five News, Independent Radio News and EuroNews. I have also done some print work writing columns for the *Financial Times* and the London *Evening Standard*, and articles for the *Guardian* and *The Times*. And I have had dealings as a regulator or as one of the regulated with Ofcom , its predecessors the ITC, the IBA, the BCC, the Radio Authority and Ofcom's counterparts in France and Germany not to mention plus a whole host of so called 'self' and 'co-regulators' the Press Complaints Commission, the Advertising Standards Authority, the British Board of Film Classification, the Authority for Television on Demand and the Internet Watch Foundation'.

No wonder that when I organised an event at City University with many of these good folk present, Michael Grade described it as a 'regulatory self-flagellation session'. So a welcome to the wonderful world of media regulation to the Right Honourable Lord Justice Leveson, Brian Leveson to his friends. And the task he and his team have been given by the Prime Minister? No less than to make recommendations:

a. for a new more effective policy and regulatory regime which supports the integrity and freedom of the press, the plurality of the media, and its independence, including from Government, while encouraging the highest ethical and professional standards;

b. for how future concerns about press behaviour, media policy, regulation and cross-media ownership should be dealt with by all the relevant authorities, including parliament, government, the prosecuting authorities and the police;

c. on the future conduct of relations between politicians and the press; and

d. on the future conduct of relations between the police and the press.

And that's just half of Part One of a two-part project. In the first days of public seminars and I suspect that what he was really trying to get from these was :

1. A bit of theatre which brought together all the key stakeholders in a public event if only for a short time. I have never seen so many newspaper editors gathered together in one place. So tick that box.

2. Due process. Giving everybody a say so they can't say they weren't asked. Surprisingly few editors had much significant to say but they did get the chance to say it.

3. Getting at least one senior editor to make some proposals for the reform of self-regulation.

It was very interesting how Paul Dacre, Editor-in-Chief of the *Daily Mail*, and Kelvin MacKenzie, former Editor of the *Sun*, chose to respond to their invitations to speak at the public hearings. They both decided to attack the inquiry itself. Paul Dacre criticised Lord Leveson's team as a 'panel of experts who – while honourable distinguished people – don't have the faintest clue how mass-selling newspapers operate'. He then moved onto their remit: 'Am I alone in detecting the rank smells of hypocrisy and revenge in the political class's current moral indignation over a British press that dared to expose their greed and corruption?'

Kelvin MacKenzie called it a 'ludicrous inquiry' and 'this bloody inquiry', and then went for the jugular, attacking Lord Leveson's own professional reputation as a lawyer: 'God help me that free speech comes down to the thought process of a judge who couldn't win when prosecuting counsel against Ken Dodd for tax evasion and more recently robbing the Christmas Island veterans of a substantial pay-off for being told to simply turn away from nuclear test blasts in the Fifties. It's that bad.'

A few days later there was an unprecedented apology from MacKenzie in his column in the *Mail* for being 'disobliging' to Lord Leveson. Maybe he and his editor at the *Mail*, Paul Dacre, realised their tactics had been over the top.

What is the Main Problem for Leveson?
It is worth asking ourselves: what is the main problem for which Lord Justice Leveson and his panel of six assessors are trying to find the solution? Is it the failure of the police to investigate properly a series of crimes? Or a failure of the system of self-regulation which the press jealously guards to itself. I suspect that the view of the average citizen is that it sounds like a bit of both. But the view of these two editors – one past and one present – is that it is primarily the former not the latter and that the failings of the police shouldn't be allowed to damage the freedom of the press.

Maybe by challenging the inquiry's purpose and personnel they were trying to encourage Lord Leveson to focus on the police part of his remit and less on the press part. And if it was encouragement with a touch of menace, well Paul Dacre and Kelvin MacKenzie both do menace well.

There is one principal problem with this strategy of 'challenge the inquiry, challenge the judge and blame the police'. It is one word: events. Specifically the publication of the 2008 legal advice to News International from Michael Silverleaf QC. Who would have expected that this far into the phone-hacking saga such new and crucial information would become available? The QC advised News International that there was 'a powerful case that there is (or was) a culture of illegal information access' at the *News of the World* and that any trial would be 'extremely damaging' to the publisher's reputation. It will be difficult for the media to keep pointing the finger at the police as the principal culprits if it can be proved that senior executives at News International failed to volunteer information to the police despite getting legal advice like this.

What Lord Leveson got from his encounter with Paul Dacre was something more lasting than a headline. You will remember that I speculated that one of his ambitions would have been to get a senior editor to put some concrete proposals for reform on the table. In one paragraph half way through his speech Paul Dacre made a dramatic change of gear. 'OK,' he said, 'enough of being defensive. The truth is we are where we are. The perception is that the PCC is broken. It needs to be reformed if it is to regain trust, so may I make several suggestions.'

Paul Dacre's Call for an Ombudsman

His plan was that the industry's own self-regulatory body, the Press Complaints Commission, should continue but there should be one extra and new body. He called it an Ombudsman, though others including some Ombudsmen have said that's the wrong term for what he has in mind. He suggested a retired judge or civil servant, possibly advised by two retired editors, should have the power to investigate what he called 'potential press industry scandals'.

He went on: 'The Ombudsman could also have the power to summon journalists and editors to give evidence, to name offenders and, if necessary, – in the cases of the most extreme malfeasance – to impose fines.' When he spoke those words there was shock and surprise all round the room. OK, nobody gasped out aloud, but editors, academics and policy-makers alike were asking themselves: 'Did I hear that right?' The disciple of total self-regulation advocating what sounded like some kind of back stop statutory regulation.

There a number of things to be said about this. One is how pleased Lord Leveson must be that it was a senior editor who has started the ball rolling on ideas for reform. Two is whether many or any of the other editors present knew of Paul Dacre's plan in advance. At the seminar I asked an open question inviting any other editor to comment on the plan, none spoke. That suggests to me this was an individual initiative not an industry one.

Thirdly it is clear that Paul Dacre does not speak for the industry because much of the rest of the industry doesn't agree with him. They don't think a statutory back-stop is necessary, they think they can win the case for continued and total self-regulation. At the event which I mentioned earlier , two respected media commentators Peter Preston and Roy Greenslade spoke out against the idea.

Dealing with the 'Desmond Problem'

Which brings us to the fourth and perhaps most bizarre thing to be said about the Dacre plan. That the only media owner who appears to be close to his position is the rival he dislikes most – and the feeling is clearly mutual – Richard

Desmond. This is the Richard Desmond of the so-called and seemingly unsolvable 'Desmond problem'. He who doesn't like the self-regulatory PCC but is happy with the statutory regulator Ofcom.

For newish readers, Mr Desmond's company, Northern and Shell, is owner of the *Daily Express* and *Daily Star*, and their Sunday equivalents, plus Channel Five. He pulled out of the Press Complaints Commission, refusing to pay the subscription. So the PCC no longer considers complaints by readers against those papers, thus exposing a serious and potentially fatal flaw in the system. Getting Mr Desmond back inside the tent to stop him doing whatever he wants to do outside the tent in the direction of the tent has been a primary focus for the PCC.

Paul Dacre addressed this issue in his speech at Leveson . But he also couldn't resist an attack on those who he said had decided that 'Richard Desmond, the businessman who'd made his money from porn, was a fit and proper person to own a newspaper'. Richard Desmond's response came in an interview with the *Guardian*. He was asked about rejoining the PCC and according to the *Guardian*, he said: 'I'm not sitting there with Dacre. Dacre goes out slagging me off; he can go fuck himself. I'm not worried about statutory regulation. I'm regulated by Ofcom for TV. I'm happy with that.'

The very public 'Desmond and Dacre Show' does the self-regulation campaign no good at all. Their mutual abuse is a kind of warning sign to outsiders flashing 'Caution, unpredictable egos still at work'. And unpredictable egos are not a great starting point for a reformed self-regulatory system. But behind the scenes there may be some more positive signs. At an event which I helped to organise at City University the editorial director of Northern and Shell, Paul Ashford, spoke – probably for the first time in public – about their decision to withdraw from the PCC last year.

He hinted that Northern and Shell might be prepared to rejoin the PCC if it was differently constituted including an independent board. At present the PCC is funded and some say controlled by something called PressBof – short for Press Board of Finance – with delegates from the organisations which represent the national and the regional press.

It is clear to me now that a key issue is the PCC's relationship with PressBof as much as the PCC itself. The PCC does not and should not stand any chance of survival unless and until it becomes a body which is truly independent from its funders, the very people whose content it is set up to judge. The Irish have shown how this can be done. Trade bodies are fine but don't let's confuse them with independent self-regulators.

But Lord Leveson does not seem obsessed with regulatory plumbing. In his latest call for evidence he highlights twelve key questions and it is noticeable that the detail of new regulatory institutions is not amongst them. Maybe he won't want to be prescriptive in his report. Maybe he will just want to welcome the reforms which the new Chairman of the PCC the Conservative peer, Lord Hunt, will quietly have put in place by then. And those reforms may also have been enough to have persuaded Richard Desmond inside the newly redesigned tent.

Half of Lord Leveson's new questions are under the heading 'culture, practice and ethics'. Now there's a lot of talk nowadays about the importance of 'newsroom cultures'. And to those of you considering a career in journalism these are issues you could face very soon. A former *Daily Star* reporter, Richard Peppiatt, gave a fascinating presentation to Leveson on what it was like working on the *Star*.

Making the Facts Fit the Story

He said: 'The skill of a journalist today is about finding facts, it is also, particularly at the tabloid end of the market, about knowing what facts to ignore. The job is about making the facts fit the story, because the story is almost pre-defined. Laid out before you is a canon of ideologically and commercially driven narratives that must be adhered to. The newspaper appoints itself moral arbiter, and it is your job to stamp their worldview on all the journalism you do.' Now, I haven't worked in a tabloid newsroom so I don't know if this is true but there were some knowing looks around the room when Richard Peppiatt sat down.

Just to frighten you a bit more here are two anecdotes from my first jobs in journalism and the newsroom cultures I encountered. Job Number One: 1968, while still at university, working Friday and Saturday shifts at a regional press agency selling stories to national newspapers and magazines. I discovered that the underlying assumption at this agency was that it was a risk worth taking to invent quotes from people who didn't exist. I was even told of the name of a road where you should claim these fictitious people lived because the road was so long that nobody would ever bother to go and check.

Another example: if time was short, instead of finding out this week's prices at the local livestock market for *Farmer and Stockbreeder* magazine, send last week's prices plus or minus a few pounds as it took your fancy. But I do remember the people at *Farmer and Stockbreeder* sounding rather startled by price trends at our local market which were the opposite of those elsewhere in the country.

Within a year Job Number Two: a very different kind of employer. Unconvinced that I was cut out for a career in tabloid papers I became one of the first three BBC news trainees doing shifts as a sub-editor in the BBC radio newsroom. My father, who worked for British Airways, rang me with a big exclusive story. Eager to impress I passed on the story – though obviously not my source – to the BBC Newsdesk. An hour later I was called in and reprimanded. The British Airways Press Office had denied the story. I had wasted the newsdesk's time.

Twenty-four hours later British Airways announced to the world what they had denied to the BBC. It was the lead story on the World at One, based on the account sent out by the Press Association wire service (the PA). So those were the newsroom cultural stereotypes of the sixties. Tabloid newsrooms made up stories. Broadcasters wanted stories served up on a plate by the PA.

Of course, neither stereotype was accurate then, and over the decades both became less and less accurate. Tabloid newspapers got more concerned about getting the facts right. Broadcasters got out and about and found more of their own stories.

Changing Newsroom Cultures

Coming back to the present, what can be done to change newsroom cultures where they need to be changed for the better? What can be done to prevent new journalists from picking up any lingering old bad habits? The former Chair of the PCC, Baroness Buscombe, suggests that adherence to the Editors' Code should be written into all journalists and editors contracts, that there should be 'industry-wide protocols on news-gathering' and 'a credible independent whistle-blowing system in place' so that what she calls 'any beleaguered journalist can have free access without fear to a second opinion as to his rights in law.

John Lloyd, of the *Financial Times* and the Reuters Institute, has suggested a Journalism Society along the lines of the Law Society for solicitors. He would love to see a day when you would be confident enough to reply: 'I'm a journalist and journalists don't do that.'

A lot of these developments could come about voluntarily in parallel during Lord Leveson's inquiry rather than as a direct result of compulsion at the end of it.

My colleague at City University, Roy Greenslade, argued in his column in the London *Evening Standard* that, therefore, maybe we don't need Lord Leveson's Inquiry after all. Hacking is over, regardless of Leveson, he pronounced.

Roy is one of those who believes that there already is and will continue to be a self-correcting mechanism going on in journalism. That nobody in the right senses, whatever the pressures on them, would now hack a phone or pay a police officer. Lord Grade, Michael Grade, has pointed out that since the premium rate phone scandal in television was fully exposed there have been no more cases. Put more bluntly, it's the fear of getting caught. And if that's one of the legacies for 'journalism after Hackgate' it might just turn out to be one of the most effective.

But just in case the path to voluntary reform doesn't run smoothly, just in case the momentum slows, just in case some new scandal is revealed, just in case somebody or something is needed to keep an eye on progress, I think Lord Leveson and his panel should not go back to their day jobs just yet.

Note on the contributor

Stewart Purvis's career is probably unique in its range across journalism, management and regulation. A local radio reporter, a regional television presenter and Sunday tabloid freelance while still at university, he was chosen as one of the BBC's first three News Trainees in 1969. He moved to ITN in 1972 where he went on to win Royal Television

Society awards for news and documentaries, two BAFTA awards as Editor of Channel Four News and a *TV Times* award. He became Editor-in-Chief of ITN and then Chief Executive. After he retired from ITN in 2003 he became City University's first Professor of Television Journalism and a Visiting Professor of Broadcast Media at Oxford University. From 2007 to 2010, Professor Purvis was Ofcom's Partner for Content and Standards, effectively the regulator of UK broadcast content, responsible for the implementation of the Ofcom broadcast code and other broadcasting regulation. In 2000 he was made a CBE for services to broadcast journalism, in 2005 he was made an Honorary Doctor of Law by Exeter University and in 2009 he received the Royal Television Society's Gold Medal for an outstanding contribution to television. Apart from teaching at City University, Professor Purvis is currently a Specialist Advisor to the House of Lords Select Committee on Communications, a regular guest speaker at the BBC College of Leadership and he advises broadcasters on strategy.

• This is an edited version of a talk given as part of the Coventry Conversations 'Life after Phone Hacking' series on 3 November 2011 in Coventry.

Journalism in the Public Interest

Phil Harding argues that it is vital for those who care about the future of good journalism and its proper role in a civic society to take the lead in defining 'the public interest'. And he warns: 'If we don't, the substantial risk is that others will do it for us and they could be people who know little and care even less about the future of journalism'

What exactly is journalism in the public interest? It's the most important question in journalism today. It's a question which lies at the heart of the Leveson Inquiry. It's a question which is hotly disputed and to which there seem to be few easy answers. Yet unless it can be answered convincingly, it is a question which threatens to destroy independent journalism in this country. In this chapter, I shall attempt to explain why the phrase is so difficult to define and put into practice, the importance of arriving at an agreed definition and some pointers as to how this might be done.

The Democratic Role of the Press

The debate about the public interest and what it is and what it is not stems back to some basic questions about the role of the media in a democracy. It was Edmund Burke who first used the term the Fourth Estate: '...there were Three Estates in Parliament; but, in the Reporters' Gallery yonder, there sat a Fourth Estate more important far than they all.' This idea that the media has an unofficial constitutional role as a part of democratic process lies at the heart of the concept of the public interest. By reporting on and laying bare the affairs of the other three estates (and the rest of public life) the Fourth Estate acts as an unofficial check on the use and abuse of power by the others.

It is widely accepted that in all democratic societies access to information is essential. It allows all citizens to make informed choices about their lives. It helps to ensure that those in charge are properly accountable to those over whose lives they have influence and control. This public role of the media is acknowledged throughout our institutions. There are specially reserved seats for the press and the media in our courts, in our council chambers and in parliament. It is widely understood that what is done in the name of the people should be reported back to them. The public interest is recognised as a defence under some of our laws.

But this privileged position of the media depends on this public role. The media has no legitimacy in its own right. It is only entitled to its special place in society and any of these privileges when it is acting *on behalf of* the public and representing their interests.

Difficult to Define

For a phrase that is so central to the debate, for one that is so often used by the media as a justification for their purpose and their methods, the public interest is a phrase that is infuriatingly difficult to define with any precision. As Chris Patten, the chair of the BBC Trust, put it at the Society of Editors' conference this year: 'It is much easier to look at specific cases rather than give a general definition' (Patten 2011) (Though, as we shall discover later, it can get very tricky even when it comes to specific cases.)

What It Is Not

It is maybe easier to start with what the public interest is *not*. Let's look at some of the propositions that have been put forward for public interest journalism. Paul Dacre, the editor-in-chief of the *Daily Mail*, in his Society of Editors lecture in 2009, argued vociferously that newspapers needed to be given the leeway to drive circulation and that of itself was in the public interest (Dacre 2009):

> ...if mass-circulation newspapers, which, of course, also devote considerable space to reporting and analysis of public affairs, don't have the freedom to write about scandal, I doubt whether they will retain their mass circulations with the obvious worrying implications for the democratic process.

And he cited two unlikely supporters to his cause in the Law Lords Lord Woolf and Baroness Hale. This is from Lord Woolf's judgment in the case of the footballer Gary Flitcroft, the captain of Blackburn Rovers, who was trying to stop the *People* revealing his affairs with a lap dancer and a nursery nurse:

> The courts must not ignore the fact that if newspapers do not publish information which the public are interested in, then there will be fewer newspapers published, which will not be in the public interest (see McNamara 2002).

And this is Baroness Hale's even more forthright opinion in the Naomi Campbell case against the *Daily Mirror*:

> One reason why freedom of the press is so important is that we need newspapers to sell in order to ensure that we still have newspapers at all. It may be said that newspapers should be allowed considerable latitude in the intrusions into private grief so that they can maintain circulation and the

rest of us can continue to enjoy the variety of newspapers and other mass media which are available in this country (see House of Lords 2004).

Even though it has eminent supporters, this argument that driving circulation through titillation is in the public interest isn't very convincing. It is circular: newspapers have to be allowed to intrude against members of the public in order to sell enough newspapers in order to be able to continue commercially and thus be able to report on other matters which are more clearly in the public interest. The media cannot claim the right to transgress just to ensure their continuing existence.

The public interest is *not* the same as what the pubic are interested in; though of course you always hope that with enough imagination and creativity you can persuade the public to be interested in your newspaper or your report or programme. But there will be a lot of things that the public will be interested in that are not what we would call in the public interest. The public interest does not mean just satisfying the curiosity of the public.

The second line about the public interest that was pushed by Paul Dacre in his Society of Editors' speech was that the media should be some kind of moral check on an individual's scandalous behaviour:

> Since time immemorial public shaming has been a vital element in defending the parameters of what are considered acceptable standards of social behaviour, helping ensure that citizens – rich and poor – adhere to them for the good of the greater community. For hundreds of years, the press has played a role in that process. It has the freedom to identify those who have offended public standards of decency – the very standards its readers believe in – and hold the transgressors up to public condemnation…What the judge [Mr. Justice Eady in the Max Moseley v the *News of the World*] case loftily calls the 'new rights-based jurisprudence' of the Human Rights Act seems to be ruling out any such thing as public standards of morality and decency, and the right of newspapers to report on digressions from those standards (Dacre op cit).

Given that such moral standards will not be universally agreed Dacre goes on to argue that the market will decide: 'If their readers don't agree with the defence of such values, they would not buy those papers in such huge numbers.'

Again this argument is circular. The media are to be allowed to breach one set of moral values – the right to privacy – in order to be able to uphold another – about individual behaviour in sex and decency. Furthermore, there is a practical difficulty with this argument: standards of decency are very subjective. One's person's view of a piece of legal sexual behaviour will be different from another's. This makes it next to impossible to frame this in a regulatory code or law.

The last thing that the public interest is *not* is that it is not the same as the national interest or the interests of the state or the government or of any ruling elite. An independent media does not exist to further the interests of any party or political grouping. Politicians will often choose to blur this distinction and argue that, at times, the media are there to further their interests. And they will be wrong. Distinguishing between the public interest and the interests of the state is crucial for a democracy. It is an important part of the job of the media to call to account governments and those in power. (And, of course, when they do so is usually when the rows start!)

This distinction is of critical importance for the public media, especially the BBC, where politicians and civil servants often feel a greater sense of ownership and confuse accountability with interference. This attempt to blur the line between the public and government interest becomes most acute when this country is involved in military action. It is no accident that the most violent rows involving the BBC and politicians have been at times such as Suez (1956), the Falklands (1982) and the Iraq war (2003).

Some Definitions

So if those are some of the things that are not journalism in the public interest, what about the current definitions of what is? To date the most authoritative are those to be found in the three existing regulatory codes: the Press Complaints Commission's editors' code of practice, the Ofcom broadcasting code and the BBC's *Editorial Guidelines*. In the current PCC code there are eleven asterisks against various sections of the code. These mark where there may be exceptions to the clause in question where it can be demonstrated that the journalism is 'in the public interest'. The code goes on to give this definition:

1. The public interest includes, but is not confined to:

    i) Detecting or exposing crime or serious impropriety.

    ii) Protecting public health and safety.

    iii) Preventing the public from being misled by an action or statement of an individual or organisation.

2. There is a public interest in freedom of expression itself.

3. Whenever the public interest is invoked, the PCC will require editors to demonstrate fully that they reasonably believed that publication, or journalistic activity undertaken with a view to publication, would be in the public interest.

4. The PCC will consider the extent to which material is already in the public domain, or will become so.

5. In cases involving children under 16, editors must demonstrate an exceptional public interest to over-ride the normally paramount interest of the child (see PCC).

Section 8 of the Ofcom code on privacy (and as we shall discuss later it is in cases of privacy that the subject of the public interest becomes most acute) says this:

...where broadcasters wish to justify an infringement of privacy as warranted, they should be able to demonstrate why in the particular circumstances of the case, it is warranted. If the reason is that it is in the public interest, then the broadcaster should be able to demonstrate that the public interest outweighs the right to privacy. Examples of public interest would include revealing or detecting crime, protecting public health or safety, exposing misleading claims made by individuals or organisations or disclosing incompetence that affects the public (see Ofcom).

The BBC, in its *Editorial Guidelines*, in the section on privacy has this:

Private behaviour, information, correspondence and conversation should not be brought into the public domain unless there is a public interest that outweighs the expectation of privacy. There is no single definition of public interest. It includes but is not confined to:

- exposing or detecting crime;
- exposing significantly anti-social behaviour;
- exposing corruption or injustice;
- disclosing significant incompetence or negligence;
- protecting people's health and safety;
- preventing people from being misled by some statement or action of an individual or organisation;
- disclosing information that assists people to better comprehend or make decisions on matters of public importance.

There is also a public interest in freedom of expression itself.

When considering what is in the public interest we also need to take account of information already in the public domain or about to become available to the public.

When using the public interest to justify an intrusion, consideration should be given to proportionality; the greater the intrusion, the greater the public interest required to justify it (see BBC).

All three definitions have a great deal in common. All deal in specifics rather than attempting an overall definition and in large part concentrate on exposing crime or protecting public health. None is definitive nor claims to be. All say the examples cited are not exhaustive. All are quite narrow, though both the BBC and the PCC say that freedom of expression itself is in the public interest. The BBC version which is the most comprehensive also carries an important additional phrase about 'disclosing information that assists people to better comprehend or make decisions on matters of public importance'. That comes close to articulating the broader principles behind the public interest argument.

Journalistic Methods and Journalistic Ends

A large part of the reason why the public interest debate is so controversial at the moment is, of course, that it is closely tied to the debate about journalistic methods some of which led to the establishment of the Leveson Inquiry. Journalism is not always a polite trade. It asks questions that people would rather not answer and it cannot always restrict itself to knocking on the front door. The boundary of acceptable practice is often determined not by the means used but by the nature of what is uncovered.

In thinking about this it is possible to put journalistic methods into three categories: the unexceptional, the unacceptable and somewhere between those two, the debatable. An awful lot of journalism is totally unexceptional – someone wants to tell the media something or at least is perfectly willing to answer questions about it. It's press conferences, it's press releases, it's reporting of public events, it's broadcast and print interviews.

At the other end of the spectrum there are methods which no sane journalist would consider using in order to get a story. To take a ludicrous extreme an example of this would be committing murder to get a story. In current circumstances – though obviously less extreme – no editor in his or her right mind would regard phone hacking as a legitimate method at the moment.

And then between these two ends of the spectrum there comes a middle 'grey' area where the methods might be questionable but in some circumstances justifiable. This might involve deception, surveillance, subterfuge, secret recording or an invasion of privacy. This is the area where editors and journalists are most likely to try to justify their methods 'in the public interest'. Within this argument there is a further understanding that there has to be a correlation between the extent of the method used and the degree of public interest invoked. The greater the public interest involved in the publication of the story, the greater can be the amount of deception or intrusion used to get it.

It is this inter-relationship between journalistic methods and public interest ends which makes it much more difficult to accept the initially beguiling suggestion that there could be a separation between the regulation of journalistic methods and content. This idea had been put forward by, among others, Onora O'Neil in her Reuters Memorial Lecture on 21 November 2011 (O'Neill 2011) when she suggested that there could be statutory regulation of methods without there being such regulation of content. The two are so linked that it would be impossible to regulate methods without regard to (and hence regulation of) the resulting content.

Privacy

Many of the most contentious cases of public interest involve invasions of privacy, be it secret recordings, long lenses or access to bank accounts.

How much can someone's privacy legitimately be invaded by a journalist in pursuit of a story in the public interest? Are there any absolute limits as to how much protection of their private lives individuals are entitled to? Again, there appears to be an accepted sliding scale. The greater the degree of invasion of privacy, the more it has to be justified by the extent of the public interest involved. But there is little widespread agreement about what sort of calibration should be used in this calculation.

There are some simple criteria that can be used when looking at invasions of privacy. First, the degree of privacy to which an individual is entitled will vary depending where the individual is. People should not expect the same degree of privacy walking down a busy high street as they would in their bedroom. Second, individuals in public life can expect a lesser degree of privacy than those who are and remain private individuals. (We shall return to what is public life in a moment.) Thirdly, individuals surrender their rights to privacy in proportion to the extent of any criminal or anti-social behaviour they may be involved in. Lastly, individuals surrender some of their rights to privacy by the extent to which they are or have been courting publicity and by the extent to which they have deliberately exposed their private life to public view.

This last point is highly contentious and comes to the fore in the debate about celebrities and their private lives. So in other words if you had to sum up the above criteria with a practical example: an unknown citizen sitting in their home living a perfectly blameless existence is entitled to a near total degree of privacy that would not be accorded to a rock star who done a home photo shoot for *Hello* magazine and who has been seen shooting up drugs in the high street.

Public Life and Private Life

Everyone is entitled to 'respect for his private and family life, his home and his correspondence'. This right is detailed in Article Eight of the European Convention of Human Rights (see ECHR 1950). But like all rights it is one that is qualified by other rights and circumstance. One of the big issues around the current debate is how much protection someone in public life is entitled to. When someone enters the public gaze how much should they be open to scrutiny by the media? I would suggest there are some important distinctions to be made here and too often they have become blurred. Again let me suggest some criteria for judging this.

First, there is an important distinction to be made between someone who deliberately chooses to enter the gaze of the public and someone who finds themselves in the spotlight by accident. This is the difference between the politician or the actress and the parents of a missing girl. This does not mean that the actress has no entitlement to protection but if she has chosen to put herself on the stage or screen that is a deliberate lifestyle choice. It might be possible to do that job without seeking any additional publicity but it would be difficult and unlikely. (The world of celebrity however does get more complicated and we shall come back to that shortly.) The parents of a missing schoolgirl, however, have not chosen to put themselves in their awful predicament. If they choose to seek publicity for the return of their daughter, say by police press conferences, they do so only because of the terrible situation they find themselves in.

Second, there is an important distinction to be made between public life and private life. But it is a distinction that is not always clear. A prime minister or a cabinet minister certainly chooses to enter public life. They ask the public to vote for them, they spend a lot of public money. They are and should be accountable for that. The media has an important role to play in that. Equally they and their families are entitled to have a life outside of the public gaze. So far so simple.

Where it gets complicated is when the public and private lives overlap. If an MP chooses to put a picture of his wife and family on his election address, then he (and it usually is a 'he') is inviting the public to draw certain conclusions about him and his lifestyle in order to get elected to public office. Among other things it sends out a message that he is a happily married man and is faithful to his wife. If it turns out his marriage is a total sham then the voters are entitled to know that as part of helping them make an informed decision as electors in a democracy. Once the MP has chosen to make his family life part of his electoral appeal, then there is a public interest in disclosing those details of what, in other circumstances, would be his private life.

Where the distinction gets much harder is when you have to judge whether a public figure, especially one who has not chosen to exploit his private or family life, is in some way being hypocritical or portraying themselves in one way in the public eye and privately doing something else.

Perhaps one of the finest lines in this argument in recent years was over the reporting of the affair of David Blunkett and Kimberley Quinn. I have tried this example out on several of what I would describe as responsible mainstream journalists and it divides opinion right down the middle. The main facts are these: Mr. Blunkett, when Home Secretary, had an affair with Mrs. Quinn when she was publisher of the *Spectator* and she had a child. He was divorced, she was married. There was a dispute over the paternity of the child which Mr. Blunkett claimed was his. Later there were allegations that Mr. Blunkett had improperly intervened to secure a visa application from Mrs. Quinn's nanny fast-tracked. But that emerged later and only after the main facts of the affair had become widely publicised in the press. Later still, it was revealed that Mr. Blunkett had given a £180 rail warrant intended for MPs' spouses to his lover, money which Mr. Blunkett repaid.

Leaving the visa issue to one side for a moment because that only came to light later, was exposing that affair in the public interest? It's a very fine line of judgment. On the hand, it could be argued, people, even those in public life who have chosen to put themselves there, do have a right to a private life, which should extend to include affairs with other people whether they are married or not. On the other hand, it could also be argued, here was a politician, avowedly of the left and holding office in a Labour government, consorting with the publisher of a magazine which was one of the fiercest right-wing critics of that government. Did the public, did the voters in Mr. Blunkett's constituency, did the members of his constituency party have a right to know that? If they did know it, would they think any differently of Mr. Blunkett or of his suitability as a politician or as a candidate?

The argument gets easier when we get to the nanny and the visa. Whatever the facts of the case (and a subsequent inquiry was inconclusive) establishing whether a Home Secretary had or had not improperly intervened to get the nanny of his lover a visa extension was most certainly a legitimate matter of public interest.

But of course this only emerged after and almost certainly because of the exposure of the affair. As has happened with many stories over the years some of the most salient facts only start to emerge after the initial story has broken. This reinforces the argument that to have a strong and independent media, essential for a healthy democracy, the balance of the argument in marginal cases should be in favour of publication. There is a lot of force in that phrase in the PCC code that: 'There is a public interest in freedom of expression itself.'

The World of Celebrity

Rightly or wrongly, the world of celebrity has become an increasingly important one in contemporary journalism – even among the more upmarket sections of the press. Red carpet photoshoots take up more of the front pages, interviews with stars occupy more of the airwaves, celebrity magazines take up more shelf space at the newsagents. These days, you can even take a university degree course in celebrity journalism.

We have seen the growth of a whole celebrity industry employing thousands of people: publicists and prs, agents, photographers, celebrity journalists, 3am Girls, show business editors and photographers and paparazzi – all involved in meeting the appetite for celebrity news. It's worth remembering that this is not just a one one-way game either. The intrusions of paparazzi are not always unwelcome. Sometimes the photographers outside the restaurant are there because they have been tipped off by the publicist working for the star or film company.

In addition, we have seen the widening of the scope of celebrity through so-called reality television programmes such as *Big Brother* where members of the public through their antics on television become staple fodder for front page stories for the red-top papers. Such figures, once voted out of the *Big Brother* house and anxious to make as much money as possible out of their fifteen days of fame, are often willing to trade a large part of their private (usually sexual) lives in return for a cheque from one newspaper or another.

Though the justification of public interest is sometimes cited to justify celebrity reporting and intrusion, this is deliberately confusing two issues: privacy, which is one and the public interest which is the other. They are inter-related but they are not the same. If celebrities and their agents sometimes blur the lines of what is private and public that is them lessening their right to privacy. It is not increasing the public interest – or, indeed, providing any public interest justification at all. In this debate it is vital to keep that distinction.

Sienna Miller, Steve Coogan and Hugh Grant have all given evidence to the Leveson Inquiry arguing that exposure of their private lives is not public interest journalism at all but nothing more than sheer prurience to sell papers. As Robert Jay QC, counsel to the inquiry, outlined in his opening submission, many critics of the press believe that editors use the justification of the public interest to excuse the inexcusable:

> Put simply, the 'public interest' is very often deployed as some form of trump card, and it is too loosely defined. It ends up with the press delving into the affairs of those who are celebrities and those who are not in a way which unethically penetrates a domain which ought to remain private (Jay 2011).

The counter-argument goes something like this: The public are interested in the affairs of celebrities particularly where there is an apparent clash between a confected public image and their private transgressions. The public are invited to buy that image, but it isn't real, it's a sham. In these circumstances the role of the press is to hunt down such hypocrisy, to expose it and to stop the public being duped into buying into a false image. On this analysis, private transgression becomes a matter for legitimate public interest.

This argument really doesn't stand up to any sort of serious scrutiny. To argue that we have a right to know whether star x or footballer y is promiscuous or adulterous because it helps the public to decide whether to buy tickets for a film or match is stretching logic to ludicrous lengths. Put another way, this is what the former Appeal Court Judge, Sir Stephen Sedley wrote recently:

> Its [the tabloids'] merchandising of voyeurism might be worth debating if that were the way it was promoted; but the eye at the keyhole is presented as that of the public moralist: because stars are role models, it is argued with a straight face, the exposure of their promiscuous sex lives will appropriately harm their image and deflate the young's perception of them (Sedley 2011).

Conclusion

The debate about the public interest has shown that it is currently far too wooly a concept to be of much practical use. Many in the industry have used it to justify pretty much anything. Those who, for a variety of motives, wish to see the media muzzled have argued for a very narrow definition.

It is time for those who care about the future of good journalism and its proper role in a civic society to take the lead. We need a much more developed definition of what journalism in the public interest actually means. It must provide an overarching rationale as well as being of practical use. While such a definition can never legislate for every circumstance it must be sufficiently clear as to what is meant to be in and out of scope.

While this chapter is not an attempt to provide that precise definition of the public interest, I would suggest the following pointers for the debate:

- In a democracy, citizens have a right to know what is being done in their name.

- Citizens in a democracy have a legitimate interest in having access to information about the workings of all branches of government and the state, its institutions and its officials. This interest also extends to private corporations and utilities and to voluntary organisations which require the public's trust or which are funded by the public.

- The media is acting in the public interest when it operates on behalf of the public as citizens and provides such information.

- Those working for or representing such organisations who, by virtue of taking on such roles, ask the public to place their trust in them should legitimately be scrutinised and held to account for their actions in carrying out such roles.

- There is a public interest in freedom of expression itself. At the margins the balance should be in favour of disclosure and publication.

- Journalism in the public interest may involve invasions of privacy. While the former may justify the latter they are separate concepts and should not be used inter-changeably.

- Because of the inter-relationship between invasions of privacy and the public interest in any future system of regulation it would impossible to regulate journalistic methods separately from journalistic content.

- The extent of any invasion of privacy should be proportionate to the extent of the public interest.

In the months to come we need to carry this debate forward and put forward an agreed definition which is generally understood and leaves little doubt. If we don't, the substantial risk is that others will do it for us and they could be people who know little and care even less about the future of journalism.

References

BBC *Editorial Guidelines*. Available online at http://www.bbc.co.uk/editorialguidelines/, accessed on 9 December 2011

Dacre, Paul (2009) Speech to Society of Editors. Available online at http://www.societyofeditors.co.uk/page-view.php?pagename=thesoelecture2008, accessed on 9 December 2011

ECHR (1950) The European Convention on Human Rights. Available online at http://www.echr.coe.int/NR/rdonlyres/D5CC24A7-DC13-4318-B457-5C9014916D7A/0/ENG_CONV.pdf, accessed on 9 December 2011

House of Lords (2004) Judgment in Campbell v. MGN Limited. Available online at http://www.publications.parliament.uk/pa/ld200304/ldjudgmt/jd040506/campbc-1.htm, accessed on 9 December 2011

Jay, Robert (2011) Submission to Leveson Inquiry. Available online at www.levesoninquiry.org.uk, accessed on 9 December 2011

McNamara, Martin (2002) Lords reject footballer's privacy bid, *Guardian*, 31 May. Available online at http://www.guardian.co.uk/media/2002/may/31/pressandpublishing.privacy, accessed on 9 December 2011

Ofcom broadcasting code. Available online at http://stakeholders.ofcom.org.uk/broadcasting/broadcast-codes/broadcast-code/, accessed on 9 December 2011

O'Neill, Onora (2011) The Rights of Journalists and the Needs of Audiences. Reuters Memorial Lecture, Oxford Reuters Institute for the Study of Journalism, 21 November. Available online at http://politicsinspires.org/2011/11/the-rights-of-journalism-and-the-needs-of-audiences-onora-oneill-on-the-rise-of-corporate-media/, accessed on 9 December 2011

Patten, Chris (2011) Journalists need own Hippocratic Oath. Society of Editors lecture. See http://www.societyofeditors.co.uk/page-view.php?pagename=Journalists-need-hippocratic-oath, accessed on 9 December 2011

PCC code of practice. Available online at http://www.pcc.org.uk/cop/practice.html, accessed on 9 December 2011

Sedley, Sir Stephen (2011) The Goodwin and Giggs Show, *London Review of Books*, 16 July, Vol. 33, No. 12 p 3. Available online at http://www.lrb.co.uk/v33/n12/stephen-sedley/the-goodwin-and-giggs-show, accessed on 9 December 2011

Note on the contributor

Phil Harding is a journalist, broadcaster and media consultant. One of his specialist areas of consultancy is in the ethics of journalism. Previously as the BBC's Controller of Editorial Policy he wrote the BBC's *Editorial Guidelines* and was involved in many contentious decisions on what sort of journalism qualifies as being in the public interest. He is a former Editor of the *Today* programme and Deputy Editor of *Panorama*.

Fear and Loathing: Media Accountability after the Phone-hacking Affair

Damian Carney proposes the setting up of a new regulatory body for the press providing strong remedies for complainants, better internal controls on ethics and complaints – and enough independence from government and industry to appease the general public

Despite frequent criticism of the evolving self-regulatory system, and calls for statutory intervention (Press Authority Bill 1953, Calcutt Review 1993) the print industry in the United Kingdom has, unlike broadcasting, been left to its own devices. However, the *News of the World* phone-hacking scandal has led to the Leveson Inquiry whose terms of reference calls for it to make recommendations '... for a new more effective [media] policy and regulatory regime' (Leveson 2011). There is broad consensus that this will lead to changes in press regulation, although there is disagreement over the form this may take (Tomlinson 2011a to c discusses many of these).

This chapter argues that the Press Complaints Commission (PCC) needs to be replaced with a statutory-backed regulator with a broader cross-section of stakeholders (including representative of journalist bodies such as the NUJ), and an enhanced set of powers. Direct government involvement should be minimised. It should be independent of government and publishing interests. At the same time it is argued that if the new regulatory system is to herald in a new age of good journalistic standards that publications themselves will be required to adopt more robust internal accountability systems, policed by the new regulator to ensure they are effective and meet minimum standards.

In reaching this conclusion the paper explains why the arguments for self-regulation of the press have failed, and why the new system will not threaten the 'independence of the press' and could actually enhance this principle and improve journalistic standards. However, it identifies some potential problems of regulation of the print media which may offer a final opportunity to those who oppose statutory regulation to undermine it.

Self-regulation of the Media: Arguments for and its Virtues.
Professions and industries tend to believe they should be left to govern themselves. They claim that only the members of the profession, or industry, have the experience and expertise capable of deciding what standards should be expected of the membership. Self-regulatory systems are usually less intrusive on the activities of those they govern than regulations imposed by the state, and are cheaper to comply with. Supporters of press self-regulation today are able to add a gloss to the latter argument by linking it to the 'death of the newspaper' thesis (*Economist* 2006), and suggest the additional costs of any statutory regulatory system would merely exacerbate the financial crisis the print media currently faces as a result of the rise of new media platforms. This is especially so if what is recommended encompasses sanctions which include compensation, administrative fines or compulsory rights of reply.

In the last forty years or so, other professions and industries have seen increasing state interference with their self-regulatory structures, with many traditionally independent professions such as the legal profession (Legal Services Act 2007) finding their own self-regulatory systems co-opted into a statutory framework (co-regulation). The print media has remained, however, in control of its own regulatory regime. Where state regulation is imposed on the media it is seen as the hallmark of authoritarianism, with supporters of the status quo drawing unflattering comparisons between the proposals for a statutory body and the government control of the media in Zimbabwe (Dacre 2011). Supporters of media self-regulation point out that it is the norm in Western Europe (Denmark is the only exception), and that an industry-wide body is not even seen as necessary in the United States (Greenslade 2011b). Furthermore, it is argued that if there are any statutory provisions for the regulation of the print industry it will have a chilling effect on journalism, limiting what the general public gets to know.

Finally, supporters argue that the current PCC system works well providing: a cheaper alternative to the court for complainants; resolving complaints quickly; a set of sanctions which are widely adhered to; guidance to the press to avoid problems using devices such as 'desist orders'. So successful is the PCC that it has even been recommended as a model to improve the performance of the Netherlands Press Council (Koene 2009).

The Current Crisis in Media Self-regulation
However, critics identify many failings. The Media Standards Trust sums up its view of the PCC as follows: 'As it currently operates and is constituted, it is insufficiently effective, largely unaccountable, opaque, and failing to reflect the radically changed media environment' (2009: 9).

The ineffectiveness referred to relates largely to the PCC's powers and how it uses them. It has five formal sanctions at its disposal: negotiation of an agreed remedy; publication of a critical adjudication; a letter of admonishment from PCC chairman to editor of the publication; follow-up actions to ensure there are no repetitions; and a formal referral of an editor to their publisher for action (PCC 2011a). The first of these, seems to be the preferred method, and though the agreed remedy may be in the form of apology or published correction, critics have questioned the degree to which such remedies get the prominence they deserve in the offending publication (MediaWise 2010: par. 4.06 to 4.09). Adjudications, which have the benefit of stating to the world at large that there has been a breach of the code and that the newspaper must do something about it, are becoming much less frequent (House of Lords Select Committee on Communications 2008: 352), and this may as a consequence help to undermine public confidence in the press at a time when public trust of journalism is very low. Some of the stronger powers, such as admonishment of the editor by the PCC chairman, remain unused. Further powers which the PCC has at its disposal, such as the ability to launch inquiry into issues of press misconduct without a complaint, have either not be used, for example the reporting of the Madeleine McCann story, or have been ineffective.

The PCC's investigation of phone-hacking at the *News of the World* (PCC 2009) is an example of the latter, and it exposes weaknesses with the powers the PCC has at its disposal (MediaWise 2010: par. 3.01). It has no power to call witnesses or demand documents; felt that as Andy Coulson had left the media he was outside the remit of its powers; and accepted at face value the assurances of News International that Clive Goodman was a rogue reporter, and lambasted the *Guardian* for suggesting otherwise. The fact that the PCC ultimately withdrew its report in 2011 when the extent of New International's deception on this issue became apparent (PCC 2011b) merely highlights the limitations of its powers.

Critics argue that the PCC is too influenced by the industry which funds it to be independent, and forceful. In the PCC's early days, the *Mirror* titles left after being criticised for publishing photographs of Princess Diana exercising in a gym, whilst the Northern and Shell group has in effect been outside its remit since 2009. Membership and compliance is therefore voluntary. Withdrawal lacks sanctions (Saloman 2011). There may be as, supporters argue, more lay members than any other media self-regulatory body in the world; but there is currently no representation on the editorial code committee which decides the standards the industry watchdog will enforce.

The public lacks confidence in journalism and the ability of the industry to regulate itself (Media Standards Trust 2010: 2), and the lack of transparency of the PCC over its funding and workings raises more suspicions about the extent to which publications as funders can influence what its supposedly independent regulator can do (Media Standards Trust 2009: 34). The industry has helped to make the PCC ineffective by starving it of the necessary funding (a budget of £1.1 million in 1991 had only increased to £1.9 million by 2009).

The PCC is not the only part of self-regulation in the print media. Publications may have codes and complaint mechanisms at their disposal, whilst the National Union of Journalists and Chartered Institute of Journalists possess codes. The PCC does not come out well in the wake of the phone hacking scandal, whilst the NUJ and CIJ seem largely peripheral to the dispute (perhaps because many national newspapers no longer recognise the NUJ). News International conducted an internal investigation which seemed to reveal widespread illegality at the *News of the World* and rather than reveal its findings to the world, or sack employees other than Clive Goodman (who had already been convicted), it engaged in a campaign of obscuration and lying which damaged the reputation of the whole industry. In comparison, when *The New York Times* found Jayson Blair had fabricated and plagiarised stories, a full investigation was undertaken and the newspaper explained the events to its readership in a series of articles (Dan Berry et al 2003) and strengthened the company's Policy on Ethics. The professional bodies in the United States condemned the breach of professional ethics and Blair appears unable to work in the traditional print media again. Clive Goodman, in contrast, was re-employed by the *Express* group as a freelance.

A Case for a New Improved Self-regulator

Several commentators accept that the PCC has failed as a regulator, but argue the problem with the system is not the principle of self-regulation, but rather the powers and structure of the PCC itself. Simply strengthen these and the criticisms will, it is claimed, disappear.

Roy Greenslade, for example, puts forward his 'PCC Plus' model (2011a). Diluting the influence of industry could be achieved by inviting non-industry people to meetings and consulting the public more regularly, whilst lay representation would be increased. It would be encouraged to use adjudication powers more than the current PCC, and would be able to investigate alleged misdoings with powers to order editors and journalists to attend meetings, with a special panel to be instigated in such cases. Whilst arguing for more robust sanctions, what these amount to are left unarticulated except that Greenslade seems opposed to fines (2011a) although he moves from a position of strong opposition in his original article to a position that these 'need careful thought' in later statements on his blog (2011c).

The Media Standards Trust has argued that the public wants 'an independent self-regulatory body, rather than a newspaper industry complaints body' (2010: 2), and its proposals for a Press Standards Commission goes much further than the 'PCC Plus' model. The commission would have a much broader role than a 'complaints body' (Media Standards Trust 2009: 7) and become a true regulator. To do this it would be more proactive in investigating breaches of the code, without the need for a complaint and be more willing to investigate following complaints from third parties (Media Standards Trust 2010: 5). This would be linked to a broader remit in which it is the custodian of the code in the public interest (ibid: 10 and 13). Its complaint system would remain, but rather than being a port of first call, and a 'method of out-sourcing internal complaints mechanisms' (ibid: 15) the expectation is that publications would develop more robust internal accountability/complaints systems which they would publicise and encourage the complainant to use.

Its suggests that the independence of the new body can be guaranteed by the chair of the PCC having a fixed term of office made by an appointments committee, rather than PresBof (the funding arm of the PCC), and that serving editors should be removed from the PCC itself (ibid: 25).

Responding to criticism of the existing system as having no means of identifying the seriousness of a breach, the proposal calls for a 'financial value' to be placed upon breaches. Based on 'rates cards' for advertisers this would not impose any direct financial penalty upon the newspaper (thereby not adding to costs of compliance) but would require the publication to decide how to publish the correction or apology based upon the cost that is attached to the ruling (ibid: 20-21). Thus it enables the publication to have a smaller amount of space devoted to the apology on a more expensive advertising position within the publication, or a larger space devoted where the rate card would be less.

The model also would also require the PCC to become a membership organisation (ibid: 20). This would make it clearer to complainants about what publications are covered, and would enhance the ability of the commission to ensure compliance, as membership would be contractual and compliance would be a term of membership. The problem with this suggestion is that there is no incentive or compulsion for publications to join. They may like, Northern and Shell, conclude the cost of membership is not worth it. Indeed it is this limitation which undermines the whole of the self-regulatory model.

This is part of the problem with media self-regulation. The incentives to join and remain committed to an industry self-regulatory regime do not exist in the same way as they do in other industries. In the City, the Panel on Takeovers and Mergers was able from 1968 to 1984 ensure that those wishing to takeover, or merge, listed companies on British stock exchanges complied with their code of practice without any statutory basis, or contractual obligations, by being able to guarantee that those who did not would be blackballed by the financial institutions whose backing would be needed to succeed. The only incentives that media companies have to join is fear of a statutory regime which will take away their self-governance and independence; or being viewed by the rest of the industry as being less ethical. The latter can be used to justify non-compliance with codes on the basis that the codes themselves infringe upon freedom of speech; and it probably only has any true impact if the non-member publication loses advertisers and/or readers as a result of its lower 'ethical reputation'.

Why Statutory Intervention is Likely

Sceptics about enhancing self-regulation abound. Mediawise argue: 'At every new crisis of confidence about press misbehaviour the public are assured *ad nauseam* about editors' commitment to self-regulation and the code of practice. It is touted as if it were a last bastion against the risk of state control and as a vital guarantor of a healthy, open democracy' (Mediawise 2010: par. 2.09).

It coincides with a commitment to strengthen not only the industry body, but the internal complaints procedures of publications (Wintour 1990, *Independent* 1990, Dacre 2011, Greenslade 2011b). Many of these, however, seem to go into abeyance or become less publicised, when the threat of statutory intervention disappears.

The print media has itself been sceptical of self-regulation in other spheres but claim special treatment for itself (McKie 1990). Claims that 'an independent press' has a special constitutional position as a 'Fourth Estate', or 'watchdog of the public', ignores the fact that other professions making constitutional claims, such as lawyers, are now subjected to a degree of state control (Legal Services Act 2007). An independent, statutorily based, legal ombudsman has replaced the complaint mechanisms that used to be provided by various legal professional bodies because these mechanisms did not adequately protect the public interest.

Despite Thatcherite beliefs in less government, the last thirty years or so has seen increasing state involvement in regulating important industries and professions as a perception has grown that self-regulation becomes too self-interested. There are many reasons to believe that print self-regulation would go the same way. The City is illustrative of how even very powerful sectors of society influence can wane. In the 1950s and 1960s concern over the manner in which takeovers took place in the United Kingdom and threats by the Labour government to introduce a statutory regime to govern it in 1968, led to the creation of the Panel on Takeovers and Mergers (a self-regulatory response). In the 1980s and 1990s, despite emerging evidence of widespread insider dealing (see the Guinness and Blue Arrow Affairs), the political influence of the City together with the dominance of Thatcherite free market theories meant that the various strands of the financial service industries were required to engage in more rigorous self-regulation.

However, when evidence of widespread criminality such as insider dealing, and the misselling of mortgage and private pensions were revealed, the public confidence in City and financial services self-regulation disappeared, and the Financial Services Authority was created imposing direct regulation upon the sector. The phone-hacking affair is about criminality, and if, as the author, suspects the criminality is revealed to exist beyond one single newspaper, it undermines the argument that self-regulation can be trusted.

In the past, the print media could rely upon their immense political power to block any statutory regulation of their industry. As the headline which greeted John Major's unexpected 1992 general election win went: 'It's the *Sun* Wot Won It'. With declining circulations the influence of the print media is not as strong as this today, and alternative media platforms are likely to grow in influence even more in the future. Whilst it could be argued that this does not matter as many owners of print periodicals are media conglomerates whose collective powers need to be respected, the relationship between politicians and the media at this moment in time is badly damaged as a consequence of a combination of the MPs' expenses scandal, and politicians' reactions to Hackgate.

Whilst allowing defendants of self-regulation to portray calls for regulation as an attempt by the political class to get revenge (Dacre 2011), this argument is being made to a public which distrusts the press more than any profession (Media Standards Trust 2009: 8-9). In these times making even well articulated arguments about press independence and constitutional roles whether to the chattering classes, or public at large, are bound to fail.

Finally, the idea that regulation curtails freedom of the press ignores the fact that broadcasting has been subjected to regulation on content since its birth, and no-one seriously contends that this has resulted in censorship, or curtailed serious investigative journalism (Barnett 2011). In an age of media convergence and conglomerates the print media are asking for special treatment without any real justification as to why they as a mass media format should be treated differently.

What Form of Statutory Regulation?

Proponents of continued press self-regulation have portrayed statutory intervention as something of a bogeyman, with the insinuation of censorship and control. They argue that an end to voluntary self-regulation will result in the state being directly involved in the determination of journalistic ethics or content of newspapers. It is highly, unlikely, that any government would want to have direct control of the media in this way, not only because of the constitutional and political issues that would arise, but because it would be economically more costly. In any case, there is no such 'binary choice' (Browne 2011), with modern day statutory regulation of industries and professions taking a variety of different forms, with some being much lighter touch than others.

The lightest is that which Paul Dacre has suggested (2011), whereby statute would ensure all in the print industry are subject to the regulatory regime, preventing opt outs such as Northern and Shell. There is no reason in theory why the latter cannot be done within a self-regulatory system based upon contract, but only statutory intervention can guarantee compliance with the self-regulatory regime unless as we have seen there is some other incentive to join. In Ireland the incentive for publications to join up to the non-statutory press council is that membership and adherence to its code will enhance their entitlement to the reasonable publication defence in defamation suits (Defamation Act 2009 (Ireland), s26(2)(f)). Whilst Dacre accepts the need for lay representation on the editorial code committee and for the creation of an ombudsman with investigating powers, the most important feature, and his main concern, was to ensure the industry remained largely in control of the system.

Dacre's limited role for the state raises the issue of what publications should be subjected to the regime. This is important as unlike Ireland there is no choice to opt out. It clearly is designed to cover traditional news publications, but should its remit extend to student newspapers or publications such as *Nature* or the *Lancet?* Should the size of circulation matter?

Dacre's proposal should be rejected because in essence it is another attempt to leave regulation largely in the hands of an industry which has shown itself incapable of operating a regulatory system which has avoided 'regulatory capture' and gaining public confidence. In his proposed scheme there is no statutory backstop like that which exists in legal services, allowing state intervention if the self-regulatory mechanisms are inadequate. Co-regulation adopts a mix of self-regulation and statutory regulation and has been used in the broadcasting and advertising industries in the United Kingdom. In all cases, Ofcom acts as a fallback regulator, having the power to intervene if the self-regulation does not work, or the powers of the self-regulators are inadequate in particular circumstances. Convergence and the online presence of newspapers add to the logic of such an arrangement, and its presence in the background could act as a Damocles sword hanging over the head of a reformed PCC or new self-regulator to force it to improve. If a background regulator is needed then Ofcom is the logical body to have this role.

An Independent Stakeholder model

The danger with applying a co-regulation approach to the print industry is that this may not dispel the perception that the industry regulator is too influenced by the commercial interests of publishers. The new regulator needs to be one in which the general public has the confidence that it will admonish publications when they do something unethical and support public interest investigative reporting. To achieve this, the make-up of the print regulator needs to be broadened. Whilst Dacre's proposal and the self-regulation options described above call for a greater role for non-industry representatives in any new press regulator, none recognize the need to involve a key stakeholder in journalist ethics, namely representatives of journalists themselves.

It is unlikely that left to their own devices the industry would ask the NUJ or other journalists' associations to come on board. Yet, in all other European countries which have self-regulatory bodies there are representatives from journalist unions and associations suggesting that this is good practice (Alliance of Independent Press Councils Europe 2011). Their involvement is important as it acts as a counterweight to the commercial pressures which editors, as representatives of industry, may be susceptible to. At the same time their knowledge and experience will add something of value to the regulator, and so would the continued presence of current editors of newspapers despite calls for them to be absent from any new or reformed regulator (Media Standard Trust 2010: 25).

Statute needs to allocate places on the new regulator to journalist association representatives, and set down criteria to ensure that the lay element of the new regulator is in the majority. It could also require other stakeholders such as the need for representatives of readers' interests and human rights groups to be represented. A regulator which has this set of balanced and competing interests, as well as individuals likely to have some common goals in regards to freedom of expression are likely to overcome suspicions that the body is too influenced by the narrow interests of the industry.

Independence from the government is also needed, and an independent appointments commission should decide who should be the independent members as is done in Ireland (Press Council Ireland 2011, Mediawise 2010: par. 3.07), with the unions, associations and industry determining their own representatives.

Furthermore, the independence of the new industry wide regulator demands a clear and transparent means of funding. A levy system based upon annual readership is an obvious way of demonstrating 'independence' of both government and industry influence, and allows a degree of differentiation between publications based upon regularity of publication and popularity. This suggests that direct government subsidy should not be forthcoming, but there is a danger that if the print industry contracts and financial pressures lead to more recall for complaints to be made then the regulator would be underfunded and unable to carry out all its roles.

The Roles of the New Regulator

There is consensus that any new press regulator must continue to act as a complaints mechanism. A variety of different options have been canvassed ranging from those modelled on the current system (albeit with strengthened powers), press ombudsmen and 'parallel legal systems' or tribunals (Browne 2011, Tomlinson 2011c). The latter is best avoided as it is likely to overjudicialise the process, increases costs and provides less economic benefits for publications (although it could be a cheaper alternative to the courts if all disputes were settled here) (Rusbridger 2011). Would-be complainants may be deterred from using the system because of the probable need to instruct lawyers and the costs associated with this, whilst the speed of resolution is likely to slow down when an adversarial process is followed. Neither the industry nor the complainants would benefit from this system, and the only real winners would be lawyers.

Either of the other two models can perform the role, although in one sense if something approaching the existing system was adopted then publications would have a good idea of what to expect, and this aspect of the PCC has been said to work well. Some critics of the current system suggest that the PCC has become a means of publications 'outsourcing complaints' and being the first port of call in a dispute between the publication and complainant (Media Standards Trust 2010: 15). The new system should discourage this. It would probably be more cost-effective and likely to secure more industry support if it was more of a backup to internal complaint mechanisms of individual publications or publication groups. This system would echo that which currently exists in the legal profession. The new regulatory system could require that publications satisfy the new regulator as to the robustness and fairness of internal complaints system, and a clause within any new code could be added to achieve this objective. There could be a requirement for each publication or publication group to present annual reports on its internal complaints handling. Publications which did not have a robust internal system, or persistently mistreated complainants, could be forced to have all complaints heard by the statutory regulator or someone appointed by the regulator and pay the costs of doing so. This creates an incentive for publications to invest in proper long-term internal media accountability systems.

These powers would improve the effectiveness of the complaints function by allowing the regulator to be more thorough in its examination of the facts, and provided these powers are used properly it might deter complainants from taking court actions. The effectiveness of the complaints system needs to be improved to restore public confidence in the system, and it is important that the regulator has a set of sanctions likely to encourage compliance with its adjudications whilst satisfying complainants. Research (Bezanson 1986) and anecdotal evidence seems to suggest that complainants in most cases are interested in an adequate apology or the redemption of their reputation rather than damages. Consequently, any new regime needs to focus on development of remedies which address these concerns rather than remedies which impose financial penalties. Two particular powers may be beneficial to the new system: the right of reply and the ability of the regulator to demand an apology with particular wording and with the ability to direct the publication as to its prominence. The former allows the wronged person the ability to put his side of the story or criticise the publication's handling of the original story, whereas the latter enables the regulator to give an indication of the seriousness of the breach of the code.

This power is not enough, and any new regulatory system needs to have a system of sanctions which grades the seriousness of the breach. Adjudications should indicate that the breach was serious, major, or minor, and the regulator should have the power to make recommendations for changes to practices (if need) and *ex gratia* payments. Compulsory financial penalties should be avoided because it is likely to face strong opposition from the print media, will be portrayed as an attempt to muzzle the press, and may encourage the use of the complaints system by those seeking compensation that have adequate alternatives in the courts.

The second role that a press regulator needs to have is to be guardian or promoter of journalistic standards. This requires two powers. The setting of a code, and the ability to have inquisitorial powers enabling the body to call witnesses and demand documents to settle individual complaints, and to carry out own initiative investigations into systematic failures of a publication or the industry as a whole. These powers would enable the regulator to exercise a control function in which its investigations could feed into the evolution of the code, and would enhance the independence of the press. For when new scandals arose the regulator would have the powers to undertake the inquiries which select committees and public inquiries are doing now and in the past.

The code of the future press regulator may be little different from the PCC code, although the addition of a 'conscience clause' is necessary. This is included because the framers/guardians of the code will not simply include industry interests (i.e. the editors), but must include other 'stakeholders' which will include both the public and journalist union and association representatives. By widening the participation of who has input into the development of the code, criticisms that it is too protective of industry or too slow to evolve can be overcome, and it gives a degree of legitimacy to the final code which the current PCC's editorial code lacks. The conscience clause itself can be utilised as something of a defence against the evolution of publication cultures in which unethical behaviour is developing, and gives the journalist or other employee of the publication a position akin to protected whistleblower if he were to bring this to the attention of the regulator. Under the existing PCC system there is no formal mechanism by which journalists can bring such matters to the attention of the body, and given the industry bias within the body probably no confidence that the complaint would be dealt with effectively.

The third role of the new regulator should be as 'guardian of freedom of the press', similar to the role performed by the Australian Press Council (Australian Press Council 2011). This role becomes much more important when one takes into account the new membership, and because of the membership what reports and contributions it makes on freedom of speech issues are likely to be given greater weight considering that it is an amalgam of interest groups. Whilst sometimes the industry, journalists and others, may seem to have competing agendas, they often share an interest in opposing legislative attempts to impose restrictions on reporting, but have proven in recent years incapable of influencing the content of new laws.

Conclusion

Whilst this proposed model is one of many options which the Leveson Inquiry might recommend, it is one which avoids many of the continued pitfalls of self-regulatory, and co-regulation options, which leaves control of regulation to the industry alone. It provides strong remedies for complainants, better internal controls on ethics and complaints, and provides enough independence from government and industry to appease the general public. Yet this regime, like many of the other proposals currently being discussed, will impose upon the print sector increasing costs. If these costs are viewed as too much, a publication has two tools at its disposal which can undermine the effectiveness of this regime.

Firstly, the publication has the ability to influence the public discussion and impression of the new regime. It can adopt a very negative response in circumstances when it finds itself on the wrong side of the regulator's ruling, appealing to the public in a language portraying the new system as authoritarian or censorial. If this is adopted widely by the sector the effectiveness and public confidence in the new regulator may be undermined. Alternatively, publications which are unhappy with this new regime have relatively simple methods of avoiding the regulatory reach of this regime. Publications can join the flight of print journals to the internet and/or offshore the centre of operations to another country beyond the press regulator's reach. Economics are likely to be the driving force, but the attractiveness of free speech havens such as Iceland or, to a lesser extent, the United States may also prove a pull for some types of publications which do not need a UK base.

References

Alliance of Independent Press Councils Europe. Available online at http://www.aipce.net/, accessed on 21 November 2011

Australian Press Council (2011) Available online at http://www.presscouncil.org.au/what-we-do/, accessed on 21 November 2011

Barnett, Stephen (2011) What redress should be available for breach of standards? Presentation to Leveson Inquiry. Available online at http://www.levesoninquiry.org.uk/wp-content/uploads/2011/11/Steven-Barnett4.pdf, accessed on 21 November 2011

Berry, Dan et al (2003) Correcting the Record; Times Reporter who resigns leaves long trail of deception, *New York Times*, 11 May

Bezanson, Randall (1986) The libel suit in retrospect: What plaintiffs want plaintiffs get, *California Law Review*, Vol. 74 pp789-808

Browne, Desmond (2011) What redress should be available for breach of standards? Presentation to Leveson Inquiry. Available online at http://www.levesoninquiry.org.uk/wp-content/uploads/2011/11/Presentation-by-Desmond-Browne-QC-PDF-20.9KB.pdf, accessed on 21 November 2011

Calcutt, David (1993) *Review of press regulation* (Cmnd 2135) National Heritage Committee

Commons media, culture and sport select committee (2007) *Self regulation of the Press* (HC 375)

Dacre, Paul (2011) The future for self-regulation? Presentation to Leveson Inquiry. Available online at http://www.levesoninquiry.org.uk/wp-content/uploads/2011/11/Paul-Dacre.pdf, accessed on 21 November 2011

Defamation Act 2009 (Ireland)

Greenslade, Roy (2011) Don't axe PCC – press must put its own house in order, London *Evening Standard*, 27 July. Available online at http://www.thisislondon.co.uk/markets/article-23973366-dont-axe-pcc---press-must-put-its-own-house-in-order.do, accessed on 21 November 2011

Greenslade, Roy (2011) Press self-regulation and press freedom go hand in hand, 5 August. Available online at http://www.guardian.co.uk/media/greenslade/2011/aug/05/pcc-lord-justice-leveson, accessed on 21 November 2011

Greenslade, Roy (2011) PCC Plus – a way to make self-regulation work in the public, and press interest, *Guardian*, 9 September. Available online http://www.guardian.co.uk/media/greenslade/2011/sep/09/pcc-leveson-inquiry1, accessed on 21 November 2011

House of Lords Select Committee on Communications (2008) *The Ownership of the News* (1st Report, Session 2007-2008) (HL Paper 122–II)

Koene, Daphne (2009) *Press councils in Western Europe*, Netherlands Press Council Foundation Amsterdam/Netherlands Press Fund, the Hague

Legal Services Act 2007

Leveson, (2011) *Leveson Inquiry: Culture, Practice and Ethics of the Press*, Terms of Reference. Available online at http://www.levesoninquiry.org.uk/about/terms-of-reference/, accessed on 21 November 2011

McKie, David (1990) Self-regulation and the Calcutt Report, *Index on Censorship*, Vol. 19 pp 2-3

Media Standards Trust (2009) *A More Accountable Press: Part 1*, London

Media Standards Trust (2010) *Can Independent Self-regulation Keep Standards High and Preserve Press Freedom?*, London

MediaWise (2010) *Getting it Right for Now*, Bristol

Press Authority Bill 1953

Press Complaints Commission (2009) *PCC Report on Phone Message Tapping Allegations*

Press Complaints Commission (2011a) About the PCC. Available online at http://www.pcc.org.uk/AboutthePCC/WhatisthePCC.html, accessed on 21 November 2011

Press Complaints Commission (2011b) Statement from the PCC on Phone Hacking following Meeting today. Available online at http://www.pcc.org.uk/news/index.html?article=NzI0Mg, accessed on 21 November 2011

Press Council of Ireland. Available online at http://www.presscouncil.ie/, accessed on 21 November 2011

Rusbridger, Alan (2011) The Importance of a Free Press: Evidence to Leveson Inquiry. Available online at http://www.levesoninquiry.org.uk/wp-content/uploads/2011/11/Alan-Rushbridger.pdf, accessed on 21 November 2011.

Saloman, Eve (2011) The Future of Self-Regulation: Evidence to Leveson Inquiry. Available online at http://www.levesoninquiry.org.uk/wp-content/uploads/2011/11/Presentation-by-Eve-Salomon-PDF-23.4KB1.pdf, accessed on 21 November 2011

Economist (2006) Who killed the newspaper?, 24 August

The Independent (1990) Downey is appointed as Readers' Ombudsman, 15 March

Tomlinson, Hugh (2011a) Media Regulation: A Radical New Proposal: Part 1, Reform Options. Available online at http://inforrm.wordpress.com/2011/09/29/media-regulation-a-radical-new-proposal-part-1-reform-options-hugh-tomlinson-qc/, accessed on 21 November 2011

Tomlinson, Hugh (2011b) Media Regulation: A Radical New Proposal: Part 2, Reform Options. Available online at http://inforrm.wordpress.com/2011/09/30/media-regulation-a-radical-new-proposal-part-2-more-reform-options-hugh-tomlinson-qc/, accessed on 21 November 2011

Tomlinson, Hugh (2011c) Media Regulation: A radical new proposal: Part 3, the Media Regulation Tribunal. Available online at http://inforrm.wordpress.com/2011/10/04/media-regulation-a-radical-new-proposal-part-3-a-media-regulation-tribunal-hugh-tomlinson-qc/ accessed on 21 November 2011

Wintour, Charles (1990) Former editor named as readers' editor, *Sunday Times*, 29 April

Note on the contributor

Dr Damian Paul Carney is Principal Lecturer in Law at the University of Portsmouth. A qualified barrister, he has published extensively on media law including the first legal academic article on phone-hacking at the *News of the World*. Currently, he is writing a monograph entitled *Anonymous Sources: A Comparative, Theoretical and Critical Analysis* that studies the use of unattributed sources by journalists and other public communicators.

The Key Questions: But Are the Right Ones Being Asked by the Leveson Inquiry?

Barry Turner dares to question the questions being asked at the Leveson Inquiry. For instance, why focus on media ethics when the hacking hacks have clearly broken the law?

The following chapter examines on a question-by-question basis the remit of Lord Leveson's Inquiry into the culture, practice, ethics and standards of the press. The key questions as they have been identified are written in italics within the text. The 'other key questions' ask if Leveson's remit will really get us to the heart of the matter and help explain why a significant section of our press is now out of control.

The reputation of the press is certainly at an all time low. Certain reporters, editors, proprietors and other individuals less often associated with newsgathering have by their conduct sullied journalism and engaged in conduct, the result of which could damage or even destroy centuries of press tradition and freedom.

The Leveson Inquiry is structured around three themes: the culture, practice and ethics of the press, standards and public interest, all subjects very familiar to both working journalists and teachers of journalism. In the section under culture, practice and ethics, the inquiry is seeking to discover the causes of the scandal that has already seen the demise of the 168-year-old *News of the World*.

The inquiry needs to understand how newsrooms operate, particularly in the tabloid and mid-market sectors. Can you provide a personal account of culture, practices and ethics in any part of the press and media?

The culture of the newsroom is the stuff of legend. Editors bullying reporters in foul-mouthed tirades have been portrayed in a hundred plus movies and TV shows. Stereotypical it may be but like most stereotypes it is based on truth. In this kind of an atmosphere is it inevitable that those working in it will become so self obsessed, so inured and desensitised to normal emotions and empathy that they will do anything for a story? The answer is probably yes.

> *Seminar debates have suggested that commercial pressures were not new, were not unique to the press, and did not impact adversely on standards of journalism or ethical behaviour. The inquiry would be interested in submissions on this, with examples where possible.*

Commercial Pressures on the Press

The statement above is, on the face of it, defensive of the press as a whole. The press has always been subject to commercial pressures but that cannot be equated with an excuse for not simply unethical but criminal behaviour. Moreover, there is one fundamental flaw in the theory linking economic decline and financial pressure to the gross breaches of the criminal law that this scandal has uncovered. The main offender the now defunct *News of the World* was one of the papers least affected by this crisis.

> *Some seminar attendees suggest reader loyalty limits competition between titles. Professional competition to be first or best with a story, though, could be a powerful force. Other participants suggested some papers put journalists under significant pressure to produce a story within a tight timeframe. The inquiry would be interested in experiences of the competitive dynamics in journalism and how that impacts on the way in which journalists operate, with examples where possible.*

The competitive dynamics spoken of here are part of the myths and legends of journalism and like many myths have an element of truth in them. Scoops, exclusives and deadlines are the very stuff of news and while on the one hand contributing to quality journalism and keeping the public informed on matters of public interest, they have a pernicious and dark side. Like the commercial pressures alluded to in the previous question above are we looking for excuses rather than a rational explanation for the conduct of some editors and journalists?

Investigative journalism often requires the journalist to go to extraordinary lengths to get a story where no other method will work. This has even excused otherwise immoral conduct such a lying, subterfuge and deception to get the story. In a free society we have to allow this to protect freedom of expression and the journalist in their role as public watchdog. Some of the best stories of the last two decades involved subterfuge where journalists went undercover, and by doing so engaged in conduct we would normally regard as reprehensible and unethical.

In *The Secret Policeman* (2003) the journalist Mark Daly joined the Greater Manchester Police in an attempt to expose racism in the ranks. Daly joined the force under his own name since to do so under a false name would certainly have been an offence. During his training he recorded conversations in which officers openly expressed their own racist and in some cases corrupt activities.

When Daly's secret life was discovered the GMP arrested him for dishonestly obtaining a pecuniary advantage by deception, fallaciously on the basis that he had obtained his police salary under false pretences. Thankfully this failed to lead to a conviction but it demonstrated the anger of the police at what many saw as a betrayal.

Courageous Reporters Exposing Serious Wrong-doing

If any journalist was subject to what Lord Justice Leveson describes in his question as *powerful forces* or *significant pressure* it must be the investigative reporter. The experiences of Daly and other courageous reporters who expose serious wrongdoing must surely outweigh the *powerful forces* of the newsroom bully and the *significant pressure* from the editor.

The culture of the newsroom is legendary and there is little doubt that competitiveness contributes to bullying and pressure put on journalists. Whether seeking confirmation of this well-known phenomenon is helpful to the inquiry is questionable. As many journalist have demonstrated working to tight deadlines, working under pressure from colleagues and editors alike and working in a competitive environment are hardly excuses for criminality or even failing ethical standards.

> *With the advent of the internet and 24 hour news as well as declines in revenue and circulation, we have heard that fewer journalists are having to do more work. The seminars also raised the issue of the casualisation of the workforce. The inquiry would be interested in experiences of how this may have changed the culture in newsrooms and what it might mean in terms of journalistic practice, with examples where possible.*

Once again the question seems to be addressing very real problems within journalism and the newsroom culture but falling short of determining these shortcomings as causes of the serious breaches of the law and ethics that have occurred. There is little doubt that the outcome of the inquiry will be a suggestion that regulations need to be strengthened.

The leap to new regulation is the typical response of recent governments to a crisis which simultaneously deflects responsibility away from those in power while making it appear that they are doing something. The press are likely to bear the brunt of most of the regulation emerging out of this affair even though all the players, rogue reporters and editors, rogue police officers and sycophantic politicians eager to curry favour with the press barons – all created this scandal in equal measure.

What kind of new regulation should we expect? Prime Minister David Cameron has already alluded to the possible models that could be put in place. The obvious one is to turn the PCC into a proper regulatory body independent of the newspapers and government and with the ability to impose sanctions on an offending newspapers and individual journalists and editors. This model would resemble the current strictures placed on the broadcast media under

Ofcom. The Ofcom model is itself flawed, based as it is on the faulty concept of balanced reporting and paternalistic protection from offence to public decency.

British Newspapers' Tradition of Partisanship

This model represents a threat to more than 350 years of newspaper tradition in that it would force editors into the ridiculous position of incorporating 'balance' into the stories they published. British newspapers have a tradition of partisanship and it is the reason people buy them. Most of our newspapers take a particular slant on issues and that is why their readers find them attractive. To introduce the concept of 'balance' will remove the very heart from each of them. To wreck centuries old traditions of the press in order to prevent the type of scandal we are now witnessing is throwing the baby out with the bath water on a grand scale. It is akin to attempting to prevent stealing by banning the ownership of property.

Another 'regulator' mooted by Ed Milliband, leader of the Opposition, is to introduce a GMC or Law Society-based professional practice model. This model also is flawed. The GMC and Law Society, more correctly the Solicitors Regulatory Authority, do not conduct their business publicly. They act as investigator, judge and jury and are hidebound with anachronistic practices and a lack of transparency, precisely the problem with the current regulators of the media.

Why do we need new press regulation at all? Since this scandal began with the arrest and eventual imprisonment of Clive Goodwin and a private investigator for tapping phones it is clear that these matters are of a criminal nature and not one of press regulation. We have adequate and well-seasoned law in place to deal with this type of criminal activity so it is the failure of the criminal law that should be in the spotlight here not the failure of press regulation. This affair is not about journalists or editors: it is about corruption in public office. The journalists and editors are playing on a much wider stage than simply that of modern journalism.

Links between Press and Politicians 'Too Close'

David Cameron did accept in his comments at a press conference on the 8 July 2011 that the problem lies with the dangerous relationships that have developed between politicians and media corporations. He accepted that for too long practices that allowed this scandal and the earlier one of MPs' expenses were well known in the corridors of power and disgracefully tolerated. He accepted that such practices represented a threat to our democracy, where the legislators who make our laws and who govern us, the police who enforce those laws and the media who inform us of how we are governed have developed an unhealthy and corrupt relationship based on kickbacks and deals entirely against the public interest.

There is now a danger that attention will be focused on the press and away from the other two key players in this disgraceful affair as if the actual hacking into private mobile phones was the heart of these crimes. Hacking is a symptom of the disease, not the disease itself. So the press will be pilloried and blamed for what are, in fact, corrupt practices involving multiple players. The common law of corruption tells us that where a person accepts material gain to discharge a duty the offence is committed by both parties. (see R v. Whittaker 1914[1]). The Prevention of Corruption Act 1906 also makes very clear that those accepting consideration as inducement or reward are as guilty as those offering it. This is at the heart of Hackgate, not press regulation. It has been for over a century an offence to bribe public officials with gratuities and cash and the official taking the money should be targeted. It is difficult to see how we can blame the newsroom culture when an individual who does not work in it is prepared to accept money from one who does.

The issue of stories that attract a high degree of press attention but subsequently turn out to be false was raised at the seminars. The inquiry would be interested in submissions from editors, reporters and subjects of such stories – why they occur (what are the pressures that drive press interest) and how they occur (what checks and balances are or should be in place to stop this happening and why do they sometimes not operate)?

Fact, Fiction and Faction in the Press

Since time immemorial stories that attract a high degree of press attention have subsequently turned out to be false. Many stories are based on fake premises. Favourite themes were red top claims about Europe banning curved bananas or the 'British banger' to ridiculous claims of Elvis found on the Moon. The fake EU stories were frequently repeated even though no evidence was ever produced showing that the European Commission had ever discussed these issues let alone made plans to legislate on them.

The pressures that drive press interest are simple: competition for circulation, translating directly into profit and the overdeveloped egos of some journalists. It has long been recognised that the large circulation newspapers can take a gamble in publishing stories with a defamatory risk on purely economic terms. This is especially true where the story involves salacious gossip or domestic rows involving celebrities. The profit-driven excesses have had for a long time a suitable remedy. In the case of Cassell & Co. Ltd v Broome [1972][2], the House of Lords recognised that a publisher could well calculate a profit from the wrongdoing might exceed any damages awarded.

One seminar attendee suggested that the National Council for the Training of Journalists does not teach ethics. The inquiry would be interested in experience of how ethics are taught and promulgated amongst journalists.

This question appears to be based on an error and needs little examination. All journalism programmes in universities and colleges across the country (including those accredited by the NCTJ) *do* teach ethics and extensive coverage is also given to the legal elements of journalism. The next question focuses more on the rule of law:

Attendees proposed that the general law, as it applies to everyone, should be the only constraint on the press. The inquiry would welcome submissions on whether, and if so why, the press should be subject to any additional constraints in relation to behaviour and standards, for example relating to accuracy, treatment of vulnerable individuals, intrusion, financial reporting or reporting on crime, other than those imposed by existing laws.

Significantly, if there is one area where the inquiry discussions are superfluous it is on the phone hacking. The media do not need to be regulated on phone hacking, it is a criminal offence.[3] Anyone who has done this needs to be fully investigated and where there is sufficient evidence prosecuted. It is entirely irrelevant whether they are journalists or private investigators. This is nothing to do with press standards.

Stringent Codes could not have Prevented Hackgate

Why then are journalism ethics and standards being questioned? The most stringent codes of practice and terms of regulation could not have prevented Hackgate. Criminals do not abide by codes of practice, regulations or even the law. It would be a wonderful world, indeed, where burglars could be regulated and drug dealers licensed!

Editors at the seminars argued that the editors' code was a good set of standards to work to. The inquiry would be interested in submissions from all parties on the coverage and substance of the editors' code including accuracy and redress for those who are affected by breaches of the code.

The editors' code represents the right balance necessary to ensure a workable and free press while respecting fundamental human rights. Journalistic cynicism and even gallows humour has often made light of this type of code but there is nothing essentially wrong in expressing a set of common rules which, in the main, are based on the decent principles.

Yet rules are made to be broken. And there is no doubt that some of the best journalism in recent decades has come from a bending of the rules. Ethical codes must be flexible and this is what clearly distinguishes them from law. The question considers accuracy and redress and few ethical codes contain adequate measures for redress.

Could the answer lie in imposing an ethical code via legislation? Would a set of ethical guidelines with sanctions attached deter rogue journalists? We perhaps only need to look at the number of solicitors struck off the roll every year or doctors up before the GMC to answer that question.[4] A few, perhaps.

Public Interest Issues

The next set of questions posed by the inquiry focus on public interest issues. Public interest is, of course, both the underpinning principle in a democratic society and an excuse for many excesses. The biggest problem with the concept is there has never been a clear definition of what is in the 'public interest'.

The inquiry has heard strong arguments for the importance of a free press in a democratic society. The inquiry would be interested in submissions on the special role to be played by the press in a democracy, what 'freedom' requirements need to be in place for that role to be played and the whether this role places any obligations or responsibilities on the press.

The free press is at the heart of our democracy. The endeavours of the earliest journalists and pamphleteers laid the foundations of modern democracy. Democracy and individual freedoms were not granted freely by the politicians and the regulators. Does this special role in democracy place any obligations and responsibilities on the press? Of course, the same ones it places on all people in a democratic society under the rule of law.

Notes

[1] 3 KB 1283; 10 Cr App R 245

[2] 1 All ER 801 (HL)

[3] Section1 (1) Criminal Law Act 1977, S.1(1) Regulation of Investigatory Powers Act 2000 S.1(2) Regulation of Investigatory Powers Act 2000

[4] Some 82 solicitors were struck off by the tribunal to 30 September 2010, 21 per cent more than the previous year

Note on the contributor

Barry Turner is senior lecturer in law at the School of Journalism, University of Lincoln.

Promoting a Democratic and Accountable Media

The Coordinating Committee for Media Reform, an umbrella organisation of advocacy groups, academics and individuals campaigning for meaningful reform of the UK media, argues that a system that monitors and challenges unaccountable formations of media power, encourages significant new news initiatives, fosters more public involvement and holds unacceptable journalistic practices to account is the least we deserve

Introduction

In 2006, the World Values Survey found that well over 80 per cent of those polled in the UK indicated that they had little confidence in the press (World Values Survey, n.d.) while an Ipsos/MRBI survey in 2010 found that a mere 22 per cent of people said that they generally trusted journalists to tell the truth (Ipsos/MRBI 2010).

In July 2011, reporters working for the *News of the World*, were found to have hacked into the mobile phone of a murdered teenager and evidence soon emerged of complicity between senior media executives, top police officers and leading government officials. Since then, it has been revealed that there may have nearly 6,000 victims of phone hacking accompanied by the systematic use of covert surveillance, blackmail, the 'blagging' of information and regular invasions of privacy.

The Co-ordinating Committee for Media Reform was formed in response to this as an umbrella organisation of advocacy groups, academics and individuals campaigning for meaningful reform of the UK media. In a debate largely dominated by vested interests, the aim of Media Reform is to engage with the discussions occurring in parliament and beyond and to draw up policies designed to sustain the public interest and foster a more democratic media system.

In a world in which there is an ever smaller number of increasingly dominant, global media institutions, we believe that their power has out-grown the regulatory infrastructure that ought to balance their rights with the rights of the individuals they report on. The phone hacking debâcle is merely the latest manifestation of a significant imbalance and the time has come for the power between the media and the people to be re-evaluated.

Some editors have suggested that the problems are all related to one single maverick company. While it may turn out to be true that illegal phone hacking was not widespread across the British press, there is no doubt that, as became absolutely clear during the Leveson Inquiry, other unethical practices are rife and that the current regulatory structure has not proved sufficiently robust to tackle this kind of behaviour. According to researchers at Goldsmiths:

> Self-regulation outsources ethical practice either to individual users who have little power to influence media content (except through their 'market power') or, overwhelmingly, to institutions who, because of competition and economic uncertainty, show little willingness to provide the space and resources to journalists to act ethically (Phillips, Couldry and Freedman 2010: 67).

The phone hacking scandal and the ethical and regulatory crisis that followed are the result both of the failure of British news publishing to implement its own rules and of structural flaws associated with the regulation and ownership of the UK media. We argue that, as with many other areas of endeavour where risk-taking is endemic, regulatory frameworks may be required that enable and foster a greater sense of public responsibility while, at the same time, ensuring that no action is taken that cuts across the essential freedom of journalists to investigate wrong-doing.

Any recommendations that come out of the Leveson Inquiry need to be aimed at tackling corporate power and not restricting the ability of journalists to do precisely this. But it is wrong to equate what *Index on Censorship*'s John Kampfner (2011) describes as a 'raucous' media in this country with one that is adequately serving its citizens. Journalists, who are under extreme commercial pressure to attracts 'hits' rather than finding important stories, may be raucous (Fenton 2010, Lee-Wright, Phillips and Witschge 2011) but if that is at the expense of adequate research and verification they will never be trusted. Journalism that is not trusted cannot adequately contribute to a democratic debate.

The more complex challenge facing society now is to set clear and realisable standards for the institutions and individuals that investigate, report and make sense of the world for the rest of us. By articulating such standards, and the principles upon which they are based, we can hope not only to prevent repetition of some of the more unacceptable practices that have been brought to light recently, but also to work towards a commonly meaningful language through which journalists, politicians and the public can reflect upon, scrutinise and assess the relationship between the media and the public interest. This will involve proposals for a right of reply, a strengthened public interest test as part of a more robust approach to media concentration in order to secure media pluralism and diversity, and for a range of alternative models—both in terms of organisational structure and revenue generation—that will help to sustain news in the public interest.

Self Regulation

Ethics are not derived from laws; laws should arise from ethics. It is a shared sense of equity and justice, rooted in something deeper than fear or mere obedience that enables a group or community to set ethical standards which its members freely agree to abide by.

The problem we face is that organisations that have differing interests and very different ways of operating do not necessarily have a shared ethical sense to which they can all refer. Journalism is sharply divided between, on the one hand, those editors and journalists who have the freedom of action and conscience to operate ethically and, on the other, those who operate within a highly structured and competitive environment in which they are under heavy pressure to deliver stories by any means possible and often without even the protection of a trade union.

Whereas the former require protection from pressures that might prevent them from investigating abuses of power, the latter require firmer rules to prevent them from using their power (and desperation to grab market share) to traduce innocent people. Those individuals working for highly competitive news organisations also need protection – of their right to exercise their conscience.

The first journalists' code of ethics in the UK was established in 1884 precisely in order to differentiate responsible journalists from those working on the 'Yellow Press'. The National Union of Journalists introduced a code in 1936 in opposition to plans for a register from which 'unethical journalists' might be struck off (Gopsill and Neale 2007).

The current editors' code, policed by the Press Complaints Commission, had no input from the NUJ (though it is clearly heavily influenced by the NUJ code) and it cannot, therefore, be said to represent the interests or concerns of ordinary working journalists. It was drafted by a team of editors, brought together by those publishers who fund the PCC. Yet it is still very often flouted by its members and no longer even represents all the newspapers since the withdrawal of the Express group in January 2011.

We suggest that a new body to regulate the press is required, the News Publishing Commission, which can represent the interests of ordinary working journalists as well as editors and members of the public.

Statutory Regulation and Press Freedom

Whenever the idea of statutory backing to press reform is considered, the argument from editors is always that it will have a chilling effect and prevent journalists from investigating wrongdoing. In reality we already have laws governing much of what journalists do. Our libel laws are so strict that people from other countries visit our law courts in order to get compensation for wrongs perpetrated in other jurisdictions. We also have laws governing the reporting of the legal process and we have a range of laws covering race hatred, bribery, electronic eavesdropping and so on.

However, proprietors and editors shy away from a simple, enforceable system that would give quick, cheap access to redress from members of the public who feel that they have been misrepresented, even though it might actually lift (or ameliorate) the threat of court action from those genuinely exposing wrongdoing.

We take the need for press freedom every bit as seriously as the editors. This is why we would like to see the concept of 'the public interest' clearly defined and enshrined in law. There will always be a 'grey area' in journalism in which editors encourage journalists to 'dig a little deeper'. That will always involve intrusion into places where those who wish to cover up wrongdoing would rather we didn't go.

Both the NUJ code of conduct and the editors' code allow the use of surreptitious means, if there is no alternative, to dig out stories in the public interest. The Guardian's investigations editor, for instance, has admitted he used material from phone-taps in the paper's exposé of bribery and corruption at BAE Systems (Leigh 2006). Leigh did so because he believed he was working 'in the public interest'.

However, an understanding of the 'public interest' must include a sense of public service. The problem for journalists is that owners (often public companies) are more concerned with serving their shareholders than with serving the public. They transmit this view to the editors they appoint (Marr 2004: 235) who, in turn, increasingly, enforce a top-down editorial line that journalists are expected to obey (Phillips, Couldry and Freedman 2010: 57). In this respect, Rupert Murdoch's definition of public service is instructive: 'Anybody who provides a service which the public wants, at a price it can afford, is providing a public service' (Murdoch 1989).

A clearly defined 'public interest' defence in law is vital to any attempt at reform because it helps us to deal with the central contradiction of journalism – the fact that ethical journalists require defence for rule breaking if they are to do their job, whereas unethical journalists attempt to use a 'public interest defence' to protect themselves against criticism.

The public interest is a concept that is well understood by both the public and journalists (Morrison and Svennevig 2002). The Human Rights Act already embodies the concept as a reasonable defence for intrusion and if there is to be any extension of the law into the realm of journalism then that concept needs to be clarified. The word 'public' in this instance embodies the notion of a whole society. For something to be in the 'public interest' it must affect the way in which we live together as a social group (Phillips, Couldry and Freedman 2010: 52). It should be information that will help us to live better together, or that will prevent us from being harmed. With a clear public interest defense in place it should be possible to ensure that codes of ethical conduct are upheld and that those who choose willfully to ignore them will face some form of legal censure.

Democracy and the Right of Reply

The public interest defence assumes that stories are being pursued for serious reasons but there is a whole mass of material written every day that is not serious and has never been intended to be serious. There is no intention here to suppress the exuberance of the British press. Many people read news for the fun of finding out what celebrities are up to or for moral tales derived from other lives. Storytelling is as much a part of journalism as reporting. Journalists, however, need to keep in mind that the stories they tell concern real people with real lives. We feel that the subjects of press intrusion also have rights and also need protection.

When information is inaccurate, unfair, or just 'made up', real people are affected and they should have an absolute right to tell their own side of the story and to correct misleading statements. And we should not underestimate the size of this problem or the distress it causes. The PCC's statistics show that in 2009, 87.5 per cent of the complaints it received concerned accuracy and opportunity to reply, and only 21.4 per cent were about privacy (PCC 2009).

As MediaWise has pointed out, a statutory right of reply need be no threat to the commercial future nor to the democratic rights of publications. It argues that a right to reply has been 'commended by the Council of Europe and offered in other perfectly healthy democracies (France, Germany, Belgium, Norway, Sweden, Greece, Austria and Switzerland)' (MediaWise 2010: 4).

There have been a number of attempts to establish a right of reply in this country. All of them have been vehemently opposed by editors who think that offering such a right would spoil the careful balance of their publications, take up too much space and introduce badly written and boring 'legal-ese' into their carefully planned publications.

The arguments were more reasonable before the advent of the internet, where the addition of a reply slot, immediately below an offending article, need not change the lay-out or look of the publication. With the addition of a mistakes and clarifications column in every newspaper and magazine – pointing out what items have been corrected and where they can be viewed in full – it should be possible for corrections to be made very quickly, with minimal fuss and without damaging the look and feel of the publication. The advantage of using the web version of a publication for the full-length correction is that it can be done within hours of publication and be immediately available to those reading the offending article. At present it can take weeks or months to negotiate a right of reply and then it will read entirely out of context.

There can be no more useful corrective to journalistic malpractice than the knowledge that any person who is unfairly traduced has the right to reply immediately below the offending article. It is to be hoped that by introducing such a statutory right, publications would very quickly take on board the need to offer a hotline for would-be complainants who could reply without needing to bring the law into play. However, in order to ensure that this right is backed up with the possibility of a sanction, complainants should be able to take their complaints further in the event that all interim attempts at redress are refused.

Ownership and Control

Diversity of news provision is more likely to come from a plurality of types of news outlets, platforms and funding models as well as a diversity of news owners. There have always been anxieties over the ownership of the media because of its agenda-setting role. Media owners have, over time, been shown to influence the way their organisations present news and in turn have some bearing on public debate and political opinion. Owners can have an effect on news output through various means including, at times, direct intervention. More frequently, however, it is likely to be via indirect means: through the appointment of like minded editors, emphasising particular business approaches, or by prioritising certain types of journalism. Owners can also influence the journalistic ethos of a news organisation and this can filter through to the processes of news production. This may derive from a certain vision of a particular owner or an editor in chief, from a particular family ownership tradition or from structural and organisational principles which impose a particular form of editorial direction. All of these can influence the types of journalism that are valued and promoted and what kinds of stories are followed.

Despite the current ownership regulations, a small group of owners in the national and regional press have a large market share, thus a limited number of people and approaches potentially dominate the media agenda and can influence public debate and political opinion.

Market share of UK national daily newspapers (%) (1997-2009)

Title/Company	1997	2001	2002	2008	2009
News International	34.4	31.8	32.2	34.8	33.8
Trinity Mirror	23.9	21.0	20.2	15.6	16.2
Northern & Shell (formerly United Newspapers)	14.3	12.5	13.8	14.9	13.5
Daily Mail & General Trust	13.6	18.7	18.5	21.2	19.9
Telegraph Group	7.7	7.7	7.3	7.4	7.3
Pearson	1.3	3.8	3.5	4.0	4.1
Guardian Media Group	2.7	3.1	3.0	3.0	3.3
Independent Print Ltd	2.1	1.5	1.4	1.8	1.9

Source: Audit Bureau of Circulations

How well does contemporary British journalism serve the public interest (as discussed above)? Journalistic approaches to the news tend to revolve around two perspectives. The first represents the political world as a game in which the attainment and retention of power is the principal goal. This account is dominated by reports of 'winners' and 'losers', strategies designed even to 'sell' unpalatable policies to an unwitting electorate and accounts of an inner political world often laced with Machiavellian manipulation and deception. Faced with such a political world, citizens come to feel like spectators, observing the skills of an opaque sport, or cynics, withdrawing in frustration from a system of political communication that rarely takes them seriously.

The second journalistic perspective is to see the democratic polity as a civic forum in which issues and policy proposals are discussed on their merits. This approach is characterised by a canvassing and sifting of competing arguments; an acknowledgement that mature democracy entails trade-offs between different preferences and values; and an historical sense that stories and events have long-term pre-histories and consequences that add up to more than a stream of isolated episodes. In this context, a clear relationship is envisaged between people as news consumers and people as reflective, monitoring, arguing, voting, active citizens.

In the real world of contemporary democracy, political communication entails a mixture of these two orientations, with politics depicted through the frames of both the competitive game and the civic forum. But the presentation and analysis of news is currently showing signs of radical imbalance, with game-oriented journalism rising and civic-oriented public-interest journalism in decline. While it cannot be denied that high-quality journalism based upon serious investigation and astute analysis can still find its way into print and broadcast news; that even some of the most populist newspapers manage to stimulate important public debates; and that a significant range of voices and perspectives can now be accessed online by those with the time to search for them, the news landscape as a whole is increasingly devoid of civically relevant content.

This serious problem for democracy is exacerbated by three pressures in the current environment. Firstly, newspaper circulation and readership levels are at an all time low and key advertising revenue has reduced sharply. The tremendous growth in the number of free newspapers, emergence of 24 hour television news and the popularisation of online and mobile platforms have presented the newspaper industry with some real challenges. Maintaining profit margins and shareholder returns is increasingly dependent upon the use of fewer journalists doing more work in less time to fill more spaces than ever (Phillips 2010). This results frequently in greater use of unattributed rewrites of press agency or public relations material and cut-and-paste practices that are now commonly referred to as 'churnalism', a practice that is antithetical to the kind of public-interest values upon which the democratic public sphere depends (Davies 2008).

Secondly, the media system is increasingly dominated by a fierce competition for public attention. Irresponsible editors push journalists to almost any lengths to break a story (Phillips, Couldry, and Freedman 2010), even when the methods adopted are ethically repugnant or, as we have seen, criminal. Political communication is increasingly shaped by this intense competition, reducing news holes for politics and placing a premium upon arresting stories rather than the cultivation of civic knowledge. One consequence of this is the creation of a particularly bouncy news agenda: what is 'the story' one week (sometimes, one day) is superseded by a different one the next week, leaving citizens with an impression of politics as an overwhelming succession of mishaps, unmanageable events, incompetent authorities and suspicious circumstances.

Thirdly, the purchase which parties and leaders once had upon the media as channels for the promotion of ideas and policies has declined. Whereas in the relatively recent past, political communication strategists had a limited range of press, television and radio bases to cover, they are now involved in multi-dimensional impression management. This leads to an inevitable loosening of their control over the political agenda, forcing politicians into a predominantly responsive mode or an attempted news-management one. To cover the broad, dynamic and often unpredictable media environment in which they now operate, political actors are compelled to adopt elaborate cross-media strategies, which may amount to little more than keeping up with the incessant flow of relevant information and hoping to spot embarrassing media content before it damages them. To help them cope with these incessant pressures, politicians have come to rely upon journalists-turned spin doctors who advise them to adapt to the logic of the media ecology, regardless of its civic defects.

There is, therefore, a need to assess concentrations of media ownership and cross-media ownership to ensure that the public media on which we rely provide pluralism of voice and opinion, sufficiently diverse sources of news and information, and diversity of cultural expression. Thus, we propose a revision of the UK public interest test to ensure that concentrations of ownership and the behaviour of those providing public media services do not operate against the public interest in terms of media plurality. The test could be applied whenever proposed media mergers or market concentration reaches a particular threshold, such as a 15 per cent share of supply in a relevant market. In such cases, a stronger public interest test than we have at present could be applied, one which would assess media ownership against a range of criteria set out in law, including, plurality of ownership and supply, cultural diversity, corporate behaviour, and content issues.

Public Intervention is not the Enemy of Independent Journalism

Commercial media organisations and industry associations representing them occasionally claim that public support for the media undermines the viability of market-based models by constraining private enterprise and crowding out commercial players. Comparative research by the Reuters Institute suggests this need not be the case and that, for example, targeted subsidies for minority newspapers in Finland, discounted rates for postal delivery in Italy, paying the salaries of 60 young journalists in the Netherlands and subsidised provision of newspapers to young people in France have all helped ensure 'the press increase its reach, helped smaller publications survive, and helped bigger ones increase both their profits and their potential to do public good' (Nielsen and Linnebank 2011: 9).

When it comes to public support constraining private enterprise, it is worth keeping in mind that media organisations commonly seen as market-based, such as private for-profit newspapers, have historically and in virtually all democracies been at the receiving end of considerable amounts of indirect public subsidies through extensive tax exemptions and other forms of regulatory relief. This suggests public support does not preclude private media, but can in fact underpin them and incentivize them to innovate in both their business practices and journalistic enterprises and encourage them to emphasize their public role as parts of democratic politics. Public policy can, in the media sector as elsewhere in society, work with commercial enterprises and need not exist at their expense.

Furthermore, public support need not privilege particular viewpoints nor marginalise others. As the authors of the recent Reuters report argue, public support for the media that operates through a series of mechanisms including subsidies, tax exemptions and promotion of public service has the 'clear advantage of being able to be instituted in a viewpoint-neutral fashion that does not give politicians or government bureaucrats ways of discriminating against particular publishers' (Nielsen and Linnebank 2011: 24).

In terms of the claim that public support may crowd out commercial players, it is important to note that even very strong license fee funded public broadcasters such as those found in Germany, the Scandinavian countries, and elsewhere in Northern Europe have, commercial misgivings aside, clearly been able to co-exist with sizable advertising and pay-TV commercial television businesses and ensured a more diverse and durable media environment than a more exclusively commercial model such as the one seen in the United States. Some industry executives see the BBC as the main obstacle to financial sustainability in online news. These include James Murdoch, News Corp Chief Executive in Europe and Asia, who, in his 2009 MacTaggart lecture, claimed that 'dumping free, state-sponsored news on the market makes it incredibly difficult for journalism to flourish on the internet' (Murdoch 2009). However, the inability of American general interest news organizations, both print- and broadcasting-based, to break even despite the absence of strong public media competitors suggests that the BBC and other publicly-funded organisations are not what stands in the way of online profitability.

The revenue attached to existing forms of subsidy is considerable. Total indirect support for US newspapers and magazines via a range of tax breaks and reduced postal rates is at least $1.2 billion a year while in the UK over half a billion pounds (£594m) is provided in public support in terms of VAT exemptions for newspapers alone. Indirect support is far more popular than direct subsidies but nevertheless the latter are still significant in countries such as France and Italy making up 10 per cent and 13 per cent respectively of total public support. (Nielsen and Linnebank 2011: 18).The problem is, of course, that the value of indirect subsidies, such as those based on non-payment of VAT on sales, is declining in direct proportion to the drop in circulation and print revenues. Yet, if they were extended to digital sales, this could amount to a considerable advantage for news organisations facing a volatile time. Surely the current situation is absurd—because VAT exemptions are only provided for print products, it actually costs more more expensive to subscribe to the digital-only version of the *Wolverhampton Express & Star* than the much more expensively produced and distributed print product.

The notion of economic incentives, or even subsidies for newsgathering may seem radical and problematic to some, but it is the case that broadcasting policy in the UK has always been based on a system of subsidies since its inception and that there remain strong reasons, based on market failure and social welfare, to continue them. The principle source of public subsidy outside the BBC has been the use of spectrum licensing as an indirect subsidy scheme. The main terrestrial 'public service' television broadcasters do not pay market prices for spectrum and the economic benefit of advertising revenues that result is used to fund news and other public service genres. Whilst it is the case that subsidies of news may entail problems of broadcaster independence it is arguably the case that the current system is already subject to such pressures.

The subsidies that currently go to large media organisations, in the shape of tax breaks and VAT exemptions, could be used along with new sources of funding, including levies on ISPs, broadcasters, mobile operators and hardware companies, to divert sums of money into funding publicly accountable media designed to increase diversity of opinion in the printed media, broadcasting and the internet. Indeed, we propose that if large news organisations are to continue receiving indirect subsidies, this *must* be conditional on their practical support for either new or existing forms of public interest news.

Any use of public money, however, must also be transparent and open to effective challenge. Interventions have to ensure that there are proper ways of accounting for public money and, above all, that the end product of public support is to enhance diversity of expression in the country. This must also be applied to the composition of any new bodies that allocate funds for public interest journalism which must include individuals with different views and from different backgrounds. Neither markets nor bureaucratic control have delivered and sustained the journalism we need. It is therefore time to try more democratic forms of organisation –including community, cooperative and charitable structures as well as the 'news hubs' advocated by the Media Trust (2010)— and to demand that major communications interests make a significant contribution to a diverse and accountable news landscape.

Furthermore, in areas of underprovision we recommend a direct subsidy to local print or digital news organisations. The subsidy would cover the salary of one journalist who must be dedicated to coverage of local politics: both in the town hall and the community. The jobs should be paid for at the entry level with the intention of providing job creation opportunities for young journalists as well as improving democratic accountability and debate at local level. Any organisation that can provide evidence of attracting a reasonable audience in the locality should be able to apply for this funding.

Conclusion

A media system dominated by a few, powerful voices and a news media increasingly run to secure financial reward or political influence has failed us when we needed it most: to alert us to the endemic insecurity of the financial system to warn us about the privatisation of the universities and the NHS and indeed, with a few honourable exceptions, to acknowledge the complicity at the highest levels between politicians, police and media executives. A system that monitors and challenges unaccountable formations of media power, encourages significant new news initiatives, fosters more public involvement and holds unacceptable journalistic practices to account is the least we deserve.

References

Davies, Nick (2008) *Flat Earth News*, London: Chatto & Windus

Fenton, Natalie (2010) *New Media, Old News: Journalism and Democracy in the Digital Age*, London: Sage

Gopsill, Tim and Neale, Greg (2007) *Journalists: 100 years of the NUJ*, London: Profile

Ipsos/MRBI (2010) *A Crisis in Trust?* Ipsos Mori. Available online at http://www.ipsos-mori.com/Assets/Docs/News/ben-page-a-crisis-in-trust-september-2010.pdf, accessed on 10 November 2011

Kampfner, John (2011) The phone hacking inquiry must shackle corporate power, not jouranlsits, Comment is Free, Guardian.co.uk. Available online at http://www.guardian.co.uk/commentisfree/2011/nov/09/leveson-james-murdoch-phone-hacking, accessed on 10 November 2011

Lee-Wright, Peter, Phillips, Angela and Witschge, Tamara (2011) *Changing Journalism*, London: Routledge

Leigh, David (2006) Scandal on Tap, *Guardian*, 4 December. Available online at http://www.guardian.co.uk/media/2006/dec/04/mondaymediasection, accessed on 1 December 2011

Marr, Andrew (2005) *My Trade: A Short History of British Journalism*, London: Pan Books

Media Trust (2010) *Meeting the News Needs of Local Communities*, London: Media Trust. Available online at: www.mediatrust.org/uploads/128255497549240/original.pdf, accessed on 10 November 2011

MediaWise (2010) *Getting it right for now*, January. Available online at: http://www.pcc.org.uk/assets/441/Mediawise.pdf, accessed on 10 November 2011

Morrison David and Svennevig, Michael. (2002) *The Public Interest, the Media and* Privacy, London: IPPR.

Murdoch, James (2009) The Absence of Trust. Speech to the Edinburgh International Television Festival, 29 August. Available online at http://image.guardian.co.uk/sys-files/Media/documents/2009/08/28/JamesMurdochMacTaggartLecture.pdf, accessed on 25 November 2011

Murdoch, Rupert (1989) Freedom in Broadcasting, MacTaggart Lecture, Edinburgh International Television Festival, 25 August

Nielsen, Rasmus and Linnebank, Geert (2011) *Public Support for the Media*, Oxford: Reuters Institute for the Study of Journalism

PCC (2009) *Annual Review 2009*: *Statistics conclusion*, London: Press Complaints Commission. Available online at: http://www.pcc.org.uk/review09/2009_statistics/statistics_conclusion.php, accessed on 10 November 2011

Phillips, Angela (2008) Journalism, Ethics and Codes of Conduct: Why Journalists Need a 'Conscience Clause'. Second Call for Evidence, House of Lords Select Committee on Communications. Available online at http://www.publications.parliament.uk/pa/ld200708/ldselect/ldcomuni/122/122we13.htm, accessed on 10 November 2011

Phillips Angela, Couldry, Nick and Freedman, Des (2010) An Ethical Deficit: Accountability, Norms and the Material Conditions of Contemporary Journalism, Fenton, Natalie (ed.) *New Media Old News: Journalism and Democracy in the Digital Age*, London: Sage pp 51-67

Phillips, Angela (2010) Old Sources: New Bottles, Fenton Natalie (ed.) *New Media Old News: Journalism and Democracy in the Digital Age*, London: Sage pp 87-101

World Values Survey (n.d.) Online data analysis. Available at http://www.worldvaluessurvey.org/index_html,accessed on 10 November 2011

Note on the contributors

The Co-ordinating Committee for Media Reform (www.mediareform.org.uk) is an umbrella organisation of advocacy groups, academics and individuals campaigning for meaningful reform of the UK media. The CCMR was established to represent the interests of civil society in the light of both the Leveson Inquiry and the Communications Review, a government-initiated consultation in advance of a future Communications Bill. In a debate dominated by vested interests, Media Reform aims to draw up policies designed to sustain the public interest and foster a more democratic media system. This chapter has been edited by Natalie Fenton, Des Freedman and Angela Phillips from content provided by a range of individuals within the CCMR.

Lightning Source UK Ltd.
Milton Keynes UK
UKOW021251240212

187858UK00001B/42/P